Schooling Students Placed at Risk

Research, Policy, and Practice in the Education
of Poor and Minority Adolescents

Schooling Students Placed at Risk

Research, Policy, and Practice in the Education
of Poor and Minority Adolescents

Edited by

Mavis G. Sanders
Johns Hopkins University

LEA LAWRENCE ERLBAUM ASSOCIATES, PUBLISHERS

2000   Mahwah, New Jersey   London

The final camera copy for this work was prepared by the author, and therefore the publisher takes no responsibility for consistency or correctness of ty-
pographical style. However, this arrangement helps to make publication of
this kind of scholarship possible.

Lawrence Erlbaum Associates, Inc., Publishers
10 Industrial Avenue
Mahwah, NJ 07430

Cover design by Kathryn Houghtaling Lacey

Library of Congress Cataloging-in-Publication Data

Schooling students placed at risk : research, policy, and practice in the ed-
ucation of poor and minority adolescents / edited by Mavis G. Sanders
    p.   cm.
Includes bibliographical references and index
ISBN 0-8058-3089-8 (cloth : alk. paper) — ISBN 0-8058-3090-1 (pbk. :
alk. paper)
1. Socially handicapped students—education (Secondary)—United
States. 2. Minorities—Education (Secondary)—United States. I. Sanders,
Mavis G.
LC4069.4.S35 2000
373.1826'24—dc21   99-048452
                                                                   CIP

Books published by Lawrence Erlbaum Associates are printed on acid-free
paper, and their bindings are chosen for strength and durability.

Printed in the United States of America
10 9 8 7 6 5 4 3 2 1

Dedicated to my beloved daughter, Shori

Contents

IV: FROM RESEARCH TO PRACTICE

Foreword

A. WADE BOYKIN
Howard University

In recent decades, few topics in American education have received more attention than the academic achievement of "minority group" students from low-income backgrounds. Yet, in spite of such concentrated attention, all too many such students continue to perform at unacceptably low levels in U.S. public schools. This is obviously cause for concern. Indeed, children from the domestic cultural groups that have fared the worse in schools constitute the fastest growing school-age population. The communities from which these students come will not be able to reap the benefits of proportionately large numbers of well-educated citizens. But, this also poses a substantial challenge to society at large. As the bar is constantly being raised for the minimal skill and knowledge needed for entry into the workforce and while preparation for the labor markets of the 21st century will require competencies that schools are only recently beginning to acknowledge and appreciate, this society must rely increasingly on a talent pool comprised of people who represent groups that this society has yet found ways to successfully educate. If this challenge is not soon met, the future productivity and well-being of American society could be severely compromised. America can ill afford to have substantial numbers of poor and "minority-group" students functioning at the educational margins.

Fortunately, recent years bear witness to an apparent paradigm shift taking place in the American schooling enterprise. Many are losing patience with academic programs, practices, and procedures that are based essentially on hunches, fashions and fads, and good will alone. There is an increased call for schooling to be based on what truly works with the claims substantiated by solid, rigorous, systematic evidence. To be sure, this documentation must be contextualized so that there is understanding of when, where, and for whom certain approaches are effective. However, this does not reduce the importance of implementing evidence-based approaches to schooling. Further, it has become obvious that programs that only focus on one or two aspects of schooling or that are piecemeal in their implementation, will have limited utility if the goal is to significantly enhance outcomes for the student populations of interest here. The call has gone out for systemic and comprehensive school reform. School change must be school wide. It must encompass all relevant aspects of the schooling enterprise. The activities also must be sufficiently coordinated around a common vision or a set of principles, so that there is consistency and coherence to the school experience for students and staff alike.

Still further, a talent sorting or "weeding" function for schooling is giving way to approaches that function more to actualize the talents and potential of all students enrolled at the school. This is to be accomplished through providing the appropriate supports and opportunities for students to grow intellectually, and to genuinely succeed in school and beyond. In a related vein, there also is a shift afoot in how students are to be viewed within the academic arena. For all too long, low-income students of color have been conceived as "at risk". Advocacy now is growing to see these students instead as "placed at risk." This is more than a mere change in labels. Referring to students as at risk effectively locates the problem of schooling "inside" the children or in their putative problematic home and community circumstances. In this manner, students and their families are conceived to have afflictions that must be cured if positive schooling outcomes are to accrue. In defining the problem of schooling this way, the prescription most often is to repair the child or fix the family in some way. Certainly if we move away from a talent sorting model of schooling, this deficit conception of children would have no place. All too often, these so-called deficient aspects of children and their families have been utilized as the basis for the sorting out of "problematic" children, and thereby limiting their access to quality educational experiences.

Poor and minority children are not without their challenges and difficult life circumstances. Programs certainly should be implemented to fortify such children as needed. Yet, by offering the notion of students placed at risk, this widens the possibilities for what could be the source of schooling problems to include schools themselves, and their attendant curriculum, instructional, organizational, and professional development practices. Indeed, using practices that are not rooted in solid evidence surely can place students at risk. Narrowing the scope of interventions to single focused efforts, or to uncoordinated collections of practices may also place students at risk. Programs and practice which function to sort children inevitably lead to the unfortunate waste of human talent.

This book brings much needed theory, research, and practical suggestions to the task of increasing the possibilities of success for students who too frequently have been marginalized by U.S. public schools. It gives greatly welcomed attention to issues that bear on the schooling of adolescents, whose concerns too often get shortchanged in discussions of achievement enhancement and school reform. This book presents conceptions and approaches consistent with the newly emerging paradigms of schooling. Important new vistas are explored and important new questions are asked. New light is shed on such crucial topics as student transitions, tracking, school engagement, and small learning communities. Attention is given to the social fabric of the schooling process, acknowledging the significance of the social transactions and patterns of participants in the schooling enterprise. Attention also is given to how the quality of students' educational experience influences achievement outcomes. Relatedly, there is focus on the necessity and consequences of teaching for inclusiveness in order to proactively accommodate students of diverse backgrounds. Furthermore, in chapters throughout the book, poor and minority students' families and communities are presented not as caldrons of deficiencies and pathologies, but as resources for activities, experiences, and competencies that can be capitalized upon in school settings. There also is focus on ways in which schools can be resources for families and community development. The challenges and opportunities of comprehensive reform and restructuring are given consideration as well.

This book is a valuable contribution to the literature on school reform and the education of students placed at risk. As such, it should be taken seriously by practitioners, policy makers, and researchers alike. This volume steers clear of offering definitive answers. Yet, it enriches our understanding of the schooling challenges that American society faces, raises questions often not asked, and sheds light on some hopeful possibilities for more successful schooling ventures. The reader who cares about the future of poor and "minority" children, the future of American schooling, indeed the future of this society, is in store for an enlightening and rewarding experience.

Preface: Research, Policy, and Practice in the Education of Poor and Minority Adolescents

MAVIS G. SANDERS
Johns Hopkins University

Since the advent of mass schooling in the United States, some populations have been better served by this nation's educational system than others. Poor and minority students have been among those for whom the system has provided unequal inputs, and who have been plagued and stigmatized by unequal outcomes. Despite years of educational reforms designed to address these disparities, the United States is still faced with substantial numbers of poor and minority students who are being failed by this nation's schools. This failure is particularly evident at the secondary level. Between 1972 and 1996, students from low-income families were more likely to drop out of high school than were their counterparts from middle- and high-income families. Furthermore, in 1996, the high school dropout rates for African-American, Latino and Native-American students were still higher than the dropout rate for their White peers. For poor and minority students who remain in school through high school graduation, their proficiency scores in mathematics, reading, and science continue to lag behind those of their White counterparts. Students who attend secondary schools with high poverty levels and high percentages of minority students also are more likely to be taught core academic subjects by teachers who did not major in these subjects than are students at more affluent schools with smaller minority populations.

These statistics[1] show that even as we, as a nation, approach the 21st century, poor and minority students are disproportionately placed at risk for school dropout, low achievement, exposure to less qualified teachers, and continued marginalization in the larger society.

This book seeks to contribute to the intellectual exchange among researchers, policymakers, practitioners, and concerned citizens on factors that influence the achievement of poor and minority youth, specifically students in middle and high schools. It also seeks to encourage increased dialogue about policies and practices that can make a difference in educational opportunities and outcomes for these students. Although the chapters in this book are not exhaustive, they represent an array of theoretical and methodological approaches that provide readers with new and diverse ways to think about issues of educational equality and opportunity in the United States.

In the first section of the book, the authors take a look back in order to look forward. Franklin, in "Students at promise and resilient: A historical look at risk," asks, What are the origins of the term "at risk"? He outlines the historical misuse of the term and cautions against the use of any term or[1] label that assumes students' failure and not success. He argues that in the future, researchers need to use an ecological approach to understanding risk and resilience in order to promote greater school success among all students. The second chapter in the section is Mitchell's "Historical trends in federal educational policies that target students placed at risk ." In it, she outlines different policies that have been enacted to address the needs of poor and minority youth. Beginning with the Elementary and Secondary Education Act of 1965, she highlights factors that alter and modify these policies as they move through the political maze toward enactment. Mitchell's conclusion considers whether educational policies enacted during the Clinton administration are likely to produce the kinds of positive changes needed to improve educational opportunities and outcomes for poor and minority youth.

This section ends with Balfanz's "Why do so many urban public school students demonstrate so little academic achievement?" In this chapter, Balfanz focuses on the importance of history and context in explaining low achievement levels among many inner city students. Noting the

---

[1]Statistics were taken from *The Condition of Education 1998*, published in Washington, D.C., by the National Center for Education Statistics.

"underappreciated importance of time and place," Balfanz discusses how both the location of a school within a hierarchy of neighborhoods, school districts, and states, and the history of the community it serves "shape students' learning opportunities and supports. . . ." He contends that researchers and policymakers who seek to improve student outcomes in urban public schools must not focus solely on group and individual characteristics of students. They also must focus greater attention on the environments that create weak and dysfunctional learning institutions, and inequalities in the intergenerational provision of learning opportunities and supports.

Part I of this book, thus, sets a stage. Franklin cautions against repeating mistakes of the past. He challenges the reader not to use terms such as "at risk" to stigmatize or explain failure, but rather to use research and improve practice to promote success among youth *placed* at risk. Mitchell and Balfanz show the value of examining current educational issues and concerns within a historical context. All three of these chapters illustrate how time and place can inform policies and research that seek to improve educational opportunities for not only poor and minority youths, but all youth.

Part II moves the discussion of the education of youth placed at risk forward with empirical studies on factors that influence the educational outcomes of poor and minority adolescents. This section begins with a chapter titled "Student-teacher relations and academic achievement in high school." In this chapter, Sanders and Jordan highlight the importance of teacher support and expectations for adolescents' school engagement and success, and the importance of sustained teacher support as students transition from one grade to the next. This chapter concludes with a discussion of the need for research to identify factors that encourage or prohibit teachers from developing and acting on high expectations, and providing support to all students.

Next, Jordan and Plank, in "Talent loss among high-achieving poor students," explore factors that influence postsecondary enrollment among students who perform well academically, but who are from low socioeconomic status (SES) families. The authors find that low SES, academically able students are less likely than are their high SES counterparts to attend colleges and universities directly after high school. Much of this effect is explained by the actions of students, their families, and schools. Students with higher SES are more likely to report having social capital in the form of guidance and support for advanced schooling than are students from lower SES backgrounds. Interviews with school counselors shed light on some factors that may reduce the social capital on which poor students can draw.

Yonezawa uncovers more about the schooling experience of poor and minority adolescents in her chapter, "Unpacking the black box of tracking decisions: Critical tales of families navigating the course placement process." In her case studies of 19 ninth-grade students and their families in a comprehensive high school in California, Yonezawa reveals how families' biographies and relationships influence the schooling process. Through four critical tales, Yonezawa shows that students in the same school may have very different schooling experiences, which are likely to result in very different post-high school opportunities.

Part III of this book includes empirical studies on factors that influence the educational experience of African-American students, currently the largest minority student population in U.S. public schools. Despite gains over the past three decades, the educational experiences of African-American youths remain illustrative of the nation's failure to extend equal educational opportunity to poor and minority students. The four chapters in this section use different methodologies and data sources to identify and examine how schools, families, teachers, and communities influence the educational opportunities and outcomes of African-American adolescents.

The first chapter in this section is titled "Gender and the effects of school, family, and church support on the academic achievement of African-American urban adolescents." In this chapter, Sanders and Herting explore how teacher support, family support, and church involvement differentially influence the attitudes, behaviors, and academic outcomes of African-American male and female adolescents. The authors find evidence that African-American male adolescents are less likely than are their female counterparts to report high levels of teacher and family support or church involvement. African-American male adolescents also report lower academic self-concepts and achievement ideologies, higher levels of school misconduct, and lower grades. These findings are discussed relative to school reform efforts that target African-American youth.

The second chapter, "African-American teachers and the roles they play," focuses on how exemplary African-American teachers use various competencies to promote the success of African-American youth. In this chapter, Mitchell analyzes life history data from eight retired teachers to explore the roles they played in their students lives and how these roles might inform teacher practice. Her conclusions draw attention to the role of professional development in educational reforms that seek to improve poor and minority students' schooling experiences.

The third chapter examines school and community factors that influence the success of African American adolescents attending elite independent schools. In "African-American students' success in independent schools: A model of family, school, and peer influences," Cooper and Datnow show the importance of school climate, and family and peer support for African-American students' success in elite independent schools. The authors conclude this chapter with insights into how the findings gleaned from their study can inform the policies and practices of public schools that serve larger populations of African-American adolescents.

The final chapter is this section is titled "Creating a climate for diversity? The institutional response of predominantly White independent schools to African-American students." In this chapter, Datnow and Cooper use interview and observational data to show factors that influence whether elite, independent schools create climates that promote the success of their African-American students. The authors contend that structural changes alone are not sufficient to create a school climate that encourages academic engagement and excellence among all students. They argue that changes in school culture also are necessary to ensure that elite independent schools are inclusive and responsive to cultural diversity.

The final section of this book moves readers from empirical research to current educational policies and practical reforms. Part IV includes chapters that describe five different reform efforts that are currently being implemented to improve educational opportunities and outcomes for poor and minority adolescents. In the first chapter in this section, "Toward an understanding of school reconstitution as a strategy to educate students placed at risk," Mintrop examines school reconstitution as one of the "get-tough" educational reform policies that are in vogue. Drawing on both theory and case study data, he explores how reconstitution policies may affect teachers' motivation and performance in schools that serve large numbers of poor and minority students. This chapter provides food for thought concerning reconstitution policies and their potential to reform at-risk schools.

The second chapter provides an overview and nascent results of a middle school reform effort. In "Talent development middle schools: Blueprints and results for a comprehensive whole school reform model," MacIver, MacIver, Balfanz, Plank, and Ruby discuss the obstacles and successes encountered at two middle schools in Philadelphia that are undertaking whole school reform. The authors also discuss the supports necessary to encourage successful implementation of the model.

The third chapter in this section describes a reform effort that is occurring in several high school classrooms across the nation. McClendon, Nettles, and

Wigfield evaluate the success of the PASS (Promoting Achievement in School through Sport) program in creating content-rich classrooms that promote high school students' achievement and resilience. They also identify factors that make these classrooms more engaging for students and that may account for the documented improvements in participating students' achievement.

Legters, in "Small learning communities meet school-to-work: Whole school restructuring for urban comprehensive high schools," describes how some high schools are pulling together specific reform practices in a schoolwide attempt to improve student outcomes. After describing the origins of these reform practices, Legters discusses their implementation in several schools that she and colleagues have worked with as part of the talent development high schools project. Legters concludes the chapter with insights into the challenges and possibilities of high school reform.

The last chapter in the section is titled, "Building school-family-community partnerships in middle and high schools." In this chapter, Sanders and Epstein discuss how secondary schools can work with students' families and communities to develop comprehensive partnership programs that focus on students' success. This chapter describes the framework of six types of involvement and the action team approach used by schools in the study to develop their partnership programs. It also discusses challenges the schools face in implementing their programs. This chapter concludes with a discussion of the ingredients necessary for the successful implementation of programs of school-family-community partnerships.

Schools in the United States must provide poor and minority students with educational opportunities that ensure that they have the tools necessary to become full and productive citizens. Meeting this challenge requires continued commitment and effort from all involved in the educational process. The chapters included in this book do not necessarily provide definitive answers on how to meet this challenge. They do, however, offer suggestions about, identify obstacles to, and provide examples of educational practices and reforms that can make a difference in the schooling and life chances of poor and minority adolescents.

ACKNOWLEDGMENTS

I would like to acknowledge the individuals who helped in so many ways to bring this book to completion. Thanks are due to the contributing authors, whose thoughtful chapters have expanded my thinking on the education of poor and minority adolescents. Special thanks are due to contributing authors, Joyce Epstein and Antoinette Mitchell, who gave not only of their wisdom, but also of themselves. I am fortunate and honored to have such concerned and talented individuals as my colleagues. I am equally fortunate to have a research assistant, Lisa Tibor, whose attention to detail, organizational skills, and willingness to tackle the unknown are unparalleled. I am indebted to her for the many ways, large and small, in which she assisted in the completion of this manuscript. I would also like to thank Leonard Rosenbaum, an exceptional indexer with an amazing eye for detail.

Thanks are also due to my family — to my parents, Grover and Vera Sanders, and to each of my four sisters, Desiree, Vetta, Pamela, and Camilla. Their support has made all the difference in my life. I also would like to thank my husband, Jeffrey Sims. Without his love, patience, and timely pep talks, this book would not have been completed. He is a source of inspiration.

I

Reframing Students Placed At Risk:
A Historical Look

1

Students At Promise and Resilient: A Historical Look at Risk

WILLIAM FRANKLIN
California State University, Los Angeles

The notion of "risk" in education is borrowed from epidemiological models. Although the epidemiological model often used in risk discourse may be helpful in identifying general student and familial characteristics that make success in school difficult, the focus is on risk and vulnerability, not promise, protection, and resilience. The ecological framework proposed in this chapter goes beyond looking at populations at risk to critically examining student/environment interactions that may place students at risk. Moreover, the perspective recognizes that in most student/environment interactions there is likely to be a continuum of risk and protective variables. Thus, the chapter endeavors to: (a) revisit risk in education to show how potentially damaging and uninformative it is, particularly with minority and poor youth; (b) demonstrate that risk is a multifaceted and multicausal construct that must be viewed from an interactive and ecological framework; and (c) argue that the research community must focus attention on how families, schools, and communities can foster the development of all youth, who should be considered more "at promise" for school success than at risk for school failure.

The impetus for this review arose while critically examining the literature on risk and protective factors for poor and minority adolescents. It became increasingly clear that the label at risk may place students more at risk than internal and external factors. Moreover, the notion of risk in education is relatively new but its widespread abuse and use to flag non-normative development, cultural "deficits," and academic problems is old and uncomfortably familiar. At risk, as a classification, disproportionately relies on broad sociodemographic criteria (i.e., race, ethnicity, social class) to predict delinquency or remediation. By definition it is incapable of explaining individual variation and serves as the latest in a long line of labels used to stigmatize classes of individuals. As Fine (1995) vehemently contended:

> The language of risk is upon us, piercing daily consciousness, educational practices, and bureaucratic policy-making. Scholars, practitioners, and activists have been quick to name, identify, and ossify those who presumably suffer at the mercy of "risk factors." (p. 76)

The argument could be made that use of the term at risk and practices engendered by the classification are synonymous with labels and behaviors now considered politically incorrect and academically damaging (i.e., culturally deprived, educationally disadvantaged, deficient). History clearly shows that when these labels were used for poor or minority children, they served as immutable referents that spoke only to inadequacies in the child and his or her family. The psychological character, physiological makeup, and cultural patterns of students were often called into question and labeled deficient, as if competence, achievement, and motivation manifested and developed solely in the home.

The current rhetoric of pathology has a new name and unless we, as educators, begin to change the discourse; to deconstruct the insidious use and abuse of risk in education, and to empower parents, schools, and communities to be more responsive to all students, we will continue to embrace a pervasive construct that potentially does more harm than good. Thus, this chapter endeavors to: (a) revisit risk in education, and show how potentially damaging and uninformative it is for poor and minority youth, namely African-American youth, whose experiences will serve as an illustration; (b) demonstrate that risk is a multifaceted and multicausal construct that must be viewed from an interactive and ecological framework; and (c) demonstrate how family, school, and community partnerships have the potential to foster the development of youth who are more at promise for success than at risk for failure.

HISTORY OF RISK IN EDUCATION

Attention to the possible applications of risk research in education has been relatively recent (Winfield, 1991). Risk research historically has been used in medical and psychopathological investigations, and historically has concentrated on patterns and rates of disease and disorder in populations

(Masten & Garmezy, 1991). Researchers in epidemiology and medicine use narrow and exacting criteria to identify and measure outcomes related to specific risk factors. Their studies focus on sensitive and specific correlates of risk and disorder. Sensitivity in risk research refers to the frequency of persons with disorders who were initially considered most vulnerable for an unfavorable outcome. Conversely, specificity refers to the frequency of normative development in persons who were not initially considered at risk (Masten & Garmezy). These criteria are most useful and reliable when risk factors and outcomes are narrowly defined.

In education, children are identified as at risk, and assumptions that there exists a higher probability for the development of psychosocial disorder and academic failure are made based on sociodemographic characteristics. Unfortunately, use of the risk paradigm in the educational setting has engendered more victim blaming and labeling as it relates to poor and minority children. In its attempt to help remediate and provide equal education for poor and minority students by identifying those who may be at risk for academic failure, it has systematically indicted many students with its "disease-model" concentration. This concentration is far too common in programs and policies that, historically, have been designed to improve academic outcomes for poor and minority youth. There are differences in individual outcomes that have been ignored by epidemiological risk research, perhaps out of necessity and by design. However, when educators use the same generalized risk conceptions on poor and minority youth, subjective and phenomenological indicators of healthy outcomes are overlooked.

Moreover, one of the claims of this chapter is that the term "at risk" is synonymous with the now politically incorrect term, "culturally deprived" (Swadener & Lubeck, 1995). Supporters of the cultural deprivation theory looked at the culture of groups and their environments as predisposing factors for academic failure. The risk paradigm engenders a similar focus on higher incidence and probability of disorder in certain populations, and thus has established an alliance with the outdated cultural deprivation theory. Both theories tend to completely exonerate schools and communities, thereby making the individual, the family, and the socialization process culpable.

Educators continue to ask, "Is the child ready for school?" and, "Is the child at risk of failing school?" The inherent danger in solely making such inquiries is that blame or credit is unduly placed on the child. Educators must also ask, "Is the school ready for the child?" and, "Is the school at risk of failing the child?" Knowledge and learning are far too complex and interdependent to place the responsibility for outcomes solely on the learner. Poor and minority youth are not homogenous, and their diverse skills and talents have been overlooked and understudied in the literature (Winfield, 1991). There is clearly a diversity of competencies, attitudes, and behaviors in these populations. Moreover, there are areas that have been overlooked in risk paradigms that must be factored in the developmental trajectory as key to adaptation and success.

RISK AND AFRICAN-AMERICAN YOUTH

The life experiences of African-American adolescents in this country are complicated by an array of issues rarely faced by majority youths. The historical vestiges of legally sanctioned exclusion and discrimination, coupled with the contemporary pervasiveness of unequal outcomes and racism, interact in complex ways and have a grave impact on educational attainment for African-American youth (Pine & Hilliard, 1990). African-American students, for example, are grossly underrepresented in academic tracks designed to prepare them for postsecondary education, and they receive inadequate amounts of math, science, and computer training while in high school (Lomotey, 1990). Despite modest gains between 1986 and 1996, African-American adolescents' academic performance while in school is still significantly below that of their White counterparts. Specifically, in 1996, African-American 17 year olds had an average reading proficiency that was equal to that of White 13 year olds. When math and science indices were noted, African-American 17 year olds performed below the level of White 13 year olds (National Center for Educational Statistics [NCES], 1998). In 1995, the percentage of African-American high school status dropouts was higher than that of Whites, 11.4% versus 8.4%, respectively. Of the African-American youth who fail to complete high school, about 1/10 have less than a 9th-grade education, and about 1/4 have less than a 10th-grade education. Given these indicators, it is not surprising that African-Americans who persist to graduation are less likely to be qualified to attend 4-year colleges and universities than their white counterparts (NCES, 1997). In summary, African-American youth are disproportionately *placed* at risk for academic failure; school dropout; and inadequate skills in mathematics, science, and technology.

African-American Youth and Academic Achievement

The relationship between poverty, institutional racism, social inequalities, and the achievement levels of African-American students has been well researched and documented (Anderson, 1984; Committee for Economic Development, 1987; Ford, 1992). These studies contend that low achievement and failure may be due to the longstanding social, political, and economic institutions that have failed to wholly address the needs of African-American youth.

Yet, despite the larger systemic barriers, the pernicious and ingrained devaluing that occurs in the school setting, and other forces that factor into the paradox of low achievement and school failure, many African-American students not only survive but excel against the odds. Developmental paradigms, however, disproportionately view poverty and many of the social ills that plague African-American youth as invariably malignant. Research on the diversity of achievement levels and competencies among poor African-American adolescents has been scarce. This is a costly oversight. Underachievement persists even in populations that do not have historical, socioeconomic, and institutional forces that conspire to hinder achievement. Because underachievement is a widespread phenomenon in the United States, analyses of African-American adolescent achievement patterns could substantially contribute to the field (Carr, Borkowski, & Maxwell, 1991).

Research on African-American youth clearly shows that these children, like virtually all children, begin school with an interest in learning and the ability to do so (Kunjufu, 1984). Somewhere in their educational trek, however, enthusiasm wanes, and school is viewed as a hostile and uncaring environment (Pine & Hilliard, 1990). Anderson (1984) argued that: "any student of Black achievement behavior should recognize at the outset that historically much discordance has reigned between Blacks' motivation to achieve and their opportunities to achieve" (p. 104). Many of the interventions and research studies have focused on improving skills and increasing motivation in the at risk student. Although these are important, educators and researchers must also concentrate on how schools and the larger society may engender failure in African-American youth (Pine & Hilliard). Research on poor and minority youth, especially those considered at risk, must be embedded in a conceptual framework that contextualizes and incorporates the complexity of structural influences operating in their lives.

AN ECOLOGICAL FRAMEWORK THAT FOSTERS AT-PROMISE YOUTH

Lewin (1951), used the term *lifespace* to describe the nexus between an individual's development and his or her environment. The lifespace of

African-American adolescents is composed of the following: (a) the adolescent, (b) the family, (c) the school, (d) the neighborhood, (e) the service community, and (f) sociopolitical structures and processes. An ecological framework goes beyond viewing populations as at risk to critically examining student/environment interactions that occur in all areas of the lifespace. The epidemiological/medical model used in risk discourse may be helpful in identifying general student and familial characteristics that make academic achievement difficult. But when used alone, the focus is on risk and vulnerability, not promise, protection and resilience. The ecological perspective recognizes that in most student/environment interactions there is likely to be a continuum of risk *and* protective factors.

Protective factors are those processes that interact with risk factors to decrease the probability that an individual experiences an adverse outcome. Rutter (1979) insisted that the scientific community has been remiss in its efforts to assist deprived and disadvantaged children because scientists have not focused on influences that ameliorate, protect, neutralize, and provide support for individuals in adverse conditions. Not all children succumb to deprivation and distress, and research on their experiences could greatly impact prevention paradigms.

Anthony (1987) coined the term *invulnerable child* to discuss his exploration of children who gain competencies despite seemingly insurmountable odds. He discovered that children of psychotic parents were protected from adverse outcomes because of their ability to remove themselves psychologically from the environment and maintain confidence in their ability. Masten and Garmezy (1991), however, maintained that the term "invulnerable" is inaccurate because it implies that individuals are somehow immune to a disorder or have escaped damage altogether. Instead, they argued that the term "resilient" is more fitting because it denotes a transactional relationship between individuals and their environment. Resilient individuals have a greater opportunity for success when protective factors increase or improve in quality, and the number of risk factors descreases.

These studies and others like them have the potential to move the research community beyond the long-standing focus on risk toward the construct of resilience. However, there is an inherent danger in viewing resilience solely as a psychological or intrapersonal trait. Crediting individuals for achieving or blaming them for failing, without considering the complex and varied influences in their environment, may be equally damaging.

Garmezy and Neuchterlein (1972) identified individual, familial, and social factors in resilient children who had been exposed to conditions of poverty.

Resilient children were highly motivated to perform well and possessed an internal locus of control. Their families were often not intact, yet there was order, discipline, and structure. Garmezy's work has helped to lay a foundation for examining the role of protective and compensatory factors in children placed at risk. It is important to note that protective resources are both constitutional and experiential. Resilient youth may display high self-esteem, acquire coping skills, and have positive experiences outside of the home. Thus, both constitutional and experiential factors impact healthy outcomes.

Werner and Smith (1982), in their study of children on the island of Kauai, emphasized that it is important to look at how "constitutional and experiential factors correlate to bring about developmental outcomes in children and adolescents" (p. 171). Their longitudinal study began in 1954 and research teams conducted follow-up visits when the youth were 2, 10, and 18 years old. During adolescence there appear to be four protective mechanisms, constitutional and environmental, that foster and enhance resilience. Resilient adolescents: (a) are more responsible; (b) appreciate and are successful in environments that provide structure; (c) have more emotional support from family members; and (d) receive more interpersonal support from members in the community (e.g., peers, ministers, and teachers). Moreover, resilient adolescents possess strong capability and context beliefs, respond well to positive influences in their lives, and are more oriented toward achievement.

McIntyre, White, and Yoast (1990) maintained that resilient youth are repeatedly identified in the literature as possessing "positive self-regard, high self-esteem, optimism, motivation to perform well and an internal locus of control" (p. 24). Hauser, Vieyra, Jacobson, and Wertlieb (1985) contended that personality, and social and familial associations, can be consistently detected in resilient youth from high-risk environments (e.g., those characterized by poverty, abuse, psychotic families, and chronic illness).

Again, it is important to note that the ecological framework allows us to examine student/environment interactions. In the above examples, risk, protection and resilience were researched and discovered in the multiple ecologies that characterize the lives of youth. Risk and vulnerability findings, on the other hand, are disproportionately limited to characteristics of students and their families. Community factors and school correlates are left essentially unexamined. According to Richardson, Casanova, Placier, and Guilfoyle (1989), the interactional approach to the study of at risk status contrasts with the model prevalent in at risk literature. These authors contended that the latter, called the epidemiological model "suggests a linear relationship between certain student characteristics and undesirable outcomes" (p. 138).

Brofenbrenner's (1977; 1989) theory of ecological development also provides insight into factors affecting student resilience. Brofenbrenner maintained that there are five environmental systems that provide a sociocultural lens of development. The five systems are (a) microsystem, the setting in which individuals live; (b) mesosystem, the relationships between microsystems or connections between contexts; (c) exosystem, experiences in a social setting, in which an individual does not have an active role, that influence what the person experiences in his or her immediate context; (d) macrosystem, the culture in which individuals live; and (e) chronosystem, patterns of environmental events and transitions over the life course (Santrock, 1996). Brofenbrenner contended that development is directly influenced by the microsystem, and by similarities and differences in patterns of interaction, resources, beliefs, and values across the various systems in one's lifespace.

A system this dynamic, interactive, and malleable paints a picture different from that proffered by the at risk paradigm. Challenging the overly deterministic nature of the at risk paradigm, Garard (1995) asserted that "not only does the student lack control and voice in determining if s/he is labeled 'at risk', s/he appears unable to change that label" (p. 4). Research studies on risk and resilience must incorporate the subjective experiences of poor and minority youth. Their perceptions of stressors and protective factors in their lifespace must be factored in to any quantitative or qualitative assessment. If a young person does not perceive elements in their environment to be traumatic and achievement limiting, then a researcher's notion of "at risk" or "resilient" may be ignoring key attributional information.

The ecological approach allows researchers to look across multiple ecologies for factors that may contribute to academic failure and success. The identification of both risk and protective factors in the family, school, and larger community and society broadens the scope of viable prevention and intervention strategies.

Families That Foster At-Promise Youth

The family is, of course, one of the most influential sources of environmental protection (Clark, 1983). The home environment shapes and reinforces the child's sense of efficacy in an academic setting by establishing positive values about education, establishing homework rituals, setting academic standards, and supporting school-related functions.

The composition of the family appears to be related to academic outcomes. The research literature is replete with information about how children who live in single-parent homes receive lower standardized test scores and attain poor marks in school (Natriello, McDill, & Pallas, 1990). Garmezy (1981), however, argued that the research evidence to support the favorable effects of a two-parent household is not unfailingly consistent. Many academically resilient children reside in homes where the father is not present, and the mother has maintained a supportive and structured environment conducive to achievement.

Research on risk and protective factors strongly suggests that a stable and nurturing family life is a mediating variable for poor and minority children and youth, regardless of the family's composition. Grossman et al. (1992) discovered that a young adolescent's perception of family cohesion and open communication with his or her parents was directly correlated with positive outcomes and adaptability. Alva (1991), in her examination of protective resources and appraisals in Mexican-American students, found that academically at-promise students experience less conflict and stress at home, and take greater advantage of the resources in their family networks. These studies and others like them point to the efficacy of good parenting and its relationship to achievement and success, even in environments that are considered high risk.

Use of the resiliency construct may cause individuals with political stakes to espouse the "bootstrap" theory. The notion that, if parents only do their jobs, poor and minority youth can overcome any environmental deficiencies ignores other important ecological influences. In far too many poor and minority communities, there are serious structural and economic challenges confronting families. The attention on resilient families in those communities should not remove the focus from improving and revitalizing our neighborhoods, schools, and cities.

Communities That Foster At-Promise Youth

Community can be defined in a number of ways, but here it means the physical composition and cultural milieu of neighborhoods in a general locale. Physical composition includes homes, landmarks, and the overall quality and character of the area. The cultural milieu focuses on the values, norms, and precepts espoused by significant others, including family members, neighborhood friends, non related adults, churches, youth organizations, and local businesses.

The community can serve as a support resource outside of the family. Even when the home is not a source of protection, community-based groups can help to buffer the child by providing the social capital needed (Coleman, 1987). To this end, community involvement consists of the formal and informal action and response of businesses, schools, churches, and social service providers to the needs of youth within their local boundaries (Nettles, 1989).

Comer (1980) contended that a support mechanism consisting of one individual or a group of individuals that motivate, inspire, and care has the capability of providing the resources children need to be resilient in the face of adversity. Lomotey (1990) argued that the entire African-American community must galvanize, accept their responsibility, and become more involved in the issues confronting their youth. Communities, therefore, can be instrumental in helping to further identify and eradicate the factors that devalue, discount, and deny equal educational outcomes for poor and minority youth.

Schools That Foster At-Promise Youth

Many scholars maintain that the school system, as it currently operates, is ill equipped to offer the support children now desperately need in light of changing family, economic, and community patterns (Coleman, 1987; Jones, 1989; Pine & Hilliard, 1990). This support is especially crucial for poor students, and in particular African-American adolescents, who continue to experience dissonance, devaluation and discontinuity in the educational system (Pine & Hilliard). Neisser (1986) argued that it may be necessary to separate the questions of *will* and *should* from that of *can*, especially as they relate to African-American students:

> Children who view the educational context as hostile to their own interests and as undermining their integrity may a) decide that what they *should* do is not what the teacher thinks should be done; b) act in a way that they *will* not do what the teacher wants, and c) display what they *can* do in ways that are not in accordance with what the teacher prescribes. (p. 79)

These behavior patterns are not at all irrational if an environment is viewed as uncaring, culturally incompetent, antagonistic, and oppressive. Unfortunately, teachers' counteractions to such behavior are usually consistent with the broader school context, and consequently poor and minority students are often labeled defiant, deficient, or unmotivated. Such labels disproportionately relegate these students to academic failure and dropout when they are placed in dead-end special education classes, suspended or expelled from school, or tracked into low-level academic courses. These are examples of the environmental unresponsiveness that engenders low achievement. Many schools fail to create environments that value and appreciate cultural differences through curricular, attitudinal, and administrative mechanisms (Pine & Hilliard, 1990; Datnow & Cooper, Chapter 10, this volume).

Teachers often view poor and minority students and the environments from which they come as adversarial, homogenous, and unchangeable. However, when armed with a different orientation, which promotes understanding of the larger structures that shape urban environments, and acknowledges the presence of protective and supportive community resources, teachers are better equipped to build bridges of trust and support so that learning can take place. To encourage this effort, teacher education programs should expand to include courses in urban history, urban sociology, community awareness, and other courses that build a greater awareness of their students' communities. When teachers begin to understand the historical and structural forces that shape communities and impact individuals, then perhaps such understanding will promote cooperation where there has been dissension, and collaboration where there has been conflict (see Mitchell, Chapter 8, this volume).

Effective schools for poor and minority students have historically shared common characteristics: a strong principal, a climate of high expectations where no child is allowed to fall below prescribed levels, and a strategy for closely monitoring scholastic progress (Edmonds, 1979; Smith & Chunn, 1989; Catterall, 1998; Crowther, 1998). Even in low-income, crime-ridden areas that have been slated for low achievement, good schools can provide the social capital students need to excel. In a study conducted by Bowser and Perkins (1991) on academically resilient African-American and Latino students, it was demonstrated that these students had at least one teacher or counselor who had been personally interested and supportive, and who believed in their scholastic abilities.

Teachers, counselors, and administrators play a pivotal role in shaping healthy achievement goals and promoting student success (see Yonezawa, Chapter 6, this volume; Jordan & Plank, Chapter 5, this volume). If they fail to acknowledge and nourish students' potential and link classroom learning to career objectives, students may fail to see the value of education. Many poor and minority students place less significance on education and its ability to fulfill promises of upward mobility, equal opportunity, and gainful employment. These students' awareness that educational attainment does not automatically ensure success in the opportunity structure must not be overlooked or downplayed (Mickelson, 1990).

CONCLUSION: PARTNERSHIPS
THAT FOSTER YOUTH AT PROMISE

Perhaps one of the most salient implications to be drawn from this review is the need for family, school, and community partnerships. The findings suggest that academic achievement, social responsibility, and achievement orientation are influenced by a variety of risk and protective factors in multiple ecologies, most notably, the family, the school, and the community. Achievement outcomes can be positively impacted through collaborative programs and services. Moreover, family, school, and community partnerships can lead to a comprehensive and responsive set of strategies to minimize risk factors and identify protective resources in students' lives.

Research findings indicate that parent involvement in schools tends to decline when students reach the secondary level due to adolescents' need for autonomy (Caissy, 1994). Further, high schools are larger and more complex, and many parents may not have the time or knowledge to become more actively involved without direct guidance and support from schools (Dornbusch & Glasgow, 1996). In light of these obstacles, creation of effective school, family, and community partnerships must begin with an assessment of what practices are appropriate and realistic. It may be helpful for schools to begin establishing partnerships by opening up lines of communication and earning parent and community trust (see Sanders & Epstein, Chapter 15, this volume).

The benefits from family, school, and community links are limitless. Families can gain knowledge and practical information about adolescent development, parenting, establishing home environments that support learning, and helping students with postsecondary planning (see Jordan & Plank). Teachers can obtain assistance from parents and community advocates on lessons and strategies that will sustain student interest and bolster academic effort. Communities can work to establish school-based health care programs, school-to-work formulas, and community resource identification and referral for families in need.

Family, school, and community links have the potential to enrich achievement outcomes, and the quality of life for poor and minority students. Moreover, these collaborative partnerships have the potential to increase our knowledge of students' lives in the context of larger structures, and may be instrumental in helping to provide an explicit understanding of how youth determine their interaction with these structures and gain the power to transcend them. Family, school, and community partnerships can play a vital role in fostering resilience by helping students identify specific factors that hinder success, and by assisting in the development of culturally competent prevention and intervention strategies and support mechanisms. These partnerships can also provide tangible evidence that will help to eradicate the fixation on the at risk paradigm. If families, schools, and communities are cognizant of and responsive to student needs, they have the potential to produce poor and minority youth who are more at promise for success than at risk for failure.

REFERENCES

Alva, S. A. (1991). Academic invulnerability among Mexican-American students: The importance of protective resources and appraisals. *Hispanic Journal of Behavioral Sciences, 13*, 18-34.

Anderson, J. D. (1984). The schooling and achievement of Black children. *Advances in Motivation and Achievement, 1*, 103-122.

Anthony, E. J. (1987). Risk, vulnerability and resilience: An overview. In E. J. Anthony & B. J. Colher (Eds.), *The invulnerable child.* New York: Guilford.

Brofenbrenner, U. (1977). Toward an experimental ecology of human development. *American Psychologist, 32*, 513-529.

Brofenbrenner, U. (1989).Ecological systems theory. In R.Vasta (Ed.), *Annals of child development: revised formulations and current issues* (pp.187-249). Greenwich, CT: JAI.

Bowser, B. P., & Perkins, H. (1991). Success against the odds. Young Black men tell what it takes. In B. P. Bowser (Ed.), *Black male adolescents.* New York: University Press of America.

Caissy, G. (1994). *Early adolescence: Understanding the 10-15 year old.* New York: Insight Books.

Carr, M., Borkowski, J., & Maxwell, A. (1991). Motivational components of underachievement. *Developmental Psychology, 27*, 108-118.

Catterall, J.(1998). Risk and resilience in student transitions to high school. *American Journal of Education, 106*, 302-333

Clark, R. M. (1983). *Family life and school achievement: Why poor black children succeed or fail.* Chicago: University of Chicago Press.

Coleman, J. S. (1987). Families and schools. *Educational Researcher, 17*, 32-38.

Comer, J. P. (1980). *School power.* New York: The Free Press.

Committee for Economic Development (1987). *Children in need: Investment strategies for the educational disadvantaged.* New York: Author.

Crowther, S. (1998). Secrets of staff development support. *Educational Leadership, 55*: 75-76.

Dornbusch, S. M., & Glasgow, K. L. (1996). The structural context of family-school relations. In A. Booth and J. F. Dunn (eds.), *Family-school links: How do they affect educational outcomes?* (pp.35-44), Mahwah, NJ: Lawrence Erlbaum Associates.

Edmonds, R. (1979). Effective schools for the urban poor. *Educational Leadership, 37*, 15-27.

Fine, M. (1995). The politics of who's at-risk. In B. B. Swadener & S. Lubeck (Eds.), *Children and families at-promise.* New York: State University of New York Press.

Ford, D. Y. (1992). Self-perceptions of underachievement and support for the achievement ideology among early adolescent African-Americans. *Journal of Early Adolescence*, 12, 228-252.

Garard, D. (1995). *Defining the at-risk student: Conceptual and theoretical considerations.* Paper presented at the SCA Conference, San Antonio, TX.

Garmezy, N. (1981). Children under stress: Perspectives on antecedents and correlates of vulnerability and resistance to psychopathology. In A.I. Rabin, J. Arnoff, A. Barclay, & R. Zucker (Eds.) *Further explorations in personality* (pp. 196-270). New York: Wiley.

Garmezy, N., & Neuchterlein, K. H. (1972). Invulnerable children: The fact and fiction of competence and disadvantage. *American Journal of Orthopsychiatry*, 42, 328-329.

Grossman, F., Beinashowitz, J., Anderson, L., Sakurai, M., Finnin, L., & Flaherty, M. (1992). Risk and resilience in young adolescents. *Journal of Youth and Adolescence*, 21, 529-549.

Hauser, S., Vieyra, M., Jacobson, A., & Wertlieb, D. (1985). Vulnerability and resilience in adolescence: Views from the family. *Journal of Early Adolescence*, 5, 81-106.

Jones, R. L. (Ed.). (1989). *Black adolescents.* Berkeley, CA: Cobb & Henry.

Kunjufu, J. (1984). *Countering the conspiracy to destroy Black boys.* Chicago: Afro-Am.

Lewin, K. (1951). *Field theory in social sciences.* New York: Harper Press.

Lomotey, K. (1990). *Going to school.* New York: State University of New York Press.

Masten, A. S., & Garmezy, N. (1991). Risk, vulnerability and protective factors in developmental psychopathology. In D. B. Lahey & A. E. Kazdin (Eds.), *Advances in clinical child psychopathology,* (Vol. 8, pp. 1-51) New York: Plenum.

McIntyre, K., White, D., & Yoast, R. (1990). *Resilience among high risk youth.* Madison, WI: Clearinghouse.

Mickelson, R. A. (1990). The attitude-achievement paradox among Black adolescents. *Sociology of Education,* 63, 44-61.

National Center for Educational Statistics (1997). *Confronting the odds: Students at-risk and the pipeline to higher education.* Washington, DC: Author.

National Center for Educational Statistics (1998). *NAEP 1996 trends in academic progress: Achievement of U.S. students in science, 1969-1997; mathematics, 1969 - 1996; reading, 1971-1986; writing, 1984-1996.* Washington, DC: Author.

Natriello, G., McDill, E. L., & Pallas, A. M. (1990). Schooling disadvantaged children: Racing against catastrophe. New York: Teachers College Press.

Neisser, U. (1986). *The school achievement of minority children.* Hillsdale, NJ: Lawrence Erlbaum Associates.

Nettles, S. M. (1989). The role of community involvement in fostering investment behavior in low-income Black adolescents. *Journal of Adolescent Research*, 4, 190-201

Pine, G. J., & Hilliard, A. G. (1990). R_x for racism: Imperatives for America's schools. *Phi Delta Kappan,* 56, 593-600.

Richardson, V., Casanova, U., Placier, P., & Guilfoyle, K. (1989). *School children at-risk.* London: Falmer.

Rutter, M. (1979). Protective factors in children's responses to stress and disadvantage. In M. W. Kent & J. E. Rolf (Eds.), *Primary prevention of psychopathology.* Hanover, VT: The University Press of New England.

Santrock, J. W. (1996). *Child Development.* Dubuque, IA: Brown & Benchmark.

Smith, W., & Chunn, E. (1989). *Black education: A quest for equity and excellence.* New Brunswick: Transaction.

Swadener, B., & Lubeck, S. (1995). *Children and families at promise: Deconstructing the discourse of risk.* New York: State University of New York Press.

Werner, E. E. & Smith, R. S. (1982). *Vulnerable but invincible: A longitudinal study of resilient children and youth.* New York: McGraw-Hill.

Winfield, L. F. (1991). Resilience, schooling and development in African-American youth: A conceptual framework. *Education and Urban Society*, 24, 5-14.

2

Historical Trends in Federal Education Policies That Target Students Placed At Risk

ANTOINETTE MITCHELL
Urban Institute

Children who live in poverty are more likely than others to experience educational difficulties that place them at risk for school failure. Recognizing this relationship between poverty and academic performance, the federal government has passed several important pieces of legislation designed to address the educational needs of poor students. Through an analysis of the Elementary and Secondary Education Act of 1965, and the Improving America's Schools Act of 1994, this chapter traces the evolution and impact of federal policies implemented to improve the academic performance of students placed at risk. In so doing, it examines both the challenges and the opportunities inherent in federal support to schools serving poor and at-risk youths.

The U.S. constitution is silent on the issue of which entity shall govern education. As a result of this silence, education is recognized as a de facto responsibility of the states. Traditionally, local governments manage school districts, while states oversee broader policy objectives. The federal government's role in education was fairly negligible until 1954, when *Brown vs. Board of Education, Topeka* and other later judicial desegregation decisions began to encroach on state and local governments' control over educational policies. The federal government's legislative commitment to the provision of equal educational opportunities for disadvantaged students was codified in 1965, with the passage of the Elementary and Secondary Education Act (ESEA). Since then, the federal role in education has been expanding.

Passed as part of then President Lyndon Johnson's "Great Society" social agenda, ESEA was designed to focus attention on the educational needs of poor and minority students. Policymakers sought to equalize educational opportunity by improving the quality of education that these students received. They strongly linked equal educational opportunities to employment and the elimination of poverty.

As a result of this legislation, federal aid to education increased from $ 0.5 billion to $3.5 billion dollars between 1960 and 1970. Similarly, the number of federal programs increased dramatically, from 20 in 1960 to 130 in 1970. The programs supported by ESEA concentrated federal funding on categorical programs that provided greater educational opportunities for economically disadvantaged youth. The most notable of these programs, comprising up to 80% of all ESEA funding, was Title I. Although the federal government provided the resources and the regulations necessary to ensure that the funding was spent as Congress intended, it left the design and implementation of the programs to state and local governments. ESEA established the federal government as an important funding source in the education of disadvantaged students. Although ESEA funding has never exceeded 10% of the total spending on education nationally, it constitutes an important effort in equalizing educational opportunities for millions of poor and minority students.

Through ESEA and many of its later amendments, the categorical nature of the programs, particularly Title I programs, was maintained and even strengthened to ensure that local educational agencies (LEAs) developed programs that addressed the needs of disadvantaged students. However, the 1983 publication of "A Nation at Risk" warned the nation of the "rising tide of mediocrity" in American schools and was a federal call to arms on behalf of education in general. The report, sponsored by the National Commission on Excellence in Education, called on the states to make voluntary reforms including more rigorous course work, longer school days, and increased teacher accountability. The report marked the beginning of a shift in federal focus from disadvantaged students to all students and moved education to the forefront of the national agenda.

After 10 years of unremarkable state-led reform, President Clinton signed into law the Goals 2000: Educate America Act (Goals 2000). A few months later, ESEA was revamped and reauthorized. These laws, passed as part of President Clinton's "Human Capital" agenda, marked the first time that the federal government established a framework for educational reform (Riley, 1994). The legislation, although voluntary and providing for local autonomy, adopted eight national goals. It strongly encouraged states to adopt standards of what students should know and be able to do based on national models, and to align their educational systems to meet these standards.

This chapter examines the evolution of federal involvement in education, concentrating on ESEA; the federal role in education during the 1980s; and current federal education policies, namely Goals 2000 and the reauthorization of ESEA in 1994. In the first section, I review the assumptions and beliefs of the policymakers who crafted the 1965 legislation, the reasons the legislation was passed, and the effects of the legislation on student achievement. In the second section, I review the role of the federal government in education during the 1980s, highlighting the report of the National Commission on Excellence in Education and the 1988 reauthorization of ESEA. In the third section, I review the philosophy behind the federal government's current educational agenda, the provisions in Goals 2000 and the 1994 reauthorization of ESEA. I also review existing critiques of the federal government's evolving role in educational reform. In the conclusion, I discuss the federal government's changing role in education, and the potential of federally funded programs to significantly influence educational opportunities and outcomes for historically underserved youth.

THE ELEMENTARY AND
SECONDARY EDUCATION ACT OF 1965

ESEA is commonly identified as one of the most important pieces of legislation to emerge from President Lyndon Johnson's Great Society, the initiative designed to eliminate poverty in the United States. This legislation enhanced the federal role in education by providing financial aid for elementary and secondary schools. The aid was distributed to states based on a formula involving the number of students living in poverty. States then gave grants to LEAs, which were primarily responsible for determining the types of projects implemented in schools. In addition to providing funds for programs to improve the educational opportunities of disadvantaged children (Title I), the legislation also provided aid for (a) school library resources, textbooks, and other instructional materials; (b) supplementary education centers and services; (c) education research and training; and (d) state departments of education. Overall, ESEA provided struggling school systems with extra funds to meet the educational needs of economically disadvantaged students.

The Passage of ESEA

A major hurdle in getting the ESEA legislation passed was the impasse between the National Education Association and the National Catholic Welfare Conference. The two competing interest groups were split on the provision of federal aid to parochial schools and on categorical versus general aid to education. The compromise agreed to was that the private/Catholic schools would receive no funds under ESEA, but LEAs that received funds would provide "special educational services and arrangements (such as dual enrollment, educational radio and television, and mobile educational services and equipment) to address the needs of disadvantaged students attending private schools" (Riley, 1994).

Beyond this compromise, historians have identified several reasons for the passage of the ESEA legislation. Kantor (1991) asserted that this legislation was part of a larger strategy by policymakers in the Kennedy and Johnson administrations to end poverty by enhancing the ability of the poor to obtain jobs and more actively participate in the economy. According to Kantor, the politicians who shaped this legislation were strongly influenced by the culture of poverty literature. The central tenet of this literature, which was popularized by the work of Lewis (1969), was that people who live in poverty are present minded; unable to defer gratification; and plagued by feelings of helplessness, dependence, and inferiority. These attitudes and behaviors, according to the literature, are passed down from one generation to the next. Although Lewis explained the existence of these traits as an adaptation to economic conditions, the general public, policymakers included, often did not recognize this aspect of the theory.

Based on the culture of poverty theory, the Kennedy and Johnson administrations decided that educational programs that "compensated" for the self-defeating attitudes and behaviors of poor youth could break the cycle of poverty. This was the philosophical underpinning of the ESEA legislation. Kantor (1991) argued that the government's reluctance to address the structural causes of poverty, including the distribution of economic resources, was the major flaw in this line of reasoning. He warned that unless educational reform is accompanied by policies that address larger structural issues in the economy, it will fail to improve educational opportunities and outcomes for poor youths.

Although Kaestle and Smith (1982) did not dispute the federal intentions described by Kantor, they did argue that the increased federal role in education between 1940 and 1980 was part of a larger centralizing trend in American educational history. They contended that centralization began in the 19th century, when states began to impose regulations on local districts. Gradually the role of states increased and the population came to accept state regulation of the educational system. Federal involvement is recognized as a continuation of this trend. Kaestle and Smith argued that the movement toward centralization has not been a linear process and is often contested by local resistance. Such resistance may or may not be an indication of local disapproval of centralization, however. For example, they assert that resistance to school desegregation in the 1960s was not against federal involvement per se, but rather against the federal government's attempt to improve the quality of education offered to African-American students.

In another account of why the ESEA legislation was passed, Kantor and Lowe (1995) argued that increased federal involvement in education occurred in the 1960s, in part, as a result of "changes in the relationship between class, race and the state in the 1930's and 1940's." They argued that the accord reached between business and labor during this period reduced pressure on the state to intervene in the labor market, and the emerging Civil Rights movement increased pressure on the government to respond to the poverty of African-Americans. Kantor and Lowe posited that in this policy context, the federal government proposed educational legislation as a politically palatable and inexpensive means of addressing the concerns of African-Americans without seriously addressing segregation and possibly offending White Democrats in both the north and the south. In a more radical analysis of the causes of the legislation, Spring (1976) asserted that the needs of the economic elite were the driving force behind the ESEA legislation. He posited that the programs that emerged from the legislation were designed to impose social order and train workers.

Although historians disagree about why ESEA was passed, they agree that it dramatically changed the role of the federal government in education by increasing its financial support and the regulatory role that accompanied such support. Whereas previously, government support to education had been very limited, suddenly, the government was providing billions of dollars to state educational funds across the country.

In fact, the allocation of funds had always been a stumbling block in earlier attempts to pass legislation involving federal support for education. ESEA was passed because an allocation formula that, while compensatory in nature, provided funds to almost every congressional district in the country was devised. Some critics argued that this formula was a political compromise that ensured the bill's passage at the expense of concentrating funds in areas where they were most needed (Peterson, Rabe, & Wong, 1988).

The Impact of ESEA

In many ways, ESEA did focus attention and resources on the needs of poor and minority students. Initially, many districts disregarded program requirements and made the funding part of the district's general funds (Wargo, Tallmadge, Michaels, Lipe, & Morris, 1972 in Borman & D'Agostino, 1996; Martin & McClure, 1969). In response to these findings, the federal government instituted more stringent program accountability measures. As a result of the new regulations, programs that targeted economically disadvantaged students in most localities were developed and implemented. These programs usually involved tutorial sessions and drills in "Title I labs." In part because standardized test scores became more public, in part because community action around education increased, and in part because of the federal monies tied to special programs for disadvantaged students, many school systems did take notice of historically underserved students.

States across the country, which formerly did not expect or anticipate either federal money or the regulatory requirements that came with it, grew to anticipate federal funding. In fact, federal monies grew to make up almost 10% of some state funding, and more in states and districts with large concentrations of poor students.

As for the legislation's effectiveness in improving the quality of education received by economically disadvantaged students, the record is less encouraging. Until the reauthorization in 1988 (discussed later), federal regulation stressed compliance to guidelines rather than quality of programs being implemented (Heid, 1991). According to Gibboney (1994), the quality of teaching and learning in these programs was (and some might argue continues to be) very low. A review of studies prepared for the 1988 reauthorization indicated that up to that point most Title I teachers had very low expectations for their students. The programs concentrated on the basics, and usually emphasized skills and facts as opposed to critical thinking and problem solving. Usually, students were pulled out of their regular classrooms and taken to the Title I lab where they completed reproduced sheets from workbooks that emphasized the memorization of detached skills.

Relative to the effectiveness of the ESEA legislation, most researchers have found the following:

1. Participating students outperformed similarly disadvantaged students who did not receive program services, but they did not attain or approach the levels of academic achievement of their more advantaged peers.

2. Students participating in Title I[1] math programs gained more than those participating in Title I reading programs.

3. Students in early elementary Title I programs gained more than students participating in later grade programs. (Kennedy, Birman, & Demaline, 1986, p. 17)

According to a meta-analysis of 17 Title I evaluation studies, Borman and D'Agostino (1996) found that the more stringent regulations written into the legislation over time have contributed to a positive trend in the educational effectiveness of Title I in the years of its existence. Although these researchers contended that Title I is supplemental and should not be considered the great equalizer, they acknowledged that Title I has slowed the rate at which disadvantaged students fall behind.

In terms of breaking the cycle of poverty, clearly the legislation has not been successful. More than 20% of children in the United States live in families whose income is below poverty level. The poverty rate increases to more than double that for African-American children. Similarly, the unemployment rate for African-Americans increased from 10% in 1960 to 13% in 1993, and during that period remained at more than double the unemployment rate of White Americans (Hacker, 1992). These statistics serve as a reminder that the war on poverty was lost for Whites and especially for African-Americans.

FEDERAL INVOLVEMENT IN EDUCATION DURING THE 1980s

During the 1970s, the federal government's role in education did not change significantly. Jimmy Carter, fulfilling a campaign promise, converted the Office of Education, which was located within Housing, Education and Welfare, into the Department of Education (Baird, 1996). In addition, spending increased, as did the number of categorical programs. But significant changes in the role of the federal government in education did not occur until the Reagan presidency.

"New Federalism" was the social agenda forwarded by the Reagan

---

[1]The program was called "Chapter 1" from 1981 until ESEA was reauthorized in 1994. In this paper I use its original and current designation of Title I.

administration during its two terms, 1980-1988. This agenda was characterized by the belief that the federal government had amassed too much power and interceded in governmental areas that should be left to the states. Through the Economic Recovery Program, the New Federalism initiative sought to shrink the size of the federal government and to give substantial power back to the states. Separate programs were combined in block grants which provided states with less financial assistance but increased autonomy. In education, this policy translated into attempts to dismantle the Department of Education, to deregulate education programs, to de-emphasize the role of the education in the federal agenda, and to decrease federal spending in education (Verstegen, 1990).

Although the 97th Congress often challenged the president's agenda, federal aid for elementary and secondary education was cut substantially. In real dollars, Title I funds were cut by 12%; accumulated reductions between 1981 and 1988 amounted to almost $7 billion. Similarly, reductions for special programs, including the elementary and secondary block grant, and funding to support magnet schools, amounted to a 28% decrease during the Reagan administration. Reductions in aid during the 1980s substantially decreased the role of the federal government in education (Verstegen, 1990).

In 1983, the Department of Education's Commission on Excellence in Education published a study on American education called "A Nation at Risk." Although no major legislation was passed as a result of this report, it highlighted a perceived decline in the standards of American education and spurred action at the state and local levels. The states went through several waves of reform in reaction to public perceptions about education fostered by "A Nation at Risk" and similar reports (Congressional Budget Office, 1993). Most significantly, the report brought education to the forefront of the national agenda. It led then President Bush to hold an educational summit in 1989 with the nation's governors, and to the announcement of six national education goals in 1990, which were later expanded into eight national goals (Riley, 1994). Clearly, "A Nation at Risk" marked an important juncture in the federal government's involvement in education.

1988 Reauthorization of ESEA

The 1988 reauthorization of ESEA is recognized as a significant point in federal involvement in elementary and secondary education. This reauthorization marked a shift in federal emphasis, moving the focus away from mere compliance with fiscal and programmatic regulations to a concentration on increased academic achievement for economically disadvantaged students.

In part because so many districts received Title I funding, and in part because of the gains, although modest, in the academic achievement of poor and minority children, Title I was perceived by many policymakers as a program worthy of reauthorization. In a review of Title I in preparation for the 1988 reauthorization, however, several criticisms of the program were noted: the program focused on basic skills and not on higher order thinking skills; the funding was spread too thin; and separate programs for individual students were deemed ineffective when entire schools were affected by large numbers of poor children (Jennings, 1991).

To address these criticisms, the Hawkins-Stafford Elementary and Secondary School Improvement Amendments of 1988 incorporated into the legislation major changes in programmatic approach and the allocation of funds. With an emphasis on results and not process, changes included the introduction of higher order thinking skills into the curriculum, a reworking of the allocation formula to concentrate spending on the neediest school districts, and an increase in the number of schoolwide Title I programs due to a decrease in required school poverty rates (from 75% to 65%).

In addition to these changes, the Hawkins amendments added a program improvement provision requiring that school districts determine program effectiveness using measurable outcomes and improve ineffective programs. State and local agencies did not want the federal government to set standards of effectiveness; in fact, each entity wanted to set its own standards of effectiveness. In response to this policy context, rather than establishing rigorous standards, the Department of Education set a minimum standard that any gain in tests scores whatsoever would meet the standard of effectiveness (Heid, 1991). By requiring that states meet this minimum requirement, the amendment lowered the number of programs that would be labeled ineffective.

This low minimum standard has been criticized as not meeting congressional intent to significantly improve Title I programs. Critics contend that the minimum standard was set to avoid identification of ineffective Title I programs, and reinforces lower expectations for poor and minority students; enables too many schools with ineffective Title I programs to continue without improving; will not help Title I programs close the achievement gap between advantaged and disadvantaged students; and sets standards for students in Title I programs which are different and lower than those of other students (Heid, 1991).

Although the program improvement provision is particularly weak, the Hawkins amendments did improve the intended curriculum of Title I programs, concentrate spending on the neediest students, and increase the spending flexibility in schools that had large numbers of economically disadvantaged youth. The Hawkins amendments moved the federal focus more into the policy arena, highlighting educational quality and process issues.

CURRENT FEDERAL EDUCATION POLICY

Goals 2000: Educate America Act

President Clinton's "Human Capital" agenda redefines the role of the federal government in education. It attempts to stimulate and guide state and local education systems to better prepare Americans for working and living in a constantly evolving economy and increasingly sophisticated democracy. Through this agenda, federal involvement in education has shifted emphasis from process and quality to quality, outcomes, and accountability. The Human Capital agenda aims to improve the quality of learning opportunities for all Americans, from early childhood education to the retraining of dislocated workers. Recognizing the importance of a well-educated and trained workforce, it highlights the significance of education to the nation's economic strength and competitiveness (Smith & Scoll, 1995).

For policymakers in the Clinton administration, three factors underscored the importance of improving the education and training of Americans (Smith & Scoll, 1995). First, there was a great deal of frustration on the part of the American public because 10 years of state-led reform efforts, started after the publication of "A Nation at Risk," had had negligible effects on student achievement, reinforcing the notion that the nation's education systems were ineffective. Second, the importance of increasing the competency of the American workforce was underscored by the increased challenges of international economic competition and a changing workplace, which demanded higher skills and greater flexibility from workers. Third, the improvement of learning opportunities for all Americans was perceived to be important for the development and maintenance of an educated and informed citizenry to make decisions about national needs and to find solutions to national problems within the context of a new economy. The Human Capital agenda is the Clinton administration's attempt to address the above concerns through an increased and different federal role in education.

Several significant pieces of legislation define the Human Capital agenda, but none more so than Goals 2000 and the Improving America's School Act of 1994, which is a reauthorization of the ESEA legislation of 1965. The purposes of Goals 2000 are threefold (Riley, 1994):

1. To promote the achievement of important national education goals by the year 2000,

2. To raise student, teacher, and parent expectations through high academic standards for all students and all schools,

3. To assist state and local education reform with grants and greater flexibility.

The legislation is a framework that defines the federal government as a supporter and facilitator of systemic, standards-based reforms. The framework outlined in Goals 2000 is based on 20 years of research about improving quality and equity in schooling. The research emphasizes four points: (a) that under the right circumstances, all students can learn challenging content; (b) that curriculum impacts instruction, and an increase in the rigor of curricula calls for an increase in professional development; (c) that changes in content have important implications for assessment; and (d) that the commitment of those centrally involved in the educational enterprise is critical to successful reform (Smith & Scoll, 1995). As a result of this knowledge, Goals 2000 codified eight national standards (King, 1994). According to these standards, by the year 2000, the following goals will be met:

Goal 1: All children will start school ready to learn.

Goal 2: The high-school graduation rate will increase to at least 90%

Goal 3: All children will leave Grades 4, 8, and 12 competent in challenging subject matter.

Goal 4: The nation's teachers will have access to programs for the continued improvement of their professional skills, and the opportunity to acquire the knowledge and skills needed to instruct and prepare all American students for the next century.

Goal 5: American students will be first in the world in science and math achievement.

Goal 6: Every adult American will be literate and will possess the knowledge and skills necessary to compete in a global economy and exercise the rights and responsibilities of citizenship.

Goal 7: Every American school will be free of drugs, violence, and the unauthorized presence of firearms and alcohol, and will offer a disciplined environment conducive to learning.

Goal 8: Schools will promote parental involvement and participation in the social, emotional and academic growth of their children.

Goals 2000 is a voluntary program that asks states to work toward meeting these goals by first developing content standards that identify the knowledge and the skills students should learn in a particular subject area, and performance standards that specifically identify what students should know and be able to do. Cognizant of the research, Goals 2000 then asks states to align their standards with national standards and to organize their entire educational systems, including curriculum, assessment, instruction and instructional materials, professional development, and parental involvement, around these standards in order to meet them (Riley, 1994). The legislation awards funds to states that develop systemic state improvement plans that include strategies to increase the academic achievement of all students, including students from poor and linguistically diverse backgrounds. The legislation also formally established the National Education Goals Panel to monitor state progress toward achieving the goals articulated in the improvement plans (Stevenson, 1995).

Significantly, the Goals 2000 legislation provides funding to states and to local school districts to both plan and implement their reform efforts. In fiscal year 1994, Congress appropriated $400 million for Goals 2000 grants. Congress authorized funds through 1998.

Two important aspects of the Goals 2000 legislation were hotly contested: the opportunity-to-learn (OTL) standards and the National Education Standards and Improvement Council (NESIC). NESIC, as written in the legislation, was designed to provide technical expertise in the regulation of state reform, although state participation in any NESIC regulatory review was completely voluntary. NESIC was charged with the responsibility of (a) identifying criteria to be used for certifying standards, (b) identifying areas where standards needed to be developed, (c) certifying content and performance standards voluntarily submitted to the council, and (d) certifying OTL standards and state assessments (Riley, 1994).

Members of Congress were wary of NESIC's regulatory role, even though states were not mandated to undergo review. They were especially uncomfortable with giving NESIC the authority to judge state assessments. NESIC itself came to be associated with increased federal regulation and political correctness. As a result, the role of NESIC was drastically reduced and no members were ever officially appointed (Lewis, 1995). Although NESIC was originally conceived to coordinate the reform effort from a national perspective, its demise lessened the national standardization of the current reform effort. For example, three different educational organizations rated state standards and arrived at radically different assessments of their rigor and utility (Archibald, 1998).

Goals 2000 also included reference to OTL standards. Recognizing that districts vary in their ability to provide equal educational opportunities to all children, policymakers sought to reduce this variability through the development of voluntary OTL standards. The inclusion of such standards in the legislation was hotly debated. Some congressional members felt that these standards were needed to ensure that all students, especially historically underserved students in low income districts and schools, who are the most vulnerable to educational failure, would have equal access to the opportunity to learn (i.e., to equal school inputs such as well-trained teachers and adequate instructional materials). They argued that these students would be adversely affected were decisions about promotion and graduation based on high-stakes tests for which students had different or inferior opportunities to learn the materials tested (Elmore & Fuhrman, 1995). Proponents of OTL standards further argued that these standards would place accountability for student learning more appropriately on the shoulders of states and school districts, and not solely on the shoulders of students. In addition, they argued that the federal focus on outcomes did not adequately address issues of equity and school improvement. They supported OTL standards because the standards focused on resources and processes.

However, opponents of OTL standards, including some members of Congress and the National Governor's Association, feared that OTL standards dealt with processes and resource allocations best left to the states. Accordingly, they supported flexibility and deregulation, arguing that OTL standards would be far too prescriptive and would stifle local creativity (Traiman, 1993). An amendment to the Goals legislation that was added to the 1996 final appropriations bill eliminated NESIC and removed all references to OTL standards.

1994 Reauthorization of ESEA

Policymakers in the Clinton administration felt that with Goals 2000, they had established a framework for federal support of elementary and secondary education. Consequently, they viewed the reauthorization of ESEA as an opportunity to place many of the programs aimed to support poor and language minority children under the Goals 2000 umbrella, and to restructure the manner in which the bulk of federal money is distributed. When the legislation was reauthorized in 1994, it included several significant changes. These changes included the following (Smith & Scoll, 1995):

1. A restructuring of curriculum and assessment for students in Title I programs. The new legislation requires that the students in Title I programs be taught the same curriculum and that their progress be measured using the same assessments used for other children.

2. A decrease in the percentage of children living in poverty that is required before a school can become a schoolwide Title I program. This percentage was lowered from 75% to 65% in the 1988 reauthorization, and from 65% to 50% in the 1994 legislation.

3. A broadening of the mission of the Eisenhower program, which expands traditional support that the program provides for professional development in math and science to include other subject areas.

4. A consolidation of technical assistance centers, decreasing the number from 65 to 15. This consolidation ensures standardized service in each location.

5. The provision of funds to support the use of technology to improve teaching and learning.

6. The addition of "safety" to the Drug-Free Schools and Communities Act, which enables schools to use funds to decrease violence in schools.

7. The provision to districts and states to request waivers from the rules and regulations of categorical programs, giving school managers the ability to consolidate funds and better integrate their programs.

Through changes in curriculum and assessment, professional development, technical assistance, and movement away from categorical programs, the legislation seeks to improve the quality of education received by children from low-income and linguistically diverse backgrounds.

The 1994 reauthorized ESEA is very different from its predecessors. It emphasizes attention to instruction, accountability for student outcomes, and a relaxing of some regulations in categorical programs. The federal movement in this direction, which actually began when ESEA was reauthorized in 1988, partly occurred in response to evaluations of the Title I programs, which continued to indicate that economically disadvantaged students' educational needs were not being fully met (U.S. Department of Education, 1992). It became clear that the quality of Title I programs could be improved.

Significantly, the federal movement toward instructional emphasis and accountability for outcomes, along with the movement away from categorical programs, is part of the Clinton administration's plan to fold concerns about equal educational opportunities for disadvantaged students into the broader context of improving the educational attainment of all students. According to high-ranking members of the U.S. Department of Education:

> By helping states develop challenging standards based on a broad consensus process for what all students need to know and be able to do through Goals 2000, and then targeting resources to children who are most in need of extra assistance to reach the standards through ESEA, we hope to help raise the level of access and achievement throughout the entire system. (Smith & Scoll, 1995)

The changes clearly bring the $11 billion worth of programs that constitute ESEA in alignment with the national goals and the movement toward systemic, standards-based reform outlined in Goals 2000.

The standards-based movement outlined in Goals 2000 and supported by ESEA is not without its critics. Theodore Sizer, founder of the Coalition of Essential Schools, believes that the standards movement will lead to test-driven instruction (Sizer, 1995). Others contend that the standards-based movement will cause schools to move away from teaching basic skills, which such critics believe are important for students' academic success (Lewis, 1995). Still others argue that there is no evidence that standards-based reform works. It is an assumption and not a proven theory that high standards create high performance for all students, regardless of their economic status (Cookson, 1995). Similarly, others have criticized the federal emphasis on outcomes at the expense of ensuring equality of inputs. According to these critics, without OTL standards, there is no guarantee that less privileged students will have the same opportunities, quality teachers, materials, facilities, as their more affluent peers, and it is possible that the former may be hurt and not helped by the high-stakes testing that often accompanies state and national standards (Elmore & Fuhrman, 1995). Finally, critics contend that the standards movement ignores intra-and interstate disparities in financial resources, which place students attending schools in poor neighborhoods at a disadvantage (Sizer, 1995; Lewis, 1995). In general, critics fear that the federal government is moving away from its original attempts to provide a safety net for economically disadvantaged and other historically underserved students (Cookson, 1995).

CONCLUSION: THE CHANGING
FEDERAL ROLE IN EDUCATION

The primary intent of the ESEA legislation of 1965 was to ". . . meet the special educational and related needs of targeted pupil groups, particularly low achievers living in relatively low income areas, who have limited English language proficiency, or who are affected by racial isolation" (Congressional Research Service, 1992). As expressed in this provision, the role of the federal government in education for most of the 1960s, 1970s, and 1980s was largely financial in scope, compensatory in nature, and categorical in the way the funding was spent. Although funding was spread to 70% of all elementary schools, the original intent of the bill was to channel resources to poor and minority students.

The role of the federal government in the education of these youths has changed in three major ways: first, the intent is no longer solely to promote equal educational opportunities; second, the role has expanded from financial support and regulation to include policy initiatives and a framework for reform; and third, the federal government is moving away from categorical funding.

The current intent of federal legislation in elementary and secondary education is to promote academic achievement for all students; promoting equal educational opportunities is a subset of the larger goal. The extent to which this change of focus will affect poor and minority students is not clear. However, the lack of attention given to inputs, as demonstrated by the demise of OTL standards, does not bode well for the equalization of educational opportunities for these historically underserved youth.

The second change in the federal government's role in education is that the federal government no longer desires to play a primarily financial role in education, leaving states and local governments to design and implement policy. It wants to influence the way schools operate in a fundamental way and is, consequently, a very strong advocate for state-run, systemic, standards-based reforms. Through new provisions in Title I, all schools that receive these funds are required to use the same standards and assessments in measuring the progress of students in Title I programs. This change could be very beneficial for economically disadvantaged and minority youths because it means that they will have access to a challenging curriculum and that their teachers and administrators will be held accountable for their achievement. The potential negative is that high-stakes testing could hurt these students if they are not provided the support necessary to meet the higher standards.

Finally, the federal government has begun to move away from categorical programs. The provision allowing waivers from some of the rules and regulations of categorical programs in the reauthorized ESEA is a response to decades of complaints about the confining regulations that prohibit local administrators from designing programs that work in the best interest of their students. This change is beneficial only if local administrators are able to creatively construct programs that meet the needs of students. Removal of some of the categorical strings may help the more creative administrators implement better programs, which would, ultimately, benefit all youth.

Standards-based reform is relatively new. States only began receiving planning grants for systemic reform in 1994-1995. Ultimately, whether it will truly bring about increased academic achievement for all students is yet to be determined. However, much of its success depends on how well states and LEAs adhere to all the objectives and principles of Goals 2000 and the 1994 reauthorization of ESEA. That is, states and local education agencies must embrace not only goals related to developing challenging standards, assessments and accountability systems, but also goals focused on effective and appropriate professional development, and the involvement of students' families and communities in the schooling process. Only through such a comprehensive approach can the needs of poor and minority students be met.

REFERENCES

Archibald, D. (1998). *The reviews of state content standards in English language arts and mathematics: A summary and review of their methods and findings and implications for future standards development.* (Report No. ED-98-PO-2038). Paper commissioned by the National Education Goals Panel.

Baird, A. (1996). *Equal educational opportunity: Project series No.1*. Washington, DC: U.S. Commission on Civil Rights.

Borman, G., & D'Agostino, J. (1996). Title I and student achievement: A meta-analysis of federal evaluation results. *Education Evaluation and Policy Analysis*, 18(4), 309-326.

Congressional Budget Office (1993). *The federal role in improving elementary and secondary education*. Washington, DC: Author.

Congressional Research Service (1992). *Redefining the federal role in elementary and secondary education: Reauthorization of the ESEA* (Update CRS Issue Brief). Washington, DC: Author.

Cookson, P. (1995). Goals 2000: Framework for the new educational federalism. *Teachers College Record, 96(3)*, 405-417.

Elmore, R., & Fuhrman, S. (1995). Opportunity-to-learn standards and the state role in education. *Teachers College Record*, 96(3), 432-457.

Gibboney, R. (1994). *The stone trumpet: A story of practical school reform, 1960-1990*. New York: State University of New York Press.

Hacker, A. (1992). *Two nations: Black and white, separate, hostile and unequal*. New York: Ballantine.

Heid, C. (1991). The dilemma of Chapter I program improvement. *Educational Evaluation and Policy Analysis*, 13(4), 394-398.

Jennings, J. (1991). Chapter I: A view from Congress. *Educational Evaluation and Policy Analysis*, 13(4), 335-338.

Kaestle, C., & Smith, M. (1982). Federal role in elementary and secondary education, 1940-1980. *Harvard Educational Review*, 52(4); 384-408.

Kantor, H. (1991). Education, social reform and the state: ESEA and federal education policy in the 1960's. *American Journal of Education, 100* (1), 47-83.

Kantor, H., & Lowe, R. (1995). Class, race and the emergence of federal education policy: From the New Deal to the Great Society. *Educational Researcher, 24*(3), 4-11,21.

Kennedy, M., Birman, B., & Demaline, R. (1986). *The effectiveness of Chapter I services*. Washington, DC: Office of Educational Research and Improvement, United States Department of Education.

King, E. (1994). Goals 2000: Educate America Act. *School Law Bulletin*, 25(4), 15-27.

Lewis, A. (1995). An overview of the standards movement. *Phi Delta Kappan*, 76(10);744-750.

Lewis, O. (1969). The culture of poverty. In D. P. Moynihan (Ed.), *On understanding poverty: Prospectives from the social sciences* (pp.187-200). New York: Basic Books.

Martin, R., & McClure, P. (1969). *Title I of ESEA: Is it helping poor children?* Washington, DC: Washington Research Project and NAACP Legal Defense and Educational Fund, Inc.

Peterson, P., Rabe, B., & Wong, K. (1988). The Evolution of the Compensatory Education Program. In D. Doyle & B. Cooper (Eds.), *Federal aid to the disadvantaged: What future for Chapter I* ? (pp. 33-60) Philadelphia: Falmer.

Riley, R. (1994). Redefining the federal role in education: Toward a framework for higher standards, improved schools, broader opportunities and new responsibilities for all. *Journal of Law and Education, 23*(3), 295- 361.

Sizer, T. (1995, April 2). Making the grade. *ashington Post Education Review* , p.12.

Smith, M., & Scoll, B. (1995). The Clintor .iman capital agenda. *Teachers College Record*, 96(3), 389-404.

Spring, J. (1976). *The sorting machin‹ Vational educational policy since 1945*. New York: Longman.

Stevenson, D. (1995). Goals 2000 and local reform. *Teachers College Record,* 96(3), 458-466.

Traiman, S. (1993). *The debate on opportunity to-learn standards.* Washington, DC: National Governors' Association.

U.S. Department of Education. (1992). *National assessment of the Chapter 1 program: The interim report.* Washington, DC: Author.

Verstegen, D. (1990). Education fiscal policy in the Reagan administration. *Educational Evaluation and Policy Analysis,* 12(4),355-373.

Wargo, M., Tallmadge, G., Michaels, D., Lipe, D., & Morris, S. (1972). *ESEA Title I: A reanalysis and synthesis of evaluation data from fiscal year 1965 through 1970.* Palo Alto, CA: American Institute of Research.

3

Why do so Many Urban Public School Students Demonstrate so Little Academic Achievement?

ROBERT BALFANZ
Johns Hopkins University

The vast majority of evidence that has been used to examine and answer the question of why so many public school students in central cities achieve so little has been ahistorical and decontextualized. This chapter posits that both the location of a school within a particular district and state and its history shape students' learning opportunities and supports in what remain largely unknown ways. In particular, there are two confounding variables intimately linked to time and place that have been largely unmeasured or unexamined in prior attempts to understand achievement patterns in urban areas. They are the geographic concentration of weak and dysfunctional learning institutions, and intergenerational school effects. Neither of these variables is invariant by place and time; rather, the effects of both variables are concentrated in particular times and in particular places. Drawing on participant observations and secondary data, this chapter presents insights that are meant to provoke and stimulate thinking regarding the limits of the dominant approaches to figuring out why so many urban public school students achieve so little. Furthermore, this chapter presents an alternative approach to the analysis of low-performing urban schools and indicates directions for future study.

Urban educational policy and practice over the past 30 years have been primarily driven by ongoing attempts to provide an answer to a single question: Why do some students who attend urban public schools achieve so little? Explicit and implicit theories on why large numbers of urban students, the majority of whom are poor and minorities, possess measured achievement levels that routinely place them 2 to 5 years behind national averages have influenced public policy. These theories have shaped desegregation plans (Orfield & Eaton, 1996), court-ordered remedies to school finance suits (Wenglinsky, 1997), and federal compensatory education strategies (Wong & Meyer, 1998), and also have been at the heart of an unending parade of urban school reforms. These reforms include the effective schools movement, school choice and privatization plans, site-based management, school restructuring, and attempts to implement culturally relevant curricula and instruction.

Recent data on urban achievement demonstrate that such reforms have been largely ineffective. Measured achievement levels are almost unfathomably low in the majority of nonselective public schools in many of the nation's central cities (Education Week/Pew Charitable Trust, 1998; Hess, 1995). More than 70% of the entering freshmen in Baltimore's nine nonselective public high schools, for example, have repeatedly failed to pass Maryland's 7th grade functional math and writing tests (Maryland State Department of Education [MSDE], 1997). Of Philadelphia's 22 neighborhood high schools, only 4 saw more than 20% of their 11th graders score at the basic level or above on the Stanford 9 reading achievement test in 1997, only 1 saw 20% of its 11th graders score at basic or above on the mathematics test, and none reached this level on the science test (Philadelphia School District [PSD], 1997). Thus, even students who persevere until the 11th grade possess achievement levels that leave them unprepared for postsecondary schooling, training, or employment. These low levels of achievement are common in many of the 25 largest central cities, which school approximately one fourth of the nation's African-American students and one third of the nation's Hispanic students (Education Week/Pew Charitable Trust, 1998; Orfield & Eaton, 1996). Low levels of achievement also are found in the smaller formerly industrial cities of the northeast and midwest. Some of these cities such as Benton Harbor, Michigan, and Perth Amboy, New Jersey are served by a single high school with estimated attrition rates of 50% or higher (Balfanz & Legters, 1998). Failure to find an answer to the question of why so many urban students achieve so little and inability to use this knowledge to fashion effective remedies have left many urban school districts in a state of continual crisis, called into question the role the federal government should play in aiding urban districts, and provided fertile ground for the continuation of racial and ethnic stereotypes (Education Week/Pew Charitable Trust, 1998).

A major reason no answer has been found is that despite all the attention devoted to the question, attempts to provide an answer have drawn on a thin and narrowly focused knowledge base. Although they are often presented as fact or common sense, in practice, the dominant explanations of why so many urban public school students achieve so little that appear in the scholarly literature, in the public policy domain, and at the school level are more often than not inferences and speculations based on limited evidence. One reason for this is that the dominant explanations of the past 30 years have ignored important variations by time and place. The role of spatial location and the impact of history have been largely overlooked. This is a critical oversight because the context within which schooling occurs helps to explain both the forces behind low achievement and the possibilities for reform.

This chapter draws on research from three ongoing projects to demonstrate how the location of a school in a particular place and at a particular time can have a strong impact on the academic achievement of its students. The first project involves participant observation in whole school reform efforts targeted at low-performing urban middle and high schools. This has involved the author (who is one of the developers of both programs) working intensively with teachers and administrators in 5 nonselective central city public middle schools and 6 nonselective central city public high schools in two large mid-Atlantic cities. It has also brought him into contact with more than 20 other low-performing central city middle and high schools located in various regions of the United States. Participant observation has included active collaboration with administrators and teachers in all of the schools over a 2-year period in attempts to change both organization and instruction; presence at faculty meetings; scores of classroom observations and visits; continual semi structured and unstructured conversations with teachers and administrators; organization and delivery of staff development and in-classroom implementation support; and access to a wealth of achievement, attendance and promotion data, as well as yearly teacher and student surveys and interviews. The second ongoing project that informs this chapter is a demographic analysis of comprehensive high schools and school districts in the 25 largest central cities. The third is a historical investigation of the evolution of urban school systems during the 20th century. These latter two projects serve to place the participant observation in a larger historical and geographic context.

This chapter first uses insights drawn from the previously mentioned projects to critique contemporary explanations of why so many urban students achieve so little. Then, it uses evidence drawn primarily from participant observation to demonstrate how some urban secondary schools actively manufacture low levels of student achievement and argues that this, in part, arises because social, economic, and geographic forces work to concentrate weak learning institutions in many U.S. inner cities. Next, it uses historical analysis to show why it also is essential to consider the impact of intergenerational school effects in any attempt to explain why so many urban students achieve so little. Finally, this chapter argues that the forces of time and place converge in largely negative ways in urban schools, and that this fact must be confronted in attempts to both explain and improve current levels of academic achievement in urban schools.

THE UNDERAPPRECIATED IMPORTANCE OF TIME AND PLACE

The vast majority of evidence that has been used to examine and answer the question of why so many public school students in central cities achieve so little has been ahistorical and decontextualized. The main strategies used by researchers to examine achievement patterns in urban public schools – statistical analysis of nationally representative data sets and case studies of either individual schools or a small collection of schools chosen to represent a given type of school – are, in many respects, not well suited to uncovering important variations by time and place. Nationally representative data sets by definition strip away context. Data are sampled from urban areas using various indicators, including population size, poverty rates, and ethnic and racial composition, and then used to examine general characteristics, trends, and relationships.

This is informative in a broad sense but the utility of the results for understanding why large numbers of students are not achieving in a particular time and place rests on the rather large assumption that schooling and learning are relatively simple and uniform phenomena that are invariant across sites with different histories and locations. In other words, the impact on student achievement of the major variables (i.e., class size, teacher experience and education, educational expenditures, amount of instructional time, and others) that have been explored through statistical analysis of nationally representative data does not account for what has happened in a given city's schools in the past. Moreover, these analyses often do not distinguish between elementary, middle and high schools, nor do they control for the geographic, social, and political environments in which schools are situated.

Another interpretive problem of statistical analysis of nationally representative databases is that such databases typically do not allow data to be analyzed at state and district levels. This means that the impact of the two most important policymaking units with regard to public education are obscured, and critical geographic and historical differences are not analyzed. State level differences, however, are often greater than differences between racial and ethnic groups, social classes, and public and private schools, which have received much more analysis, in part, because of the greater availability of data.

In the 1990s, for example, the National Assessment of Educational Progress (NAEP) began reporting some data at the state level for the first time (by federal statute it is not allowed to report data at the district level). These data show that on critical opportunity-to-learn variables, such as the percentage of eighth grade students taking algebra (shown in Fig. 3.1), state differences are greater, often considerably so, than differences between students from different social, economic, and ethnic backgrounds (National Center for Education Statistics [NCES], 1997).

Recent efforts to equate state-level performance on the NAEP eighth grade mathematics and science tests with national performance on the Third International Mathematics and Science Study (TIMSS) further indicate that the range in achievement across states is as great as the range across the nations participating in the TIMSS study. Achievement in Iowa and Minnesota is at world class levels (in particular for students in the bottom half of the distribution), whereas performance in Mississippi is on par with the lowest performing nation (Jordan) in the TIMSS study (NCES 1998).

The inability to examine educational trends in a comprehensive manner at state and district levels, moreover, has tended to shift analysis of why so many urban public school students achieve so little away from factors that are influenced by state and district actions and characteristics, and more towards individual ascribed characteristics such as race; income; parental socioeconomic status; and urban, suburban, or rural residence. The problem is that schools are not organized and do not run along these lines.

Case studies are superb at providing a strongly contextualized analysis of the learning conditions within a school or a set of schools in a particular time and place. By their very nature, however, they are labor intensive, and as a result most researchers typically study one school or a small set of schools, and often for only a period of 1 to 3 years. The results are often highly informative snapshots that leave the generalizability of their findings unknown. Does examination of 4 elementary schools in a single, northern, deindustrializing city, with strong teachers' unions give us an accurate understanding of how learning opportunities are shaped within all schools in

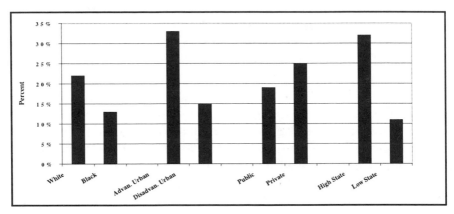

Figure 3.1: Percentage of eighth-grade students taking algebra, 1992.

a district; in all cities with similar characteristics; or in all cities? It is also unknown whether the case study captured relationships and processes that have endured or will endure at the school for a decade or more, or whether it happened to capture an idiosyncratic period in the school's history that is not representative of its past or future. Few case studies revisit schools several years after the initial analysis and those that do have often found large changes. Urban schools in particular, are characterized by high rates of mobility of superintendents, principals, teachers, and students. The nature of city schools can and does change rapidly.

Finally, both case studies and statistical analyses of nationally representative data sets often downplay essential differences between schools for different age groups of students. Findings based on data from elementary schools or high schools are often generalized to schools in general (Barr & Dreeben, 1983; Elmore, Peterson, & McCarthey, 1996). Preschools, elementary schools, middle schools, and high schools, however, engage students at different stages in their life course, historically have had different missions, organize teachers work in different manners, have different expectations for students, and, in cities, draw students from different neighborhoods. In addition, there is evidence that the factors that shape learning opportunities and supports at each level of schooling are not the same or operate through different mechanisms (Entwisle, Alexander, & Olson, 1997, NCES, 1998). Three recent studies, for example, that have employed widely divergent methodologies have all found significant differences between elementary and middle schools in the impact of educational expenditures, the effects of class size, the connections between student attitudes and mathematics achievement, and the allocation of resources within a large urban school district to high poverty schools (Berne & Stiefel, 1994; Ma & Kishor, 1997; Wenglinsky, 1997).

Answers, however, to questions with huge policy and educational significance, such as the impact of educational expenditures, class size, school climate, grade retention, sitebased management, school restructuring, professional development, and tracking on student achievement to name only a few – continue to be formulated based on data drawn from only one level of schooling. This is due, in large part, to the fact that the pressing magnitude of the problem is not balanced with the data needed to solve it. No nationally representative data on educational expenditure and student achievement at the district level have been collected since the Coleman Report in 1966 (Wenglinsky, 1997). Attempts to measure expenditures at the classroom and student level remain on the drawing board (NCES, 1998). A nationally representative study that follows a cohort of students from kindergarten through the fifth grade will start in 2000 and several nationally representative data sets have followed students through the upper secondary grades (Bobbitt, Quinn, & Dabbs, 1992). To date, however, there is no data set available (nor is one immediately contemplated) that follows students through the middle grades.

Even more significant than the spottiness of nationally representative data is the fact that there are currently no data available that would allow researchers to situate classrooms within schools and schools within their districts across a large number of districts or states. In other words, data that would allow a researcher to examine, for example, the distribution, correlates, and causes of student achievement at the school level across elementary, middle, and high schools within known school districts and states are not presently available.

In lieu of these data, the question of why so many urban public school students achieve so little continues to be answered with fragmented nationally representative data, a relatively small number of case studies, and meta-analysis of tens or hundreds of smaller studies which have statistically examined relationships within one locale, at one time, and typically for one level of schooling. These meta-analyses use a variety of approaches to examine how often a significant relationship has been found. The fact that they almost always find that sometimes a relationship has been found and sometimes it has not strongly hints at the importance of time and place, but does not fully reveal it (Burtless, 1996).

A recognition of the importance of time and place, however, is essential. Without contextual and comparative data from a large number of school districts, we will likely never gain a deep or even moderate understanding of why so many urban public school students achieve so little. Learning occurs in places – schools and homes – that are situated in a hierarchy of other places – neighborhoods, school districts and states – and each place has its own history. This chapter posits that both the location of a school within this hierarchy of places and the history of the community it serves shape students' learning opportunities and supports in what remain largely unknown ways. In particular, there are two confounding variables intimately linked to time and place that have been largely unmeasured or unexamined in prior attempts to understand achievement patterns in urban areas. These are the geographic concentration of weak and dysfunctional learning institutions, and intergenerational school effects. Neither of these variables is invariant by place and time; rather, the effects of both variables are concentrated in particular times and in particular places.

CONFOUNDING VARIABLE 1: THE (POTENTIAL) GEOGRAPHICAL CONCENTRATION OF WEAK AND DYSFUNCTIONAL LEARNING INSTITUTIONS

The school effects and school restructuring literature has identified a number of characteristics found in schools that, at least in some respects, can be classified as strong and effective learning institutions. These are schools which beat the demographic odds and produce higher and more widely dispersed student achievement than is typical for schools with similar student populations and resources. The identified characteristics include, but are not limited to, an able principal who provides strong leadership; a shared vision; clear goals; a sense of community and professionalism among teachers; high expectations for all students; high quality teachers; small size; a common core curriculum; and school, home, and community partnerships (Teddlie & Stringfield, 1993; Darling-Hammond, 1997).

The dominant response to these findings has been an attempt to achieve these characteristics, often in piecemeal and serial fashion, in low-performing schools. Much less attention has been paid, however, to the nature of weak and dysfunctional learning institutions themselves. This is a critical gap in the knowledge base because, at least in the 15 or so low-performing middle and high schools located primarily in two large mid-Atlantic cities that I have worked in or observed over the past 2 years, the inability to provide students with strong learning opportunities and supports is brought about by much more than the absence of a good principal, a shared vision, clear goals, professional communities, and high expectations for all students. In fact, many of these low-performing schools have had some of these elements in place, and in a few, all have been present to, at least, a modest degree. All of the schools, for example, have school improvement teams that include a range of stakeholders and school improvement plans, which, in theory, provide the schools with a shared vision, direction, and benchmarks. As it turns out, the weakest high school, which routinely loses one third of its students in a year, has the best plan, at least on paper. Most of these schools have also, by and large, eliminated tracking and at least formally attempt to offer all students the same common core of academic courses.

The low-performing schools I have worked with actively manufacture low levels of student achievement. This direct role in producing low levels of student achievement is often not intentional and almost never openly recognized. It is, more typically, the result of weak, dysfunctional, and self-defeating institutional and collective responses to a difficult and complex environment characterized by competing demands, limited information, and constant change.

Some Primarily Middle School Examples

In the low-performing middle schools I have observed and worked in, little attention has been paid to the development and maintenance of strong and effective instructional programs. The technical core of schooling (Bryk, Sebring, Kerbow, Rollow, & Easton, 1998) has been ignored. Common curricula and instructional materials across grades, and even across teachers in a grade, are rare. Thus, teachers seldom know what their peers are doing, and as a result, they have only vague notions of what students have learned or been exposed to in earlier grades. The lack of common materials that build upon each other grade by grade, the limited information on students' prior work, and the significant number of students with weak prior preparation all lead to a situation in which limited time is spent moving students forward. The bulk of teacher effort is spent on remediation and going over essentially the same material grade after grade. In one school, for instance, nearly every mathematics teacher in every grade spent the first few weeks working on place value.

This is not simply the result of low teacher expectations but is due to competing demands. Many teachers believe that their fundamental obligation is to ensure that students have command of the basics. When they note that some students appear not to demonstrate command of what is assumed to be an elementary skill, such as being able to recognize and manipulate simple fractions, teachers often stop presenting grade-level material and have the whole class review fractions, frequently for a significant period of time. This individual judgment call, and not indefensible decision, when repeated throughout the school leads to collective failure. In an environment in which teachers do not know what their peers are doing, it creates a chain reaction that significantly limits students' opportunity to learn.

When fifth-grade teachers spend much of their time reviewing elementary skills, it means they do not cover much of the fifth-grade material. Thus, when students enter the sixth grade, the teacher soon notices gaps in some students' knowledge and stops moving forward in order to remediate the whole class. Moreover, because different teachers are making different decisions on which skills to remediate, and which ones not to cover (one teacher does not teach data to remediate fractions, another does not cover decimal operations to remediate division, etc.), teachers in the next grade face an ever-shifting composition of knowledge gaps. Over time, this creates the perception that students know little and leads to even more unnecessary remediation. Perhaps this is why students in some cities like Baltimore and Philadelphia appear to fall further behind each year they are in the school system (MSDE, 1997; PSD, 1997).

Unnecessary remediation also helps to promote another observed characteristic in these low-performing middle schools: ritualized success. Both teachers and students like to believe they are succeeding and doing well in school. In a situation in which significant numbers of students have knowledge and skill gaps, as is the case in these urban middle schools, there is a strong temptation, often unacknowledged, to give students below grade-level tasks. One particularly common and self-defeating example is the pervasive use of round-robin reading in English language arts classes. Students collectively read a short story or more commonly a few paragraphs by taking turns reading one or a few sentences aloud. Students are often enthusiastic because they like to be praised and acknowledged for their ability to read the sentence. Teachers like it because it gives them a sense that everyone is achieving and participating (Useem, 1998). The cost, however, is that students do not get an opportunity to develop their ability to read silently in a sustained fashion. In a narrow sense, the students are successful because they have shown that they can read a sentence but the success is more ritual than real. It does not propel them forward.

What is lacking in both cases is instructional leadership. Teachers are making judgment calls that make sense to them in the context of their classrooms but are deleterious for the student body as a whole. The problem, in these low-performing middle schools, is that there is seldom anyone available to provide this leadership. In the middle schools where I work, for example, the district provides a principal and a vice-principal. Then, out of their budgets, principals often pay for house or small learning community leaders (who often have to teach, at least part time) and a program support teacher, who serves as kind of a general ombudsman. In the high schools, there is typically a principal and from three to five assistant principals depending on the size and budget of the schools. In addition, there are often several teachers who serve in quasi-administrative or disciplinary roles (who are sometimes placed in these roles because they have strong administrative abilities, but weak instructional skills). In the observed schools, all of these individuals were consumed by competing demands that left little time for them to focus on instructional leadership.

It is common now to proclaim that principals are the instructional leaders of a school building. This has a nice rhetorical ring to it but it ignores the reality of principals' heavy and increasing workloads. Site-based management has given principals a whole new realm of responsibilities and typically no additional resources with which to meet them. Principals and their administrative teams in the schools where I have worked are now ultimately responsible for the budget, personnel management, student discipline, community relations, parent contact, organizational design, and instructional decisions in middle schools that can have 1,000 students and 100 employees (less than half of whom are teachers), and high schools that can have 2,000 or more students and over 250 employees. In truth, the time and energy of principals and their administrative teams are consumed by their fiscal, personnel, discipline, and parental responsibilities, as well as by an unending stream of district and state requirements and day-to-day emergencies, both small and large. These are all demands that typically cannot wait. Unfortunately, instructional leadership can and frequently does wait.

The absence of instructional leadership also means that critical decisions on instructional materials usually are made in a haphazard, hasty, and uninformed manner, often by a single individual. Yet, selection of the right materials matters, particularly when the goal is to teach advanced and complex cognitive skills to large numbers of students with weak preparation. One middle school I work with invested in three different mathematics series in three years. With little thought, the school selected a poorly conceived commercial series that purported to use a cooperative learning model. To make matters worse, it was implemented without training or support and soon was perceived to be a failure. This led to the purchase of a more traditional text, even though the school knew that the following year it would be adopting a whole school reform model that used a third standards-based text with an emphasis on problem solving. Thus, in the course of three years, teachers will have been forced to use three widely divergent approaches and materials, further supporting many teachers' belief that reform, too, is ritual.

At the end of the academic year in one high school, I was told by a group of exhausted ninth grade teachers, who had been delegated the task of selecting a new algebra textbook, that I should make the decision because I was the only person with time to examine the different choices. The delegation of critical decisions about instructional materials to unprepared, overburdened, and unsupervised staff also means that essential tasks such as ordering textbooks, submitting grants, or delivering materials once they have arrived often are not done in a timely manner. As a result, teachers in these schools have come to expect that critical supplies will not be present at the start of school and, at best, may trickle in during the course of the year. This haphazard approach to the selection, ordering, and delivery of instructional materials reinforces to teachers the message that they are on their own and further encourages them to do their own thing.

An additional factor that works against the development of strong instructional programs in these schools is the constant mobility of administrators and faculty, as well as annual changes in teaching assignments. Several of the schools in which I have worked have had three or four principals in the space of 1 or 2 years. Others have had staff turnover rates of 20% or more per year. In the middle schools, it is common practice for teachers to change subjects and grade levels on an almost yearly basis. Teaching assignments are often made based on seniority, the impact of faculty transfers, and a host of other factors (including internal school politics), which seldom have much to do with instructional needs. This prevents the development of a stable teaching core with specialized skills, makes it more difficult for teachers to know their students, and negatively affects the impact of professional development. It is not uncommon for teachers who receive special training to be unable to make use of it because they end up teaching a different subject or grade level (Useem, Christman, Gold, & Simon, 1997). This also means that promising reforms tend to have short shelf lives in these schools because key leaders and implementers leave before such reforms are firmly established. This, in turn, further cements the notion that nothing works and makes it very difficult to judge the effectiveness of school improvement efforts.

Some Unique Features of Low-Performing High Schools

At the high school level, the often subtle forces previously mentioned are joined by more overt actions, which work to push poorly prepared students out of school. Paramount among these is the game that is played on a yearly basis between these high schools, their districts, and their staff with regard to student enrollment figures and class size. It works like this: Districts know that, historically, these high schools lose between 20 and 30% of their students during the course of the year, and have daily attendance rates between 60 and 70%. Thus, they do not staff the schools for their actual opening enrollments, but rather use an estimate of the surviving population later in the year. Consequently, teachers often begin the year with 40 or more students on roll and in their classrooms during the opening weeks. Classes of this size do not encourage teachers to work on promoting student attendance or student success, especially when they are housed in rooms with desks for only 30. Sixty percent of 40, or 24 students, represents a much more manageable class.

Sometimes, when *natural* attrition is not enough, or when the actual enrollment is significantly more than predicted, these schools rely on more direct actions. One high school, which was staffed for 1,900 students but found itself with 2,200 in attendance at the start of the year, did not provide 200 students with a schedule for 2 months. Instead, it told them to shadow a buddy. Another school scheduled students into classes without teachers that were covered by a succession of substitutes, aides, and, at times, no one at all. These maladaptive responses by the districts, the schools, and the teachers to what they perceive to be difficult, trying, and fluid circumstances actively work against providing all students with a strong learning environment. A recent study in Philadelphia high schools found a direct link between this turbulence and student performance. Students who experience two or more (a) classes in which there were not enough chairs for all students, (b) classes in which there were not enough textbooks for all students, (c) classes in which there was more than one teacher during the term, and (d) having their schedule changed were found to be "at significantly greater risk of failure than students who do not" (Neild & Weiss, 1999, p. 43). Cumulatively these actions send a signal to many students that districts and school staff do not really want them in school.

In a much less obvious manner, a similar signal is sent to students attending high schools such as these, which typically have three to five times as many freshmen as seniors. A common pattern among these schools is to have about 1,000 freshmen, 500 sophomores, 300 juniors, and 200 seniors.

Teachers in each class and at each grade level tend to give a distribution of grades that is skewed to the low end: a few As and Bs, and many Cs and Ds (Neild & Weiss). Interviews with teachers reveal that this stems, in part, from ad hoc curved grading systems in classes that are filled with large numbers of poorly prepared students. Many teachers believe that if they truly graded to a secondary school standard few students would get higher than a D. On the other hand, they believe that they cannot totally abandon standards and grade purely on a curve or give students undue credit for effort, improvement, or attendance. Thus, they tend to create ad hoc assessment schemes and lower their perceived secondary standards to such a degree that some students get As and Bs (Natriello, Riehl, & Pallas, 1994). The 500 9th graders who make it to the 10th grade typically are the A, B, and C students. However, since the 10th grade teachers also give a normal distribution of grades that is skewed to the low end, the surviving C students from the 9th grade typically earn Ds and Fs and former B students earn Cs. This continues throughout the grades so that at every transition many students get lower grades for similar levels of effort and are sent the signal that they do not have what it takes to continue (Wood, 1994).

All these examples are meant to illustrate the kinds of maladaptive institutional and collective responses that exist or have existed in the low-performing schools I have worked in over the past 2 years, which work to actively manufacture low levels of student achievement. They are not, however, the only reasons these school are low performing. All of the schools I have worked in could use more instructional resources. In most of the high schools, teachers work without basic tools such as overhead projectors, and students use class sets of outdated textbooks. Libraries or "media centers" are often atrocious. In one school the media center is an empty room lined with dilapidated bookshelves that are less than one quarter full. In addition, all the schools have to make do with too many provisionally certified teachers and long-term substitutes, who do not have the knowledge to teach challenging academic skills or the ability to manage challenging classrooms (Darling-Hammond, 1997). Consequently, many students experience blank years in which little or no instruction occurs in a subject (Corbett & Wilson, 1997).

Some of the schools could clearly use stronger and more effective principals, as has been highlighted in the effective schools literature. But my experience working in these schools indicates that this would not be enough. If the schools received an infusion of instructional supplies, certified teachers, a restocked library, and a new principal, the achievement of some students would improve. It is unclear, however, whether such inputs would cause the schools to begin systematically producing high levels of student achievement. This is because these low-performing central city middle and high schools do not simply lack adequate resources but are caught up in a vortex of institutionalized chaos. This vortex is not simply the result of inferior management, and hence cannot simply be solved by getting a better principal, but results from dysfunctional and counterproductive institutional and collective responses to complex and difficult situations marked by high levels of uncertainty, stress, and social distance.

Are Weak and Dysfunctional Learning Institutions Geographically Concentrated?

Do the subtle and not-so-subtle institutional and collective actions observed in these schools, which actively work to manufacture low levels of student achievement, exist in other central city schools? In other schools in these cities? In schools outside central cities? I do not know. But these concerns are worth considering and investigating in any attempt to answer the question of why so many urban public school students achieve so little. This is because the forces that appear to drive dysfunctional institutional and collective actions in the small sample of observed low-performing urban middle and high schools – uncertainty, stress, exhaustion, social distance, and constant mobility – are heightened and geographically concentrated in the schools of some central cities in the United States.

The magnitude and scale of social change that has occurred in many northern and mid-western cities during the second half of the 20th century is difficult to imagine. The central cores of industrial cities have become depopulated, impoverished, and have seen the social and human capital of their citizens diminished. The experience of Milwaukee is typical for other large formerly industrial cities such as St. Louis, Baltimore, Detroit, Philadelphia, Chicago, and Cleveland. It also reflects the situation in many smaller formerly industrial cities such as Benton Harbor, Michigan; Camden, New Jersey; and New Haven, Connecticut (Rusk, 1996).

In Milwaukee, four statistics reflect much of the social change that has occurred in the northern industrial cities. In 1950, 137,428 individuals lived in Milwaukee's inner city, of which 91% were White and 8% were African-American. In 1985, only 69,522 people lived in the inner city, of which 6% were White and 87% were African-American. In 1950, 19% of families that lived in the inner city had an income between 0 and 49% of the city's median. By 1985, this number had grown to 42%. In 1950, the percentage of the population that was school aged in the inner city and in the city at large were nearly identical at about 20%. By 1980, 40% of the inhabitants of the inner city were school aged compared to 25% in the city as a whole. In 1950, there were 120,108 blue-collar manufacturing jobs in Milwaukee. By 1985, this had declined to 72,900. Thus, by the 1980s, the central core of Milwaukee was inhabited by poor children living in a depopulated area of a deindustrializing city with a falling revenue base (Zipp & Levine, 1993).

This social change and reactions to it have created schools that have historically unique school populations. In many formerly industrial northern cities, most schools serve students who come from urban neighborhoods with levels of concentrated and long-term poverty unprecedented since the advent of mass secondary schooling in the United States (Miller, 1995). In Philadelphia, for example, a middle school can have 75% of its students eligible for free lunches and yet receive no Title I money because there are 30 other middle schools with higher poverty rates. In Milwaukee, the poverty rate of public school students nearly doubled between 1977 and 1987 (Zipp & Levine, 1993). In 1990, only 7 of the 118 elementary schools in Baltimore had less than 25% of their students eligible for meal subsidies (Entwisle et al., 1997).

This is highly significant because the concentration of poverty in schools has a stronger association with student achievement than does poverty at the individual level (Orland, 1994). This is borne out by the fact that in all of the cities previously mentioned, more than half the high schools have estimated attrition rates of 50% or higher (Balfanz & Legters, 1998). This means that most of their public school students attend high schools where failure and leaving school is the norm.

It seems reasonable to hypothesize that concentrated and long-term poverty, and persistent and pervasive educational failure of this magnitude, might work on at least three levels to create conditions that promote weak and dysfunctional learning institutions. First, the social distance between students and teachers is vast. With few exceptions, teachers in these schools are college graduates; many have graduate training, and despite their often legitimate claims of being underpaid, they are thoroughly middle class. In many central cities, the majority of urban students in nonselective middle and high schools will not graduate from high school, only a relatively small percent will go to college, more than half are eligible for free lunch, and many live in neighborhoods where the modal pattern for adults 25 to 64 is to be a high school dropout. Very few teachers live in the neighborhoods of their students or send their children to similar schools. In short, students and teachers are not a part of the same communities, nor do many of the students share a common life course with their teachers. Teachers, by and large, also were successful students in school. In nonselective, high-poverty schools in many central cities, the majority of middle school students are several years behind grade level, and most high school students receive Cs, Ds, and Fs (Neild & Weiss, 1999).

This social gulf between students and teachers, which cuts across racial and ethnic lines, manifests itself in a multitude of subtle and largely deleterious ways. It makes it easier for some teachers to devote most of their energy to a relatively small set of students whom they believe have a chance to succeed. It encourages other teachers not to send textbooks or even inexpensive workbooks home with some students for fear they will not be returned. Moreover, such a social gulf makes it more likely that teachers will succumb to a "pedagogy of poverty" and focus on low-level skills that are perceived to be necessary for students' imagined futures (Anyon, 1997; Haberman, 1994).

Second, teachers and administrators in high poverty schools face more complex demands and a wider range of pressing student needs. Poverty exacerbates social frictions. A multitude of family and neighborhood disputes, tensions, and tragedies spill over into the school and the classroom. They also contribute to attendance patterns that disrupt instruction. In seven of Baltimore's nine nonselective neighborhood high schools, 70 to 77% of the students missed 20 or more days of schooling during the 1996-1997 school year (MSDE, 1997). High-poverty and nonselective schools also face greater regulatory burdens and intrusions. Teachers in these schools often must administer Title I, state, and district assessments, which when combined with preparation for the tests, can consume a month or more of instructional time. It is not atypical for schools to devote most of an administrator's time to all the paperwork that comes with high poverty and low performance – Title I reports, district school improvement plans, state compensatory education requirements, and reconstitution edicts. In central cities, nonselective middle and high schools also must educate a proportion of special education students much higher than that found in other schools. In most schools where I have worked, special education students constitute about 20% of the school's population. This coupled with large classes and many students with poor prior preparation, is a recipe for teacher and administrator exhaustion. It also leaves little time or energy for professional development or collaborative reform efforts.

Finally, in addition to social distance, stress, and exhaustion, schools that educate large numbers of students from central city neighborhoods with concentrated and long-term poverty are fraught with uncertainty. The high mobility rates of these neighborhoods make it difficult for administrators to estimate yearly enrollments. In addition, each summer brings high rates of teacher turnover. As a result, schedules are not completed until the last moment, and returning teachers often do not know what or who they will be teaching until they arrive at school for the start of the new year. Also, the high concentration of high-poverty and low-performing schools in central cities means that the districts, as a whole, are characterized by pervasive and persistent failure. This, as noted earlier, often leads to short tenures for principals and superintendents, and a revolving door of new reform plans and district initiatives.

One partial answer, then, to the question of why so many urban public school students achieve so little may be that during the past 30 years many of them have attended schools in cities where rapid social change and high concentrations of central city poverty created conditions that have left teachers and administrators ill prepared and unequipped to create strong learning institutions. Furthermore, these conditions have led to the dysfunctional institutional and collective responses previously described, which have made matters worse. In short, a constellation of social, economic, political, and institutional forces in a particular time and particular place have led to the geographic concentration of weak and dysfunctional learning institutions in the very locales that need strong institutions the most (Coleman, 1994).

Clearly, this is not the only reason urban public school children achieve so little. It may not even be a significant factor in some cities. A different constellation of forces may be at work in cities with high immigration rates or in cities with larger middle classes. Enough poor and minority students, however, attend school in formerly industrial cities to seriously skew an analysis of academic outcomes that does not take into account the geographic concentration of weak and dysfunctional schools.

CONFOUNDING VARIABLE 2: INTERGENERATIONAL SCHOOL EFFECTS

A second variable, which confounds prior attempts to understand why so many urban public school students learn so little, and which varies by time and place, is intergenerational school effects. That is, the academic achievement of current students in a given time and place is influenced by the educational opportunities and learning supports available to their parents, grandparents, relatives, and the wider adult community with whom they interact (Miller, 1995). To understand the contemporary impact of different school inputs, practices, and policies on student achievement, researchers have attempted to control for the role of home or community effects by including measures of parental education, income, and family composition. Although this might make sense from a short-term public policy or program evaluation perspective, it has created the impression that these home effects are primarily the result of individual, community, or social motivations or behaviors. In fact, there is substantial evidence that most of the commonly employed social and economic status variables are influenced by the educational opportunities and learning supports provided to parents and family members (Miller). Thus, what is being controlled for is not just the educational opportunities and learning supports provided to students in their homes, but also their parents' ability to provide these opportunities and supports given the quality and the quantity of schooling they received. This obscures the intergenerational impact of state and district level variations in the quantity and the quality of schooling provided to different social and economic groups throughout the 20th century.

Northern Industrial Cities

The middle and high schools I have been working with over the past 2 years are located in two mid-Atlantic cities. These cities, like many of the formerly industrial cities in the north and midwest, primarily educate low-income, African-American students in their public school systems (Education Week/Pew Charitable Trust, 1998). Because of historical patterns of migration, racial discrimination, and the historical development of urban comprehensive high schools, multiple generations of these students' families generally have been denied equal access to high-quality educational opportunities and learning supports.

Prior to the 1930s, northern and midwestern industrial cities had relatively small African-American populations. During the first half of the 20th century, most African-Americans (90% in 1910, 77% in 1940) lived in the south and by law attended segregated schools (Miller, 1995). Some recent historical scholarship has demonstrated that a number of African-American communities were able to provide students with high-quality educational experiences despite segregation and disenfranchisement (Walker, 1996). Generally, however, African-American students attended segregated schools that provided grossly unequal learning opportunities (Margo, 1990; Anderson, 1988; Orazem, 1987).

In 1920, for example, African-American students in the south attended school, on average, 41 fewer days per year than did all students and attended schools with an average of 56 students per teacher, far more than the average of 32 students per teacher for all students (Miller, 1995). One historical irony is that, by the 1950s when African-American migration from the south to northern industrial cities was in full swing, a half century of effort by African-Americans in the south to secure more equitable learning opportunities was bearing fruit, and the gaps between the resources provided to African-American and White students was beginning to decline considerably (Margo, 1990). In northern cities, however, African-American immigrants from the south were being pushed, through restrictive housing practices and other discriminatory tactics, into racially segregated neighborhoods with inferior schools.

Although the educational history of industrial cities in the northeast and midwest has been much less well documented than that of the south, the historical research that has been conducted in Chicago (Homel, 1984; Mohraz, 1979), Milwaukee (Rury & Cassell, 1993), Detroit (Angus and Mirel, 1993; Mirel 1993), Providence (Perlmann, 1988), Indianapolis, and Philadelphia (Mohraz) paints a remarkably similar picture. The similarities provide insight into the educational opportunities and learning supports provided to African-Americans from the south when they arrived in northern industrial cities. Until about 1930, when African-Americans typically composed no more than 12% of the population in the cities studied, it appears that African-Americans were provided roughly equal educational opportunities at the elementary school level, often in integrated settings (Mohraz). At this time, public schools in industrial cities were in many respects some of the best in the United States. Achievement test data from Buffalo, New York, for the 1929-1930 school year, for example, indicate that the median performance of students in Buffalo exceeded the national mean in every subject tested, and in every grade from fourth to ninth. By ninth grade, the typical student in Buffalo exceeded the national mean on the Stanford Achievement test by a full grade level.

By the 1930s, as the first large wave of southern African-American immigrants began arriving in northern cities and mass secondary schooling was becoming a reality, the quality of schooling provided to African-American students began to change on two levels. First, African-American students began to attend increasingly segregated schools (Homel, 1984; Mohraz, 1979). Second, African-American high school students were directed primarily into the burgeoning general track of studies in emergent comprehensive high schools (Angus & Mirel, 1993). This track had limited academic requirements and a weak academic focus. It was designed for students who were not college bound. In many cities, high school students in this track needed to take only 1 year of general mathematics to meet graduation requirements.

By the 1940s urban ghettos were firmly established, and weak learning institutions were beginning to emerge. Homel (1984) in his study of the African-American schooling experience in Chicago prior to 1950 stated that in the 1940s,

> Most commentators believed that the high proportion of beginners and the smaller share of veterans in ghetto schools meant less-effective instruction. One teacher asserted that the high turnover rate at her predominately black school fostered disorder among pupils and low morale among the faculty. She explained, "The new teachers only expect to be there a year so they don't care. When you know that you are going to be some place a long time... you plan and work to make the place better. (p. 67)

He also noted that African-American students disproportionately attended extremely large schools. In the early 1940s, half of the 24 African-American elementary schools in Chicago had over 1,200 students, and 5 had more than 2,000 students. Less than one fifth of White elementary schools had more than 1,200 students, and only 1 had more than 2,000.

More significantly, these enrollments seriously overshot capacity in most of these schools. New school construction did not keep pace with the rise in enrollments in African-American neighborhoods. This led to several deleterious effects including larger class sizes, housing of students in makeshift facilities, and, most damaging of all, the adoption of double schedules. Under this system, some students attended school from 8 a.m. to 12 noon and others from 12 noon to 4 p.m. This meant that many African-American students received 4 hours of schooling per day instead of 5 hours. By one estimate, "three-quarters of the children at black elementary schools on the South Side spent 20 to 40 percent fewer hours in class than did their counterparts in white areas" (Homel, 1984, p.82). Double schedules, along with larger classes, and poor facilities also further encouraged tired and frustrated teachers to leave these schools as soon as possible.

As African-American migration to northern cities from the south increased in the 1950s and early 1960s, discrimination in housing and employment created larger and larger segregated neighborhoods that contained weaker and weaker schools. By 1961, Conant, in a study of "slum" schools (as he called them) in New York, Chicago, Detroit, Philadelphia, and St. Louis, found the following conditions:

Let me describe a slum that might be in any of one of the several large cities I have visited. The inhabitants are all Negroes and with few exceptions have entered the city from a state in the deep South anytime within the last month to the last three years. Often the composition of a school grade in such an area will alter so rapidly that a teacher will find at the end of a school year that she is teaching but few pupils who started with her in the fall. (p.18)

Conant added that he had seen the results of a questionnaire sent out by school authorities in one neighborhood, which revealed the following:

Only 10 percent of the parents had graduated from high school and only 33 percent had completed the elementary school (K-8). Contrast this situation in which a third of the parents have completed elementary school with that in a high-income suburb where as many as 90 percent of the parents have bachelor's degrees, if not graduate degrees from a university. (p.19)

Conant further reported that most schools he visited had approximately 40 professionals per 1,000 students, compared to up to 70 professionals per 1,000 students he found in affluent suburbs. This, he stated,

. . . is further complicated by the fact that the turnover rate of teachers in the slum schools is very high. Teachers who have achieved some seniority rights often apply for transfer to schools away from the slum neighborhoods, where working conditions are at best difficult. (p.68)

Conant also stated that in the neighborhoods he visited it was typical for students to be 2 to 4 years behind in reading achievement and for half or more of the students to drop out in 9th or 10th grade.

It is important to remember, however, that in the early 1960s, long-term and concentrated poverty, and persistent and pervasive school failure did not dominate the populations served by many northern cities' public schools, as they do today, nor did all African-American students live in neighborhoods with poor schools and limited human, social, and economic capital. A report on Philadelphia public schools in 1965 (Pennsylvania State Department of Public Instruction, 1965), for example, noted that:

According to locally constructed tests, less than one-third of the seventy-seven schools with 70 percent or more Negro pupils reached expected city-wide median sixth grade level achievement in reading and arithmetic as compared with over 90 percent of 93 schools with 30 percent or less Negro enrollments. (p.58)

Thus in 1965, about half the students in Philadelphia, including a substantial number of African-Americans, were meeting city standards in mathematics and English. What these data and the prior discussion also show, however, is that by the 1960s, there were a large number of African-American students in northern industrial cities, who were performing below grade level, attended segregated and weak schools, and came from families that for generations had been denied access to strong learning opportunities and supports. By and large, it was these students who remained in the inner city and became the parents and grandparents of the succeeding generations that would come to dominate the public schools of northern industrial cities over the next 30 years (Boeger &Wegner, 1996).

This thumbnail sketch of the public schooling provided to African-Americans in northern industrial cities during the first two thirds of the 20th century falls far short of a full accounting, but it does illustrate a key point. If one takes an intergenerational viewpoint and examines the flow of learning opportunities and supports that have been provided to families over several generations, one reaches the inescapable conclusions that (a) there have been great inequalities in these provisions and (b) history, economics, and racial discrimination have worked together to concentrate families with high and low flows of intergenerational school effects to different locations in the United States. One of these concentrations is currently found in the inner core of formerly industrial northern cities. Thus, another partial answer to why so many urban public school students achieve so little is that members of their families, over multiple generations, have not been provided with strong or even adequate learning opportunities or supports. There are few people in their homes, their extended family, or their communities to help them, for example, learn algebra. No one they know may have ever been exposed to it.

CONCLUSION

Time and place matter. What I have proposed in this chapter is that we have been unable to find an answer to the question of why so many urban public school children achieve so little and unable to use this knowledge to develop effective remedies because our analytic lens has been narrowly confined by the data at hand. Such data have directed our attention to individual and group characteristics, and away from close analysis of environments that create weak and dysfunctional learning institutions. They also have prevented us from fully realizing how wide inequalities in the intergenerational provision of learning opportunities and supports (in some places and at some times) have been. Finally, the existing data have worked against recognition that these two forces now overlap in many central cities in the United States, and are tightly confounded with the more commonly explored variables of race, poverty, and school expenditure.

Consequently, the attention of educators has been misdirected. Focusing on the association between race, poverty, and school performance, largely at the national level, has led to rather diffuse, crude, "one size fits all" attempts to improve urban academic achievement. It has also directed research and reform efforts toward students with given characteristics – low income (Title I pullout programs), attendance at a racially segregated school (court-ordered desegregation), or residence in a neighborhood with low socioeconomic status (adult and parental education classes) – and away from a contextualized understanding of why schools in central cities do not work.

In order to refine the understanding of why so many urban public school children achieve so little, more and better data are needed. Data sets from which to analyze academic achievement and other student outcomes in schools within known districts and states need to be constructed. Such data must include contextual variables and find a means to at least proxy the impact of intergenerational school effects. This is critical because if the insights in this chapter can be confirmed and refined, they point to a different approach to school reform in high-poverty neighborhoods. A number of the more prescriptive whole school reform efforts of the past decade, such as, Success for All, the Edison Project, the Talent Development Model, and Direct Instruction have had small-scale success in providing the instructional and organizational leadership and tools needed to get high-poverty schools to focus on their technical cores.

This is a big step forward, but the means by which to reliably transform high-poverty schools into strong learning institutions on a large scale remains to be developed (Stringfield, 1995). The only way we will overcome the social and economic difficulties caused by the unequal and geographically based distribution of prior investments in the quantity and quality of schooling, however, is by building strong learning institutions in high-poverty neighborhoods. This requires, first, that reform efforts address contextual factors that negatively affect teacher and administrator functioning, and second, that these efforts be sustained over time to create generations of individuals who have had opportunities to learn challenging material in supportive school environments. Finally, the improvement of high-poverty schools requires a better understanding of history and the spatial distribution of weak and dysfunctional learning institutions so that efforts can be targeted and concentrated to the locales most in need.

REFERENCES

Anderson, J. D. (1988). *The education of Blacks in the south, 1860-1935.* Chapel Hill: University of North Carolina Press.

Angus, D. L., & Mirel, J. E. (1993). Equality, curriculum, and the decline of the academic ideal: Detroit, 1930-68. *History of Education Quarterly,* 33(2), 178-207.

Anyon, J. (1997). *Ghetto schooling: A political economy of urban educational reform.* New York: Teachers College Press.

Balfanz, R., & Legters, N. (1998). Unpublished common core data tabulations.

Barr, R., & Dreeban, R. (1983). *How schools work.* Chicago: University of Chicago Press.

Berne, R., & Stiefel, L. (1994). Measuring equity at the school level: The finance perspective. *Educational Evaluation and Policy Analysis,* 16(4), 405-421.

Bobbit, S., Quinn, P., & Dabbs, P. (1992). *Filling the gaps: An overview of data on education, grades K through 12.* Washington, DC: National Center for Education Statistics.

Boeger, J., & Wegner, J. (Eds.). (1996). *Race, poverty and American cities.* Chapel Hill: University of North Carolina Press.

Bryk, A., Sebring, P., Kerbow, D., Rollow, S., & Easton, S. (1998). *Chartering Chicago school reform: Democratic localism as a lever for change.* Boulder, CO: Westview Press.

Burtless, G. (Ed.). (1996). *Does money matter?* Washington, DC: Brookings Institute.

Coleman, J. (1994). The concept of equality of educational opportunity. In J. Kretovics & E. Nussel (Eds.), *Transforming urban education* (pp. 18-31). Needham Heights, MA: Allyn & Bacon.

Conant, J. B. (1961). *Slums and suburbs.* New York: McGraw-Hill.

Corbett, H., & Wilson, B. (1997). *Cracks in the classroom floor: The seventh grade year in five Philadelphia middle schools.* Philadelphia: Philadelphia Education Fund.

Darling-Hammond, L. (1997). *The right to learn.* San Francisco: Jossey-Bass.

Education Week/Pew Charitable Trust (1998). *Quality counts '98: The urban challenge - public education in the 50 states* (Vol. XVII, No. 17). Washington, DC: Author.

Elmore, R.F., Peterson, P. L., & McCarthey, S. J. (1996). *Restructuring in the Classroom.* San Francisco, CA: Jossey-Bass.

Entwisle, D. R, Alexander, K. L., & Olson, L. S. (1997). *Children, schools, & inequality.* Boulder, CO: Westview Press.

Haberman, M. (1994). The pedagogy of poverty versus good teaching. In J. Kretovics & E.J. Nussel (Eds.), *Transforming urban education.* Needham, MA: Allyn & Bacon.

Hess, G. A., Jr. (1995). *Restructuring urban schools.* New York: Teachers College Press.

Homel, M. W. (1984). *Down from equality: Black Chicagoans and the public schools: 1920 - 1940.* Chicago: University of Illinois Press.

Ma, X., & Kishor, N. (1997). Assessing the relationship between attitude toward mathematics and achievement in mathematics: A meta-analysis. *Journal for Research in Mathematics Education,* 28(1), 26-47.

Margo, R. A. (1990). *Race and schooling in the south, 1880-1950: An economic history.* Chicago:University of Chicago Press.

Maryland State Department of Education (1997). *Maryland school performance program report.* Baltimore: Author.

Miller, L. S. (1995). *An American imperative: Accelerating minority educational advancement.* New Haven, CT: Yale University Press.

Mirel, J. (1993). *The rise and fall of an urban school system: Detroit, 1907-81.* Ann harbor, MI: University of Michigan Press.

Mohraz, J. (1979). *The separate problem.* Westport, CT: Greenwood Press.

National Center for Education Statistics. (1997). *Developments in school finance 1997.* Washington DC: Author.

National Center for Education Statistics. (1998). *Linking the National Assessment of Educational Progress (NAEP) and the Third International Mathematics and Science Study (TIMSS): Eighth-grade results.* Washington DC: Author.

Natriello, G., Riehl, C., & Pallas, A. (1994). *Between the rock of standards and the hard place of accommodation: Evaluation practices of teachers in high schools serving disadvantaged students* (Rep. No. 47) Baltimore: Johns Hopkins University Center for Research on Effective Schooling for Disadvantaged Students.

Neild, R., & Weiss, C. (1999). *The Philadelphia education longitudinal study (PELS): Report on the transition to high school in the school district of Philadelphia.* Philadelphia: Philadelphia Education Fund.

Orazem, P. F. (1987). Black - White differences in schooling investment and human capital production in segregated schools. *American Educational Review, 77*(4), 714-723.

Orfield, G., & Eaton, S. (1996). *Dismantling desegregation.* New York: The New Press.

Orland, M. E. (1994). Demographic of disadvantage: Intensity of childhood poverty and its relationship to educational achievement. In J. I. Goodlad & P. Keating (Eds.), *Access to Knowledge* (pp. 43-58). New York: The College Board.

Pennsylvania State Department of Public Instruction (1965). *Report of the study of the public schools of Philadelphia.* Philadelphia: Author

Perlmann, J. (1988). *Ethnic differences: Schooling and social structure among the Irish, Italians, Jews & Blacks in an American city, 1880 - 1935.* New York: The Cambridge University Press.

Philadelphia School District. (1997) *Philadelphia school report cards.* Philadelphia: Author.

Rury, J. L., & Cassell, F. A. (1993). *Seeds of crisis: Public schooling in Milwaukee since 1920.* Madison: University of Wisconsin Press.

Rusk, D. (1996). *Baltimore unbound.* Baltimore: The Abell Foundation.

Stringfield, S. (1995). Attempting to enhance students? Learning through innovative programs: The case for schools evolving into high reliability organizations. *School Effectiveness and School Improvement, 6*(1), 67-96.

Teddlie, C. & Stringfield, S. (1993). *Schools make a difference.* New York: Teachers College Press.

Useem, E. (1998). *Teachers' appraisals of Talent Development Middle Schools training, materials, and student progress: Results from focus groups* (Report No. 25) Baltimore, MD: Center for Research on the Education of Students Placed at Risk.

Useem, E. L., Christman, J. B., Gold, E., & Simon, E. (1997). Reforming alone: Barriers to organizational learning in urban school change initiatives. *Journal of Education For Students Placed At Risk, 2*(1), 55-78.

Walker, V. S. (1996). *Their Higher Potential.* Chapel Hill: University of North Carolina Press.

Wenglinsky, H. (1997). *When Money Matters.* Princeton, NJ: Educational Testing Service.

Wong, K. & Meyer, S. (1998). Title I schoolwide programs: A synthesis of findings from recent evaluation. *Educational Evaluation and Policy Analysis, 20*(2), 115-136.

Wood, L. A. (1994). An unintended impact of one grading practice. *Urban Education. 29*(2):188-201.

Zipp, J. F., & Levine, M. V. (1993). A city at risk: The changing social and economic context of public schooling in Milwaukee. In J. Rury & F. Cassell (Eds.), *Seeds of crisis.* (pp. 42-72). Madison: University of Wisconsin Press.

II

Factors Influencing Resiliency and School Failure

4

Student-Teacher Relations and Academic Achievement in High School

MAVIS G. SANDERS
WILL J. JORDAN
Johns Hopkins University

This chapter examines the relationship between students' perceptions of teacher-student relations and their academic achievement. Using panel data drawn from the National Educational Longitudinal Survey of 1988, the authors explore the degree to which teacher-student relations, measured as teacher expectations and teacher supportiveness at grades 10 and 12, influence 12th-grade students' educational investments and academic achievement. Multiple regression is used first to model the effects of students' perceptions of their relationships with teachers as predictors of their investment behaviors, and then to analyze the concurrent effects of teacher-student relations and student investments on academic achievement. Research on teacher-student interaction provides the conceptual framework guiding this study. The authors find consistent evidence that teacher-student relations have a positive and significant influence on adolescents' educational investments, measured as school conduct, classroom preparation, and avoidance of maladaptive behaviors. The authors also find that positive teacher-student relations and prosocial investment behaviors among students enhance academic achievement, measured as both standardized test scores and grade point averages. The regression results remain constant when controlling on background characteristics of students such as their race/ethnicity, gender, prior learning, and socioeconomic status, as well as contextual factors such as school sector and academic track. Implications for research and practice are discussed.

Adolescence is a period in an individual's life in which a major transition is made from late childhood to adulthood. Many choices and decisions about school that can have critical effects on adolescents' educational and life chances are made by adolescents and their families (Elmen, 1991; Kramer, 1991; Lipsitz, 1981). For example, the decision to put forth little academic effort while in school, or conversely to work hard in school, can have a major impact on the kind of adult life an adolescent will lead. Researchers have found that for many adolescents, there is a gradual decline in various indicators of motivation, behavior, and self-perception that can lead to lower academic achievement and increased rates of school dropout (Eccles & Midgley, 1988).

Schools, however, can play a role in offsetting maladaptive behavior, and in promoting engagement and academic success among adolescents. One way in which schools influence students is by fostering supportive relationships between and among students, teachers and other caring adults (Brophy & Good, 1974; McPartland, Legters, Jordan, & McDill, 1996; Wehlage, Rutter, Smith, Lesko, & Fernandez, 1989). It is well documented in the social psychology literature that social relationships with nonparental adults influence the social and cognitive development of children and adolescents, and, in many cases, their success or failure in societal institutions such as school (Coleman, 1987; Dryfoos, 1990; Nettles, 1991). A considerable amount of this research is focused on the relationship between teachers and students, and its effects on student outcomes (Brophy and Good, 1974; · Irvine, 1990). These studies generally support the position that positive teacher-student relations lead to higher student achievement.

The present study extends previous literature on the importance of positive teacher-student relations. It seeks to determine whether and how the nature of the relationship between teachers and students influences the academic performance of high school students. To this end, the authors explore the degree to which teacher-student relations (measured as students' perceptions of high support and expectations among teachers) influence the level of student personal investment in school (measured as student conduct, avoidance of maladaptive behavior, and classroom preparation) and academic achievement at Grade 12. We further examine whether an intervening relationship between teacher-student relations, student investments, and student achievement exists. We hypothesize that, to some extent, teacher-student relations affect the personal investments students make in their schooling, which, in turn, influence their level of achievement.

REVIEW OF LITERATURE

There is considerable research suggesting that the relationship between teachers and their students can affect student achievement and overall educational success. Popular media provides many examples of teachers, who through affirming relationships with students, helped students to improve their academic performance and, in some cases, achieve well beyond expectations. The case of Jaime Escalante in the film *Stand and Deliver* is one such example. Escalante was an exemplary mathematics teacher who successfully taught scores of poor, Hispanic students in Los Angeles to excel in calculus against the odds. This example illuminates how high teacher expectations, along with nurturance, can foster academic excellence among all students. On the other hand, low expectations among teachers and school staff, as well as impersonal or negative teacher-student relations, can produce low student engagement and achievement in school (Fine & Zane, 1989; Irvine, 1990; Kelly, 1991). Thus, students' experiences within schools are related to their level of psychological investment (motivation), their emotional well-being, and their academic achievement (Clark, 1995). Research has shown that adolescents often are motivated to improve their academic and social behaviors as a result of their interpersonal relationships with teachers (see Sanders & Herting, chap. 7, this volume). This is especially prevalent among students who have had a history of bad schooling experiences or who come from families whose socioeconomic conditions place them at risk of school failure (Sizemore, 1981).

Irvine (1990) contended that teachers play a central role in the school performance of youth because the relationship between a teacher and a student "rivals the relationship between a parent and a child " (p. 47). This assertion is not unwarranted because good teachers often form close bonds with their students. In a study of high school teachers and students, students were asked who had influenced them to become the kind of people they were, and 58% named one of their teachers (Csikszentimihalyi & McCormack, 1986).

Previous studies also report evidence that teacher caring and supportiveness are important attributes that are significantly related to student achievement. For example, Sanders (1998) found that students' perceptions of teacher support have a positive and significant influence on the classroom behavior and academic achievement of African-American eighth-grade students. In another study, low income, African-American adults, aged 18-34, were asked to identify the characteristics of the teachers who had influenced them the most. The respondents selected social and interpersonal skills, affective characteristics, and temperament. These respondents identified the following attributes as characteristic of influential and memorable teachers: approachable, pleasant, easy to relate to, accepting, tolerant, helpful, concerned, caring, thoughtful, and perceptive of and sensitive to the needs of their students (Irvine, 1990).

Nearly a decade earlier, researchers asked some 11,000 high school students to state what they considered to be among the most important differences between "good teachers" and "bad teachers" (Sizemore, 1981). The results suggested that, regardless of their ethnicity, adolescents seek out teachers who care about and support them, and view them as being good students. Sizemore concluded that it is necessary for teachers to remain conscious of the importance of developing supportive relationships with students in order to foster their cognitive and social growth. He further argued that without caring and supportive teachers many students might not benefit from even the most sophisticated instructional techniques.

Teacher support, caring, and nurturance, however, ought to be embedded in high expectations for students in order for positive academic outcomes to be realized. Friendly, caring teachers who do not encourage their students to achieve at realistically high levels may do little to affect intellectual growth. Since the now classic "Pygmalion in the Classroom" study (Rosenthal & Jacobson, 1968), educational research has sought to determine the significance of teacher expectations for student academic success (Brophy & Good, 1974; Dusek, 1975). Although researchers may disagree on explanations of how and why teacher expectations influence student outcomes, the prevailing view is that differential expectations of students are likely to have a significant impact on learning (Dusek, 1985; Jordan, 1993). More plainly, in schools where expectations are high, student achievement tends to be higher than in schools where expectations are low (Bamburg, 1994; Paredes, 1993).

Life histories and work experiences of individual teachers add to the existing research literature on the potential effects of teacher expectations on student learning and educational success (Hassenpflug, 1994; Mitchell, chap. 8, this volume). Research also sheds light on factors, such as class size and school organization, that influence whether teachers develop and act on high expectations for their students (Bamburg, 1994; Gollub & Sloan, 1978) .

This chapter contributes to the literature by examining how teacher-student relations, measured as both teacher expectations and teacher supportiveness, influence student achievement (measured here as standardized test scores and grade point averages) through its effects on student investments (student conduct, classroom preparation, and maladaptive behavior). The study takes advantage of a national longitudinal data set to explore the effects of teacher-student relations on student outcomes over time. The analysis has two steps. The first step is an investigation of the effects of teacher-student relations in Grades 10 and 12 on student investments in Grade 12. The second step is an analysis of the effects of teacher-student relations and student investments on 12th-grade students' academic achievement. The results of these analyses are used to infer the existence of causal relationships between the attitudes and actions (or student's perception of attitudes and actions) of key adults in the school, and student's academic success. In essence, they provide an empirical test of the simple causal relationships depicted in Fig. 4.1.

DATA AND METHODS

The data for the present study were drawn from the National Educational Longitudinal Study of 1988 (NELS:88), which is supported by the National Center for Educational Statistics of the U.S. Department of Education. NELS:88 provides abundant information on the experiences of adolescents, such as their school-related attitudes, behaviors, and achievement from the 8th grade onward. The NELS:88 design used a two-stage, stratified random sample of over 25,000 8th-grade students in 1,000 schools, who were followed up at 2-year intervals. In addition to student data, two of each student's teachers, the school's principal, and a parent were administered detailed questionnaires. In the present study, we analyze student data collected in 1988, 1990, and 1992. The baseline data, collected in 1988, were used only to provide a measure of students' prior achievement level. The independent variables, teacher expectations and teacher supportiveness, were derived from the 1990 (10th-grade) and 1992 (12th-grade) data. Finally, student investment and achievement variables, school context variables, and variables measuring student background characteristics were gathered from the 1992 data, during Grade 12. After application of appropriate weights to the sample, the minimum number of cases in the longitudinal sample for any equation was approximately 13,600 students; the average number of cases was approximately 15,000.

We used multiple regression analysis to examine the pattern of relationships outlined in Fig. 4.1. The initial set of equations model student perceptions of teacher expectations and teacher supportiveness at Grades 10 and 12 on adolescents' psychological investment in school (measured as their school conduct, maladaptive behavior, and classroom preparation).

Teacher-Student Relations →	Student Investments →	Academic Achievement
• High Expectations	• Student Conduct	• Standardized Tests
• Teacher Supportiveness	• Maladaptive Behavior	• Grade Point Average
	• Preparation for Class	

FIGURE 4.1: Simplified schematic of causal relationships

Statistical controls on both student background characteristics and school context are included in these equations. Subsequent equations build on the initial set by modeling the effects of teacher-student relations, or student perceptions of teacher expectations and teacher supportiveness, together with student investments, as predictors of academic achievement.

Construction of Teacher-Student Relations Scales

Teacher expectations (at Grades 10 and 12) were measured by a single item asking students whether their favorite teacher expected them to go to college immediately after high school. Here we use expectations for college synonymously with high academic expectations. We do so because teachers who expect their students to go to college are likely to support them and hold them academically accountable in ways different from students who are not viewed as college bound.

Teacher supportiveness was measured slightly differently at Grades 10 and 12. At Grade 10, it was measured by a six-item scale. The scale measured students' perceptions of the support, encouragement, and praise they received from their teachers, and it included items such as "Students get along well with teachers" "Teachers are interested in students" and "When I work hard, teachers praise my effort." The internal reliability of the scale was high (α =.81).

Only two of the six items were asked again at Grade 12. As a result, teacher support at Grade 12 was measured by the following two items: "Students get along well with teachers" and "Teachers are interested in students." The internal reliability of these two variables was .75. Together, teacher expectations and teacher support serve as measures of teacher-student relations.

Construction of Student Investment Scales

Students' educational investments in school were conceptualized in three ways for the purposes of this study: (a) conduct in school, (b) preparation for class, and (c) avoidance of maladaptive behavior. The first scale, student conduct, consisted of six items that measured behavior during school. This scale included questions such as "How many times were you late for school?" "How many times have you been put on in-school suspension?" and " How many times did you cut/skip classes?" The internal reliability for this scale was .74. Items in the student conduct scale were reverse coded so that a high score indicated better behavior.

The second student investment scale, student preparation, contained two items that measured the level of preparation for class. Students were asked simply how frequently they attended class without having their pencil, paper, and books (α = .76). These items also were reverse coded so that a high score on the scale indicated that students attended class prepared for school work.

Finally, the maladaptive behavior scale contained five items that measured the frequency of students' use of alcohol, marijuana, and cigarettes. Students were asked, for example, "How many cigarettes do you smoke a day?" and "In the last 12 months, how many times did you use marijuana?" The reliability coefficient (α =.73) suggested that maladaptive behavior among adolescents tended to cluster. That is, students who engaged in one of these activities such as smoking marijuana were likely to engage in other maladaptive behavior as well. A high score on this scale indicated students' frequent involvement in the maladaptive behaviors measured.

Background Characteristics

Statistical controls on race/ethnicity, gender, socioeconomic status, and family composition were drawn from the 12th-grade sample. Students' race/ethnicity was coded as a dummy variable, with White students as the reference category. Gender was coded as a dummy variable for females. A composite measure of SES that takes into account a student's household income, mother's education, father's education, and mother's and father's occupation was used. This SES composite was created by NCES, National Center for Educational Statistics, and placed on the NELS:88 data files. Family composition was coded as a dummy variable comparing students who live in a single female-headed household to those who have some other arrangement (single-parent household = 1, other = 0). Standardized reading test scores at grade 8 were used as a measure of prior achievement.

School Context

Academic track and public versus private sector were items from the 1992 data used to gauge the contextual climate for students in the study. Academic track was coded as a dummy variable (college preparatory = 1, non-college preparatory = 0), and sector was a dummy variable for public schools. The contextual variables in this study were meant not to provide an exhaustive account of social organizational influences, but instead to control on the effects of two key aspects of the school environment.

Academic Achievement

Two measures of student achievement were used in the study: standardized test scores and cumulative grade point averages (GPA). Standardized test scores were drawn from the 12th-grade sample, and represented the mean results on the NELS:88 cognitive test in reading, mathematics, science, and social studies. GPA, also measured at Grade 12, was a self-reported average of high school grades in English, mathematics, science, and social studies. Each dependent variable provided important information about the academic success of a student. Standardized achievement was the least subjective measure of academic performance available in NELS:88. In addition, although considerable variability in grading procedures within and across schools exists, GPA served as a good measure of teachers' ratings of students' academic efforts and productivity as compared to their classmates. Taken together, standardized achievement and cumulative GPA complemented each other and provided a clearer picture of a student's academic achievement in high school than either variable could do alone.

RESULTS

The primary purpose of this study was to determine whether positive teacher-student relations influenced academic achievement among high school students. We further examined whether this occurred because positive interactions between teachers and students offset maladaptive behaviors and fostered student investments in school, and whether adolescents benefitted from having positive relations with teachers for multiple years. More specifically, we analyzed the effects of teacher expectations for college, as well as teacher supportiveness at Grades 10 and 12 on student school conduct, maladaptive behavior, and class preparation, to explore the relationship between these two sets of variables (teacher-student relations and student investments) and academic achievement.

Table 4.1 shows the effects of teacher-student relations on student conduct. As indicated, student perceptions of teacher supportiveness at Grade 10 (β = .15; T = 17.19, $p<.001$), and Grade 12 (β = .12; T = 13.49, $p<.001$) were positive and significant predictors of student behavior at Grade 12. The finding that teacher support affects the conduct of older adolescents, who have more established patterns of behavior than do younger students, highlights the significance of this variable. Of further interest is the suggested sustained effect of teacher support on students' behavior. That is, although the coefficient drops from Grade 10 to Grade 12, it remains positive and significant.

The effect of teacher expectations at Grade 12 on students' conduct also was positive and significant (β = .11; T = 12.82, $p<.001$). The small, negative effect of teacher expectations at Grade 10 on students' 12th-grade behavior possibly can be explained by the inclusion of four moderately correlated teacher-student relations variables[1] in the same equation predicting student behavior. The weakest of the four teacher-student relations variables, teacher expectations at Grade 10 was either nonsignificant or negative when regressed on the 12th-grade student investment variables (see Tables 4.2 and 4.3). However, when added to the equations predicting students' 12th-grade achievement, a dependent variable with far greater variance, teacher expectations at Grade 10 had a significant effect that was in the expected direction (see Tables 4.5).

The statistical controls suggest that Hispanics, African-Americans, males, students from low SES backgrounds, low achievers, and adolescents living in single-parent households struggled more with school conduct than did other students. Whereas students in college preparatory tracks tended to exhibit better school conduct, no statistical difference between adolescents in public and those in private schools existed.

The same equation was used to model maladaptive behavior and classroom engagement among students; these results are presented in Tables 4.2 and 4.3, respectively. As illustrated in Tables 4.2, student perceptions of teacher supportiveness at Grade 10 (β = -.14; T = -16.53) and Grade 12 (β = -.10; T = -11.73) were associated with lower levels of maladaptive behavior among students. These results also were statistically significant at $p<.001$ and suggest that teacher support has an influence on students' out-of-school

---

[1]The highest correlation between teacher support at Grades 10 and 12 was .411. The teacher expectations variables at Grades 10 and 12 were correlated at .319.

behavior, as well as their in-school behavior (see Table 4.1). Teacher expectations at Grade 12 ($\beta = -.14$; $T = -16.53$, $p<.001$) also reduced students' reported involvement in behaviors such as drinking alcohol and smoking. As discussed previously, the teacher expectations variable at Grade 10 was too weak to contribute significantly to the model predicting students' maladaptive behavior. Both SES and single-parent household revealed a small but positive association with maladaptive behavior ($\beta = .04$; $T = 4.27$ and $\beta = .02$; $T = 2.81$, respectively).

The last of the initial equations is presented in Table 4.3. It models the effects of teacher-student relations on students' preparation for class. These findings were similar to those just reported. Both student perceptions of teacher expectations for college and student perceptions of teacher supportiveness at Grade 12 were found to be positively associated with 12th-grade students' class preparation ($\beta = .07$; $T = 8.40$, $p<.001$; $\beta = .09$; $T = 10.31$, $p<.001$). Students who felt supported by their teachers and who believed that their teachers had high expectations for them were more likely to come to class ready to learn. Furthermore, students who reported positive teacher support in Grade 10 also were more likely to come prepared for their

TABLE 4.1: Effects of Student Perceptions of Teacher-Student Relations on Student Conduct at Grade 12

Independent Variables	Regression Coefficient	
	β	T
Teacher-student relations at Grade 12		
High teacher expectations	.11***	12.82
High teacher supportiveness	.12***	13.49
Teacher-student relations at Grade 10		
High teacher expectations	-.02**	-2.95
High teacher supportiveness	.15***	17.19
Background characteristics		
Hispanic	-.03***	-4.16
African-American	-.04***	-4.36
Female	.13***	16.23
SES	-.04***	-4.20
Prior achievement (Grade 8)	.07***	7.48
Single-parent household	-.02	-2.39
School context		
College preparatory track	.04***	4.29
Public sector	.02**	2.98
Degrees of freedom/residual		15509
R^2		.10

Note. *$p<.05$. **$p<.01$. ***$p<.001$.

TABLE 4.2: Effects of Student Perceptions of Teacher-Student Relations on Student Maladaptive Behavior at Grade 12

Independent Variables	Regression Coefficient	
Teacher-student relations at Grade 12	β	T
High teacher expectations	-.09***	-10.31
High teacher supportiveness	-.10***	-11.73
Teacher-student relations at Grade 10		
High teacher expectations	-.02	-1.76
High teacher supportiveness	-.14***	-16.53
Background characteristics		
Hispanic	-.04***	-5.09
African-American	-.11***	-13.45
Female	-.13***	-16.16
SES	.05***	4.96
Prior achievement (Grade 8)	-.04***	-4.70
Single-parent household	.02**	2.74
School context		
College preparatory track	-.02	-1.83
Public sector	-.04***	-4.48
Degrees of freedom/residual		15509
R^2		.09

Note. *$p<.05$. **$p<.01$. ***$p<.001$.

classes than were students who did not experience such support ($\beta = .06$; $T = 7.22$, $p<.001$). Female students reported being prepared for class much more often than males and, in fact, exhibited the largest magnitude of results in this equation ($\beta = .19$; $T = 24.72$). Hispanic students reported being slightly less prepared for class than were students of other racial/ethnic backgrounds ($\beta = -.03$; $T = -3.00$, $p<.01$). SES, prior achievement, and single-parent household did not have significant effects on student preparation. Among contextual items, assignment to a college preparatory track was positively associated with preparation for class ($\beta = .02$; $T = 2.26$), whereas the public versus private sector had no significant effect.

The final stage of this analysis extends the initial models previously discussed by adding student investments as independent variables and regressing them, together with student perceptions of teacher expectations and teacher supportiveness on academic achievement. To isolate the effects of student perceptions of expectations and supportiveness we carried out this stage of the analysis using two equations, both with and without the measures of student investments (under the same control conditions). Both equations are presented in Table 4.4.

As shown in Table 4.4, Equation I, student perceptions of teacher supportiveness at Grades 10 and 12, and teacher expectations at Grade 12 are positively and significantly associated with composite standardized test scores. The regression coefficients for the variables are as follows: teacher support at Grade 10 ($\beta = .05$; $T = 8.56$, $p<.001$); teacher support at Grade 12 ($\beta = .07$; $T = 11.59$, $p<.001$); and teacher expectations at Grade 12 ($\beta = .04$; $T = 7.78$, $p<.001$). These findings indicate that students who felt supported by their teachers and who believed that their favorite teachers had high expectations for them were more likely to achieve at higher levels. As in the initial models, these results took into account student background characteristics and school context. Consistent with prevailing research, the best predictors of composite, standardized achievement were prior achievement ($\beta = .63$; $T = 103.20$) and SES ($\beta = .15$; $T = 24.28$). Also, college preparatory track had a significant, positive association with achievement ($\beta = .12$; $T = 21.82$).

TABLE 4.3: Effects of Student Perceptions of Teacher-Student Relations on Student Preparation for Class at Grade 12

Independent Variables	Regression Coefficient	
Teacher-student relations at Grade 12	β	T
High teacher expectations	.07***	8.40
High teacher supportiveness	.09***	10.31
Teacher-student relations at Grade 10		
High teacher expectations	.01	1.07
High teacher supportiveness	.06***	7.22
Background characteristics		
Hispanic	-.03**	-3.00
African-American	-.02	-1.74
Female	.19***	24.72
SES	.00	.24
Prior achievement (Grade 8)	.00	-.01
Single-parent household	.00	.01
School context		
College preparatory track	.02*	2.26
Public sector	.01	1.53
Degrees of Freedom/Residual		15509
R^2		.07

Note. *$p<.05$. **$p<.01$. ***$p<.001$.

TABLE 4.4: Effects of Student Perceptions of Teacher-Student Relations and Student Investment on Composite Achievement at Grade 12				
Independent Variables	Equation I		Equation II	
Teacher-student relations at Grade 12	β	T	β	T
High teacher expectations	.04***	7.78	.03***	5.74
High teacher supportiveness	.07***	11.59	.05***	9.31
Teacher-student relations at Grade 10				
High Teacher Expectations	.01	2.40	.02**	2.72
High Teacher Supportiveness	.05***	8.56	.03***	5.77
Background characteristics				
Hispanic	-.03***	-5.84	-.03***	-5.85
African-American	-.10***	-17.48	-.10***	-18.14
Female	-.11***	-20.65	.01***	1.03
SES	.15***	23.91	.15***	24.83
Prior achievement (Grade 8)	.62***	102.94	.61***	103.07
Single-parent household	.00	.64	.01	1.03
School context				
College preparatory track	.12***	21.30	.12***	20.99
Public sector	.02**	3.47	.02**	2.88
Student Investments				
Student conduct			.05***	7.69
Student preparation for class			.03***	5.61
Maladaptive behavior			-.05***	-8.45
Degrees of freedom/residual		13651		13666
R^2		.64		.64

Note. *$p<.05$. **$p<.01$. ***$p<.001$.

Student investments in school were entered as a second block of variables. These together with teacher-student relations, background characteristics, and school context variables, form Equation II in Table 4.4. As presented in Table 4.4, when the student investment block was introduced into the model, the effects of the teacher-student relations variables dropped slightly. This held true for all the teacher-student relations variables except teacher expectations at Grade 10, which was nonsignificant in Table 4.4, Equation I, but became significant in Table 4.4, Equation II ($β = .02$; $T = 2.72$, $p<.01$). Thus, we can assume that the independent effects of teacher expectations at grade 10 can be explained not by students' investments at Grade 12, but perhaps by other variables not investigated in the study.

The student investment block did not contribute to the R^2. The most likely reason for this is that prior achievement is such a strong predictor of Grade 12 achievement that little variance is left unexplained (R^2 = .64, Table 4.4, Equation I). Nonetheless, Equation II in Table 4.4 suggests that student perceptions of teacher expectations and teacher supportiveness over time, as well as student educational investments, are significantly associated with student scores on standardized achievement tests. Of these investments, student conduct and class preparation were found to have significant, positive effects on achievement (β = .05; T = 7.69 and β = .03; T = 5.61, respectively), whereas maladaptive behavior had a significant, negative influence (β = -.05; T = -8.45).

The equations modeling GPA as the dependent variable revealed a similar set of results. As presented in Equation I (Table 4.5), student perceptions of teacher expectations at Grades 10 and 12 (β = .04; T = 6.33 and β = .11; T

TABLE 4.5: Effects of Student Perceptions of Teacher--Student Relations and Student Investment on Cumulative Grade Point Average at Grade 12

Independent Variables	Equation I		Equation II	
	β	T	β	T
Teacher-student relations at Grade 12				
High teacher expectations	.11***	16.04	.09***	12.67
High teacher supportiveness	.05***	7.51	.02***	3.52
Teacher-student relations at Grade 10				
High Teacher Expectations	.04***	6.33	.05***	7.40
High Teacher Supportiveness	.12***	16.82	.08***	11.88
Background characteristics				
Hispanic	-.03***	-4.61	-.03***	-4.28
African-American	-.09***	-12.95	-.09***	-13.59
Female	.10***	15.47	.07***	10.35
SES	.16***	21.38	.18***	24.20
Prior achievement (Grade 8)	.36***	49.01	.35***	48.88
Single-parent household	-.04	-5.55	.03***	-5.00
School context				
College preparatory track	.12***	17.82	.12***	17.40
Public sector	.01*	2.14	.01	1.12
Student Investments				
Student conduct			.18***	25.50
Student preparation for class			.01	2.53
Maladaptive behavior			-.07***	-10.20
Degrees of freedom/residual		14366		14366
R^2		.42		.46

Note. *$p<.05$. **$p<.01$. ***$p<.001$.

= 16.04, respectively), and their perceptions of teacher supportiveness over time were positively associated with GPA (β = .12; T = 16.82 and β = .11; T = 16.04). The control variables in the equations on GPA and the equations modeling standardized achievement also had a similar pattern, although there were two key exception. First, whereas female high school students had lower standardized test scores than did males (see Table 4.4, Equation II: β = -.11; T = 20.65), the GPAs of females were slightly higher (Table 4.5, Equation II: β = .10; T = 15.47). In addition, it is interesting to note that living in a single-parent household had no observable effect on standardized achievement, net of SES (β = .00; T = .64), but had a significant, negative effect on GPA (β = -.04; T = -5.55). Again, as we anticipated, prior achievement was the best predictor of both achievement outcomes.

When the student investments block was entered into Equation II in Table 4.5, the effects of student perceptions of teacher supportiveness and teacher expectations on grades were slightly reduced (note the exception of teacher expectations at Grade 10 as previously described). This reduction may be explained by the effects of teacher supportiveness on the student investments measured, specifically student school conduct and involvement in maladaptive behaviors. Among the student investment variables themselves, student conduct had a strong, positive effect on grades (β = .18; T = 25.50). Conversely, maladaptive behavior among 12th-grade students reduces their GPA (β = -.07; T = -10.20).

SUMMARY

This chapter examined the degree to which teachers foster achievement among students by holding high academic expectations for them, and by acting as supportive and caring adults within the school. We conducted our analysis by initially investigating the relationships between students' perceptions of their teachers' expectations and supportiveness, and their level of investment in school (measured as student conduct, class preparation, and maladaptive behavior). The results of this initial analysis show that teacher support was positively and significantly associated with student conduct and preparation for class, and negatively and significantly associated with maladaptive behavior, such as alcohol use, among students. Furthermore, the findings suggest that the effects of teacher support from year to year were, to some extent, independent, and that students benefitted from having teacher support in both Grades 10 and 12. The effects of teacher expectations were also positive and significant. Twelfth-grade students who reported that their favorite teachers expected them to go to college also reported being better prepared for class, better behaved in school and less involved in maladaptive behavior in and out of school than were students who did not report high teacher expectations. These findings suggest that positive teacher-student relations can improve student school behavior, increase student classroom preparation, and reduce student engagement in maladaptive behaviors - educational investments that are associated with higher student achievement.

The second stage of this analysis examines the effects of teacher-student relations, as measured by teacher expectations and teacher supportiveness, on student achievement. We also added measures of student investments into the equation in order to observe their effect on the relationship between teacher-student relations and academic achievement. We found that teacher-student relations had a positive effect on student achievement. Some of the variability in this relationship may be attributed to the level of student investment in school. However, our findings indicate that teacher-student relations had some significant effects on student achievement that were not explained by the student investments measured.

DISCUSSION AND CONCLUSION

This study supports the findings of previous research underscoring the importance of building nurturing school communities with high expectations to foster student engagement and academic success. Indeed, Clark (1995) argued "school connectedness" is an important protective factor against behaviors that place many adolescents at risk for school failure or dropout. She stated that school connectedness is promoted where students feel important, supported, and cared for, and where students are expected to do well academically.

This chapter adds to a body of research suggesting that at least two ingredients – high expectations and supportiveness – are needed to establish an optimal learning environment for all students. Our findings also affirm that teachers play a critical role in providing these ingredients. Yet, despite this research, at still far too many high schools, "teachers tend to relate to students in a universalistic, specific, and impersonal way. They tend to treat all students alike, relate to students primarily in terms of subject matter, and have weak affective ties with students" (Isherwood & Ahola, 1981, p.175). Many current school reforms are attempting to change the school environment by encouraging more interpersonal interaction between teachers and students. These reforms include efforts to reduce school size using a schools-within-school model, and to extend class periods to give teachers more instructional time and direct contact with students (Legters, chap. 14, this volume; McPartland, et al., 1996). An underlying principle of these efforts is that given the opportunity and time, teachers and school staff can build more caring and trusting relationships with students, and better help them achieve their fullest potential.

Many schools that serve poor and minority adolescents, however, might lack the resources and personnel necessary to provide students with the personal support and guidance they may need to avoid stumbling into maladaptive behaviors, low school engagement, and poor achievement. Such schools, however, are not wholly without resources. Caring adults in these adolescents' families and communities can work with teachers and other school personnel to support and guide these youth (Nettles, 1991; Sanders & Epstein, chap. 15, this volume). Many reform efforts that seek to create caring learning environments for students are encouraging more parent and community involvement to achieve this goal (Dryfoos, 1998; Lucas, Henze, & Donato, 1990; McDonnell, 1989; Stephen, Varble, & Taitt, 1993).

These and other reform efforts must be supported and continually evaluated and improved to ensure that all students are appropriately served by schools. Further research delving into ways of possibly maximizing teacher expectations and support is needed. Such research should investigate how school and class size influence interpersonal relationships between teachers and students; what organizational and contextual factors influence the development of teacher expectations; and how best to support teachers in developing and sustaining high expectations for all students, irrespective of class, race, and gender. In addition, more research on how families and communities can best partner with schools to create supportive learning environments is needed. Findings from such studies could further inform and improve reform efforts in American high schools.

REFERENCES

Bamburg, J. (1994). *Raising Expectations to Improve Student Learning.* Washington, DC: Office of Educational Research and Improvement.

Brophy, J. E. & Good, T. L. (1974). *Teacher-student relations: Causes and consequences.* New York: Holt.

Clark, P. (1995). Risk and resiliency in adolescence: The current status of research on gender differences. *Equity Issues,* 1(1): 1-13.

Coleman, J. (1987). Families and schools. *Educational Researcher* 16(6), 32-38.

Csikszentimihalyi, M., & McCormack, J. (1986). The influence of teachers. *Phi Delta Kappan* (67), 415-19.

Dryfoos, J. (1990). School based social and health services for at-risk students. *Urban*

Education, 19(1): 53-76.

Dryfoos, J. (1998). *Safe passage: Making it through adolescence in a risky society.* New York: Oxford University Press.

Dusek, J. B. (1975). Do teachers bias children's learning? *Review of Educational Research,* 45(4), 661-684.

Dusek, J. B. (1985). *Teacher expectancies.* Hillsdale, NJ/ London: Lawrence Erlbaum Associates.

Eccles, J. & Midgley, C. (1988). Stage environment fit: Developmentally appropriate classrooms for early adolescents. In R.E. Ames & C. Ames (Eds.), *Research on Motivation in Education* Vol.3, pp.139-180. New York: Academic Press.

Elmen, J. (1991). Achievement orientation in early adolescence: Development patterns and social correlates. *Journal of Early Adolescence* 11, 125-151.

Fine, M. & Zane, N. (1989). On bein' wrapped tight: When low-income females drop out of high school. In L. Weis, E. Farrar, & H. Petrie (Eds.), *Dropouts from school: Issues, dilemmas and solutions.* Albany: State University of New York Press.

Gollub, W. L., & Sloan, E. (1978). Teacher expectations and race and socioeconomic status. *Urban Education,* 13(1), 95-106.

Hassenpflug, A. (1994, January/February). Notes from an English teacher: In pursuit of great expectations. *The Clearinghouse,* 161-162.

Irvine, J. (1990). *Black Students and School Failure.* New York: Praeger.

Isherwood, G., & Ahola, J. (1981). School life: A conceptual model, or where you stand depends on where you sit. In J. Epstein (Ed.), *The quality of school life,* 173-177, Lexington, MA: Lexington Books.

Jordan, W. J. (1993). *The influence of teacher perceptions on minority student success.* Unpublished doctoral dissertation. Columbia University, New York.

Kelly, D. (1991). *High school is like a soap opera: Gender and disengagement in two continuation high schools.* Unpublished doctoral dissertation, Stanford School of Education, Stanford, CA.

Kramer, L. (1991). The social construction of ability perceptions, *Journal of Early Adolescence,* 11, 340-362.

Lipsitz, J. (1981). Educating the early adolescent. *American Education,* 17(8), 13-17.

Lucas, T., Henze, R. & Donato, R. (1990). Promoting the success of Latino language-minority students: An exploratory study of six high schools. *Harvard Educational Review,* 60(3), 315-340.

McDonnell, L. M. (1989). *Restructuring American schools: The promise and the pitfalls.* New York: Columbia University, Institute on Education and the Economy.

McPartland, J. M., Legters, N., Jordan, W. J., McDill, E. L. (1996). *The Talent Development High School: Early Evidence of the Impact on School Climate, Attendance, and Student Promotion.* (Rep. 2). Baltimore and Washington, DC: Johns Hopkins University and Howard University, Center for Research on the Education of Students Placed at Risk.

National Center for Educational Statistics. (1988). *National educational longitudinal study of 1988.* Washington, DC: Author.

Nettles, S. (1991). Community contributions to school outcomes of African American students. *Education and Urban Society* 24(1), 132-147.

Paredes, V. (1993). *School correlates with student persistence to stay in school.* Paper presented at the Annual Meeting of the American Educational Research Association, Atlanta, GA.

Rosenthal, R. & Jacobson, L. (1968). *Pygmalion in the classroom: Teacher expectations and pupils' intellectual development.* New York: Holt, Rinehart & Winston.

Sanders, M. G. (1998). The effects of school, family and community support on the academic achievement of African American adolescents. *Urban Education,* 33(3),385-409.

Sizemore, R. (1981). Do Black and White students look for the same characteristics in teachers. *Journal of Negro Education,* 50(1), 48-53.

Stephen, V. P, Varble, M. E., & Taitt, H. (1993). Instructional and organizational change to meet minority and at-risk students' needs. *Journal of Staff Development,* 14(4), 40-43.

Wehlage, G., Rutter, R. A., Smith, G. A., Lesko, N., & Fernandez, R. R. (1989). *Reducing the risk: Schools as communities of support.* New York: Falmer Press.

5

Talent Loss Among High-Achieving Poor Students

WILL J. JORDAN
STEPHEN B. PLANK
Johns Hopkins University

Many high school graduates having the academic ability to continue their schooling do not pursue higher education. This phenomenon has been referred to as talent loss. The challenges involved in financing higher education partially contribute to talent loss and its pervasiveness among poor students, but they fall short of providing a complete explanation. This chapter explores other possible sources of talent loss. The authors use multiple methodologies to examine critical sources of talent loss among students who perform well academically, but are placed at risk of academic failure because they also are from low SES families. Drawing from national panel data as well as eight in-depth interviews with guidance counselors from an urban school district, the authors suggest that social capital, operationalized as the interactions and exchanges between students and significant adults in their schools and families, exposure to a high content curriculum, and the availability of school resources all play a part in determining postsecondary trajectories.

Many young adults who have the academic ability to continue their schooling beyond high school do not enroll in postsecondary educational institutions (PEIs). The term *talent loss* is often used to describe this phenomenon and there are complex reasons that it occurs (Plank & Jordan,

1996). It has been well-documented in the research literature that talent loss is concentrated among poor and minority students. Studies from several decades reveal an inverse relationship between socioeconomic status and talent loss (Hanson, 1994; Manski and Wise, 1983; U.S. Department of Health, Education, and Welfare, 1969). The financial costs of higher education partially explain talent loss and its pervasiveness among poor students, but they fall short of providing a complete explanation. This chapter explicates additional sources of talent loss by combining an analysis of recent national survey data and interviews with high school counselors.

The present study[1] is a continuation of earlier research on the impact of information, guidance, and certain actions of students, schools, and parents on postsecondary enrollment. The previous research (Plank & Jordan, 1996) examined the National Educational Longitudinal Survey of 1988 (NELS:88) data to investigate the likelihood of students reaching one of four statuses within the first 2 years after high school: (a) enrollment at a 4-year college or university, either full or part time; (b) full-time enrollment at a 2-year college or university; (c) part-time enrollment at a 2-year college or university; or (d) no enrollment at a postsecondary school.

We used multinomial logistic regression models to estimate the effect of SES on postsecondary enrollment, over and above a set of background variables including student performance on standardized tests. The effect of SES on the likelihood of an individual's ending up in a 4-year school rather than falling into one of the other three categories was strongly positive and significant. We then added three successive blocks of variables to the model to see what effects measures of parental, school, and student actions would have on enrollment in higher education. Furthermore, we examined the degree to which these successive blocks of variables were intervening mechanisms through which part of the relationship between SES and postsecondary enrollment operated.

The regression models in Plank and Jordan (1996) showed very strong effects of several measures. These measures included (a) the level and timing of discussions between adolescents and their parents about school events and postsecondary plans, (b) parent-school communication, (c) parent communication with other parents, (d) parental encouragement to prepare for the Standardized Achievement Test (SAT) or American College Test (ACT), (e) early planning and subsequent taking of the SAT or ACT, and (f) specific

[1] This research was supported by the US Department of Education, Office of Educational Research and Improvement (OERI). The opinions expressed are the authors' and do not necessarily represent OERI positions or policies.

types of guidance and help from the school in investigating and applying for financial aid and college admission. These intervening variables explained as much as 35% of the relationship between SES and postsecondary enrollment in terms of odds.

The initial study of talent loss inspired several important research questions addressed in this chapter. The first set of questions relates to the potential effects of focusing solely on students in the highest achievement group across the full spectrum of SES. The highest achievement group comprises a set of students who, given current admission standards, should all be academically prepared for postsecondary education. Would the relationship between SES and postsecondary enrollment be especially salient for these students? Would aspects of information and guidance for these students help explain any observed relationship between SES and postsecondary enrollment? Would a model that predicts postsecondary enrollment be similar in appearance to the full longitudinal panel or would it be different in important ways? Second, based on the focus on information and guidance, what more can be learned about the timing, quality, and quantity of information and guidance students receive during the high school years? Specifically, what can be learned about the relationships between students and high school guidance counselors? In this chapter, we explore each of these questions in turn. Before doing so, however, we provide a conceptual foundation from which to understand the importance of relationships and information for students' academic success and enrollment in postsecondary institutions.

SOCIAL CAPITAL

The conceptual framework of the present study is drawn from social capital theory. Coleman (1988) defined social capital as a resource available to a person that exists in the structure of his or her relationships with others, and that facilitates certain activities or actions. As an example of the influence of social capital, academic progress can be enhanced when the parents of students form a network of friends. Such a network can foster trust, expectations, and communication between adolescents and significant adults in their lives. Through the relationships formed and reinforced within the network, common and consistent messages about schooling can be transmitted to guide and monitor students' academic development. Stanton-Salazar and Dornbush (1995) conceived of social capital in a similar manner. They defined social capital as relationships from which an individual is able to derive institutional support, particularly support that includes the delivery of knowledge-based resources.

Our preliminary investigations suggest that talent loss, and the relationship between SES and talent loss, can be explained to some extent by students' lack of social capital. Discussions between adolescents and their parents about school events, encouragement from parents to prepare for the SAT or ACT, conversations between parents and school personnel about a student's postsecondary plans, and assistance from the school to a student in preparing college applications cannot occur for students without a certain level of social capital. That is, these items will be available only when relationships have been established to provide information and guidance. We hypothesize that when such relationships have been forged, they can be effective in reducing talent loss because they allow the knowledge and resources of adults and institutions to benefit adolescents who would not otherwise possess such knowledge and resources. When such relationships have not been established – and we expect that they often will not have been for students placed at risk – talent loss can be expected.

DATA AND METHODS

The present study uses multiple methodologies to explore critical sources of talent loss among students who perform well academically, focusing specifically on relationships among social capital, SES, and postsecondary enrollment. We draw from national panel data as well as from a small set of in-depth interviews with practitioners within an urban school district. First, we present an analysis of the NELS:88 data, where a combination of multinomial logistic regression models and descriptive statistics are used. This quantitative component is followed by interviews with eight counselors conducted at four urban, comprehensive high schools during spring 1997. The flow of this chapter is somewhat unconventional in that we begin with an analysis of the statistical models, followed by descriptive statistics, and finally an analysis of interview data. The justification for organizing the chapter in this manner is that although the counselor interviews are less generalizable than are the national data, the former offer a more refined perspective on student-counselor relationships and other factors that influence the process of student preparation, application, and enrollment in higher education, which is a core aspect of the study.

Multinomial Logistic Regression

As mentioned earlier, this research builds on a recent study that used multinomial logistic regression models to predict the postsecondary enrollment of a nationally representative sample of the graduating class of 1992 (Plank & Jordan, 1996). In examining the entire population (both high and low achievers), we found that one of the reasons many young adults do not continue their formal education immediately after high school is that they lack basic information about the necessary steps involved in the application and enrollment processes. This lack of critical information about higher education reflects a possible absence of effective school guidance and familial support. In the present study, we employ the basic structure of the models used in our earlier work to focus more closely on information and guidance as predictors of higher education enrollment for the highest achieving students – a subsample of students achieving in the top quintile, nationally.

Deciphering the Effects of SES

The next component of this study is a further analysis of the top achievement quintile of students in the NELS:88 longitudinal panel, approximately 2,500 weighted cases. Descriptive statistics are presented to shed light on the contexts within which students live and learn. Several factors that measure school and family-related sources of support for students are presented by SES quartiles. Focus is placed on the information, guidance, and support for postsecondary enrollment provided to students, and on how these resources vary across different levels of SES.

The Counselor Interviews

Finally, we summarize interviews with eight guidance counselors in four urban, comprehensive high schools in a mid-Atlantic school district. Each interview was audiotaped and lasted approximately 60-90 minutes. The interviews were conducted in spring 1997 at the counselors' schools, most often in the counselors' offices. The primary purpose of the interviews was to add insights gained from experienced practitioners, whose main focus is to serve poor and minority adolescents. The overwhelming majority of students in these high schools do not progress directly to college after graduation.

RESULTS

High-Achieving Students in NELS:88

Within the top achievement quintile, just as throughout the achievement continuum, talent loss is concentrated among low SES students. Specifically, as shown in Table 5.1, only 50% of students who were in the lowest SES quartile but the top quintile of high school achievement nationally enrolled in 4-year postsecondary schools as their first enrollment within the first 2 years after high school. About 22% enrolled full-time at 2-year schools; 5.3% enrolled part-time at 2-year schools; and 22.6% did not enroll in any postsecondary school within the first 2 years after high school. In contrast, talent loss was much less severe among high SES students in this top achievement group. Fully 86.6% enrolled in 4-year schools. About 8% enrolled full-time at 2-year schools; 2.8% enrolled part-time at 2-year schools; and only 2.7% never enrolled in a postsecondary school.

An analysis of information and guidance as predictors of postsecondary enrollment was presented in our earlier study (Plank and Jordan, 1996). That study examined effects on students throughout the achievement distribution. Table 5.2 summarizes the independent variables in those models and presents an outline of the major findings. For each model, the estimated direct effects of SES on the odds of an individual's enrolling in a 4-year postsecondary school relative to each of the other three options are shown. These effects are shown first for the full longitudinal panel, and then for the highest achievement quintile.

The estimates for the highest achievement quintile were generated solely for the present study and have not been analyzed or reported previously. For our present purposes, we are primarily interested in two questions. (a) What is the magnitude of the SES effect when initially introduced in Model II? and (b) What proportion of this initial SES effect is explained by the variables of Models III through V, which measure specific school, family, and student actions that support postsecondary enrollment? In each case, we answer the questions with reference to the estimates seen for the full longitudinal panel.

Table 5.1: Postsecondary Destinations for the top Achievement Quintile by SES Quartiles

SES Quartile	Proportion of top Achievement Quintile[a] 4-yr		2-yr FT	2-yr PT	Never Enrolled
High	52.7	86.6	7.9	2.8	2.7
High-mid	26.0	69.6	16.2	6.4	7.9
Low-mid	16.2	57.3	19.8	3.3	19.5
Low	5.2	50.0	22.1	5.3	22.6

[a] Proportions do not sum to 100% due to rounding.

The magnitude of the SES effect is somewhat larger for the highest achievement quintile than for the full longitudinal panel. Specifically, the effect of SES on the odds of enrolling in a 4-year school rather than enrolling full time in a 2-year school was 24% stronger when Model II was estimated for just the top achievement quintile than when it was estimated for the full longitudinal panel (2.20/1.78 = 1.24). The effect of SES on the odds of enrolling in a 4-year school rather than enrolling part-time in a 2-year school was 18% stronger when Model II was estimated for just the top achievement quintile than when it was estimated for the full longitudinal panel (1.86/1.57 = 1.18). The effect of SES on the odds of enrolling in a 4-year school rather than never enrolling in a postsecondary school was 22% stronger when Model II was estimated for just the top achievement quintile than when it was estimated for the full longitudinal panel (4.14/3.39 = 1.22).

With regard to the proportion of the initial SES effect (Model II) explained by variables of Models III through V, it is quite comparable for the highest achievement quintile and the full longitudinal panel. To the extent a difference exists, it is in the relatively greater proportion of the SES effect being explained for the highest achievement quintile. More specifically, by adding the variables of Models III through V, the effect of SES on the odds of enrolling in a 4-year school rather than enrolling full-time in a 2-year school was reduced to 85% of what it had been in Model II (1.88/2.20 = 0.85) when estimated for the top achievement quintile. This reduction is identical to that seen between Models II and V when estimated for the full sample (1.52/1.78 = 0.85). The reduction in the effect of SES on the odds of enrolling in a 4-year school rather than enrolling part-time in a 2-year school was 76% between Models II and V when estimated for the top achievement

Table 5.2: Overview of Independent Variables in Multinomial Logistic Regression Models and Summary of Effects of SES

Model I (Baseline)	Model II (Introduction of SES)	Model III (Introduction of Student, Parent, and School Discussion)	Model IV (Introduction of SAT/ACT Preparation and Taking)	Model V (Full Model)
Intercept	Variables of Model I	Variables of Model II	Variables of Model III	Variables of Model IV
Asian/Pacific Islander	SES	Parent-student discussion (LH)	Parent-encouraged SAT/ACT Prep	Guidance and help from school
Hispanic		Parent-student discussion (LL)	Prep course for SAT/ACT	Visited a PEI with parent
Black		Parent-student discussion (HL)	Prep manual for SAT/ACT	Financial aid information sources
Native American		Parent-school communication	Exam planning/taking (NY)	Applied for financial aid
Female		Parent discussion with other parents	Exam planning/taking (NN)	Applied to a PEI
Number of siblings			Exam planning/taking (YN)	
Urban				
Rural				
Public				
Prior test scores				

In models estimated for full longitudinal panel (Plank & Jordan, 1996):

Estimated direct effect of SES on:	Model II	Model III	Model IV	Model V
($P_{4\text{-yr}}$ / $P_{2\text{-yr FT}}$)	1.78	1.68	1.48	1.52
($P_{4\text{-yr}}$ / $P_{2\text{-yr PT}}$)	1.57	1.45	1.25	1.26
($P_{4\text{-yr}}$ / $P_{\text{Never Enrolled}}$)	3.39	2.92	2.29	2.23

In models estimated for highest achievement quintile:

Estimated direct effect of SES on:	Model II	Model III	Model IV	Model V
($P_{4\text{-yr}}$ / $P_{2\text{-yr FT}}$)	2.20	2.03	1.79	1.88
($P_{4\text{-yr}}$ / $P_{2\text{-yr PT}}$)	1.86	1.72	1.51	1.42
($P_{4\text{-yr}}$ / $P_{\text{Never Enrolled}}$)	4.14	3.39	2.77	2.53

quintile (1.42/1.86 = 0.76). This reduction is slightly greater than the reduction to 80% seen when estimated for the full sample (1.26/1.57 = 0.80). The reduction in the effects of SES on the odds of enrolling in a 4-year school rather than never enrolling in a postsecondary school was 61% between Models II and V when estimated for the top achievement quintile (2.53/4.14 = 0.61). Again, this reduction is slightly greater than the reduction to 66% seen when estimated for the full sample (2.23/3.39 = 0.66).

In summary, the regression models for high-achieving students confirm the association between SES and postsecondary enrollment. The results also provide evidence that social capital, operationalized as certain interactions and exchanges among school personnel, students, and parents, explains a large part of this association. As the regression equations indicate, these relationships are significant net of SES.

HIGH-ACHIEVING TWELFTH-GRADE STUDENTS: A CLOSER LOOK

The previous section described how multinomial logistic regression models were used to better understand factors that influence the initial enrollment in postsecondary educational institutions for students in the top achievement quintile. A major finding was that although SES accounts for much of the variation in postsecondary enrollment, several of the variables that measure information, guidance, and actions were significant predictors, net of SES. A limitation of these statistical models, however, is that it was not possible to include a number of potentially important aspects of information, guidance, and actions because of the methodological challenges, such as multicollinearity, it would create. In other words, there are considerable SES differences across various measures of preparation for, and information about, postsecondary enrollment that, although not included in the logistic regression analysis, should be described further.

Table 5.3 depicts students' planning, preparation, and taking of college board exams by SES quartiles. Several patterns emerged from this cross-tabulation. In looking across the first row of Table 5.3, it is apparent that 69% of high SES students had taken the Pre-SAT by 1992, compared to 42.3% of the low SES students, a 27% difference. Furthermore, there is a steady progression across the four SES quartiles.

The next rows of Table 5.3 relate to whether a student planned to take the SAT or ACT as of 1990, and whether he or she actually had taken one of these exams by 1994. This comparison suggests that students in the highest

SES quartile are much more likely to have early and sustained intentions to take college admissions tests, and actually to take them, than are those in the lower quartiles, who often become interested only during their later grades of high school or not at all. Fully 89.4% of the students in the high SES group had planned to take the SAT or ACT by 1990 and had done so by 1994 (Yes-Yes), as compared to 69.7% of their counterparts in the lowest quartile.

In contrast, and reflecting a different postsecondary orientation, low SES students were more likely than high SES students to have taken the military entrance exam, ASVAB, by 1992. Nearly 44% of the low SES group had taken this exam by their senior year of high school, as compared to only 15% of the highest quartile.

In addition, the bottom three rows of Table 5.3 show that students in the high SES quartile exhibit a greater tendency to take advanced placement (AP) tests while in high school. About 21% of the highest quartile, compared to only 5% of the lowest, had taken an AP test in at least one subject. This tendency may reflect the greater likelihood that high SES students attend high schools that offer AP courses. Higher SES students also were more likely to prepare for the SAT or ACT by taking a preparatory course as well as using manuals. However, here, the lowest rate of using these two methods of preparation exists among the lower middle SES quartile, rather than the lowest quartile.

Table 5.3: Exam Planning, Preparation, and Taking by SES Quartiles

	Low SES	Low-mid	High-mid	High SES
Had taken pre-SAT by 1992 (N=2725)	42.3	52.8	56.5	69.0
SAT or ACT planning/taking (No -Yes)	8.6	9.3	11.2	6.3
SAT or ACT planning/taking (No - No)	9.5	5.0	1.9	1.0
SAT or ACT planning/taking (Yes - No)	12.2	10.9	8.2	3.3
SAT or ACT planning/taking (Yes - Yes)	69.7	74.8	78.7	89.4
Had taken ASVAB by 1992	43.7	31.7	27.3	15.0
Had taken an AP test by 1992	5.2	6.4	10.3	20.8
Had taken prep course for SAT/ACT by 1992	19.0	16.4	23.5	35.4
Had used prep manual for SAT/ACT by 1992	59.1	48.9	52.4	67.8

Note. Values are expressed as percentages.

A pattern that emerges throughout these cross-tabulations is that adolescents in the high SES quartile were exposed to more information and engaged at a much higher rate in actions aimed at postsecondary enrollment. This pattern is exemplified by the progression of cases from low to high SES. Although there were no statistical controls at this phase of the analysis, one factor that remained constant is that all the students fall into the highest achievement quintile.

Table 5.4 shows various aspects of assistance students might receive with regard to applications for postsecondary admission and financial aid. There are few differences in the level of help with filling out postsecondary admissions applications. However, not surprisingly, the percentage of lower SES students who receive help with financial aid applications is greater than that of students in the highest quartile, 43.6% versus 32%; percentages for students in the middle two quartiles are slightly higher than the percentage in the lowest quartile. Also, because Talent Search, Upward Bound, and similar programs are geared toward helping low SES students, more than four times as many low SES as high SES students participate in such programs, 8.5% as compared to 2%.

Items related to sources of information about applying for financial aid are presented in Table 5.5. As anticipated, low SES students seek out financial aid opportunities at a somewhat greater rate than do their high SES counterparts. In the case of talking with a teacher or guidance counselor about financial aid, students in the lower three SES quartiles were very similar (69.2, 67.8, and 69.4%, in the low to higher middle categories, respectively), whereas the highest quartile was about 10% lower, 58.1%. Over half the low SES students (51.2%) had talked to a vocational/technical school or college representative about financial aid, which is about 7% more than students in the high SES quartile (44.5%). Also noteworthy is that 13% more of the students in the low SES, as compared to the high SES quartile, read information about financial aid published by the U.S. Department of Education (40.3% vs. 27.4%), and nearly 21% more pursued financial aid information through learning about military service.

In addition to guidance factors, the school itself, by marshaling its resources and providing meaningful experiences for students, can be a significant influence on enrollment in higher education. Certainly high-achieving, middle class students often attend schools that can be very different from the schools attended by high-achieving poor students. To examine some critical differences in resources designed to increase actions and information that encourage enrollment in postsecondary schools, we considered and tabulated several items by SES quartiles. The results, drawn

Table 5.4: Student's Assistance with Applications for PEI Admissions and Financial aid by SES Quartiles				
	Low SES	Low-mid	High-mid	High SES
Received help at high school filling out voc/tech or college applications (N=2704)	48.7	46.9	49.0	50.0
Received help at high school filling out financial aid forms	43.6	47.5	47.3	32.0
Received assistance at high school in writing essays for voc/tech school or college applications	21.7	27.0	30.4	39.2
Received days off from high school to visit voc/tech schools or colleges	41.1	47.4	41.5	48.4
Participated in Talent Search, Upward Bound, or similar program	8.5	3.7	2.0	2.0

Note. Values are expressed as percentages.

from the NELS:88 Administrator Component, are presented in Tables 5.6.

Table 5.6 depicts items related to the school's emphasis on actions geared toward postsecondary enrollment. Here, again, several advantages, influenced by the schools they attend, are present for high SES students. Eighty-two percent of the high SES students attended schools that reported that the staff often encouraged 12th-grade students to visit colleges, as compared to about 71% of students in the lowest quartile. In a similar vein, about 54% of the high SES students attended schools that reported that their staff often contacted parents regarding college selection, and 91% often assisted students with college applications, representing about 20 and 11%, respectively, more students than in the lowest SES quartile. For the other items shown in Table 5.6, most notably assistance with financial aid applications, there is not a great deal of variation across different levels of SES.

Families also can be instrumental in helping their children progress through high school and proceed into postsecondary schooling. The combination of schools and families working together for the sake of the student forms an even more potent source of needed support and encouragement (Epstein, 1995). Drawing from the student and parent components of NELS:88, Tables 5.7 and 5.8 show cross tabulations of parent-school communications, and parent-student discussions related to the student's postsecondary plans.

These tables reveal striking SES differences in the ways in which parents participate in their children's decision making during the critical, closing years of high school.

In Table 5.7, the first two items relate to the degree to which parents were contacted by their teenager's school about postsecondary plans and course selection. More than half the parents of high SES students had been contacted at least once by the school regarding their teenager's postsecondary plans, and 35% had been contacted about course selection. Together, these percentages are an average of 18% higher than those for parents of students in the low SES quartile. The third and fourth items show a similar pattern, that high SES parents also contact their child's high school in regard to the same issues, and the average difference of these items is also 18%.

However, the largest differences exist in the final two items shown in Table 5.7, parents attending programs on educational opportunities and on financial aid. There is nearly a 30% difference between the highest and lowest SES quartiles in parents attending programs about educational opportunities for their teenagers. Fully 55.2% of the high SES parents had

Table 5.5: Sources of Information About Applying for Financial aid by SES Quartiles				
	Low SES	Low-mid	High-mid	High SES
Talked with a high school teacher or guidance counselor (N=2694)	69.2	67.8	69.4	58.1
Talked with a representative from a voc/tech school or college	51.2	45.3	45.1	44.5
Talked with a loan officer at a bank	4.4	5.0	3.7	3.3
Read U.S. Department of Education information	40.3	31.0	33.1	27.4
Read information from a voc/tech school or college	56.5	53.2	54.9	54.2
Read about aid available through military service	38.9	25.2	22.2	18.1
Talked to a knowledgeable adult	62.8	66.6	70.1	67.3

Note. Values are expressed as percentages.

Table 5.6: School Actions Geared Toward Postsecondary Enrollment by SES Quartiles

	Low SES	Low-mid	High-mid	High SES
Students who were in schools in which high school staff OFTEN...				
Encouraged 12th-grade students to visit colleges (N=2370)	71.4	70.1	79.0	82.1
Contacted parents regarding student college selection	33.4	41.7	39.6	53.6
Assisted 12th-grade students with college applications	80.3	85.4	86.2	91.1
Assisted 12th-grade students in completing financial aid applications	67.5	73.8	68.2	68.9
Contacted college representatives for 12th-grade students	73.2	75.0	75.3	75.8
Provided letters of recommendation to colleges and universities	92.5	92.6	93.9	96.8

Note. Values are expressed as percentages.

attended such programs, as compared to only 25.4% of their counterparts in the low SES quartile. Similarly, 21% more of the high SES parents had attended programs on financial aid. In other words, low SES students are claiming to have sought more financial aid information than high SES students have, but low SES parents have done so less than high SES parents have. Many low SES parents, therefore, may have limited information about postsecondary preparation and enrollment to transmit to their adolescents.

Indeed, there is greater parent-student discussion about schooling and encouragement about postsecondary plans reported among students in the high SES quartile. The parent-student discussion items shown in Table 5.8 measure whether the level of discussion about topics such as course selection, grades, preparation for the SAT or ACT, and whether to apply for college was high or low in 1990, and high or low in 1992. Twice as many students in the low SES quartile were low at both time points as compared to those in the high SES quartile, 41% versus 19%. Conversely, the pattern was reversed for early and sustained discussion, where the high SES percentage was nearly twice as high as the low SES percentage, 51% versus 27%. Furthermore, approximately 11% more of the parents of high SES students encouraged preparation for the SAT or ACT than did those in the low SES quartile, and 41% more visited a college or university with their teenager.

Before we turn to the discussion of the interviews with guidance counselors, a point about the descriptive analysis of national data in this section should be restated. That is, although the comparisons we discussed were primarily at the extremes (that is, low SES versus high SES), in most cases there was a consistent progression from low SES, to lower middle, to higher middle, and to high SES. Although these are bivariate relationships, without the benefit of statistical controls, taken as a whole they tell a

Table 5.7: Parent - School Communications Concerning Postsecondary Plans by SES Quartile				
	Low SES	Low-mid	High-mid	High SES
Parents were contacted by high school AT LEAST ONCE about teenager's plans after leaving high school (N=2523)	28.5	34.6	45.1	51.1
Parents were contacted by high school AT LEAST ONCE about teenager's course selection for entry into college, or vocational or technical schools	21.6	31.0	40.4	35.1
Parents contacted high school AT LEAST ONCE about teenager's plans after leaving high school	37.7	47.8	53.7	58.1
Parents contacted high school AT LEAST ONCE about teenager's course selection for entry into college, or vocational or technical schools	24.7	35.1	46.5	39.8
Parents attended a program on educational opportunities after completing high school	25.4	37.8	46.0	55.2
Parents attended a program on financial aid for colleges, universities, or vocational or technical schools	30.1	42.5	51.5	51.5

Note. Values are expressed as percentages.

Table 5.8: Parent - Student Communications about Postsecondary Plans by SES Quartiles

	Low SES	Low-mid	High-mid	High SES
Parent - student discussion (Low - High)	15.5	19.1	15.5	14.3
Parent - student discussion (Low - Low)	40.9	38.8	29.8	19.4
Parent - student discussion (High - Low)	17.2	17.7	17.3	15.9
Parent - student discussion (High - High) (N=2743)	26.5	24.4	37.3	50.5
Parent-encouraged SAT/ACT prep	76.3	75.8	84.1	87.2
Parent-encouraged ASVAB prep	16.6	13.3	8.4	3.8
Visited a PEI with parent	41.3	54.9	67.3	82.5

Note. Values are expressed as percentages.

persuasive story about the relevance of SES, students' actions, and social capital in students' navigation of the path from high school to higher education.

INTERVIEWS WITH GUIDANCE COUNSELORS

The analysis of national data in the previous sections casts light on the importance of social capital, or information, guidance, and support from schools and families in helping high-achieving, poor students pursue and enroll in postsecondary educational institutions. However, this analysis misses some important insights of guidance counselors, practitioners who spend considerable time working to help students graduate from high school and to prepare them for life beyond high school. In this section, we discuss insights gained from interviews with eight counselors in four comprehensive urban high schools, located in a mid-Atlantic school district.

The interviews were conducted in spring 1997. Counselors in urban, public high schools that serve at-risk students, who could speak on a variety of important issues, were chosen. The size of these schools ranged from about 1,200 to 2,500 students. Each school serves predominately low-income, inner-city students, most of whom are African-American; but poor White, Hispanic, Asian and Native-American students attend these schools as well. The racial composition ranged from about 65% African-American (in two of the schools) to about 98% in the remaining two. Furthermore, since each of these is a regular, comprehensive high school, there are no admission standards. Students who attend these schools come from specific zones or catchment areas within the district. Although each of these schools is unique with regard to tradition and cultural organization, one characteristic they have in common is that, in each, the overwhelming majority of 12th-grade students do not go on to higher education when they graduate.

Moreover, most students in these schools do not progress to the twelfth grade in a lockstep fashion from 9th grade to 10th grade and so on. For example, at one of the sites, 47% of the students were in the 9th grade, 24% were in the 10th grade, 16% were in the 11th grade, and only 13% were in the 12th grade. Many of the students were retained, some transferred between schools, some dropped out of school, and still others met uncertain fates. The pyramid-like structure of the student body, of which nearly half are in the 9th grade, exists in the three other schools in this study and is common within most of the comprehensive schools in this district.

Scope of the Guidance Counselor Interviews

The primary purpose of the guidance counselor interviews was to add their insight to the analysis of national data previously described, and to learn more about processes at urban high schools that influence students' postsecondary enrollment, specifically the interaction between guidance counselors, and students and their families. In addition to general questions about length of service, organization of work, and the nature of interaction with students, the interview protocol covered three major areas: (a) how college-bound students are identified, (b) how college-bound students are guided and supported through the college application and enrollment process, and (c) how the guidance staff view postsecondary education.

To maintain confidentiality and participant anonymity, we use pseudonyms for both counselors and schools. The four high schools are referred to as Adams, Cooley, Taft, and Wilson. Mr. McCrae is a counselor in a career academy and Ms. Winfield is the guidance head at Adams High. At Cooley High, Ms. Gathers is the head of guidance and Mr. Bentley is the 10th-grade counselor. At Taft, Ms. Garrett is the 12th-grade counselor. Finally, at Wilson High School, Ms. Hutchins is the guidance head and Ms. Heywood is the 12th-grade counselor. Mr. Cunningham is a counselor for the College Bound program, and works at Wilson as well as three other schools in the district.

The Organization and Nature of Guidance

Except for the specialized college advisor, who was newer to the profession, the guidance counselors in the study were all seasoned veterans with more than 15 years of professional experience. Some of the interviewees had spent their entire professional careers serving high schools, whereas others had worked in middle schools and even community colleges. The specialized college advisor, referred to as the "college bound advisor," regularly floats among several schools, helping students, both individually and in select groups, prepare and apply for postsecondary admission.

There was some variation in the structure and size of the guidance departments of the schools in the study. In some cases, guidance was simply organized around grade levels. Typically, one staff member is assigned one grade, but the 11th and 12th grades are combined because they are numerically smaller and more manageable than are the lower grades. Across the four sites, counselors report case loads of between 300 and 500 students. Although no school reported having a designated college advisor, the senior class counselor often takes disproportionate responsibility for helping students with postsecondary plans. However, all of the counselors say that helping students negotiate the complexities of high school and advising them about postsecondary options are part of their regular activities.

Paperwork

The size of the caseloads and amount of paperwork take their toll on the degree to which counselors can develop relationships with students and help them negotiate the path to postsecondary schooling. Paperwork was a salient concern in each of the interviews. Some counselors reported spending as much as 60 to 70% of their time on paperwork. Several of them mentioned that they often do their paperwork at home to better focus on personal interactions with students during the school day. Ms. Hutchins, at Wilson, explained that:

> We are pro-student orientated, we have to relate to the students first. Paperwork does prevent us from going out and being as proactive as we would like to be, but we are reactive [also]. Whenever they [students] come in, you know, we stop what we are doing to satisfy their needs. But there is a tremendous amount of paperwork involved.

Her colleague, Ms. Heywood, added that:

> One of the reasons why we have so much (paperwork) is because our goal is to individualize kids. And because of that we have to examine each individual record, and we have to work with the student, and that is what creates a lot of the paperwork.

The need for vast amounts of paperwork itself is perceived differently by counselors. Some see it as a necessary evil because it reflects on a student's progress, whereas others question the logic of some of it. In any case, because so much of the counselor's job is managing students' records (and caseloads are often very high) it is sometimes difficult for counselors to establish close personal ties with students. Mr. Bentley, at Cooley High School, said that as result of paperwork, which he reported occupies 60% of his time at work, and his caseload of 400 students:

> My making contact with them (students) is fleeting, but they know where I am. And, believe me, they find me when they feel they need me. Like I mean now I get a lot of requests for credit checks. And, that's a very interesting request because all I do is recount what they (the students) already have on their report cards. But for some reason they want me to interpret for them.

However, the amount of time a counselor spends with a student increases with the student's duration in school. At Taft, Ms. Garrett estimated that 9th grade students are seen by guidance staff, on average, about twice a term, and this increases over time. As students approach Grade 12 and graduation, the amount of contact with guidance counselors increases with the need for credit checks and verification of other graduation requirements.

The Nature of Counselor-Student Relationships

In the interviews with counselors, we discovered no hard and fast pattern of interaction between counselors and students. Because most were inundated with their workload, these eight counselors tended to react to the most pressing problems of their students rather than actually being proactive and preventive in their approach. The head of guidance at Adams High School, Ms. Winfield, contends that the staff must see their primary job as doing whatever is needed to keep students attending high school. Of the counselors, she maintains:

They're not privileged to shut the door, because as soon as you shut the door, there's a knock. And I always say to them [the guidance staff] 'you have to answer that knock' because you don't know. And we don't ever want to be guilty of ignoring real emergencies.

The need to help students prepare for and apply to postsecondary schools was not the highest priority for any of the counselors we interviewed; the highest priority was helping students navigate their way through high school.

Counselors are aware that many of their students encounter serious problems within their personal lives that impact their schooling and future educational goals. In light of this fact, staying in school until graduation is a major triumph for many students placed at risk. Financial strain, of course, is a condition with which many students in these schools grapple. According to Ms. Winfield:

If money [for higher education] were there for everyone, at least for the first year, I think that we would have more students graduate. Students worry about that. It's constantly here. And, when I say worry about that because they're worrying about their survival, sometimes now even in their homes. Enough food, not necessarily clothes because they get clothes. And, when I say they get clothes, people always talk about, "Oh, they go buy their stuff." No. They borrow each other's clothes, they use each other's clothes, and they look out for each other. But, the light bill, I got to pay mine, you know, the phone being on, things in the refrigerator, or it looks like grandma's running short on her medication, if the check doesn't come, when the mailman is late. And they've lived through this for periods of . . . . And people always say, "Oh, they're accustomed to it." They never get accustomed to it! They don't like it but they have to; they don't have any other way to go.

The primary assistance given by counselors was helping students cope with the daily stressors of high school. This involved doing many things for the benefit of students such as scheduling their classes, buffering external problems that can interfere with school performance, and advocating for student services. Helping students cope with daily stressors often limited counselors' ability to help students focus and develop their postsecondary plans.

The Student's Role in Postsecondary Planning

Most of the guidance counselors interviewed for this study reported maintaining an open-door policy for students. As they see it, students share some of the responsibility in seeking help for planning their future. This is especially true for assistance with college preparation and application. Although counselors do a great deal of outreach to students within the schools about deadlines, events, and activities regarding college, the burden of follow-up is often left to the students. Counselors believe that many students simply drop the ball. On the topic of providing information to students about postsecondary opportunities, Ms. Garrett asserted:

And then sometimes it's just a fact that students don't follow through. Once you do the advertising, go to classes, and say "the financial aid forms are due, come and get your financial aid," we give the financial aid forms out . . . [and] many students do not turn them in, or get the paperwork in on time. So, therefore, what's left is the community college.

Mr. McCrae, at Adams High School, sees the lack of student follow-through as perhaps more detrimental than even the lack of finances for college. When asked how important cost was in the college enrollment equation, he replied:

Actually, though, that's really not the primary issue because if a student has a 2.5 average and good attendance, that kid can go to any school in the state school (system), and get a free ride. . . . We go around in the fall and give that information to the students, and hand out the forms, but they don't come back. I don't think I got any this year. And, even the top kids. . . many times they're late getting the stuff in. But they are told over and over again: "If you want to go to college, the money is there. The money is there." But of course they have to meet the criteria. And, that's, of course, taking the right classes, getting the right grades, and being motivated; but they can get in. That's a great opportunity; a lot of kids don't take advantage of that opportunity.

Aside from academic achievement and financial assistance to cover costs, student motivation, ambition, and internal drive can be critical factors related to graduation from high school and a successful progression into higher education, according to some counselors. Counselors in the study believe many of their students lack these critical attributes. Several maintained that when students have no interest in pursuing higher education there is probably very little that can be done to persuade them to reconsider their educational goals. In describing a student who was high achieving, but from a poor family, Ms. Hutchins stated:

I understand that this child doesn't want to go to college, is qualified, but wants to go to work. And, I don't push college personally. If a child wants to go to work, and is geared toward work, I figure that, alright, let him go to work this year and maybe they will find out that they don't want to do this for the rest of their lives, but maybe they do. . . . And I personally feel that college, the purpose of college is to get a job, to earn some money. To get a job and work in an area where you're interested. Now, if you have that already without the college education, I don't push it, because, you know, it has to be their [the students'] decision. You let them know what is available, the pros and cons of various things, and leave the decision up to them.

Her colleague, Ms. Heywood, at Wilson High School, added, "I find that when you push a student, and they're not motivated, they're not going to do well anyway."

To be sure, there was a perception among counselors that motivation was an extremely important asset for a college-bound students to possess. Highly motivated students were believed to be more likely to take demanding academic courses, exploit the full range of school resources (such as SAT preparation courses and college visits), and seek advice and help when needed. In essence, self-motivated and ambitious students were perceived to be more likely to take the necessary steps to build a competitive application for college. However, counselors say they do not see the enthusiasm and zest for learning and higher education among students at a level that they would like. Typically, blame is placed on the students themselves; the school system; the lack of social capital provided by their families, neighborhoods, and broader communities – or all of the above. In Mr. McCrae's opinion:

I think a lot of these kids. . . would be first-generation college grads. And, a lot of the parents, like a lady I saw that came in today, she just wanted to see her daughter finish high school. Finish high school, and then she thinks she'll go into the service. She didn't mention postsecondary. But many just want to see these kids get out of high school. I think there's no sense of going ahead to sort of blaze a trail for them and also becoming an example. . . . If they can get out of high school, they figure that's a prize and that's an achievement.

And even those who, as I said, were very bright and who could do well if they go to school, they could go to a two-year college. . . . Many of them also, they aren't academically orientated. I mean, they think that if they pass a class it's fine. . . there's no motivation. Studying, I say, is out and . . . students are not very ambitious. They don't care that much about education; it's not a priority in their lives. And, we just have to change that; I mean, that's the key.

Counselors' Views on Beating the Odds

In discussing why so few high-achieving poor students beat the odds and make it into college, the counselors provided several reasons for this. Mr. Cunningham, the College-Bound counselor at Wilson High, said candidly:

> Not all of my colleagues would agree with the things I have to say about the school system. However, I cite the school system on curriculum matters. . . . I think that we need to take a child and push that child to the highest and most strenuous degree. . . . You know, I know what it is to come through that strenuous curriculum. But I think if you take a 5-year-old [child], and you tell a 5-year-old to do X, Y, and Z, by and large a 5-year-old does it. So tell that 5-year-old to perform excellent and they will do it. And, keep that 5-year-old performing excellently through 8, through 10, through 12, and through 15 and they will do it because they are already used to doing it. Because that's a way of life for them. . . .

Nearly every counselor mentioned parents and families as being instrumental for the success of students in reaching postsecondary educational institutions. The counselors believed that a supportive, nurturing, and involved family can offer a strong foundation for students, and that the absence of this places them at a tremendous disadvantage. However, counselors and teachers, they believed, cannot be the functional equivalent of wise parents and supportive families. Ms. Gathers, the guidance head at Cooley High School, explained that:

> We have recognized that without involving our parents, we are not going to see a significant difference in the success of the students. So, we formed the family-support center. So, at the same time as I'm counseling, I'm trying to develop and refine a program that we could put in place to offer the parent. So, we could get more parental involvement and have something to offer them, and at the same time, share with them what's going on in the school, what their kids are doing, how they can help us at home with their child. And I think when the kid sees the parent in the school, then I expect down the road. . . to see a change in the [student] population, in their performance, in their attitude, and in their behavior, because we will involve parents.

Because of the critical role parents play, Ms. Gathers places considerable effort in building family, school, and community partnerships. Her colleague, Mr. Bentley, agrees that informed, assertive parents can be an asset in helping students act on their interest in higher education. According to Mr.

Bentley:

> Parents, when they are committed to their child going to college, they come in
> and they are like white on rice; they are like pitbulls; they don't relent. They
> want to know, "How do I help my child get to where I want my child to go?"

However, counselors, generally, were not satisfied with the level of parent
and family involvement aimed at helping students reach higher education.
When asked how involved were parents in the whole process of college
exploration, application, and selection at her school, Ms. Hutchins replied:

> Not as involved as we would like for them to be, and that's part of the problem,
> with the poorer children, as we say. Because many of them are not aware of
> what is needed, they may not even be pushing college, they may be more
> interested in their children going to work. So, they are interested in those
> things. . . . When we invite them [to information sessions], we may have one
> third, or one fourth of the ones we invite . . . come in and ask questions and .
> . . seem to be interested.

CONCLUSION

The present study represents a continuation of research on reducing talent
loss among contemporary high school students. Picking up where previous
work left off, it began with a multinomial logistic regression analysis of
various factors predicting initial enrollments in postsecondary educational
institutions. Only students in the top achievement quintile of the national
sample were included in this analysis. However, similar to the earlier study
which analyzed a full longitudinal panel extending 2 years beyond high
school and incorporating all levels of achievement, we found that SES was
a major predictor of whether a student attends college and the type of college
or university he or she is likely to attend.

In exploring possible sources of the high SES advantage, we analyzed
similarities and differences across various aspects of preparation for and
application to postsecondary institutions. This analysis revealed that high
SES students talk more often to teachers and guidance counselors about their
future plans. In addition, high SES students attend schools where they are
more likely to receive help with applications, visit colleges and universities,
be contacted by a college representative, and be encouraged to attend a
postsecondary school. But perhaps the most salient factor in the analysis was
the role of parents in steering their teenager toward college. This suggests

that high SES parents are more likely than their low SES counterparts to actively support, through conversation and guidance, their adolescents' enrollment in higher education.

Adding further insight into the postsecondary enrollment process for high-achieving, poor students, the second component of this study is based on interviews with guidance counselors from a large, urban school district. For complex reasons, creation of an environment in which every student is encouraged to pursue higher education and given the needed support was not a priority in any of the schools that participated in the study. Although we found little evidence that students were ever dissuaded from considering college, the focus was placed upon having them set "realistic" goals – goals that adults believed students might actually attain.

Guidance counselors in the present study identified several barriers to higher education for poor, high-achieving students, including weak academic preparation (an ineffective curriculum), limited school resources for college-related activities, few staff resources to provide individualized help, a general lack of student motivation, and low levels of social capital. Although emphasizing the importance of social capital, counselors contended that providing social capital can help only insofar as the students are academically prepared to survive in college. Providing students with the information, guidance, and support needed to apply to college without teaching them the skills, knowledge, and work habits they will need in order to be successful is tantamount to setting them up for disappointment and frustration.

Despite their best efforts, counselors are able to reach relatively few high-achieving poor students. Because student:counselor ratios often exceed 400:1, and resources aimed at helping students reach higher education are limited, many students who have the academic potential to do well in college are overlooked. Although we anticipated that counselors might adjust to their workloads and limited resources by focusing on students who they deemed most likely to be successful, there was little evidence of this. However, we found that the bulk of the emphasis on pursuing higher education tended to be placed on 12th-grade students, students nearest graduation, who can be seen as part of an elite group of survivors in the study's schools. Unfortunately, most of what was done to help students happened late and infrequently, rather than early and often.

Evidence from both the national data analysis and interviews with counselors underscores, among other factors, the importance of families and communities in providing students with the support necessary to pursue higher education. In the statistical analysis, the logistic regression models present clear and consistent evidence of the benefits of higher SES families' social networks, together with direct parental involvement in school, on postsecondary enrollment. However, according to the counselors, school, family, and community connections were weak in the schools we visited, and they are generally lacking in comprehensive high schools throughout the district. Although there was widespread agreement among counselors that parents and communities can be invaluable allies for schools, real-world constraints such as logistics, poor communication between families and school staff, and lack of resources impede the degree to which linkages are formed and cemented. Weak school, family, and community connections may be especially disadvantageous for students attending comprehensive high schools in the district. Because of the concentration of poverty and the small proportion of parents who have attended college, the amount of information about postsecondary opportunities, and thus, the guidance, families are able to provide their adolescents without assistance is limited. It seems certain that to break the cycle of educational failure and talent loss, and to help open the doors to higher education for at-risk students, strong interventions that unify parents, schools, and communities for the sake of the students must be established and maintained.

REFERENCES

Coleman, J. S. (1988). Social capital in the creation of human capital. *American Journal of Sociology,* 94 (Suppl.), S95-S120.

Epstein, J. L. (1995). School/family/community partnerships: Caring for the children we share. *Phi Delta Kappan*, 76(9), 701-712.

Hanson, S. L. (1994). Lost talent: Unrealized educational aspirations and expectations among U.S. youths. *Sociology of Education*, 67(3), 159-183.

Manski, C. F., & Wise, D. A. (1983). *College choice in America.* Cambridge, MA: Harvard University Press.

National Center for Educational Statistics. (1988). *National educational longitudinal study of 1988.* Washington, DC: Author.

Plank, S. B., & Jordan, W. J. (1996). *Reducing talent Loss: The impact of information, guidance, and actions on postsecondary enrollment* (CRESPAR Rep. 9). Baltimore, MD, and Washington, DC: Center for Research on the Education of Students Placed at Risk..

Stanton-Salazar, R.D., & Dornbusch, S. M. (1995). Social capital and the reproduction of inequality: Information networks among Mexican-origin high school students. *Sociology of Education*, 68(2), 116-135.

U.S. Department of Health, Education, and Welfare (1969). *Toward a Social Report.* Washington, DC: U.S. Government Printing Office.

6

Unpacking the Black Box of Tracking Decisions: Critical Tales of Families Navigating the Course Placement Process

SUSAN S. YONEZAWA
Johns Hopkins University

The present study reports findings from a multiple case study of 19 racially and socioeconomically mixed ninth-grade students' and their families' course-taking experiences as the students transitioned from the eighth to the ninth grade. It documents four distinct processes – asserting entitlement, penetrating privilege, passing through, and opting down – that the families engaged in when navigating course placements. The processes, illustrated in the critical tales of 4 families, reveal the ways in which families' biographies and their relationships with significant others in the school and community affected their approach to course placement and their ability to secure seats in higher track classes.

Over the past decade, a plethora of research has indicted tracking, that is, grouping students by perceived ability into courses marked by differentiated curriculum, as educationally harmful to students placed in the lowest tracks (see Oakes, Gamaron, & Page, 1991). Enrollment in a college-preparatory track makes it more likely that a student will attend college. It also increases the likelihood that the student will complete high school (Gamaron & Mare, 1989). Vocational tracks, in contrast, fail to increase students' chances for "securing employment related to training, avoiding unemployment, or securing higher wages than those of non-vocational high school graduates" (Oakes, et al., 1991, p. 593). Thus, tracking, the type of academic program a student selects or is selected for, has grave consequences for both opportunities to learn and educational outcomes.

Despite educators' contentions that neutral indicators such as standardized test scores, previous grades, and teacher and counselor recommendations determine track placements, research suggests that other variables may also be at work. For example, Dornbusch (1994) found that the proportion of Black and Hispanic students enrolled in college-preparatory math and science courses is less than half that of White and Asian students when controlling for previous grades. Oakes and Guiton (1995) found that in racially mixed high schools, White and Asian students are 10 times more likely to be in college-preparatory math than are African-American and Latino students with similar test scores.

For over two decades, researchers have been unearthing some of the pieces of this puzzling process of student placement. It is now suspected that preconceptions about certain students may influence who educators select as "appropriate" for particular classes (Cicourel & Kitsuse, 1963; Erickson & Schultz, 1982; Oakes & Guiton, 1995; Paul & Orfield, 1994). It is believed that some parents and families play an active role in guiding their children through the maze of courses offered (Gamaron, 1992; Lareau, 1987; Useem, 1992). It is also speculated that students (as peers and individuals) help construct – either positively or negatively – their education (MacLeod, 1995; Willis, 1977).

Unfortunately, because the literature on tracking is extensive, many people incorrectly assume that all there is to know about the track placement process is known. They conclude that because the outcomes of tracking (who ends up in what tracks) are known, the process of tracking (how these students are placed) is fully understood. This is not the case.

A multitude of research has been compiled concerning the outcomes of tracking and, to a lesser degree, separate factors affecting track placement. However, the extant research does not clearly show how different factors influencing placement – some of which have been identified, such as the home, school, and peer group, and some of which remain hidden – interactively create the observed placements. It is recognized that placement occurs differently for students depending on their race and socioeconomic status (SES), but, yet to be identified are the mechanisms by which these variations occur. It is possible to tease out the different placement processes that students of different race and class groups undergo.

To better illuminate these placement processes, this chapter[1] presents

---

[1]This research was supported by a grant from the Spencer Foundation. However, the opinions expressed are the author's and do not necessarily represent the positions of the Foundation.

examples of the ways in which students' and parents' social locations – positions often bounded by race, class, and, to a lesser degree, gender – and their resulting social networks helped shape the ways in which they approached the process of track placement. I examine how the past experiences of the study's participants shaped their outlook on school. I also examine how students' and parents' social relationships affected their ability to manipulate placement.

The findings are organized into four different placement processes that the families employed. These processes are labeled *asserting entitlement, penetrating privilege, passing through*, and *opting down*. The processes are defined by the families' modes of gathering information, sense of self-efficacy and self-worth, and actions. The groupings refer to more than the attitudes and agency of students and their parents. They refer to the complex processes by which multiple agents (school officials, peers, and siblings as well) interacted with their local system to fashion the students' placement positions.

THEORETICAL FRAMEWORK

This paper employs feminist standpoint theory and network theory to show the interaction between people's social locations and the relationships that influence their placement strategies. Standpoint theorists propose that people gain knowledge through their positions or social locations. They use the term *positionality* to capture how people's positions in the larger social structure (e.g., race, class, gender, and sexuality) influence what they are aware of and their interpretations of events (Banks, 1995). Although thought is not determined primarily by, for example, class or gender, individuals located in different positions within the social structure are believed to have different experiences that make them privy to distinct constructions and interpretations of the world around them.

Although standpoint theorists recognize the power of socially constructed categories such as race, class, and gender on the shaping of individuals' positions, they try not to reify or essentialize them. Rather, they focus on the actual lived experience of each person and the conditions of his or her life (Harding, 1993). They also privilege the social locations or positions of marginalized individuals to expose the structural and cultural obstacles they encountered within institutions (Harding). Standpoint theorists assert that it is important to comprehend how students and parents come to know themselves and to understand their place in society through past and daily experiences in order to gain an understanding of why they act in the ways they do.

Yet, paying attention to an individual's position or social location is insufficient to fully explain course placement processes. One also must consider how individuals are linked to meso and macro "patterns of life" (Erickson & Schultz, 1982). Network theory helps to reveal how the positions and biographies of individuals interact with their social relations to create large-scale, macro patterns of course placement.

Network theory posits that individuals exist within established contexts of social interaction through which ideas, opportunities, and information flow (Granovetter, 1973; Lin, 1990). This theory rests on two important assumptions: that people are influenced by their social interactions, and that people's interactions are constrained by their environment. Network theory examines how connections among subgroups within a given community influence the ways in which information and mobility opportunities are distributed. Of particular importance are the weak ties that link individuals and communities that are socially distant from one another, and convey rare and important information to which an individual otherwise might not have access (Granovetter, 1973).

Educational research has used network theory to suggest that middle-and high-income parents' information networks are an important source of social capital (Coleman, 1987) that give such parents an edge in the gathering of information with regard to their children's retention, promotion, and placement decisions (Lareau, 1987; Useem, 1991; 1992). For instance, Lareau's (1989) study aptly titled *Home Advantage* highlighted how upper-middle-class elementary school parents used neighborhood networks to maneuver within the school system. Through such networks parents developed strong relationships with their children's teachers by volunteering as homeroom helpers or field trip chaperones (Lareau, 1989). Subsequent work has revealed that race, in addition to class, may significantly affect people's opportunities to form useful relationships with key school agents (Lareau & Horvat, 1999; Stanton-Salazar & Dornbusch, 1995; Wells & Crain, 1994).

Network theory, thus, helps to reveal how parents, students, and counselors gather and make sense of placement information. The theory also helps to show how information is distributed and when and where (if at all) weak ties inform less knowledgeable students and parents about course taking. In addition, it clarifies how factors such as race and SES shape interactions among students, families, educators, and significant others (including neighbors, extended family members, etc.) to enhance or diminish the flow of information and support families receive (Granovetter, 1973; Mehan, 1992).

STUDY SETTING AND METHODS

The data in this Chapter were collected over an 18-month period from fall 1995 to winter 1997. All the data were qualitative and were collected to provide insight into the placement processes of the 19 student-parent-counselor cases.

The Setting

Edmonson High School[2] is a West Coast, suburban comprehensive school with a population of 2,500 students in grades 9 through 12. The student population is diverse: 40% White, 35% Latino, 12% African American, 10% Asian and Asian Pacific American, and 3% unknown. There are distinct neighborhoods in the school's attendance zone that are identifiable by the residents' race or SES. White, well-educated, and wealthy families reside north of Springfield Avenue. Middle- and low-income, immigrant and African-American families live south of Springfield.

Edmonson enjoys a reputation as a physically safe and an academically competitive school. Yet, despite its strong academic showing, the school has struggled to provide the same educational opportunities to all its students. For example, in 1995-96, the school's 20 advanced placement courses were 85-90% White and Asian, whereas its dropouts were 60-70% Latino and Black.

Student and Family Sample

Qualitative methodologists use both theoretical and purposive sampling when selecting cases. Theoretical sampling involves selecting cases for their potential to replicate, extend, or create theory (Eisenhardt, 1989). For example, one might seek out polar type cases that defy statistical generalizations. Purposive sampling, on the other hand, involves the use of preset characteristics (e.g., race, class, gender) to select a sample (Merriam,

---

[2]The name of the school, city, and all the study participants have been changed to preserve confidentiality.

1988).

Students were selected for this study through a combination of purposive and theoretical sampling. Race, gender, SES, and past academic achievement were preselected as important characteristics to ensure a diverse group. Students were then randomly selected from a list of all the school's incoming freshmen according to these preset characteristics. Once a purposive sample had been identified, theoretical sampling was conducted. For instance, polar types such as African-American students in honors geometry were identified and added to the list. Finally, the students and their parents were contacted. The majority (all but three) of the students and all but one of their parents agreed to participate.

The final sample consisted of 10 boys and 9 girls; of the 19 students, 5 each were African American, White, and Latino, and 4 were Asian American. Some were A students, others were B and C students, and still others had difficulty finishing middle school. Some families qualified for free-lunch programs, and some had six-figure incomes. Most of the Latino and African-American families had less money and prior education than the White and Asian families. Traditional dual-headed households accounted for 11 families; single mothers headed 6 of the families; 1 family was divorced, with both parents sharing child-rearing responsibilities; and, in 1 family, the mother worked and managed the household, while the father worked abroad, providing financial support.

Twelve of the 19 families were headed by at least one parent new to the United States. All 5 Latino families, 3 of the 4 Asian families, 3 White families, and 1 Black family had at least one recent immigrant parent. At least one family's immigration status was undocumented. Many of the Latino and Asian immigrant parents were more comfortable in their native language than in English; therefore, I used a translator when interviewing 4 of the 5 Latino families.[3] In 1 Korean family, the parents understood but did not speak English, and their son translated. All but two of the students were born in the United States. All spoke English fluently.

Data Collection

Qualitative case studies typically use a number of data collection techniques, including interviews, observations, and document analysis (Eisenhardt,

---

[3] I am grateful to Irene Serna, who helped conduct the interviews in Spanish, and managed the transcription and translation.

1989). Not all case studies employ all data sources available, but methodologists generally agree that multiple sources of evidence are essential to high-quality research (Adler & Adler, 1994; Yin, 1984), because they enhance data triangulation and result in more "believable and trustworthy" conclusions (Merriam, 1988).

In this study, semistructured interviews, observations, and documents were the primary sources of data. Each of the 19 students and at least one (sometimes both) of their parents were interviewed about their past histories and knowledge of the student's course placements. Parent meetings, faculty meetings, open house activities, and extracurricular events were observed for the ways in which information might be conveyed from the school to families. All 19 students were observed in their classes and interacting with their peers during lunch. All 7 school counselors and 5 academic department heads were interviewed regarding placement policies and strategies. Counselor-student (and sometimes parent) placement sessions were observed for the 19 students. School documents and policies were reviewed. All interviews were recorded and transcribed verbatim. All observations were recorded as field notes.

Data Analysis

Researchers conduct data analysis in a number of ways. Some use their original theoretical propositions to test their data (Yin, 1984). Others generate categories and propositions out of the data gathered via a grounded theory approach (Strauss & Corbin, 1990). However, all versions of analysis seek the same goal: to develop reasonable conclusions based on the preponderance of the data (Merriam, 1988).

Data analysis for this study fell somewhere between that of methodologists who believe that one's theoretical framework should drive data analysis (Merriam, 1988) and that of those who ascribe to grounded theory (Strauss & Corbin, 1990). Theoretical concepts (i.e., positionality and information networks) were revisited to help unpack the data and to provide useful analytic categories for organization. Propositions, categories, and patterns within the data were sought out as well (Marshall & Rossman, 1989). Analytic memo writing, diagram designing, and revisiting of the relevant literature in the research area stimulated analysis (Bodgan & Biklen, 1992; Strauss & Corbin).

During the initial stages of data analysis, it became clear that central to each student's course taking process were a series of interrelated critical moments that affected how the student transitioned between specific courses or track levels. These critical moments were created by the actions and interactions of specific students, parents, and educators. Thus, analysis of students' placements eventually took the form of capturing these critical moments as episodic narratives. Lawrence-Lightfoot (1994) advocated a similar approach she termed "portraiture." Van Maanen (1988) referred to such an approach as the writing of "critical tales."

CRITICAL TALES OF FOUR PLACEMENT PROCESSES

Because each student's critical tale is quite detailed, presenting all 19 in one paper is difficult; therefore, this paper includes 4 critical tales, 1 per placement process.[4] The tales expose the interaction of social location and networks on families' abilities to navigate the course placement process.

Process One: Asserting Entitlement

Four of the 19 cases reveal how students and their parents asserted their entitlement to the best courses and teachers Edmonson offered. By asserting entitlement, I mean that these 3 upper-middle-class White and 1 upper-middle-class Asian-American families tapped into cultural values of individual competition, innate ability, and merit to convince themselves and educators that their teenagers deserved more – more attention, more chances, and more privileges – than other adolescents.

The students from these families did well academically, but their high grades and strong teacher recommendations do not completely explain why they received the courses they did. Indeed, the families came to the placement process equipped with the means to demand that the school system do more for them. Their power came from their highly educated and wealthy social locations. It also stemmed from the extensive information networks they built with other families who occupied similarly powerful positions in the local political economy (Granovetter, 1973; Stanton-Salazar, 1997; Stanton-Salazar & Dornbusch, 1995). These families' social location and social networks enabled them to convince educators that their children were inherently smarter and, thus, more deserving than other students (Brantlinger,

---

[4]The 4 cases I present should be viewed as indicative, but not representative of the process as experienced by the other 15 families. I chose these four tales for the ways in which they fit together as well as for the ways in which they illustrate the larger processes. However, each of the 19 families' critical tales was unique and cannot be wholly captured by these 4 critical tales.

Majd-Jabbari & Guskin, 1996; Oakes, Wells & Associates, 1996; Wells & Serna, 1995).

Dan Billings: A Parent's Plea for Honors Geometry. Dan Billings lived north of Springfield with his parents, John and Nancy, and his two younger brothers. Identified with attention deficit hyperactivity disorder (ADHD) in the third grade, Dan had struggled in school, particularly in his English courses. Math and science, however, came easier to Dan, who found these subjects more enjoyable. Therefore, when Dan entered Edmonson High School, he happily enrolled in honors geometry and biology, and regular English. Dan's parents, John and Nancy, were pleased about his math placement, but less so about the regular English. Still, they agreed to send Dan to Edmonson because his father had gone there. They figured that as long as he stayed in honors math, he would be fine.

In the fall, Nancy Billings visited Dan's teachers and counselors, as she did at the beginning of every year. She also volunteered to help distribute the English department magazine. Each time she met with his teachers her visits were purposeful: to convince them that her son was "really very, very, very bright in math," despite his poor behavior and tendency to "just sit there." A soft-spoken, college-educated homemaker, Nancy advocated for Dan because she felt it was her responsibility to "make sure things are going in the right direction." Also, her husband often told her that it was her "job," and that their children's grades were her "grades too."

Despite Nancy's best efforts, however, Dan received a C- in his honors geometry class at the end of the first semester. School policy clearly stated that any student with a C or lower could not continue in honors courses. Dan would not be able to re-enroll in honors geometry for the second semester, but would drop to regular geometry. Nancy was aware of this policy because of a conversation she had had with Dan's counselor, Mrs. Cummins, earlier in the semester.

> I had been talking with her trying to figure out the system. You know, what are the criteria? What do people do? What are the options? And she was very clear on what his options were.... If Dan didn't get an A or B that semester there was no way he could stay in honors geometry.

Despite these strong declarations by Dan's counselor, Nancy strategized to get her son back into honors math. She knew that the key difference between being in regular geometry and honors geometry as a freshman was not merely the pace of the curriculum, which was slower in the regular class. Rather, it was the fact that honors geometry was reserved specifically for ninth-grade students who mostly went on to honors intermediate algebra as sophomores and calculus as juniors. Leaving the honors math track meant more than moving a bit slower through the book, it also meant moving off the pathway followed by the school's academically elite freshman, and into multigrade classrooms filled with students working above and below grade level.

Nancy also decided to "go back and fight" because she operated from a social location and within a network that told her that Dan had a "right" to be in honors classes. Her brother, a principal, reassured her that honors geometry was the proper place for "a kid like Dan", that "he would just be bored" in a regular math class. Her north-of-Springfield neighbors warned her that Edmonson was a "bad place" for nonhonors kids. Dan's private tutor contended that he was "brilliant" in math. Those around Nancy convinced her that Dan "belonged" in honors math.

Nancy began her campaign for honors geometry by calling Dan's math teacher. She also placed calls to the school's assistant principal and principal. Meanwhile, she laid out her strategy and put together a proposal that she thought might convince the teacher to let Dan back into her class.

When Ms. Bechler, Dan's teacher, returned Nancy's calls, Nancy immediately found herself negotiating a policy that for everyone else was supposed to be fixed. The teacher, however, patiently listened as Nancy pitched her proposal, which promised everything from increased home monitoring to placing Dan back on hyperactivity medication:

> I explained who I was and that [Dan] really did know the material and that he goes to a tutor who teaches him out of the book. I said, "If you noticed his grades, he's been coming home with all Bs since I've gotten the tutor." She said, "You know, he doesn't do his homework." So we set up this whole guideline program for him. We have him working with two other students, once a week each. Possibly getting him back on medication if I can do that. Keeping on top of it, making sure his homework's done. And working on his very lackadaisical attitude.

Ms. Bechler soon became convinced that she should let Dan remain in the class. A key selling point on Dan's behalf was his parents' decision to hire Dan's private tutor. This tutor in particular was well known and reputable among the school's math department. Nancy had hired her based on the recommendations of her neighbors in her elite neighborhood network. The teacher had gotten to know this tutor personally from years of sharing the same pupils, and the two women often called each other at home to discuss their students. Ms. Bechler liked and respected the tutor and felt that if the tutor worked with Dan at home, Dan might be able to keep up.

By pushing hard, enlisting the help of well-respected educational allies such as Dan's tutor, and using her son's ADHD status as a proxy for his specialness, Nancy caused the teacher to question her own motives for sending Dan to a lower track geometry class:

> With the parents pushing and his medical condition and everything...I just felt like if I didn't give this kid a second chance, maybe I was just being too hard. Maybe I wasn't doing my job, and that's giving people chances and teaching them. Maybe I was just booting him for my own convenience. I didn't want that to happen. I didn't want to be that way. I guess I was kind of worried that my own perspective might not be right. So, I decided to go the other way and just say, 'Boom! I'm giving this kid a chance. If he falls on his face now it's his fault, and it has nothing to do with me.'

Thus, even though Dan should have been moved out of honors geometry, Nancy was able to win her son another chance to prove himself. Her efforts succeeded because she was able to convince his teacher that Dan somehow deserved a second chance. In this way, the success of Nancy's plea is more than an example of an attentive parent and an open-minded educator. It is a manifestation of how elite privilege and power play themselves out in the day-to-day life of schools. Without his mother to lobby on his behalf, Dan would have sunk quickly and quietly out of the high track and into regular level geometry. With his mother behind him, Dan's space in the high track was reserved, even when he failed to meet the department's preset, high-track standards.

Process Two: Penetrating Privilege

Students and families penetrating privilege occupied economic, social, and political locations markedly different than families asserting entitlement. For instance, none of the five penetrating privilege students and their families lived north of Springfield Avenue; only one of these students was White (the others were African American or Latino); only one came from a two-parent home; and only one had a parent with a 4-year university degree. In addition, all five of the students penetrating privilege fell solidly into the middle track – into regular English, physical science, and algebra or unified math (prealgebra) placements.

Because these students and their families operated in the middle track and came from low-to-middle-class, non-White social locations, the kinds of knowledge they gathered and the ways they learned to use that knowledge differed from those of families asserting entitlement. First, those penetrating privilege often were only able to gather information from school officials, who provided what they considered relevant to the students given their social locations. Second, these families' social networks (e.g., neighbors, peers, and coworkers) were composed of "people like them," individuals of similar race, SES, and prior track placements, who provided them with little new information.

Some students and parents in this group attempted to reach beyond their social locations and bridge weak ties with elite families because they knew making such connections was important (Granovetter, 1973). Although these students and parents often had greater success than families who did not make such efforts, their success came with a price – the alienation they experienced when interacting with elite families. These less knowledgeable families were reminded in subtle and not-so-subtle ways that their lack of status labeled them trespassers in the elite's information inner circle. Such families were unable to reflect the "style of life" – the viewpoints and culture – of the entitled families (Weber, 1978). Their lack of fit was characterized by their fewer economic resources and educational credentials. It was also characterized by their reluctance to exude an aura of entitlement. Other families and educators saw them as not requiring or deserving of such information. Consequently, these families penetrated the privileged discourse and demanded more educational opportunities only to obtain improved, but not necessarily elite, placements.

In this next section, I describe the story of Michael Cantrell and his mother, Virginia. Michael's story reveals how he and his mother operated from social locations of less power and prestige, yet attempted to gather information to help beat the system. Their efforts to gather this information from elite family networks illustrate how difficult this task is for families such as the Cantrells who often find themselves less than welcome in the elite inner circle.

Michael Cantrell: Sneaking in from the Margins to Do Battle for Honors English. Michael Cantrell was a White permit[5] student who had been enrolled in the Edmonson district since the sixth grade, when he began attending a middle school science magnet program. He lived in a nearby

---

[5]According to district policy, a limited number of students who lived outside of Edmonson's boundaries could attend Edmonson schools by permit in certain circumstances. Students who received permits might include those whose parents worked in Edmonson, those who had siblings attending Edmonson, or those who wanted to participate in a school program not offered in their home district.

middle-to-working class neighborhood with his adoptive mother, Virginia Cantrell, a Scottish woman in her 50s. Michael's adoptive father, a Hungarian immigrant, had passed away 4 years ago.

A hard-working student, Michael appeared motivated, but continued to struggle in many of his courses. In fact, his year-end grade in eighth-grade Algebra was so low that his ninth-grade geometry and biology placements were in jeopardy. And despite repeated attempts throughout middle school, Michael had never managed to secure a spot in honors English. The Cantrells suspected that the regular track was not the best place for him. However, determining how to prevent him from being placed in the regular track in math, science, and English was not easy.

Virginia had not worked since before her husband passed away, and she had not been schooled in the United States. She wasn't quite sure how to go about ensuring that Michael would be placed in the most challenging classes possible. What Virginia did know from talking to other parents who hung around the elementary and middle schools was that her presence would help shape whatever educational opportunities Michael would have. Each time she visited with educators or attended parent meetings, Virginia kept her ears and eyes open for additional information that might help Michael:

> [I went] to all these meetings.... I went to the middle school PTA meeting, [and] the science magnet who had their own PTA meetings. I tried to go to the high school and whatever meetings were available. And I'd always find somebody said something that may not be anything to the main topic, but I'd just pick up these bits of information from people... It was just because I had happened to be talking to this one and that one. It was not that I [was given] the information. This is the way it seems to be if you don't just hang around you just don't hear [anything].... So it was not that we were told about it, always stuff has been just by chance. I happen to hear somebody say something and then I go out and [as she raises her arm thrusting it forward in a sword like motion] do battle!

As Virginia attended more meetings and listened in on more conversations, she found that her information network overlapped with families asserting entitlement. This gave her increased access to information that she otherwise would not have had. It also made her, a naturally introverted woman, uncomfortable, as it meant interacting with people whom she did not like and whom she knew did not like her. Still, Virginia pressed on, forcing herself to attend these meetings, because she believed it to be, "My job, my responsibility. I have to do this."

One morning Virginia's efforts paid off. She overheard talk of a parents' group who called themselves "the academic parents," a group of 20 White, north-of-Springfield mothers who met with Edmonson's principal once a month on behalf of their honors-student children. She attended the meeting unannounced and apparently (in the eyes of the other women) uninvited:

> *Virginia:* Well that [academic parents meeting], that was something that I just found out about, because they're not terribly welcoming at these places.
> *SY:* Yeah how did you find out about that?
> *Virginia:* I don't know. I must have heard somebody mention it.
> *SY:* And you just showed up?
> *Virginia:* Yeah. And, well as I say they're not terribly welcoming. [They said] "This is for honors students!" ...[It's] a closed shop.... It's a clique you see. And a lot of [th]em have been around for years because they've had older children who've been through and this is their second or third child. So, as I say, I only go because I pick up information. But I'm no good with these kind of creepy [people].

Despite her discomfort at these meetings, Virginia doggedly attended them as well as Edmonson PTSA meetings (run by nearly the same cohort of north-of-Springfield mothers) to gather information. She interacted with the women she referred to as the "super efficient females" because she knew that they possessed the know-how to get her son into the most challenging classes. Michael, meanwhile, pumped his friends and classmates for information on alternative honors pathways.

Virginia and Michael's networks told them that his best chance for a seat in honors English lay in avoiding the middle school English chair, Mrs. McNally. A couple of Michael's friends who had gone through the process earlier alerted them that Mrs. McNally did not advocate for students she had not taught. Michael and Virginia found this information easy to believe because this teacher had refused to let him into seventh-grade honors English or to consider his portfolio for eighth-grade honors English. She had also treated Michael and his mother rudely when they had inquired about honors English in the past. "She threw us out... ripped up all his papers, threw them down and flounced away. I had never seen anything like it," recalled Virginia bitterly.

More importantly, however, Virginia had learned through her contacts that a summer process of English honors review existed for students just entering the district and that this process did not include middle school teachers (because they were on break and difficult to convene). Mother and son decided not to submit his portfolio in the spring of eighth grade to the regular placement committee. Instead, they waited until the summer to submit his portfolio directly to the high school's English department chair.

> I said, 'Michael is not going to go back and give her [the middle school teacher] the pleasure of putting her big red F, well forget it.' Well later on I decided to speak to the assistant principal in charge of counseling at Edmonson because [I heard that] there must be some mechanism at the high school for students coming out of the district to take the test. And she said, 'Oh yeah sure. Come whenever.' So we bypassed [Mrs. McNally] altogether you see. He did it through the high school.

Process Three: Passing Through

A third group of eight students and their parents approached placement by passing through; that is, they did little to actively navigate the track structure. These families rarely contested the placements school officials doled out, and instead let the school mediate or channel outside political and economic forces such as racial or class-based stereotyping into their children's schedules (Lamphere, 1993).

All eight of these students lived either south of Springfield Avenue or outside of the district's boundaries. Three were Asian, two were Latino; one was Black, from Guyana; one was White, of French descent; and one was African-American. The students' placements ranged from honors geometry and English to unified math and regular English.

The action, or rather inaction, of these students and their parents was tied to their social locations and social networks. Linguistic and cultural differences made it difficult for most of the parents to help their children with the specifics of placement. Many spoke little English and knew even less about educational practices in the United States. The isolation they experienced is common between schools and nonmainstream families (Delgado-Gaitan, 1991; Lawrence-Lightfoot, 1978; Ogbu, 1974).

However, the lack of action by these parents does not mean that they lacked agency. On the contrary, many of these parents gathered information via their children, relied on educational experiences from their home countries, or networked with families of similar backgrounds to help them understand the current system.

Moreover, these parents' decision not to act was often consciously made. The parents refrained from micromanaging their children's schedules because of their fear that doing so would hurt their parent-child relationships. Their fears grew out of memories of child-rearing practices they had experienced at the hands of their parents and their desire to provide their children with the freedom they thought was characteristic of American parents.[6]

The children, most of whom were second-generation immigrants, did their best to bridge the divide between their home and school. Engaging in what Wells, Hirshberg, Lipton, and Oakes (1995) call "border crossing" and Phelan, Davidson, and Yu (1993) call the spanning of "multiple worlds," the students received some information (albeit not systematically) from like-minded peers and educators, and intermittently conveyed this information to their parents. This unsystematic approach left the students at a disadvantage, however, as neither they nor their parents fully understood the placement process. As a result, Edmonson educators had significant influence over the composition of these students' course schedules.

Lana Tran: Understanding Students who Pass Silently Through the System*.* Lana was an American-born Vietnamese girl who lived in a two-bedroom apartment on the south side of Edmonson with her petite, 35-year-old mother, Thuy. Thuy came to the United States as a Vietnamese refugee in 1976 and worked as a postal supervisor and the sole breadwinner for herself and her teenage daughter. Lana's father, a first-wave Vietnamese immigrant as well, returned to Vietnam shortly after his wife filed for divorce in 1989, the last year Lana saw him.

Thuy Tran rarely involved herself in her daughter's placement decisions. Her lack of involvement in course selection was not an accurate measure of her desire to see Lana well educated. On the contrary, Thuy believed, based on her own life experiences as a single mother, that educational credentials bring financial and psychological rewards, which she believed were essential for any woman's independence. Long ago, as a newly married woman, she had thought differently, espousing what she now called the "old-fashioned ideal" that "it's better to have a man with education...to have the children look up to their dad as the leader of the family." Now that she was alone, without financial or emotional support from her ex-husband and ostracized by her strict Catholic, Vietnamese parents for divorcing her husband, Thuy thought differently. She believed that education was the key to her daughter's future autonomy.

Thuy tried to convey to Lana that education was a worthy goal by showing her "how my life is without education" in the hope that this would then

---

[6]Other parents, who wanted to have greater influence over their children's decisions, felt that even if they exerted pressure on their sons and daughters, they would be undermined by American cultural standards that viewed their child-rearing practices as too harsh.

"trigger" Lana to "do her own research." She also devised numerous and sometimes unconventional ways to motivate her daughter. For example, Thuy dated college-educated men even when she wasn't interested in them as one way to ensure that her daughter had educated role models with whom to interact. She wanted Lana to understand that "education is knowledge, and knowledge is power." And, for the most part, Lana heard her mother's message:

> Education means everything to [my mother]. She wants me to be better than she is. Like she says, "I want you to excel in life. I don't want you to have to depend on a husband to compensate you. I want you to be really independent. And when you grow older and do what it is that you want to do – your dream – then you won't have to depend on your husband or anything like that. And you can leave him. It's not like you have to stay with a terrible husband just because he has the money." And that's exactly how I feel.

Yet, despite her desire to see her daughter succeed academically, Thuy refused to help Lana make decisions about course placement. Thuy resisted taking on this role because, although she had graduated from high school in the United States, she lacked detailed knowledge that she suspected her daughter needed. Thuy questioned her ability to advise Lana because she "never was in college" and "doesn't know what to base it [her advice] on." "Who am I to say, 'Okay you don't take this, you're going to take that?'" Thuy asked. Gathering information was out of the question for Thuy because her job, as a postal supervisor, required her to start work at 4:00 a.m. Lana confirmed that her mother knew very little about the way courses were structured at the high school.

Thuy also resisted micromanaging her daughter's course schedule because of her own experiences growing up in a "mentally abusive" family, where children were expected to obey their parents' or risk being denigrated. Those experiences made Thuy strive to be an "Americanized mother," one that gave her daughter the freedom to "make her own mistakes" and "make her own choices." They also caused Thuy to fear that if she overadvised her daughter, Lana would grow "distant" from her or "resent" her. Lana, meanwhile, never questioned her mother's decision to bow out of the placement process. In fact, in many ways, she preferred her mother's less visible position: "I prefer that she not be so involved, because I think some parents are [too] involved."

Without Thuy's influence, Lana's friends and educators became even more significant in shaping her placements. Her peer group was particularly important, because it had changed significantly when she entered high school. No longer was it the high-achieving White student group that she hung around with at the northernmost middle school. Lana had picked up with the "Asian clique," a group of about 20 Asian-American students who sat during lunch on campus in an area called "ABC (American-born Chinese) land" or off campus at a nearby food chain. This group, which mimicked a softcore gang culture and espoused a philosophy called Asian pride, comprised middle-achieving Asian-American students from the high school, as well as an influx of low-achieving Asian-American students from a continuation high school.

Although the group consisted of Asian-American students from Korean, Vietnamese, Japanese, and Chinese backgrounds, they, in many ways, operated from social locations similar to Lana's. Like Lana, these students were also left on their own to figure out the educational system. Like Lana, these students lacked the inside information on how to work the system in their best interest.

The Asian clique did not provide Lana with information on the details of getting around course placement requirements; however, they did provide encouragement and support for academic achievement. Getting average grades (Cs or Bs) was acceptable to these students, but falling below that average was not.[7] Group discussions sometimes focused on what they believed one must do to gain entry into competitive universities. They talked about what kinds of classes Lana would have to take and the grades that she would need to enter a high-status college. In this way, the Asian clique gave Lana some encouragement and information to pursue higher education.

Although the Asian clique did add to Lana's storehouse of placement knowledge, the clique also made it more difficult for Lana to develop ties to other, potentially more knowledgeable, friends. Specifically, Asian clique members disapproved of Lana's White middle school friends and pressured her to break off her ties with those 'White people." If she refused, clique members would tease, "Oh you're so white-washed" or "yellow and white don't mix." Lana's White friends also questioned her association with the Asian clique: "They don't really like White people, so why are you hanging around them if you're our friend?"

It disturbed Lana that her newfound Asian-American friends "put this wall around themselves and... wouldn't let anybody of another race come in," but she chose to spend increasing amounts of time with them because she said

---

[7]Lana expressed her concern for some of the male Asian students whose grades had fallen considerably since their freshman year. She stated that many of the Asian students have parents who will curb their freedom to spend time with the group should their grades fall much below a B-to-C average.

belonging to the Asian clique provided her with the social support network and sense of family that she wanted. "They're like my older brothers. They'll call me sister Lana in Chinese.... And then I call them brother in Vietnamese. They're like brothers I've never had," said Lana. Consequently, Lana grew distant from her White friends, those who had connections with elite information networks, and remained bereft of good, detailed information on course placement. This made Lana increasingly dependent on her educators for guidance.

Fortunately for Lana (but unfortunately for many other low-income, Latino, and African-American students), race, class, and gender affected how her counselors and teachers judged her need to take higher level courses. In Lana's case, her being Asian and all the connotations that this carried influenced her interactions with her counselor and English teacher. In this way, Lana benefited from what some researchers have described as "the model minority myth (Lee, 1996).

Lana, like all Edmonson students, had regular counseling sessions with her assigned counselor. Such sessions varied in the level of information provided, dependent on the individual counselor and student. In Lana's case, observations confirmed that her counselor – a young, energetic man – provided her with a great deal of information and guidance. In a 20-minute session, the counselor pressed Lana to raise her algebra grade from a C-, encouraged her to try out for honors English next year and to sign up for a foreign language, and reminded her that a foreign language was an important prerequisite for college. He also gave her advice about summer school courses that would best prepare her for college entrance.

However, Lana's successful counseling session was not a simple interaction between student and counselor. It was also affected by Lana's social location as an Asian student and by the counselor's desire to be sensitive to her cultural situation. More specifically, the counselor's efforts to provide Lana with information regarding college were due, in part, to his belief that all children deserved such information, but also because he felt it important to help her fulfill her parents' expectations. "When I'm dealing with an Asian student, I'm taking that into consideration," he stated, "For Asian students, and for their parents, every child's supposed to get straight As." In this way, Lana's social location shaped the way in which she and her counselor interacted.[8]

---

[8]Of course, laying blame on the counselor for being too helpful, on the one hand, and ignorant about Lana's family circumstances, on the other, would be unfair. Counselors have far too many students to avoid occasional generalizations entirely when making decisions or offering suggestions. They have even

Lana's ninth-grade regular English teacher, Mrs. Ponessa, also harbored similar beliefs. She approached Lana and offered to help her prepare for her honors portfolio because she liked to help strong students advance, and because she believed that "Lana felt a lot of pressure from her family," and that "[Lana's] parents were more strict" than most Edmonson parents. She helped Lana by giving her and several other targeted students extra assistance on their honors portfolios, proofreading their papers, and providing after-school tutoring. Specifically, Mrs. Ponessa made these assumptions despite the fact that she had never spoken with Lana's mother. In the end, Lana was headed for an honors curriculum, despite the fact that neither she nor her mother had worked actively to assure Lana's place in those courses.

It is important to note that although such placement processes work for some students, they do not work for others. Many other students and parents who followed similarly silent placement processes ended up moving down rather than up the track ladder.

Process Four: Opting Down

The critical tales of the final three families reveal how the interplay between social location and relationships at school and at home affected students' academic advancement. The three low-income, minority students, their parents, and educators interacted in ways that reinforced beliefs that the students belonged in low-track classes.

These two Latino and one African-American families differed from those in the other groups in that they often questioned the students' abilities to compete in regular or advanced classes. All three of the students in this group lived either outside the Edmonson area or south of Springfield. They entered Edmonson in the lowest track, and came from social locations that afforded them little knowledge and low self-efficacy. Even when counselors and teachers suggested to these students that they move up the track ladder and try harder classes, these students were skeptical of their ability to do so. Sometimes the students believed themselves incapable. Other times they attributed their failure to a sense of lethargy that they found difficult to explain. Many of them had internalized their low-track status (Harker, 1984; MacLeod, 1995).

Part of the reason these students were unable to take advantage of

---

less time and resources to connect one on one with students' families. Recognizing these external constraints, however, it is still important to note how the counselor interacted with Lana in ways that affected her course placement based on assumptions about her social location.

opportunities for higher track placements was that their experiences in school had told them that they could not compete with their peers. This is not to say that these students – given the policies in place at the high school – should have received higher placements than they did. The students in this section did poorly in school and had done so for years. However, regardless of the fit between the students' past performance and the classes they received, the process of placement these students experienced was inequitable on three counts:

First, because of their social location in the institutional and societal structure, these families lacked access to knowledgeable networks and had little good, detailed information about placement. Second, strained parent-child relationships made it difficult for the families to share education information among themselves, which further hampered the families' ability to shape the students' placements. Third, the students' placements undermined their self-efficacy and self-esteem, and tied their social relationships to the low track, which made it difficult for students who wanted to leave the low track to do so. As Willis (1977) noted, these families "willingly accepted their restricted opportunities" and even took the lead in limiting such opportunities further because doing so "seemed sensible to them in their familiar world as it was actually lived"(p.172).

Renita Macias: Working the System to her Disadvantage. Renita Macias, a wide-eyed, rambunctious Latina with light-skin and long brown hair, lived in a low-to-middle-income area outside of Edmonson with her mother, father, and younger brother. She attended Edmonson on permit because both her parents, Cesar and Margie, worked nearby. A weak student, Renita had never done well in school. She frequently received Ds and Fs and was constantly in trouble for fooling around in class. Renita chalked up her poor performance to her "immaturity," "laziness," and "lack of smarts." As a freshman, Renita was enrolled in Edmonson's lowest courses, including Math 9.

Cesar, an automobile upholsterer, and Margie, a grocery clerk, had emigrated from Mexico as adults over two decades ago, before meeting and marrying in the United States. Both parents understood English, although Cesar spoke more fluently than Margie did. Both also had some education: Cesar had nearly completed high school, and Margie had finished the eighth grade. Although neither parent had much knowledge of the American educational system, they had heard from their customers that Edmonson had a reputation as a safe, good school. They had little other information about Edmonson, however, because their jobs and the distance between their home and the school made it difficult for them to meet with teachers or attend meetings. "It's very hard, especially with Margie working so late. It's been very difficult. We try. We try our best. But it's very hard to go to all of those meetings," said Cesar.

Renita and her parents had a rocky relationship, which made it difficult for them to communicate about school. Most of the tension occurred between Renita and her father. Renita often complained about Cesar, "[It's the] same thing all the time. I get a big lecture on why I don't [do my work]. He always asks me the same questions." Some of her complaints could be attributed to typical teenager-parent problems. Others seemed to indicate a more serious element: "He's done some things in the past that got to my mom and me. And he does some things to my mom that I don't really care for," said Renita. She continued coldly, "So it's not like it's really important to me what he thinks."

The tension between father and daughter made talking about Renita's schooling difficult. Renita rarely volunteered information about school to him. Letters or flyers from school were invariably lost or misplaced. Weekly progress reports, which her parents had requested, never surfaced. College fairs and counseling sessions came and went. Even Cesar and Margie hesitated to bring up school issues for fear that their conversations would turn quickly into confrontations. Cesar lamented the tension between them:

> Renita says she has a hard time talking to me. [Sighs] I don't know... I don't know. I don't know what to make of it. Because when I say certain things, and I ask her the hard questions, I won't get any feedback. She just gives me the usual, "I don't know. I don't know. I don't want to, or I don't know how." ... I'd like it to be different, but I can only say so many things. And I can only do so many things to get her to [talk to me]. I don't want to force her. How can you force a child to be confident with you? You can't.

Given Renita's low motivation, low performance, and low parental involvement, it was surprising that as she moved from the 9th to the 10th grade, she also moved out of the lowest math track and into a middle math track. The remainder of this critical tale documents how Renita's supportive, though short-lived, relationship with her 9th-grade math teacher and a brief relationship with a senior boyfriend helped motivate her to move up and out of the low track, only to draw her back a short time later.

Mr. Valencia, a teacher in his 20s, had emigrated from Mexico as a teenager, studied, and eventually obtained a math degree from a well-known university. He had an affinity for students whose attitudes toward self and school placed them at risk of school failure, and taught low-level Math 9 and unified math courses taken by the school's more challenging students.[9] "My job is more than just teaching," explained Mr. Valencia, "I also try and help boost their self-esteem. I try to get them to see, 'Hey, this is not so bad. It's not so hard to get through this stuff. Maybe I'll do okay.'"

Mr. Valencia held high expectations for his students, but he coupled this with a flexible teaching style that suited Renita. In other, more traditional classrooms, Renita's can't-sit-still behavior made for a constant battle between herself and her teachers. Mr. Valencia purposefully constructed his classrooms to fit these types of "more fidgety" students, however. He said, "as long as she kept quiet while I was talking, I was okay with her, she could get up and move around if she liked or work with other students."

But even more important than his flexible teaching style was the teacher's ability to relate to Renita because of their similar backgrounds. Usually, he did not make a conscious effort to use his ethnicity to build relationships with Latino students. But, if his ethnic background became important to the student, Mr. Valencia welcomed such interactions. In Renita's case, she felt a particular affinity for Latino educators and, thus, for Mr. Valencia. Being around other Latinos made Renita feel as though she belonged. Being around Mr. Valencia made her feel that she belonged in a math class.

At the same time, Renita also had a brief, but important, relationship with a senior named Armando. Armando planned to enlist in the Army after graduating from Edmonson and often talked over his plans with Renita. From these discussions, Renita learned that the Army recruiters were interested in grades, particularly math grades. This made her think about her future beyond high school, a period of her life she had never contemplated before. "I was thinking about going into the Marines. That'd be cool. But you have to be good in math, so that's what I'm trying to do," said Renita. She slowly became convinced that math was a worthwhile subject: "The only thing that I do know that you need for sure is the math."

Once she saw the link between math and her future, Renita decided to retake prealgebra during summer school. She was already taking summer school to repeat first semester freshman English, which she had failed. If she repeated prealgebra and passed it, there was a chance that she might be able to take algebra in the fall, an option that a counselor had told her about the previous year, but that Renita had then turned down.

Before meeting with her counselor to select her 10th-grade classes, Renita sat down and wrote out her class selections. The moment the counselor

---

[9] He also sometimes taught the school's only upper level mathematics courses for Spanish-speaking students (e.g., immersion geometry and intermediate algebra).

mentioned Renita's math placement, Renita firmly stated that she wanted to take prealgebra during the summer. The counselor agreed enthusiastically with her decision: "Good! That's just what I was going to ask you.... If you pass it, you can go into algebra." Over the summer, Renita took and barely passed prealgebra. She enrolled as a sophomore in algebra.

Renita's relationship with Mr. Valencia and the encouragement and information she had received from Armando propelled her forward. Yet these ties did not equip her with the social capital that she needed to negotiate nonremedial terrain. Her relationships did not prepare her for what Mr. Valencia described as the "sink or swim" culture rampant in many Edmonson college-preparatory math classes. Midway through her sophomore year, Renita was receiving an F in algebra.

Frustrated and alone, Renita had reverted to her old ways of interaction within the classroom. Her algebra teacher was known in the department as a "this-is-what-you-do-here-you-go" kind of teacher, which made Renita uncomfortable. Instead of asking for help when she got stuck, Renita sat silently in her chair, believing that "[The teacher's] not going to come to me just to listen to me!"

Midway through the fall semester and faced with failure, Renita opted down. She approached Mr. Valencia and asked him to take her into his unified math class. Mr. Valencia refused. He encouraged Renita to remain in the algebra class because although he worried about her skill level and knew she was struggling, he also recognized that moving up and out of the lower track math classes was a rare opportunity that one could not take lightly. Moreover, his unified math class had more than 35 pupils and was already too large.[10] "I've been trying to make a stand on my end of it," said Mr. Valencia. "I usually have a cutoff point. Two or three weeks into the semester and I'm not going to take any more students." Renita returned to the algebra class, received an F, and repeated the class the following year as a junior.

Renita's short-lived but encouraging relationship with a teacher and an older peer motivated her to pursue a higher math track. Yet Renita quickly found, as do many students who advance from the low track, that she did not have the skills and social capital necessary to negotiate the challenging world of college-preparatory classes. She also did not have the academic or political parental backing to support her marginal placement in these classes. More importantly, her school did not have the institutional support structure to

---

[10]Mr. Valencia stated that although his Math 9 and unified math classes usually began the year with more than 35 students, by the end of the year, the enrollment often dropped to the mid-20s.

assist her move upward. Thus, although Renita's social location and social relations caused her to move up the tracking hierarchy, they also precipitated her move downward. This downward movement reinforced Renita's and her parents' qualms about her ability to compete with more advanced students.

CONCLUSION

Taken together, the 19 Edmonson high ninth-grade students I studied, including the 4 that I highlight in this chapter, reveal the impact of race and class stratification in the local and societal contexts that propel students automatically into their "earned" places in high school. In this way, my overall findings cohere with sociological theory and prior empirical evidence about the reproduction of inequality.

But my data also delve further and show the rich texture of people's lives that cannot be reduced to modal patterns and outcomes. The relationships enjoyed or, in some cases, endured between parents and students or between educators and families also influenced the students' placements. These relationships were strained or supported by larger contextual factors such as income levels and race, and provide a micro-example of how the biographies of the students, and their parents and educators interact within social and economic institutions and cultures to fashion track structures. The students' and their parents' social locations – their socioeconomic backgrounds, race and family structures, and cultures – worked with one another and within larger societal structures and cultures to alter the information these students and their families were privy to and their actions toward the course placement process.

What these stories fundamentally reveal is that the process of unequal educational opportunity and social and economic reproduction (Bourdieu & Passeron, 1977; Bowles & Gintis, 1976), as illustrated in track placements, is deeply rooted but not wholly deterministic. Schools do not work like simple sorting machines pumping out low-track and high-track students based solely on measured merit or their parents' race and socioeconomic class. Students, parents, and educators do not pass through schools like pawns. Rather, the process of inequity is shaped by the complex interaction between people's past histories, group and individual identities, self-efficacy and self-esteem, and their relationships with one another and the ever-changing structures and cultures in which they find themselves.

What has also been learned from this study is that the process of tracking does not have firm beginning and ending points. This is because tracking is a continuous process. It occurs through repeated retracking – year to year, semester to semester, day to day – as students, parents, and educators interact in ways that co-construct the kinds of learning opportunities available to students.

That the tracking process is interactive and ongoing raises a complex question: How can this information be used to disrupt the tracking process's reification of privilege? I offer two responses here. The first provides some insight into how these findings can inform the broader debate about detracking reform, which concentrates on effecting broad-scale structural and cultural change in today's educational system. The second response provides suggestions on ways to disrupt the process for individual students struggling to find their place in today's tracked system.

When tracking is approached as an interactive process, it becomes clear that any effort to detrack, or reduce the number of tracks at a school site, must address more than the individual student and his or her decision to enroll in a higher or lower level course. Efforts to reduce the stratification inherent in track systems must address all decision makers – students, parents, teachers, counselors, and peers – at points where they regularly connect. That is, detracking cannot be about just altering teachers' classroom practices or schools' master schedules. Detracking attempts must also attend to how parents interact with school sites, how students interact with counselors, and how parents interact with their children around academics.

Unfortunately, studies of detracking efforts, as documented by Oakes et al. (1996) and Smith-Maddox and Wheelock (1995), reveal that such efforts often are only about changing the decision-making strategies of individual students. In other words, educators sometimes define detracking as opening doors to high-track classes and encouraging students through them – or at least not hindering their passage (Yonezawa, Wells, & Serna, 1996). Very little attention is paid to changing the ways in which teachers interact with the students who move into higher track classes or to helping parents understand their child's movement into more challenging courses so that they might give them additional support at home.

If the tracking process is viewed as recurrent (without a clear beginning or end), there may be many points in students' careers where low-track placements can be disrupted. The critical tales of the families and educators told in this chapter help to demonstrate how these disruptions could occur. Recall how Virginia Cantrell was able to disrupt Michael's placement in regular English and algebra versus honors English and geometry by taking advantage of summer school programs and circumventing the regular honors English enrollment process. Recall how Mr. Valencia in the case of Renita

Macias was able to do the same by encouraging Renita to remain in algebra rather than opt down to regular math. The experiences, efforts, and interactions of the people in this study show that the interactive and ongoing nature of tracking practices must make educators vigilant, but also bring hope. This hope lies in the realization that because tracking happens via the micro interactions of people within particular structural and cultural contexts, it may also be altered by attending to those very same interactions.

REFERENCES

Adler, P. A., & Adler, P. (1994). Observational techniques. In N.K. Denzin & Y.S. Lincoln (Eds.), *Handbook of qualitative research* (pp. 377-392).Thousand Oaks, CA: Sage.

Banks, J. (1995). The historical reconstruction of knowledge about race: Implications for transformative teaching. *Educational Researcher*, 24(2), 15-25.

Bodgan, R. C. & Biklen, S.K. (1992). *Qualitative research for education: An introduction to theory and methods* (2nd Edition). Boston: Allyn & Bacon.

Bourdieu, P., & Passeron, J.C. (1977). *Reproduction in education, society, and culture.* London: Sage.

Bowles, S., & Gintis, H. (1976). *Schooling in capitalist America.* New York: Basic Books.

Brantlinger, E., Majd-Jabbari, M., & Guskin, S. L. (1996). Self-interest and liberal educational discourse: How ideology works for middle-class mothers. *American Educational Research Journal*, 33(3), 571-597.

Cicourel, A.V., & Kitsuse, J. I. (1963). *The educational decision-makers.* Indianapolis, IN: Bobbs - Merrill.

Coleman, J. S. (1987). Families and schools. *Educational Researcher*. 16(6), 32-38.

Delgado-Gaitan, C. (1991). Involving parents in the schools: A process of empowerment. *American Journal of Education,*100(1), 20-46.

Dornbusch, S. M. (1994, February). *Off the track.* Presidential Address to the Society for Research on Adolescence, San Diego, CA.

Eisenhardt, K. M (1989). Building theories from case study research. *Academy of Management Review*, 14(4), 532-550.

Erickson, F. & Schultz, J. (1982). *The counselor as gatekeeper: Social interaction in interviews.* New York: Academic Press.

Gamaron, A. (1992). Access to excellence: Assignment to honors English classes in the transition from middle to high school. *Educational Evaluation and Policy Analysis*, 14(3), 185-204.

Gamaron, A., & Mare, R. D. (1989). Secondary school tracking and educational inequality: Compensation, reinforcement, or neutrality? *American Journal of Sociology*, 94(5), 1146 - 1183.

Granovetter, M. (1973). The strength of weak ties. *American Journal of Sociology*, 78(6), 1360-1380.

Harding, S. (1993). Rethinking standpoint epistemology: "What is strong objectivity?" In L. Alcoff & E. Potter (Eds.), *Feminist epistemologies* (pp. 49-82). New York: Routledge.

Harker, K. (1984). On reproduction, habitus, and education. *British Journal of Sociology of Education*, 5(2), 117-127.

Lamphere, L. (1993). *Structuring diversity: Ethnographic perspectives on the new immigration.* Chicago: University of Chicago Press.

Lareau, A. (1987). Social class and family - school relationships: The importance of cultural capital. *Sociology of Education*, 56, 73-85.

Lareau, A. (1989). *Home advantage.* London: Falmer Press.

Lareau, A., & Horvat, E. (1999). Moments of social inclusion and exclusion: Race, class, and cultural capital in family-school relationships. *Sociology of Education*, 72, 37-53.

Lawrence-Lightfoot, S. L. (1978). *Worlds Apart.* New York: Basic Books.

Lawrence-Lightfoot, S. (1994). *I've known rivers: Lives of loss and liberation.* New York: Penguin.

Lee, S. (1996). *Unraveling the "model minority" stereotype: Listening to Asian American youth.* New York: Teachers College Press.

Lin, N. (1990). Social resources and instrumental action. In R. Brieger (Ed.), *Social mobility and social structure* (pp. 247 - 271). Cambridge, UK: Cambridge University Press.

MacLeod, J. (1995). *Ain't no makin it.* Boulder, CO: Westview Press. Reprinted version from 1987.

Marshall, C., & Rossman, G. B. (1989). *Designing qualitative research.* Newbury Park, CA: Sage.

Mehan, H. (1992). Understanding inequality in schools: The contribution of interpretive studies. *Sociology of Education*, 65(1), 1-20.

Merriam, S. B. (1988). *Case study research in education: A qualitative approach.* San Francisco: Jossey-Bass.

Oakes, J., Gamaron, A., & Page, R. (1991). Curriculum differentiation: Opportunities, outcomes, and meanings. In P. Jackson (Ed.), *Handbook of research on curriculum* (pp. 570-608). New York: Macmillan.

Oakes, J., & Guiton, G. (1995). Matchmaking: The dynamics of high school tracking decisions. *American Educational Research Journal*, 32(1), 3-33.

Oakes, J., Wells, A.S., & Associates (1996). *Beyond the technicalities of school reform: Policy lessons from detracking schools.* Los Angeles: University of California, Los Angeles.

Ogbu, J. (1974). *The next generation.* New York: Academic Press.

Paul, F., & Orfield, G. (1994). *High hopes, long odds: A major report on Hoosier teens and the American dream.* Policy report funded by the Lilly Endowment and disseminated by the Indiana Youth Institute.

Phelan, P., Davidson, A. L., & Yu, H. C. (1993). Students' multiple worlds: Navigating the borders of family, peer, and school cultures. In P. Phelan & A.L. Davidson (Eds.), *Renegotiating cultural diversity in American schools* (Pp. 52-88). New York: Teachers College Press.

Smith-Maddox, R., & Wheelock, A. (1995). Untracking and students' future: Closing the gap between aspirations and expectations. *Phi Delta Kappan*, 77(3), 222-228.

Stanton-Salazar, R. D. (1997). A social capital framework for understanding the socialization of racial minority children and youths. *Harvard Educational Review*, 67(1), 1-40.

Stanton-Salazar, R. D., & Dornbusch, S. M. (1995). Social capital and the reproduction of inequality: Information networks among Mexican-origin high school students. *Sociology of Education*, 68, 116-135.

Strauss, A., & Corbin, J. (1990). *Basics of qualitative research: Grounded theory procedures and techniques.* Newbury Park, CA: Sage.

Useem, E. L. (1991). Student selection into course sequences in mathematics: The impact of parental involvement and school policies. *Journal of Research on Adolescence*, 1(3), 231-250.

Useem, E. L. (1992). Middle schools and math groups: Parents' involvement in children's placement. *Sociology of Education*, 65, 263-279.

Van Maanen, J. (1988). *Tales of the Field*. Chicago: University of Chicago Press.

Weber, M. (1978). Class, status, party. In Charles Lemert (Ed.), *Social theory: The mulitucltural and classic readings* (pp. 126-136). San Francisco: Westview Press,

Wells, A. S., & Crain, R. L. (1994). Perpetuation theory and the long-term effects of school desegregation. *Review of Educational Research*, 64(4), 531-555.

Wells, A. S., Hirshberg, D. H., Lipton, M., & Oakes, J. (1995) Bounding the case within its context: A constructivist approach to studying detracking reform. *Educational Researcher*, 24(5), 18-24.

Wells, A. S., & Serna, I. (1995). The politics of culture: Understanding local political resistance to detracking in racially mixed schools. *Harvard Educational Review,* 66(1), 93-118.

Willis, P. (1977). *Learning to labor: How working class kids get working class jobs.* New York: Columbia University Press.

Yin, R. K. (1984). *Case study research design and methods.* Newbury Park, CA: Sage.

Yonezawa, S., Wells, A. S., & Serna, I. (1996, April). *Choosing tracks: "Freedom of choice" in detracking schools.* Paper presented at the Annual Meeting of the American Educational Research Association, San Francisco, CA.

III

Focus on African-American Students

7

Gender and the Effects of School, Family, and Church Support on the Academic Achievement of African-American Urban Adolescents

MAVIS G. SANDERS
Johns Hopkins University

JERALD R. HERTING
University of Washington

This study examines the effects of gender on the relationships between institutional support, school-related attitudes and behaviors, and academic achievement for 826 African-American adolescents in an urban school district in the southeastern United States. The results of regression and interview analyses suggest that the school, family, and church simultaneously influence academic achievement through their effects on academic self-concept and school behavior, even when controlling on background characteristics of students. Differences between the male and female populations exist. These differences appear to be related primarily to the attributes female African-American adolescents bring to school relative to males (e.g., more parental support or more church involvement), as opposed to strong differences in the effects of these attributes on the attitudinal and behavioral variables tested, and their relationship to academic achievement. This study's findings are discussed relative to improving the educational experience of male and female African-American urban youth through school, family, and community partnerships.

Over the past two decades, educators and social scientists have challenged assumptions of homogeneity among African-American youth (see Consortium for Research on Black Adolescence, 1990). Research studies have increased our awareness and understanding of the variation that exists within this population. This has been especially true in the field of education and, in particular, in the area of academic achievement. Gender is one of the primary factors found to account for differences in the school success and educational attainment of African-American youth.

Research has consistently shown that African-American female adolescents have higher academic achievement than do their male counterparts (Ford, 1992; Lee, Winfield, & Wilson, 1991; Scott-Jones & Clark, 1986). In addition, studies have shown gender differences in social and academic support networks, and in school-related attitudes and behaviors (Hare, 1979, 1985; Smith, 1982). For example, Coates (1987) found that African-American female adolescents look to parents and other family members more often for guidance and nonmaterial support than do their male counterparts. In addition, some authors (Allen, 1979; Lewis 1976) have argued that African-American girls experience more restrictions on behavior and higher expectations for academic achievement than do African-American boys. However, less is known about similarities and differences in the relationships between these variables for African-American male and female adolescents.

This research study addresses this gap by examining the effects of gender on the relationships between institutional support, school-related attitudes and behaviors, and academic achievement for African-American, urban youth. This study, thus, broadens the understanding of differences in the educational experiences and outcomes of African-American male and female adolescents, and, consequently, provides educators and policymakers additional knowledge with which to address the educational needs of these populations.

To achieve its objectives, this study compares the results of separate analyses for male and female eighth-grade students in an urban school district in the southeastern United States. The primary causal relationships analyzed are depicted in Fig. 7.1.[1] The model's focus on the effects of multiple institutions on the academic achievement of African-American adolescents reflects a growing awareness of the overlapping influence that institutions of socialization have on the success and well-being of youth (Epstein, 1995).

---

[1]This study uses cross-sectional data, which makes it difficult to argue causality. However, the direction of the relationships posited in Fig. 7.1 is supported by both formal theory and past longitudinal research.

OVERLAPPING SPHERES OF INFLUENCE

Epstein's theory of overlapping spheres of influence draws attention to the effects of family, school, and community environments on educational outcomes (for a detailed discussion, see Epstein, 1987, 1992). This theory emphasizes the simultaneous influence that institutions that socialize and educate children have on certain goals of mutual interest, such as student academic success. Pictorially, this perspective is represented by three spheres that symbolize school, family, and community, the relative relationships among which are determined by the attitudes and practices of individuals within each context (Epstein 1992). Epstein's theory of overlapping spheres of influence provides the framework with which this study examines the effects of three institutions of socialization – the school, the family and the church – on the academic achievement of African-American male and female adolescents, focusing on the effects of gender.

School, Family, and Church as Overlapping Spheres

In a previous study, Sanders (1998) found that school, family, and church influence African-American adolescents' academic achievement through their effects on academic self-concept, achievement ideology, and school behavior. More specifically, the study found that the primary effect of church involvement on academic achievement is through its positive effect on academic self-concept, the primary effect of parental support is through its positive effects on school behavior and academic self-concept, and the primary effect of teacher support is through its positive influence on school behavior.

Additional analyses were conducted to determine whether the combined effects of family, school, and church support are stronger than the independent effect of each on the attitudinal and behavioral variables measured. It was found that when a student receives support from all three institutions, the effects on his or her academic self-concept and school behavior are magnified. Thus students are triply benefitted when all three contexts are working toward the same goal of helping them succeed in school. The results of these analyses underscore the "overlapping" influence of these institutions of socialization, and the importance of communication and cooperation between these institutions for students' increased opportunities to learn and achieve in school.

However, the just-mentioned findings are for the total population, and research has shown that African-American male and female adolescents interact with and are affected by family, church, and school differently. For example, Irvine (1990) and Grant (1982) found that teachers respond differently toward students based on factors such as gender, race, and grade level. Tinney (1981) and Coates (1987) focused on the lower attendance and participation of African-American male adolescents and adults in the black church. And several researchers (Allen, 1979; Kelly & Wingrove, 1975; Starrels, 1994) have posited that there are gender differences in the socialization and parent-child relations of African-American children that may account for differences in school-related attitudes, academic effort, and achievement. These studies underscore the need to explore gender effects when examining factors that influence the educational experience and academic outcomes of African-American youth.

METHODS

This study's sample consisted of 828 (female, 443; male, 378; missing, 7) African-American, eighth-grade students attending 8 of 19 middle schools in an urban school district in the southeastern United States. Students completed a five-point, Likert-type questionnaire administered between October 1993 and January of 1994. Students were not required to write their names on the questionnaires, which took, on average, 30 minutes to complete.

Instrument Scales

Six primary variables were measured by the survey. The *teacher support* scale ($\alpha = .82$) measured students' perceptions of teachers' encouragement of academic endeavors and achievement. Students were asked to rate their agreement to statements such as, "When I need help with my homework, I feel comfortable asking my teacher."

The *parental support* scale ($\alpha = .76$) measured students' perceptions of parents' encouragement of academic endeavors and achievement. The scale consisted of items such as, "My parents praise me when I do well in school."

The *church involvement* scale ($\alpha = .73$) measured students' levels of participation in church and related activities. Students were asked to respond to items such as, "I am a member of at least one church group" and "I attend church services frequently."

The *achievement ideology* scale (α = .71) measured students' perceptions of the importance of schooling and academic achievement for future success. The scale included items such as, "I work hard in school now because I know it will help me get a good job later."

The *academic self-concept* scale (α = .74) measured students' perceptions of their ability to succeed in school. Students were asked to respond to questions such as, "Forget for a moment how others grade your work. In your own opinion, how good do you think your work is?"

The *school behavior* scale (α = .85) measured students' conduct in school. The scale consisted of items such as, "I get sent from the classroom for misbehaving" and "My parents have had to come to the school because of my behavior." (For a more detailed description of each scale, see Sanders, 1998).

A mean score of students' self-reported grades in social studies, science, English, and mathematics was used as the measure of academic achievement. The letter grade reported by students for each of the above academic subjects was converted to a number based on a four-point scale, and an academic grade point average was calculated.

Background Variables

The instrument also contained items to measure several background variables – poverty level, family structure, sex, and age. Students participating in the free or reduced lunch program (*n* = 532) were identified as living at or below poverty level, and students not receiving free or reduced lunches (*n* = 288) were identified as living above poverty level. A dichotomous variable was created: students living at or below poverty level were coded as 1, and students living above poverty level were coded as 0. Although this measure offers a limited range of variance, it does avoid the error inherent in student reports of parent education and occupation. It also permits an examination of the effects of poverty on the educational experience of African-American, urban youths.

In addition, students reported on their household structure. Forty-eight percent of students reported living in single-parent households (*n* = 392), almost all with their mothers, 44% reported living with two parents (*n* = 360), and 9% reported living with relatives serving as legal guardians (*n* = 71). A dichotomous variable was created to represent family structure with single-parent households coded as 1, and all others as 0.

A dichotomous variable for students' sex was also created: male students (n = 378) were coded as 0 and females (n = 443) as 1. Finally, students reported their ages, which ranged from 12 to 17. Approximately 1% of the students were 12 (n = 10), the majority – 60% – were 13 (n = 494), an additional 29% were 14 (n = 240), approximately 9% were 15 (n = 72), and 1% of the sample were 16 or 17 (n = 9). Of the students reporting ages 15 years or older, the majority (68%) were males. Given that all participants were eighth-grade students, age, in this analysis, serves as a proxy measure of student retention.

Interviews

After the administration of the questionnaire, 40 students (male, 16; female, 24) were selected for in-depth, semistructured interviews (see Sanders, 1997). These students differed in achievement level, and were recommended by school counselors and teachers. Student interviews were conducted privately and students were assured of anonymity. These interviews averaged 1 hr each and covered topics such as beliefs about schooling; school and out of school activities; future educational and employment plans, and relationships with teachers, family, and peers. The interviews supplemented and enriched the surveys, and aided in interpreting the quantitative data.

ANALYSIS

Multiple regression and path analytic techniques were used to examine the pattern of relationships outlined in Fig. 7.1. The results presented are for males and females pooled as a single group and for separate analyses of males and females. Differences in effects are examined by including a variable for gender (female = 1, male = 0), and all interactions between gender and other independent variables in the model (e.g., Church involvement x Gender). This allows for a direct comparison and statistical test of gender differences in the effects of the independent variables on each dependent variable in the regression.

The initial set of equations model student perceptions of teacher and parental support, along with church involvement on three attitudinal and behavioral variables: academic self-concept, achievement ideology, and school behavior. Statistical controls on student background characteristics – age, poverty level, and household structure – are included in these equations.

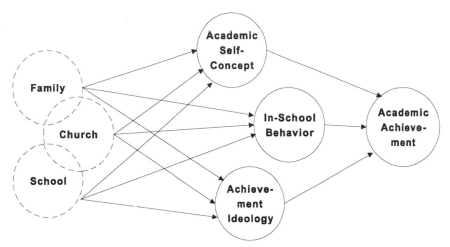

Fig. 7.1: Model of the relationships between institutional support, attitudes/behaviors, and academic achievement for African-American adolescents.

The final equations build on the initial set by modeling the effects of student perceptions of support from the family, church, and school, together with students' school-related attitudes and behaviors, as predictors of academic achievement. These analyses depict academic self-concept, school behavior, and academic ideology as mediators through which family, church, and school indirectly influence academic achievement in adolescents (i.e., church involvement leads to better school behavior, which, in turn, leads to higher achievement).

RESULTS

Table 7.1 shows the means, standard deviations, and minimum and maximum values of the variables measured. Mean differences between males and females were assessed using t-tests. As indicated, there are statistically significant differences between male and female adolescents on each of the seven variables in the study. Females reported greater parent and teacher support, more church involvement, less disruptive school behavior, more positive achievement ideologies and academic self-concepts, and higher grades. In general, females bring to school attributes more conducive to academic achievement. Females have higher levels of positive factors (e.g., positive achievement ideology) and lower levels of disruptive factors (e.g., negative school behaviors) than do their male counterparts. These differential attributes help produce the general male/female difference in academic achievement.

To explore the effects of gender further, the relationships between the background variables; the support variables, and the mediating factors of academic self-concept, school behavior, and achievement ideology are examined in separate regression analyses for males and females in the study. These factors are then examined for their effects, and potential gender difference in effects, on academic achievement.

Academic Self-Concept

For the total sample, both church involvement and parental support positively and significantly influence academic self-concept (see Table 7.2). That is, academic self-concept for both male and female adolescents in the study is affected by the support that these students find in their families and in the church. Within each group, parental involvement is the strongest standardized effect ($\beta = .204$ for males, $\beta = .210$ for females), followed by church involvement. There were no significant gender differences, based on

Table 7.1: Variable Means, Standard Deviations, and Minimum/Maximum Values for Males and Females								
Variable Name	*Mean*		*Standard Deviation*		*Minimum Value*		*Maximum Value*	
	M	F	M	F	M	F	M	F
Teacher support	3.6	3.7**	0.88	0.86	1.0	1.0	5.0	5.0
Parental support	4.3	4.4***	0.70	0.62	1.4	1.4	5.0	5.0
Church involvement	3.4	3.6**	1.25	1.16	0.0	0.0	5.0	5.0
Achievement ideology	4.4	4.5***	0.60	0.48	2.2	2.7	5.0	5.0
Academic self-concept	3.8	3.9*	0.58	0.46	2.2	2.8	5.0	5.0
School behavior	3.8	4.3***	0.83	0.65	1.0	1.0	5.0	5.0
Academic achievement	2.1	2.6***	0.84	0.78	0.0	0.25	4.0	4.0

Note.* $p<.05$. **$p<.01$. ***$p<.001$.

Table 7.2: Regression Model Predicting Academic Self-Concept for African-American Male and Female Adolescents

Independent Variables	Total Sample[a]	Males	Females
	b / β (t value)[b]	b / β (t value)	b / β (t value)
Support variables			
Church involvement	.106 / .157 (4.42)	.130 / .177 (3.37)	.079 / .128 (2.64)
Parental support	.184 / .204 (5.58)	.190 / .202 (3.82)	.184 / .210 (4.14)
Teacher support	.014 / .022 (0.63)	-.019 / -.028 (-0.54)	.038 / .070 (1.43)
Background variables			
Single-parent household	-.065 / -.063 (-1.83)	-.034 / -.030 (-0.58)	-.097 / -.106 (-2.24)
Age	-.098 / -.133 (-3.85)	-.130 / -.169 (-3.28)	-.068 / -.092 (-2.00)
Poverty level	-.001 / -.001 (-.023)	-.072 / -.061 (-1.17)	.066 / .070 (1.47)
N	781	351	430
R^2	.127	.150	.121

Notes. a) *b*, unstandardized regression coefficient; β, standardized regression coefficient.
b) t value greater than 1.65 is significant at .05 level 1-tail test; 1.96 at .05 level 2-tail test.

the regression with gender interactions included; the effect of teacher support is in opposite directions for males and females but not significantly different from zero for either group. Of the background variables tested, all are negatively correlated with academic self-concept for the total sample of students. However, for male students, age ($\beta = -.169$, $p<.01$) has a significant effect on academic self-concept. For female students, living in a single parent household ($\beta = -.106$, $p<.05$) and age ($\beta = -.092$, $p<.05$) significantly influence academic self-concept. The effect of poverty is not significant for either group. The variance explained by the model is 15% for the male population and 12% for the female population.

School Behavior

As indicated in Table 7.3, for the total sample all three support variables are positive and significantly related to school behavior (positive scores on school behavior equal less disruptive school conduct). Teacher support has the strongest relation ($\beta = .251$, p<.001), followed by parental support and the weaker, but significant, effect of church involvement. Only teacher support ($b = .325$, $\beta = .333$ for males, $p<.01$ and $b = .183$, $\beta = .234$ for females, $p<.001$) has a significant effect on the school behavior of the African-American eighth-grade students in the study when looking at each gender group separately; this reflects the smaller sample sizes and lower power compared to the total sample. Interestingly, the male coefficient ($b =$

.325) for teacher support is significantly larger than the female coefficient (b = .183), which indicates a much stronger positive response by males to teacher support.

Each of the background variables tested has a negative effect on the school behavior of both male and female students. Age is a negative and significant predictor of school behavior for both male and female adolescents, but there is no statistically significant gender difference in the effect. This finding indicates that students who are older (possibly reflecting grade retention) are more likely to report disruptive school behavior than are younger students.

Living below poverty level, however, is a negative and significant predictor of school behavior for girls only. This finding may reflect different norms of behavior for African-American female adolescents living below and above poverty level. In a classic sociological work, Ladner (1971) noted the difficulties that African-American girls face growing up and the forced acceleration of growing up in low-income, urban areas. Similarly, Campbell (1987) reported that females growing up in low-income, urban neighborhoods are exposed and must respond to the crime and violence that increasingly characterize these areas (Kotlowitz, 1991; Majors & Billson, 1992). Rejecting many of the stereotypes of middle-class femininity, some low-income female adolescents value traditionally masculine attributes such as assertiveness and physical toughness (Campbell). These qualities may, in turn, translate into more disruptive classroom behavior, and greater student-

Table 7.3: Regression Model Predicting School Behavior for African-American Male and Female Adolescents

Independent Variables	Total Sample[a]	Males	Females
	b / β (t value)[b]	b / β (t value)	b / β (t value)
Support variables			
Church involvement	.057 / .057 (1.65)	.046 / .044 (0.86)	.036 / .040 (0.84)
Parental support	.127 / .094 (2.64)	.105 / .078 (1.51)	.099 / .080 (1.58)
Teacher support*	.251 / .275 (7.95)	.325 / .333 (6.58)	.183 / .234 (4.79)
Background variables			
Single-parent household	-.048 / -.032 (-0.93)	-.080 / -.049 (-0.97)	-.038 / -.029 (-0.62)
Age	-.196 / -.179 (-5.32)	-.147 / -.135 (-2.66)	-.144 / -.137 (-2.98)
Poverty level	-.124 / -.078 (-2.29)	-.082 / -.048 (-0.95)	-.191 / -.141 (-2.96)
N	781	351	430
R^2	.169	.184	.126

Notes. a) b, unstandardized regression coefficient; β, standardized regression coefficient.
b) t-value greater than 1.65 is significant at .05 level 1-tail test; 1.96 at .05 level 2-tail test.

Table 7.4: Regression Model Predicting Achievement Ideology for African-American Male and Female Adolescents			
Independent Variables	Total Sample[a]	Males	Females
	b / β (t value)[b]	b / β (t value)	b / β (t value)
Support variables			
Church involvement	.020 / .029 (0.87)	.022 / .030 (0.55)	.021 / .032 (0.71)
Parental support	.300 / .318 (9.36)	.316 / .330 (6.56)	.271 / .292 (6.26)
Teacher support	.171 / .267 (8.10)	.177 / .253 (5.16)	.170 / .294 (6.52)
Background variables			
Single-parent household	-.062 / -.058 (-1.80)	-.066 / -.057 (-1.16)	-.057 / -.059 (-1.35)
Age	-.032 / -.041 (-1.29)	.004 / .006 (0.12)	-.030 / -.030 (-0.68)
Poverty level	.014 / .013 (0.41)	.059 / .049 (1.00)	.066 / .070 (1.47)
N	781	351	430
R^2	.244	.229	.256

Notes. a) b, unstandardized regression coefficient; β, standardized regression coefficient.
b) t value greater than 1.65 is significant at .05 level 1-tail test; 1.96 at .05 level 2-tail test.

teacher conflict. African-American females living below poverty level, thus, may require additional support to effectively negotiate home and school environments that may clash over behavioral expectations and norms. Eighteen percent of the variance in male school behavior and 13% of the variance in female school behavior is explained by the regression model.

Achievement Ideology

Table 7.4 shows that both parental support and teacher support were found to significantly predict achievement ideology for males and females in the study; this can be seen both in the total sample and for each sample analyzed separately. There are no gender differences in the magnitude of these effects. Whereas parental support (β = .330) appears to play a slightly stronger role relative to teacher support (β = .253) for males, both factors basically are of equal strength for females (β = .292 and .294, respectively).

Of the background variables tested, age and poverty level are not related to students' achievement ideology. Household structure has a negative and significant effect on achievement ideology for the total sample. There are no gender differences in the effects of these background factors. The model tested accounts for 23% of the variance in achievement ideology for males and 26% for females.

Academic Achievement

The final models predicting academic achievement are shown in Tables 7.5 and 7.6. Table 7.5 shows the results of the support and background variables on academic achievement for the total sample, and for the separate analyses of males and females. Table 7.6 adds to these equations the three mediating variables: academic self-concept, school behavior, and achievement ideology. The results for the total sample show the significant and positive effects of church involvement ($b = .107$, $\beta = .098$, $p<.01$) and teacher support ($b = .091$, $\beta = .092$, $p<.01$) on student achievement as measured by academic grades. In addition, each of the background factors is significant and negatively related to academic achievement. Age is the strongest factor and continues to represent the influence of the older students, those most likely retained, on educational outcomes.

Table 7.6 shows that addition of the three mediating factors substantially increases the explained variance (from .12 to .28). It is also evident that the effects of the support variables are no longer significant once academic self-concept, school behavior, and achievement ideology are entered. Specifically, school behavior ($\beta = .179$, $p<.001$) and academic self-concept

Table 7.5: Regression Model Predicting Academic Achievement for African-American Male and Female Adolescents

Independent Variables	Total Sample[a]	Males	Females
	b / β (t value)[b]	b / β (t value)	b / β (t value)
Support variables			
Church involvement	.107 / .098 (2.75)	.053 / .050 (0.92)	.115 / .108 (2.21)
Parental support	.075 / .052 (1.40)	.037 / .027 (0.50)	.072 / .048 (0.93)
Teacher support	.091 / .092 (2.57)	.043 / .044 (0.83)	.119 / .127 (2.56)
Background variables			
Single-parent household	-.099 / -.060 (-1.72)	-.047 / -.028 (-0.53)	-.173 / -.112 (-2.32)
Age	-.292 / -.246 (-7.09)	-.295 / -.267 (-5.05)	-.213 / -.171 (-3.63)
Poverty level	-.128 / -.074 (-2.12)	-.221 / -.128 (-2.42)	-.084 / -.052 (-1.07)
N	781	351	430
R^2	.123	.122	.097

Notes. a) b, unstandardized regression coefficient; $\beta=$ standardized regression coefficient.
b) t-value greater than 1.65 is significant at .05 level 1-tail test; 1.96 at .05 level 2-tail test.

Table 7.6: Regression Model Predicting Academic Achievement for African-American Male and Female Adolescents: Effects of Academic Self-Concept, School Behavior, and Achievement Ideology

Independent Variables	Total Sample[a]	Males	Females
	b / β (t value)[b]	b / β (t value)	b / β (t value)
Support variables			
Church involvement	.031 / .029 (0.87)	-.035 / -.034 (-0.69)	.062 / .059 (1.29)
Parental support	-.061 / -.041 (-1.16)	-.095 / -.070 (-1.36)	-.055 / -.037 (-0.72)
Teacher support	.031 / .032 (0.91)	.006 / .006 (0.12)	.069 / .074 (1.50)
Background variables			
Single-parent household	-.052 / -.031 (-0.98)	-.019 / -.012 (-0.24)	-.108 / -.070 (-1.54)
Age	-.193 / -.162 (-5.02)	-.193 / -.175 (-3.60)	-.148 / -.118 (-2.67)
Poverty level	-.103 / -.060 (-1.87)	-.173 / -.100 (-2.10)	-.090 / -.056 (-1.22)
Behavioral and attitudinal variables			
School behavior	.194 / .179 (5.29)	.142 / .139 (2.74)	.163 / .137 (2.96)
Academic self-concept	.596 / .369 (10.96)	.605 / .417 (8.19)	.614 / .358 (7.66)
Achievement ideology	.013 / .009 (0.24)	.023 / .016 (0.16)	-.018 /-.011 (-0.22)
N	781	351	430
R^2	.278	.302	.231

Notes. a) b, unstandardized regression coefficient; β= standardized regression coefficient.
b) t-value greater than 1.65 is significant at .05 level 1-tail test; 1.96 at .05 level 2-tail test.

(β = .369, $p<.001$) are strong predictors of academic achievement, and all other factors, except age and poverty, operate indirectly through these mediating variables. The age effect remains negative and relatively strong (b = -.193, β = -.162, $p<.001$).

Shown in Table 7.5 for males, age (b = -.295, β = -.267, $p<.001$) and poverty level (b = -.221, β = -.128, $p<.01$), are negative and significant predictors of academic achievement as measured by grades. Male adolescents who have been retained in school and who live below poverty level are less academically successful than males at modal grade age who live above poverty level. None of the support variables tested was significant.

When the block of behavioral and attitudinal variables are included in the regression equation, the variance explained by the model increases from about 10% to about 30% (see Table 7.6). Both school behavior (b = .142, β = .139, $p<.01$) and academic self-concept (b = .605, β = .417, $p<.001$) are positive and significant predictors of male students' academic achievement. These two variables aid in the understanding of the significance of church involvement, parental support, and teacher support for the academic achievement of African-American male adolescents. Church involvement and parental support are significant predictors of male adolescents' beliefs about their academic abilities, and teacher support has a positive and significant influence on male adolescents' school behavior. Table 7.7 shows the indirect effects of church, parental, and teacher support on academic achievement, and their significance for the total sample and the male and female populations separately (Bollen, 1989).

Each indirect effect is significant, although the indirect effect of teacher support is weak ($\beta = .038, p<.10$) for males (see Table 7.7). The standardized indirect effect of church involvement and parental support through self-concept and behavior is .085 ($p<.01$) and .099 ($p<.01$), respectively, and is similar in magnitude to the direct effect of poverty and school behavior. Thus, the findings of this study support Epstein's theory of overlapping spheres of influence. Supportive adults in the homes, communities, and schools of youths simultaneously affect their school success through their influence on students' behaviors and attitudes.

As indicated in Table 7.6 for the male sample, school behavior and academic self-concept weaken the effects of poverty and age on the academic achievement of African-American male youths; however, both remain significantly negative and relatively strong in their effect. The strong effect of age indicates that older African-American male adolescents are possibly disengaging from school; this is seen in the effect of age on their behavior, as well as on their achievement. Given that over two thirds of the students who were between ages 15 and 17 in the eighth grade were males, this finding has important implications for the way we educate and provide academic and social support for African-American male students, especially those who live below poverty level.

Table 7.7: Indirect Effects of Church, Parental, and Teacher Support on the Academic Achievement of African-American Male and Female Adolescents

Independent Variables	Total Sample[a]	Males	Females
	b / β (t value)[b]	b / β (t value)	b / β (t value)
Support variables			
Church involvement	.075 / .070 (4.65)	.088 / .085 (3.51)	.053 / .050 (2.69)
Parental support	.137 / .096 (4.92)	.132 / .099 (3.34)	.128 / .087 (3.41)
Teacher support	.058 / .060 (3.11)	.037 / .038 (1.45)	.050 / .054 (2.13)

Notes. a) *b*, unstandardized regression coefficient, β, standardized regression coefficient.
b) t value greater than 1.65 is significant at .05 level 1-tail test; 1.96 at .05 level 2-tail test.

As shown in Tables 7.5 and 7.6, and as indicated by the nonsignificant effects of the gender interactions for the total sample, the regression results for the female population are similar to those for the male population. As Table 7.5 shows, church involvement ($b = .115$, $\beta = .108$, $p<.01$) and teacher support ($b = .119$, $\beta = .127$, $p<.01$) are significant predictors of academic achievement as measured by grades for the female group. It is interesting that, despite no significant gender interactions, the unstandardized regression coefficients for each of these are about double those observed for males (e.g., for church involvement compare .053 to .115). That these variables reached significance may be explained by the larger number of females ($n = 431$) than males ($n = 353$) participating in the study. In addition to teacher support and church involvement, age ($\beta = -.171$, $p<.01$) and living in a single-parent household ($\beta = -.112$, $p<.01$) have negative and significant effects on female students' academic achievement. As with their male counterparts, female adolescents who have been retained in school also appear to disengage and perform less well. Different from males, however, for female adolescents, the effect of living in a single-parent household is also a negative and significant predictor of academic achievement.

When we add the behavioral and attitudinal variables block in the regression equation predicting academic achievement, we find that the beta coefficients for church involvement ($\beta = .059$) and teacher support ($\beta = .074$) are substantially reduced and are no longer significant. This again indicates that much of the influence of the support variables is mediated by school behavior and academic self-concept. The indirect effects (see Table 7.7) of church involvement, parental support, and teacher support on female adolescents' academic achievement are all significant and show how these effects operate indirectly. That is, church involvement, parental support, and teacher support are important for both male and female adolescents because this support influences behaviors and attitudes that positively and significantly influence academic achievement. Also, as indicated by the changes in the beta coefficients and significance levels, controlling for school behavior ($\beta = .137$, $p<.01$) and academic self-concept ($\beta = .358$, $p<.001$) reduces the influence of age and living in a single-parent household on the academic achievement of African-American adolescent females; only age remains a significant predictor once controlling for the three additional mediating factors. When the block of behavioral and attitudinal variables are included in the regression equation, we find that the variance explained by the model increases from about 10% to over 20% – a substantial and statistically significant increase (see Tables 7.5 and 7.6).

Finally, it is interesting to note that achievement ideology, although positively correlated to academic achievement, is not a significant predictor of academic achievement for the male or the female population. This finding may be best explained by Mickelson's (1990) distinction between abstract and concrete attitudes. According to Mickelson, whereas abstract attitudes reflect the dominant ideology, concrete attitudes – which are "rooted in life experience" (p. 44) – inform achievement behavior. If in their households and neighborhoods, African-American adolescents are not exposed to individuals who confirm the possibility of mobility through education, they may possess an abstract belief in the importance of schooling, but not a concrete one.

For example, in the school district studied, only 7% of African-American adult males and 19% of African-American adult females have B.A. degrees or higher, and 24% of African-American males and 15% of African-American females age 20 and older have not completed high school (U.S. Census Report, 1990). These statistics suggest that in the school district studied, a number of African-American students may not have family members who have completed high school or attended college.

DISCUSSION

Interview data were analyzed to enhance and aid in the interpretation of the questionnaire data. The interview excerpts highlighted in the following discussion were selected to further clarify key quantitative findings relative to the importance of church involvement, and teacher and parental support for student achievement. One such finding is that although parental support is important for the school success of both male and female African-American adolescents, the latter report greater parental academic support than do the former. This finding may indicate a need for African-American parents to reassess the ways in which they socialize their sons. Of the students interviewed, girls discussed spending more time with family members such as aunts and grandparents after school than did boys, who spoke of spending more time with their peers. Females also reported more restrictions on their time, greater responsibilities at home, and higher expectations for achievement. As a result of stricter supervision and higher expectations, behaviors of female adolescents may be more reflective of the norms and desires of their parents than are those of male adolescents.

Of additional interest is the effect of age on parental support for males in this study. When poverty level, family structure, and age are regressed on parental support, age ($\beta = -.16$, $p<.01$) is the only variable that is a significant predictor of parental support for the males in the study. None of the background variables tested has a significant effect on the parental support reported by females in the study. Thus, in addition to males reporting less parental support than females, the support that they do receive may wane as male adolescents age, and need adult support and guidance the most. This is an issue that schools, families, and communities must address.

A previous paper (Sanders, 1998) highlighted the importance of church involvement for student academic self-concept. Student interviews indicate that the church provides them the opportunity to engage in a number of activities that require school-related skills – such as public speaking, and reading and analyzing texts – in a supportive, nurturing environment. The present study emphasizes this finding and further highlights the significant influence of church involvement on the academic self-concept of both male and female students. Given the significance of institutions such as the church for the academic confidence and success of youth, a primary question that faces these institutions is that of how to attract and fully engage more young people, especially young African-American males, so that they may receive the benefits that such institutions provide.

This study also emphasizes the importance of teacher support for male and female students' school behavior. Although male students report less teacher support than do their female counterparts, the effect of teacher support on male adolescents' behavior was stronger than on female adolescents' behavior. When discussing how teachers have influenced his school conduct, one male eighth-grade student, age 14, states:

Teachers think that they scare you when they write you up, some students don't get scared. If teachers care, though, I'll do my work and behave. A teacher did me like that last year. She liked me; she started helping me and all that, and I made a good grade.

However, many students, especially male adolescents, do not feel supported by their teachers. The following were reported by two different male eighth-grade students, both age 13:

Sometimes the boys are treated worse than the girls. . . . The way that the boys are treated, it's unfair. Like my friend Eric, he got written up and got sent to the office today, and it's the first time this year that he's got written up, and he got in-house suspension. A girl was also written up, she didn't get anything. . . .

We do have a few teachers who care, but most don't. Some of the young, White teachers coming here seem to lack care for Black children. They will write you up in a second, whereas a Black teacher will try to talk to you and try to make you understand the situation.

Thus, in addition to acknowledging the positive influence that teachers can and do have on the academic performance of African-American youths, this study also highlights areas that require special attention. The relationship between urban, African-American male students, and their often White, suburban, or female teachers is such an area. As indicated in interviews, male respondents may perceive their teachers as unduly harsh and exhibiting less patience with them than with female and non-Black students.

Student-teacher conflict also occurs with female students, especially those whose environments may promote behavioral and attitudinal norms that differ from or contradict those expected by the school. For example, this study highlights the negative effects of living below poverty level on the school behavior of female adolescents. The following low-income, female eighth-grade student, age 13, illustrates how student-teacher conflicts can develop. She explains:

Some of these teachers [have] got problems; they grab you and stuff and I am not trying to be rude or nothing, but if you grab me, I am going to jerk away from you.... If I am not going to let someone my own age hit me, why should I let a teacher grab on me; she should know better than to grab on me.... And then they say that we are disrespecting the teacher.

This student voices an interpretation of respect, and possesses expectations of both student and teacher behavior that may differ from those held by teachers at her school, and that may cause conflicts which negatively affect teacher job satisfaction and student learning. This study, thus, suggests that the present and future teaching force be made more aware of the varying norms, attitudes, and expectations of their students, including African-American urban adolescents, and be better trained to deal with conflicts that may arise (see Mitchell, chap. 8, this volume). This can be effectively achieved, in part, through greater communication with adults in students' families and communities. School, family, and community partnerships, therefore, are needed to enhance each sector's ability to better address the needs of adolescents and to ensure their well-being and success.

CONCLUSION

This study's population was selected to provide a representative sample of African-American youth in the urban, southeastern U.S. school district studied. Further studies with a broader cross section of the African-American population are needed to promote greater generalizability of the findings and also to allow for comparative analyses. This study also highlights the need for future research on differences in the socialization and social capital (Coleman, 1987) of male and female African-American adolescents.

For example, the findings of this study highlight the importance of student affiliation in stable, adult-supervised, community-based organizations such as the church; family support of and high expectations for school achievement; and teacher support for student learning for the academic success of African-American male and female urban youth. Female adolescents in this study perceive more family and teacher support, and are more active in the church than are male adolescents. It is not surprising that African-American females also report more positive academic self-concepts and achievement ideologies, less disruptive school behavior, and higher achievement than the male students surveyed.

Given this study's findings, it is important that schools, families, and community agencies and organizations use their combined resources and expertise to ensure that both females and males have the opportunity to benefit from positive contact with caring, supportive adults. Because schools, families, and communities differ relative to their resources and the needs of their students, there is no one-size-fits-all formula of activities in which these institutions should engage. School, family, and community partnerships can take a variety of forms, and focus on a variety of goals linked to students' success. For example, some schools have joined with community institutions to implement mentoring and tutoring programs to reduce dropout among low achieving students (McPartland & Nettles, 1991; Nettles, 1991). Other communities and schools have partnerships to provide integrated health and welfare services to students and their families (Dryfoos, 1994). Still other schools are working closely with families to identify and develop the skills needed for both institutions to be more responsive to their adolescents' changing social, emotional, and academic needs (Lucas, Henze, & Donato,

1990). All of these activities could directly benefit students through the support provided to them or their families – support that, in turn, can positively influence attitudes and behaviors linked to academic success.

Such interactions between the overlapping spheres that influence a child's growth and learning are important early in, and throughout, a child's development and educational career. With this combined support, perhaps fewer youths will develop the patterns of school failure that negatively impact their school behavior, beliefs about their academic ability, and, ultimately, academic achievement. This study further suggests that well-designed and implemented partnership activities, which are part of a comprehensive program of school, family, and community partnership (see Sanders & Epstein, chap.15, this volume), may be especially important for subsets of the African-American male and female student populations. These include students who live below poverty level and those who are older than modal grade age.

REFERENCES

Allen, W. (1979). Family roles, occupational statues, and achievement among Black women in the United States. *Journal of Women in Culture and Society*, 4, 670-686.

Bollen, K. (1989). *Structural equation with latent variables*. New York: Wiley.

Campbell, A. (1987). Self definition by rejection: The Case of gang girls. *Social Problems*, 34(5), 451-466.

Coates, D. L. (1987). Gender differences in the structure and support characteristics of Black adolescents social networks. *Sex Roles*, 17(11/12), 667- 687.

Coleman, J. S. (1987). Families and Schools. *Educational Researcher*, 16(6), 32-38.

Consortium for Research on Black Adolescence. (1990). *Black adolescence: Current issues and annotated bibliography*. Boston: G. K. Hall & Co.

Dryfoos, J. (1994). *Full service schools: A revolution in health and social services for children, youth and families*. San Francisco: Jossey-Bass.

Epstein, J. (1987). Toward a theory of family-school connections: Teacher practices and parent involvement. In K. Hurrelmann, F. Kaufmann and F. Losel (eds.), *Social intervention: Potential and constraints* (pp.121-136). New York: DeGruyter.

Epstein, J. (1992). School and family partnerships. In *Encyclopedia of educational research* (pp. 1139-1151). New York: MacMillan.

Epstein, J. (1995). School/family/community partnerships: Caring for the children we share. *Phi Delta Kappan*, 76 (9), 701- 712.

Ford, D. Y. (1992). The American achievement ideology as perceived by urban African American students: Explorations by gender and academic program. *Urban Education*, 27(2), 196-211.

Grant, L. (1982, September). *Black females' place in desegregated classrooms*. Paper presented at the American Sociological Association annual meeting, San Francisco, CA.

Hare, B. (1979). *Black girls: A comparative analysis of self-perception and achievement by race, sex and socioeconomic background* (Rep. No.27). Baltimore, MD: Center for the Social Organization of Schools. The Johns Hopkins University.

Hare, B. (1985). Reexamining the achievement central tendency: Sex differences within race and race differences within sex. In H.P.McAdoo & J.L.McAdoo (Eds.), *Black children: Social, educational, and parental environments* (pp.139-155). Beverly Hills, CA: Sage.

Irvine, J. (1990). *Black students and school failure*. New York: Praeger.

Kelly, P. E., & Wingrove, C. R. (1975). Educational and occupational choices of Black and White, male and female students in a rural Georgia community. *Journal of Research and Development in Education*, 9, 45-56.

Kotlowitz, A. (1991). *There are no children here*. New York: Anchor Books.

Ladner, J. (1971). *Tomorrow's tomorrow: The Black woman*. Garden City, New York: Doubleday.

Lee, V. E., Winfield, L. F., & Wilson, T. C. (1991). Academic behaviors among high-achieving African-American students. *Education and Urban Society*, 24(1), 65-86.

Lewis, D.L. (1976). The Black family: Socialization an sex roles. *Phylon*, 36(3), 221-237.

Lucas, T., Henze, R,. & Donato, R. (1990). Promoting the success of Latino language-minority students: An exploratory study of six high schools. *Harvard Educational Review*, 60(3), 315-340.

Majors, R. and Billson, J. (1992). *Cool Pose: The Dilemmas of Black Manhood in America*. New York: Lexington Books.

McPartland, J., & Nettles, S. (1991). Using community adults as advocates or mentors for at-risk middle school students: A two-year evaluation of project RAISE. *American Journal of Education*, 99, 568-586.

Mickelson, R. (1990). The attitude achievement paradox among Black adolescents. *Sociology of Education*, 63, 44-61.

Nettles, S. (1991). Community contributions to school outcomes of African-American students. *Education and Urban Society*. 24(1), 132-147.

Sanders, M. G. (1997). Overcoming obstacles: Academic achievement as a response to racism and discrimination. *Journal of Negro Education*, 66(1), 83-93.

Sanders, M. G. (1998). The effects of school, family and community support on the academic achievement of African-American adolescents. *Urban Education*, 33(3), 385-409.

Scott-Jones, D., & Clark, M. L. (1986). The school experiences of Black girls: The interaction of gender, race, and socioeconomic status. *Phi Delta Kappan*, 520-526.

Smith, E. J. (1982). The Black female adolescent: A review of the educational, career and psychological literature. *Psychology of Women Quarterly*, 6(3), 261-287.

Starrels, M. E. (1994). Gender differences in parent - child relations. *Journal of Family Issues*. 15(1), 148-165.

Tinney, J. (1981). The religious experience of Black men. In L. Gary (Ed.), *Black Men*. Beverly Hills, CA: Sage.

U.S. Census Bureau. (1990). Washington, DC: Author.

8

African-American Teachers and the Roles They Play

ANTOINETTE MITCHELL
Urban Institute

Using the oral histories of eight recently retired school teachers, this chapter identifies the multiple roles they played as they worked effectively with African-American students. These roles included teacher as mediator, activist and active supporter of student growth and development. In playing these roles, teachers addressed the social, economic and political circumstances of their students. Through these roles, the teachers increased student motivation and promoted student resiliency. The teachers, thus, present models for effective teacher-student interaction that could be used to help prepare all teachers to work more effectively with African-American and other minority youth.

The educational achievement and attainment of African-American students has long lagged behind those of their White peers, as is demonstrated by national test scores, grades, and designation in special education (National Center for Educational Statistics [NCES], 1997). In addition, African-American students' rates of college attendance are below the national norm, and high school dropout rates have been and continue to be disproportionately high (NCES, 1996a; NCES, 1997). Over the years, numerous theories have sought to explain these disparities. These theories range from macro- to micropolitical and include deficits in the students, their families and communities (Hernstein & Murray, 1994; Jensen, 1969); low expectations and discontinuities in the relationships between teachers and students, and between students and schools (see Erickson, 1984; Giroux, 1983; Ogbu, 1987; Rist, 1970; Smitherman, 1977); weaknesses in the organization and governance of schools (Hess, 1993; Oakes, 1985; Tyack, 1990); and inequalities in the structure of society (Bourdieu & Passeron,

1977; Bowles & Gintis, 1976).

Since the 1980s, efforts to decrease these disparities and to increase levels of educational achievement among all students have involved systemic reform – the reorganization of schools around national standards; the alignment of curriculum and assessment; and increased accountability. This reform movement has also proposed changes in professional development that aim to enable teachers to help their students meet high standards through developing greater expertise in content, methods, and assessment (O'Day & Smith, 1993). Less attention has been given, however, to what teachers do in the affective domain to establish and maintain student motivation and engagement.

This is a significant oversight given that student motivation has been long recognized as an important aspect of academic achievement. Motivation propels students to behave properly in class, to pay attention to the teacher, and to exert effort in learning situations (Glasser, 1996; Senecal, 1995). It has been identified as a key factor in theories explaining the resilience of at-risk students, and the high achievement of students who excel in academic and other settings (Chambers, 1994; Dorsey, 1995; Gordon, 1995). Often, the most effective teachers not only are well versed in areas of content, methods, and assessment, but are also capable of motivating and engaging their students. Some theorists posit that minority teachers are particularly adept at motivating and engaging minority students because they often bring a certain knowledge of student backgrounds to the classroom that enhance their educational experience (Foster, 1995; Irvine, 1990a; Michael-Bandele, 1993). The teaching approach that emerges from this knowledge is often referred to as *culturally relevant pedagogy*.

Using oral history interviews as the primary data source, this chapter examines aspects of the culturally relevant pedagogy of eight recently retired African-American teachers[1]. It explores the roles they played as they worked effectively with African-American students over the course of their careers. Situated in the affective domain of teaching, these roles include teacher as mediator, teacher as activist, and teacher as active supporter of student growth and development. This chapter posits that living and understanding African-American experiences in the context of a society that is painfully conscious of race enhances one's ability to perceive the necessity of and successfully interpret these teaching roles. Through their explicit discussion

---

[1]This research was supported, in part, by a grant from the American Educational Research Association (AERA). However, the opinions expressed are the author's and do not necessarily represent the positions of AERA.

of these roles, the focal teachers provide examples of behaviors and attitudes that can enable teachers of other racial and ethnic backgrounds to work more successfully with African-American students, and indeed with all students in U.S. schools.

FRAMEWORK: AFRICAN-AMERICAN TEACHERS AND CULTURAL PEDAGOGY

The number of African-American teachers in the U.S. teaching force has been declining since the 1960s (King, 1993). At the same time, the percentage of African-American students in the nation's public schools has been increasing (Pallas, Natriello, & McDill, 1989). In urban (central city) schools, although almost 30% of the students are African-American, only 15% of the teachers are (NCES, 1996b). This disparity has been a cause for concern for several reasons (Carnegie Forum on Education and the Economy, 1986; King, 1993; Zeichner, 1993). Greater representation of minority teachers would provide positive role models and highlight minorities in positions of authority (Michael-Bandele, 1993). There are also pedagogical benefits (Villegas, 1991). Minority teachers often bring to the classroom cultural understanding that informs their pedagogical approach and improves their ability to work effectively with African-American students (Hollins, 1992; Ladson-Billings, 1994).

The works of Ladson-Billings (1992, 1994), Foster (1990, 1993a, 1993b), Villegas (1997), and King (1993) best describe the practical and theoretical underpinnings of culturally relevant pedagogy. In her exploration of pedagogy, which incorporates various aspects of the students' culture into the schooling process, Ladson-Billings (1992, 1994) found that teachers who were family oriented, cultivated relationships beyond the classroom, encouraged collaborative learning through building a community of learners, and created an atmosphere of trust and support were successful with African-American students, largely because of the greater match between these teaching techniques and the cultural background of the students. Ladson-Billings (1995), in a theoretical work, articulated three criteria for culturally relevant pedagogy: the pedagogy must be aimed at academic achievement, must demonstrate respect for and encouragement of students' ability to operate within the context of their culture, and must develop the students' ability to critique social inequalities. From this perspective, culturally relevant pedagogy recognizes the primacy of learning and academic success, but also acknowledges the significance of cultural competence and critical thought.

Similarly, Foster (1990, 1993a, 1993b), in her series of interviews with successful African-American teachers, attributed these teachers' success to shared community norms with their students that were reflected in their classrooms. These teachers worked well in the affective domain, challenging negative attitudes and helping students understand the significance of academic achievement in the context of past and present African-American struggles for social equality (Foster, 1993a). King (1993) studied African-American teachers, who through "emancipatory pedagogy," encouraged students to think critically about issues of social justice as it related to their cities, neighborhoods, and families.

Drawing on breakthroughs in cognitive science that have demonstrated that learning is an interactive process that builds on prior knowledge and experiences, "both individual and cultural," Villegas (1997) posited that minority teachers who are familiar with the cultural backgrounds of students are better able to build necessary bridges between home and school. When minority teachers are properly trained to translate their cultural knowledge into pedagogical approaches, they are able to help students integrate the school learning experience into their lives outside of school. She noted that the teaching profession as a whole stands to gain from the infusion of expertise about minority cultures, perspectives, and experiences that minorities possess.

This chapter[2] examines minority teachers' understanding of how social and economic background factors affect student behavior. It further examines how some minority teachers work in the affective domain, assuming expanded teacher roles that encourage engagement and achievement among minority youth. The findings presented in this chapter suggest that African-American and other minority educators can enhance the teaching profession by providing input and role models for teachers of different backgrounds.

METHODS

Setting

The study's site, the District of Columbia, was selected because demographic changes that have occurred in the city over the past three decades are in many ways representative of changes that have occurred in many urban

---

[2] This is an expanded version of a paper published in *Education and Urban Society*, 31(1), pp. 104-122, November 1998.

communities and school districts throughout the country. In the 1960s and 1970s, middle-class White, and later African-American, families moved to the suburbs, leaving behind predominantly African-American communities plagued by unemployment and poverty, and the concomitant social ills of teen pregnancy, crime, violence, and drug abuse.

Participants

To conduct the study, interviews were conducted with eight secondary school teachers who retired from the District of Columbia system between 1990 and 1995. Each had 25-30 years of teaching experience in the district. The focal teachers had received several honors and distinctions over the course of their careers, and were identified by peers, students and administrators as highly effective. Six of the teachers were female and two were male. This is representative of both national and local ratios of female to male teachers. Five migrated from the South to the District in the 1950s, one was born in Pennsylvania and came to the District in 1949, and two were born in the District. Several of the teachers were reluctant to give their ages, but the years they entered teaching indicate that all respondents were between 60 and 75 years old. Although they were all secondary school teachers, six of the eight taught exclusively at the junior high school level, one taught at both the junior and senior high levels, and one taught only at the senior high school level. They taught a variety of subjects, including English, social studies, science, and music.

Interviews

With the in-depth narrative interviewing techniques described by Seidman (1991), each participant was interviewed for 60-90 minutes on at least three occasions. The first interview was used to gain an understanding of the participants' backgrounds as they related to their professional lives, thereby establishing a context for their narratives. In the second interview, participants were encouraged to tell the story of their careers, with special emphasis on the roles they played with students, parents, administrators, and other teachers. In the final interview, participants were encouraged to reflect on the meaning of their experiences. Thus, they were asked about their perceptions of their professional interactions, and the significance and societal consequences of their teaching roles. Each participant generated 80-100 pages of transcribed text.

Analysis

The interviews were coded and analyzed based on emergent themes. The analysis involved reading and rereading of the transcribed text and identification of themes within and across the interviews. These themes revolved around the roles that the teachers played as they engaged students in academic activities and critical dialogue related to their growth and well-being.

I conducted all interviews and analyses. As an African-American woman and former teacher in the DC school system, I brought an intimate knowledge and awareness to the research topic. I approached the study with the assumption that each teacher would have a unique story to tell, but that the underlying themes would be similar to and enhance our understanding of culturally relevant pedagogy.

FINDINGS

In thinking about their interactions with students, particularly in the 1980s and 1990s, the teachers noted that the students became more distracted by outside influences, particularly the prevalence of drugs and violence in their communities. As a result, the teachers often had to work more than they had previously in the affective domain to engage students in classroom learning. They identified several roles that they found themselves playing, including teacher as cultural mediator, teacher as activist, and teacher as supporter of student growth and development. In describing these roles, the teachers, in their own voices, tell of the expanded nature of their work.

Teacher as Cultural Mediator

The focal teachers often operated as cultural mediators, interacting with students and families based on a two-pronged philosophical understanding. On the one hand, they acknowledged student backgrounds, which often included poverty and the related problems of unemployment and underemployment, drug trafficking and abuse, homelessness and violence. The teachers recognized the negative effect that these environmental hazards can have on student growth and development. On the other hand, they related to their students as children who could and wanted to learn, but who had to overcome environmental hazards in the process. The teachers worked diligently to promote individual and collective agency aimed at transcending these barriers. This duality was expressed by most of the teachers interviewed.

The teachers clearly recognized the problems that plagued student neighborhoods and the ways in which these problems affected students in schools. This recognition is best summarized by one teacher, who said:

By the time the '80's rolled around, I was working with just a special segment of the school population, the students who were supposed to have been high achievers. But I had some, I had one or two classes of students, who were achieving below average. They [all of the students] had more problems to deal with. Well, in the '60s and '70s, they had the drugs and the pregnancy, but it wasn't as widespread as in the '80s. Then AIDS started coming into the picture. Then homelessness became an issue for the students in the '80s. We had students who had trouble with the law in shelters and in group homes. The community around [the school] has many group homes and students were not living with their families. All of these things escalated. We had just a smattering of that kind of problem earlier on. But now, the community problems really impacted the schools by the time the '80s came . . . . (Carolyn Price)[2]

Another teacher compared the neighborhoods of today with the neighborhoods of 20 years ago and said:

The difference I think is when you look at the violence in the neighborhood; that's the difference. . . . I would say that the change really came about somewhere around 1988. That's when they really started with the killings and then we really lost kids to school, because they were busy with the business of surviving. That became the number one thing. (Anita Evans)

In these quotes, the teachers describe aspects of the students' neighborhoods that did not foster their academic and social development, but rather caused instability in students' lives and in some ways negatively affected their orientations toward school. It is important to note that the teachers recognized that some students were more adversely affected by community problems than others and that the students' communities included some positive aspects as well as negative influences.

In their roles as mediators, the teachers recognized several ways that students' backgrounds, particularly their socioeconomic status, affected them

---

[2]Pseudonyms have been used throughout the text to protect the anonymity of the teachers interviewed.

in the school setting. The teachers recalled situations in which students' behavior was adversely affected by factors outside of the school. One teacher recalls a student who had a record of poor behavior:

> I had one student who was very bright, a very bright girl. But she was so on edge. I mean if you looked at her wrong, she wanted to fight. I used to talk to her. I'd say, "You know, you're very talented, you're very bright, you have a lot of potential, but you'll never get to develop it unless you let people work with you. You have to stop being so difficult." Then I realized that this poor child lived in one shelter after another, and sometimes she traveled long distances to get to King. . . . She traveled all that way and sometimes by foot. (Anita Evans)

One teacher remembers a student who was very listless in class:

> We had a girl during my last year [she] was just downright hungry. We sent her down to the nurse. She told the nurse that the problem was she really just hadn't had any food. Well, some of them have tickets to eat free lunch, and some of the kids tease them, and they have too much pride to go in and get it. (Cheryle Thomas)

Another recalled that students often seemed tired and did not complete their homework.

> There are so many single-parent households. That's the major thing right there. A lot of children have to work to help the family. Some of them have jobs after school. Some of them work on the weekends. The parents need them to work. I know they need that extra money that the students are making to make ends meet. (Hazel Jones)

Another teacher, in discussing her understanding of student behavior and motivation, said:

> I believe that students want to learn. They don't come to school necessarily to cause problems. They may have a lot of things going on in their lives that come out as disruptive in the learning situation, but basically students want to learn. (Anita Evans)

In understanding certain aspects of student behavior as consequences of their backgrounds, the teachers demonstrated an awareness of the larger, underlying problems in the students' lives. The teachers' understanding often helped them to respond to the various situations with the appropriate sensitivity, and enabled them to provide support that helped students better negotiate the demands of home and school. One teacher, in discussing the students in the context of disintegrating neighborhoods, said:

> I think the worse things got around them, the more children needed guidance. They really did. They needed people to talk to them about where they were in all of this, and where they were going, and if they had a future in all of this. This is what we tried, I tried, to do with them. Talk to them, keep them going. Let them see that there was something ahead for them. (Rainie Michaels)

This teacher remembers absenteeism as a problem with many of her students and how she dealt with it. She said:

> I guess we had maybe half and half living in the projects. Sometimes children wouldn't come to school because of that. So I told them, "You are not responsible for that situation. You are not responsible for where you live. Because you live in a project or in a low-income housing unit does not mean that you are low. Okay, and so you have to conduct yourself in a way that says, 'I'm as good as the next person,' because you are." (Rainie Michaels)

According to another teacher:

> A lot of times they would come, didn't have bus fare, didn't have food, so you would go into your pocket and buy lunch for them. If you had some extra clothing, whatever, at home, you brought it in. You tried to make the child feel cared for. We had some very good-minded kids, but when you're hungry, you're wondering where your next meal is going to come from and you're wondering where you're going to sleep. . . how could a child think? You know? So we tried to do what we could to make it better for them. (Carolyn Price)

Another teacher recalls how parental drug abuse affected one student and his response:

> I used to have a girl in my class whose mother was on drugs. Now she was disruptive in the class but I knew why. Someone [another teacher] had given me the information. She was disruptive in another class. I passed that information on to that teacher. And that teacher redirected this [student misbehavior] and had no problem. (Roland Collins)

Other children were more directly affected by drug use. One teacher recalls talking to her students about drug use:

In my last homeroom, I had 23 or 24 kids. . . . Many of them were on drugs. They would come in and crash on you. They didn't have the energy for anything. They'd tell you they were smoking [marijuana]. They said it feels good, that they can forget everything. I'd say to them, "Boy, stop smoking that nasty weed – [you're going to] get your brain all mixed up." They'd say, "What you talking 'bout?" And then they'd come on out and tell on the other one. I don't know if it [talking to them] worked, but they didn't hide it from me. I used to talk to them about it. (Cherlye Thomas)

In these quotes, the teachers anchored their understanding of students in the reality of the students' lived experiences and in the possibilities of the students' potential as learners. Not only did the teachers recognize that the behavioral problems that manifested themselves in schools were symptoms of larger problems in the students' lives, they also attempted to help students deal with these problems. Through providing advice, sharing information with other teachers, giving students support and encouragement, and, in some instances giving clothing, lunch money, and tokens for transportation, the teachers played an active role in the lives of the students, understanding the complexity of student behavior and attempting to mediate between the needs of home and school.

The teachers also acted as mediators in their interactions with parents. First, they understood that parents are interested in their children's education and want to be involved, even at the junior and senior high school levels. But the teachers also understood that parents cannot and do not always demonstrate their interest in traditional ways. According to the teachers:

You know, it's a simple thing. It pays to listen to what a lot of the parents say. A lot of the parents are young parents and I think they feel alienated from the school. You see, they are parents who dropped out to have children and they didn't get a chance to go back; so the last thing they think about is coming to the school. So you have to work with those parents, try to build a bridge to get them back in here. (Rainie Michaels)

A woman trying to make it with three or four kids? She doesn't have time to get up to school. (James Scott)

Although there was parent support to a certain degree, the parents were not readily available because of their own life demands and what not. (Anita Evans)

I don't remember having a problem with parents when I called them. Some teachers said they turned them off, "They [parents] gave me the cold shoulder!" But my parents were nice. They really were. But they wouldn't come to PTA meetings. (Cherlye Thomas)

Demonstrating an understanding of and respect for their students' parents, the teachers were able to actively engage more of the traditionally "hard to reach" parents in the schooling process. They encouraged parents to participate in a number of ways.

I guess I would see a lot of parents, because I would tell them [the students], "Your mama doesn't show up, you're in trouble!" And I said, "You take this stuff [PTA notices] home." See, I was one who would call the people. They said, and I think a lot parents would say, "You know, Ms. Michaels, you're the first teacher who's ever called me about my child."... We talked about everything. I would always let the parents know. I told them I would tell them what we're going to do. I would send home things. I had a lot of cooperation with my parents because I would try to clue them in on things that we were doing. When we started taking field trips, they would go along with me – a lot of them. (Rainie Michaels)

Sometimes a call [to the students' parents] will affect the way a student behaves, because they tell you just what they're going to do to the child.... One little boy's mother told me in my presence that he wasn't coming back until he improved. And that little boy became so nice! He was just the best little kid. And kept asking, "Have I improved? Have I improved?" [laughter] (Cherlye Thomas)

One of the teachers encouraged an administrator to visit the parents in their homes.

She went out [into the public housing complex where many of the school's children lived]. I said to her, "You've got to go there." She said, "I'm taking your advice; I'm going." She started going and she would go every week. That's how it happened. It was an eye opener. She just had to go down there because they weren't going to come up. So they [the administrative team] went. They used to go every Friday in the van. They would go over there and talk about different things that they were doing [at the school]. She really filled the gap between parents and the school, and that was good. (Rainie Michaels)

Another teacher encouraged parental involvement by creating organizations, such as the booster club, that parents could join and see immediate benefits for their children. According to this teacher:

The purpose of the booster club was to support instrumental music organizations like band. You need the support financially, because there are so many areas that the school or the school board does not fund. If you have active organizations like I've had through the years – like a concert band, the marching band, and especially the marching band – you need funds. So we'd get the parents together and we'd work for the children. . . . We'd do various projects like bake sales, raffles, and any other types of activities that you can think of. And it was to help the band sponsor their trips. . . . (Hazel Jones)

Through their understanding of parental orientations toward school, and their ability to interact with and help parents with negative orientations move beyond them, the teachers acted as mediators between home and school. Their willingness to call homes, invite parents on field trips, send information home, and encourage their colleagues to interact with parents demonstrated their ability to act as a link between the home and school communities.

Teacher as Activist

The teachers also played the role of activist. They took actions that they believed supported students' rights and often gave of their own time to advocate for certain issues. One teacher refused to join the teachers' union because she believed that the union protected weak teachers, and diluted teachers' responsibilities to students and parents. She said:

> I think the union caused some of the breakdown in teachers not doing their job. Before the union came, the principal was in charge. . . . It seems to me that after the union came, the union said that you don't have to do this, like keeping records for so many things. You don't have to go to but so many PTA meetings at night. That's to me one of the breakdowns – the union just came in and gave a crutch to a lot of people who weren't going to do well anyway. That's my personal opinion. It's how I feel. I never joined the union. (Joanna Simms)

Another teacher was asked by an administrator to identify students who were suspected of drug dealing. She did so, because she believed that these students were disrupting the school. She recalls:

> And I said, "I don't know what you can do, but these are basically the people, who were doing most of it." . . . . [The new principal] told the dealers, "Now if I see any of you I'm going to have you arrested. If I see any of you with any drugs in this building, I'm going to have your number." Well, they didn't believe her and they went back to business as usual. And the next thing we saw was the cops coming and the dealers going out in handcuffs. (Rainie Michaels)

Other teachers attended meetings of the Board of Education to raise concerns about various issues.

> I was always one to go to board meetings. I would go sometimes as a representative of the PTA and sometimes just as a teacher. I complained about the books, the lack of books or about how old they were. Sometimes I felt that the content was ridiculously easy and I complained about that too. The kids were getting shortchanged and I wanted to make some noise, see what could be done. (Carolyn Price)

> Some of us also complained about not having full-time nurses anymore. It used to be if we thought a child was on drugs or something, we sent him or her to the nurse. But the nurses were rarely in the building. That was dangerous for everyone in the school, teachers and other students. (Joanna Simms)

One teacher remembers going to the board about an incompetent administrator, who had lost control of the school completely.

> She was there for 3 years and we did all kinds of things to get the Board of Education to, please, replace her. I mean, the building was crumbling in every [sense] of the word, especially the morale of the teachers and the discipline of the students. We had all kinds of meetings with the regional superintendent. (Anita Evans)

The teachers also appealed to the board about other teachers who administered standardized tests incorrectly to boost student test scores. One teacher said:

> Then they started giving the teachers the tests [in advance]. Some of them [teachers] would give the kids the answers. Others erased the children's answers and put the right answers down. They did it to make themselves look good. . . . The attitude was, "If the kids can't learn, they could at least teach the test, right?" . . . So the kids are not as prepared as they used to be. We get our 7th graders in and they are scoring 10th, 9th, 7th grade level on the test. And you get the child in the classroom that's been tested, and you see what the child knows and he doesn't know anything. He's nowhere near reading or doing anything that the test says he's doing. Now some teachers want to say that he loses it over the summer. But I don't see how a child loses that much over the summer. They come in, they can't even write a paragraph. I mean, that's ridiculous. So they are not as prepared as they were years ago. Older kids, when they came out of high school, they had a good education. . . . Kids come out of high school now and they can't write a sentence. It's just terrible. What

happened to the system is that everybody wants to make himself look good. A few of us made some noise about that, but nothing ever came of it. (Cheryle Thomas)

This teacher was chair of her department and often participated in selecting books. According to Ms. Thomas:

The books that teachers use have changed. I have an English book that's 20-some odd years old, and it's on grade level. It's a 7th grade English book, and it gives you 7th grade English work. And it is more complicated than the books, the new books. So everybody watered everything down. The book companies have high-interest, low-level books. And they flooded the markets with those. Bringing the levels down so you can teach the kids. Everybody's in this thing.

It was from this perspective that she selected books and interacted with book companies. She considered herself an advocate for children in this capacity. Another teacher advocated on behalf of her students with other teachers. She encouraged her colleagues to understand the context in which the students lived before judging them:

A lot of kids – you have to give them a lot of credit for it, because they would come in with their homework, and sometimes teachers would look at their work and say, "I'm not going to take this." It might have grease or whatever on it. I used to ask them [the teachers], "Have you ever been to their houses? Have you ever been there?" . . . . You open the living room door, there's a mattress on the floor. And you look around and [there are] no tables – no place where the children can sit. So I said, "This is what you need to do; you need to go and find out what our children have to deal with on a daily basis, all day and all night." (Rainie Michaels)

Ms. Michaels took the teachers to visit some of the students' homes. She stated that after the visit, the other teachers "were grateful to me for taking them down there.... They got a different perspective of the children and for that I was happy."

As demonstrated by the previous quotes, the teachers went beyond their classroom responsibilities to advocate for students at school board meetings and in a variety of school contexts. In large part, the teachers took on this activist role because they cared about their students, and wanted to work toward ensuring that their students were educated in safe and effective schools.

Teacher as Active Supporter
of Student Growth and Development

The teachers also worked diligently to develop and support students' intellectual, social, and political growth. They helped students think critically about local and national events. They tried to serve as role models, and, perhaps most importantly, they always maintained and communicated high expectations for student behavior and academic success.

In this role, teachers helped students notice, understand, and analyze events both inside and outside of school in ways that were personal and political. Rather than narrowing class discussion to the prescribed curriculum, the teachers encouraged students to actively engage in thought and dialogue about events and situations occurring in their communities. Many of the teachers knew that some of their students were smoking marijuana. One teacher discussed police reaction to drug use by the students. She remembered:

> Some of them were smoking. I said, "The police know this. They see you smoking this stuff." I can't say that this is true. But I did believe that there was an attitude [on the part of the police] that said, "Go ahead and let them do what they want to do." I said [to the students], "A person who's on drugs is no threat to anybody. But that person is a threat to himself." (Rainie Michaels)

These teachers talked with their students about why they used drugs, the dangers of drug use to the students' physical and intellectual well-being, and the larger political implications of widespread drug use in the African-American community. One teacher expressed her belief that the police were being intentionally neglectful, challenging students to think critically about law enforcement in their communities. This teacher went on to say to her students:

> You watch what's happening in your neighborhoods and every Monday when we come back here we're going to discuss what goes on over the weekend." After the weekend, things would get so bad that these children could hardly stand it. I mean every drug that was out was there. (Rainie Michaels)

In her discussions with students on these issues, this teacher, like others in the study, challenged students with questions such as, "Why are drugs so prevalent in our communities? What are the effects? What will be the consequences if you don't study?" By engaging students in this type of dialogue, the teachers were attempting to raise the students' consciousness and help them to think critically about issues that directly affected them.

As supporters of student growth and development, the teachers also served as role models to the students. According to one teacher:

> It's always been my understanding that as a teacher, you were the role model. You wanted students to look up to you and to know what's right, and you did that or didn't by setting an example. The first example was the way you carried yourself. You added to that with personality, that kind of thing. (Carolyn Price)

Another teacher, in thinking about how younger teachers have changed, revealed a hidden aspect of teaching that she and other teachers of her generation considered very important.

> . . . Teachers used to dress up to go to work. They made the kids look up to them. Now, what do they wear? Slick sweaters, no ties, dungarees – tennis shoes. That kind of thing has had a great effect on kids. One child said to me, "If you can make any amount of money, why do teachers dress so shabbily?" If you really inspire a child to get an education then you were supposed to buy a nice car and have nice things. Then the children see, yes, education is worth my trouble to get. (Cheryle Thomas)

The teachers in the study saw themselves as role models, as examples of how obtaining an education could be beneficial to students later in life. They supported the students' academic development through demonstrating their own economic stability and well-being.

Finally, the teachers' educational philosophies inspired them to embrace the role of teacher as supporter of student growth and development. These philosophies were steeped in the notion that the ability to learn is innate and that it was their job, as teachers, to nurture that innate ability. The teachers said:

> Different people see different things in children. I see that they're eager to learn. They're going to carry on a whole lot of foolishness before they get down to the business, but when you really start with those children, they want to learn. And they are great learners, great learners. . . . I had all kinds. I had some of the worst students and some of the best students. They knew one thing – when they came into that 201, they were going to do their work and they were going to learn. (Rainie Michaels)

> My philosophy, even back then, was that children can learn. There was a teacher who used to tell me, she'd say, "Hazel can teach the devil!" [laughter]

That's the reputation I had, that those hard-to-teach children could learn under me. . . .(Hazel Jones)

The teachers manifested their philosophies through maintaining high expectations and creating situations in which the students felt comfortable and nurtured. According to the teachers:

I had a group of boys once, about 12 boys, and they could not read. I suggested to the principal that we just put them together and work with them so they wouldn't be embarrassed in front of their peers. I would have those boys come in at 8:00 in the morning and they would be there. They were all in the same boat. "Nobody's here to embarrass anybody else." You just have to be frank with them and let them know you understand. You don't have to let them pretend – some of them are very good at pretending they know how to read when they don't – and at masking it for a long time. Once they realized it [this class] was not threatening to their self-esteem, they would come. I'd have a pot of hot chocolate and doughnuts in the morning and a bowl of apples – it's amazing what children will work for. (Anita Evans)

In the classroom, you have to roll with the punches. You make the adjustments. You get your students in and you find out where they are. You know you better get down where they are in order to bring them up. So you just tell them your expectations. Your expectations are high. And you motivate them. You have to say, "I know you can do well." (Cherlye Thomas)

The teachers were willing to find out where the students were and to teach at that level, maintaining high expectations but remaining sensitive to students' academic self-concepts and fragile egos. The teachers also taught to the whole child – the academic, the social, and the emotional. One teacher talked about teaching at the junior high school level, where the children were at a "crossroads." According to this teacher:

. . . [Students at this level] need that extra encouragement and friendship; they also need the discipline to help them to make the right decisions. Education is giving students the tools to make the right decisions. Ultimately, the decisions are theirs to make, but if they have the foundation, they usually end up doing what is in their own best interest. And I think that's what being a teacher is all about. (Anita Evans)

Significantly, all of the teachers expressed a deep level of commitment to supporting the growth and development of their students. This is best summarized by one teacher, who, in discussing her relationship with students, said:

You think about those that you know if you could just give them the right stroke, that it would send them in the right direction. You're always hoping that you would do this. . . . In a year's time, or we used to have a section for three years, there's a kind of bond that develops that's hard to break. They become, they really become, an extension of yourself. They're part of your family. And you're so used to doing things with them; the same things that you're doing for your children, you're hoping you're doing for them. (Rainie Michaels)

These quotes reveal the level of caring that the teachers felt toward their students.

DISCUSSION

Haynes and Comer (1990), in an article that argues that many African-American students perform poorly in schools because their psychological, socioeconomic, and emotional needs go unmet, wrote:

Children who are hungry, who feel unsafe, or who lack a sense of belonging are most concerned about getting their hunger, safety and belonging needs met. They are least concerned about deriving self-esteem or self-actualization through high academic achievement (p.108)

As stated by Haynes and Comer, and acknowledged in many of the previously cited quotes, students who live in poverty sometimes are distracted by primary needs that are unfulfilled and find it difficult to put forth extended academic effort. This chapter has explored the expanded roles that African-American teachers played as they worked to meet the varied needs of students in predominantly African-American urban environments.

In assuming expanded roles, which included acting as mediator, activist, and supporter of student growth and development, the teachers demonstrated a sophisticated understanding of how student economic and social backgrounds often created barriers to academic achievement. The teachers also demonstrated a deeply felt belief that the students could achieve despite of these barriers. They struck an interesting balance between acknowledging social forces that contribute to student attitudes and behaviors, and recognizing students as actors who, through individual agency and with the proper guidance, can make independent choices based on a logical assessment of the rewards and consequences of their decisions. A part of the teachers' role was helping students understand these rewards and consequences.

Adverse social and economic conditions place many of the students that the focal teachers worked with at risk of school failure. Research on students placed at risk has identified three groups of protective factors that promote resilience, or the ability of the students to achieve academic and personal success despite seemingly overwhelming odds. Categories of protective factors include (a) caring and supportive relationships; (b) positive and high expectations; and (c) opportunities for meaningful participation, including the encouragement of critical thinking about current social issues (Benard, 1995; Garmezy, 1991; Sarason, 1990; Weis & Fine, 1993; Werner & Smith, 1989). Through their understanding, activism, and demonstration of caring and support for student growth and development, the teachers in this study provided the protective factors that helped students overcome risks and develop both academically and socially. In other words, the teachers encouraged the resilience of their students through expanding their professional identities to include the roles described in this chapter.

The focal teachers' encouragement of student resilience is, in part, a product of their biographies. With the exception of one, who grew up on a farm, the teachers were raised in urban environments. Because of segregation, they were all raised in predominantly African-American communities that included families of differing economic backgrounds. The teachers described themselves as having been strongly influenced by community norms and values, which were instilled in them through their interaction with individuals in their families, churches, schools, and neighborhoods. These individuals and institutions taught them to behave in ways that reflected the social mores that were accepted and expected in their communities. Consequently they learned, among other things, to interact with one another with respect; to work hard at whatever they did; to respect adult authority; and to value and acquire education as a means of social, racial, and economic uplift and empowerment.

Recognizing the significant role their communities played in their development, the teachers had a keen awareness of what was missing in the lives of their students. One teacher said:

> And they don't get that support from all the contacts in their lives as I got it. Went to church, they said, "Get your education." Went home, they said, "Get your education." Your neighbors, "Get your education." That was the theme, you know. But that theme is not there anymore. You have students involved in so many things that sometimes they miss out on what they should be about. They miss out on the their childhood. (Anita Evans)

As a result of this personal knowledge, the teachers sought to compensate for what the students did not receive by providing more support in the affective domain. Research has demonstrated that motivation and engagement increase when students work with teachers who care about their well-being (Dev, 1997; Gordon, 1995; Miserandino, 1996; Noddings, 1992).

In their roles as cultural mediators, the focal teachers demonstrated an understanding of students' communities and helped them to overcome or better negotiate difficulties at home and at school. They showed concern about students' primary needs and attempted to address those needs. They also attempted to work with students' parents, despite the difficulties of engaging parents whose orientation toward schools was often negative.

The teachers' role as activist was also a product of their biography. Educators have long been at the forefront of political struggles in the African American community (Irvine, 1990b). Many of the teachers in this study were active during the Civil Rights movement and had fought injustices on national and local levels. Activism on behalf of their students was, in part, an extension of their broader political involvement. The teachers believed that there are powerful economic and political forces that pose barriers to the academic achievement of poor and minority students, especially in urban areas. And just as they tried to help students transcend the more immediate barriers in their lives, the teachers also tried to affect change through advocating for youth in and outside of the school.

In addition to being student advocates, the teachers were also active supporters of student growth and development. The teachers realized the relationship between race and the socioeconomic realities in which the students lived. Consequently they considered it vital to teach students to think critically about issues of social equality and about the ways in which decisions that they made every day could affect their futures. Thus they talked openly with students about teen pregnancy, crime, violence, and drug and alcohol abuse in their communities. In addition, the focal teachers attempted to act as role models, demonstrating that a certain level of economic stability and well-being could be obtained by making appropriate decisions, including doing well and completing school.

Critical to their role as supporters, the teachers had educational philosophies that valued each child's ability to learn. Yet, they considered teaching to be much more than the transferring of academic knowledge. They were engaged in the business of shaping lives. Teaching to them was meaningful and engaging work that had ramifications for student lives far beyond their time with students in the classroom. In addition, the teachers considered the students to be extensions of themselves, in many instances like their own children. Consequently, they possessed high levels of commitment and caring that propelled them to struggle with and on behalf of their students, even in the face of significant constraints.

CONCLUSION

Recent literature on African-American teachers often focuses on their ability to work effectively with African-American students, using their bicultural knowledge to inform teaching practices. Often this literature concentrates on elementary school teachers and students. This study has concentrated on the roles played by secondary school teachers as they interacted with predominantly low-income African-American adolescents in an urban school district.

These teachers were committed to the academic achievement of their students, but they understood the increased need to work in the affective, as well as academic, domain. The teachers realized that as students mature, environmental factors become more influential in their growth and development. Most significantly, the teachers understood the need to establish a caring relationship with students as a vital factor in their ability to engage students in academic learning. This knowledge and the practices that it inspired encouraged student resilience, and can be used by teachers of all racial and ethnic backgrounds.

One way to communicate the collective knowledge of the focal teachers is through professional development. In the current wave of reform efforts, researchers and educational policymakers have reconceptualized teacher education. Once viewed as a discrete time period encompassing college, and perhaps the initial years of teaching, professional development is now considered a continuous process that begins when one is accepted into a teacher training program and ends when one retires (Wood & Thompson, 1993). This career-long process of professional development is seen as being essential to keeping teachers abreast of educational change, and encouraging constant and habitual professional growth (American Association of Colleges for Teacher Education, 1995).

The current study suggests that professional development should be expanded to include methodologies that would help teachers better interact with the students that they teach. First, teachers need to gain personal knowledge of the communities in which their students live. They need to see the resources, interact with community members, and initiate or participate in, whenever possible, community activities. Second, teachers need a clinical understanding of key theories on student motivation (see Covington, 1992, for a review of these theories), and practical knowledge about how and when to use these theories to motivate students. Third, teachers need an understanding of the effects of negative environmental and social factors, such as violence and drug and alcohol abuse, on students' school behavior and performance. This understanding should always be current so professional development in this area should be flexible and responsive to significant national and local trends. Finally, teachers need to be trained in how to work more effectively with parents, especially at the secondary school level (see Sanders & Epstein, chap. 15, this volume). If professional development were redefined to be inclusive of this knowledge, then all teachers would be better prepared to assume the roles played by the African-American teachers in this study. Teachers would understand their students from a uniquely professional perspective that would help them establish the mutual trust and respect necessary for successful teaching and learning.

REFERENCES

American Association of Colleges for Teacher Education (1995). *RATE: Teaching teachers: Facts and figures.* Washington, DC: Author.

Benard, B. (1995). *Fostering resilience in children.* Urbana, IL: ERIC Clearinghouse on Elementary and Early Childhood Education.

Bourdieu, P., & Passeron, J. (1977). *Reproduction in education, society and culture.* Beverly Hills, CA: Sage.

Bowles, S., & Gintis, H. (1976). *Schooling in capitalist America.* New York: Basic Books.

Carnegie Forum on Education and the Economy. (1986). *A nation prepared: Teachers for the 21st century. Report of the Carnegie task force on teaching as a profession.* Washington, DC: Author.

Chambers, K. (1994). What makes students improve? *Teacher Education,* 6(1), 9-19.

Covington, M. V. (1992). *Making the grade: A self-worth perspective on motivation and school reform.* New York: Cambridge University Press.

Dev, P. C. (1997). Intrinsic motivation and academic achievement: What does their relationship imply for the classroom teacher? *Remediation and Special Education,* 18(1), 12-19.

Dorsey, M. S. (1995). Afro-American students' perceptions of factors affecting academic performance at a predominantly white school. *Western Journal of Black Studies,* 19(3), 189-195.

Erickson, F. (1984). School literacy, reasoning and civility: An anthropologist's perspective. *Review of Educational Research,* 54(4): 525-546.

Foster, M. (1990). The politics of race: Through the eyes of African-American teachers. *Journal of Education,* 172(3), 123-41.

Foster, M. (1993a). Educating for competence in community and culture: Exploring the views of exemplary African-American teachers. *Urban Education,* 27(4), 370-394.

Foster, M. (1993b). Urban African-American teachers' views of organizational change:

Speculations on the experiences of exemplary teachers. *Equity and Excellence in Educations*, 26(3), 16 24.

Foster, M. (1995). African-American teachers and culturally relevant pedagogy. In J. Banks & C. McGee Banks (Eds.) *The handbook of research on multicultural education* (pp. 570-581). New York: Macmillan.

Garmezy, N. (1991). Resiliency and vulnerability to adverse developmental outcomes associated with poverty. *American Behavioral Scientist*, 34, 416-430.

Giroux, H. (1983). Theories of reproduction and resistance in the sociology of education: A critical analysis. *Harvard Educational Review*. 53(3), 257-293.

Glasser, W. (1996). Then and now: The theory of choice. *Learning*, 25(3), 20-22.

Gordon, K. A. (1995). Self-concept and motivational patterns of resilient African-American high school students. *Journal of Black Psychology*, 21(3), 239-255.

Haynes, N., & Comer, J. (1990). Helping black children to succeed: The significance of some social factors. In K. Lomotey (Ed.), *Going to school: The African-American experience* (pp.103 - 112). Albany: State University of New York Press.

Hernstein, R. J., & Murray, C. (1994). *The bell curve: Intelligence and class structure in American life*. New York: Free Press.

Hess, M. (1993). "Why do I have to read?": Multiplying perspectives through peer response. *English Education*, 25(3), 148-156.

Hollins, E. (1992). The Marva Collins story revisited: Implications for regular classroom instruction. *Journal of Teacher Education*, 33(1), 37-40.

Irvine, J. J. (1990a). *Black students and school failure: Politics, practices and prescriptions*. Westport, CT: Greenwood Press.

Irvine, J. (1990b). From plantation to school house; The rise and decline of black women teachers. *Humanity and Society*. 14(3), 244-256.

Jensen, A R. (1969). How much can we boost I.Q. and scholastic achievement? *Harvard Educational Review*, 39, 1-23.

King, S. H. (1993). The limited presence of African-American teachers. *Review of Educational Research*: 63(2), 115-149.

Ladson-Billings, G. (1992). Reading between the lines and beyond the pages: A culturally relevant approach to literacy teaching. *Theory into Practice*: 31(4), 312-320.

Ladson-Billings, G. (1994). *The Dreamkeepers: Successful Teachers of African American Children*. San Francisco: Jossey-Bass.

Ladson-Billings, G. (1995). Toward a theory of culturally relevant pedagogy. *American Educational Research Journal*, 32(3), 465-491.

Michael-Bandele, M. (1993). *Who's missing from the classroom: The need for minority teachers* (Trends and Issues Paper No. 9) Washington, DC: ERIC Clearinghouse on Teacher Education, American Association of Colleges for Teacher Education.

Miserandino, M. (1996). Children who do well in school: Individual differences in perceived competence and autonomy in above average children. *Journal of Educational Psychology*, 88(2), 230-211.

National Center for Educational Statistics. (1996a). *Digest of education statistics: 1996*. Washington, DC: U.S. Government Printing Office.

National Center for Educational Statistics. (1996b). *School and staffing survey, schools and staffing in the United States: A statistical profile, 1993-94*. Washington, DC: U.S. Government Printing Office.

National Center for Educational Statistics (1997). *The condition of education 1997*, Washington, D C: U.S. Government Printing Office.

Noddings, N. (1992). *The challenge to care in schools: An alternative approach to education*.

New York/London: Teachers College Press.

Oakes, J. (1985). *Keeping track: How schools structure inequality.* New Haven, CT: Yale University Press.

O'Day, J. A., & Smith, M. S. (1993). Systemic reform and educational opportunity. In S.H. Fuhrman (Ed.), *Designing coherent education policy: Improving the system* (pp. 250-312). San Francisco: Jossey -Bass.

Ogbu, J. (1987). A cultural discontinuities and schooling. *Anthropology and Education Quarterly*, 18(4), 290-307.

Pallas, A., Natriello, G., & McDill, E. (1989). The changing nature of the disadvantaged population. *Educational Researcher*, 18(5), 16-22.

Rist, R. (1970). Student social class and teacher expectations: The self-fulfilling prophecy in ghetto education. *Harvard Educational Review*, 40(3), 411-451.

Sarason, S. (1990). *The predictable failure of educational reform.* San Francisco: Jossey-Bass.

Seidman, I. E. (1991). *Interviewing as qualitative research.* New York: Teacher College, Columbia University.

Senecal, C. (1995). Self regulation and academic procrastination. *Journal of Social Psychology*, 135(5): 607-619.

Smitherman, G. (1977). *Talkin' and testifying.* Boston: Houghton Mifflin.

Tyack, D. (1990). Restructuring in historical perspective: Tinkering toward Utopia. *Teachers College Record*, 192(2), 170-191.

Villegas, A. (1991). *Culturally responsive pedagogy for the 1990s and beyond. Trends and Issues* (Paper No. 6). Washington, D C: ERIC Clearinghouse on Teacher Education.

Villegas, A. (1997). Increasing the racial and ethnic diversity in the US teaching force. In B. Biddle, T. Good, & I. Goodson (Eds.), *International handbook on teachers and teaching* (pp. 297 - 335). Dordrecht: Kluwer.

Weis, L., & Fine, M. (Eds). (1993). *Beyond silenced voices: Class, race and gender in the United States schools.* New York: State University of New York Press.

Werner, E., & Smith, R. (1989). *Vulnerable but invincible: A longitudinal study of resilient children and youth.* New York: Adams, Bannister, and Cox.

Wood, F. H., & Thompson, S. R. (1993). Assumptions about staff development based on research and best practice. *Journal of Staff Development*, 7(1), 52-66.

Zeichner, K. (1993). *Educating teachers for cultural diversity.* East Lansing, MI: National Center for Research on Teacher Learning.

9

African-American Student Success in Independent Schools: A Model of Family, School, and Peer Influences

ROBERT COOPER
AMANDA DATNOW
Johns Hopkins University

This chapter examines survey and interview data collected from African-American students in 15 independent schools in Baltimore to analyze the relative importance of family, peers, and the school in influencing students' school success, defined as college enrollment. The data presented in this chapter show that despite the culture shock experienced by many African-American students when they first enter these institutions, many of them have developed a strong network of support to overcome the unique academic, social, emotional, and psychological challenges they encounter in these environments. A combination of family, peer group, and school factors help these students to be both academically and socially successful. This chapter reports data that explain the contribution of each of these factors in the success of African-American students at elite, independent schools.

Numerous studies and national reports have documented the continuous decline of public education, particularly in urban areas. This decline has caused many African-American parents in urban centers to seek alternative educational options for their children. Historically, the alternatives to public education for African-American students have been severely limited. Prior to the 1960s, the attendance of African-American students at some of the nation's most elite independent schools was prohibited. Today, however, large numbers of African-American students are taking advantage of private school education. Many attend parochial schools, and an increasing number of African-Americans are enrolling in elite independent schools (Datnow & Cooper, chap. 10, this volume). These schools offer some advantages: higher expectations, a wealth of resources, and higher achievement and college attendance rates (Coleman & Hoffer, 1987). However, for many African-American students, these schools also pose a unique set of academic and social challenges.

Some African-American students enter these environments with less academic preparation than their majority counterparts. This lack of preparation often stems from the limited resources and lower expectations that characterize the schools they previously attended (Datnow & Cooper, 1996). This is contrary to the conclusion drawn by some of their classmates, who believe that African-American students' poor preparation stems from their limited intellectual capabilities. This misperception contributes to the difficulties faced by some African-American students in independent schools. On the one hand, they acknowledge a gap in their knowledge base and, in some cases, work twice as hard to compensate for that gap. On the other hand, for certain students, the gap is so wide in their knowledge base that although they work twice as hard as their fellow classmates, it takes several years before their hard work becomes evident in their academic performance (Datnow & Cooper, 1996).

Furthermore, African-American students represent a racial, and sometimes social class, background that is different from that of the majority of the school's population. Consequently, the normal pressures on young adolescents to fit in with their peers are heightened. Common adolescent issues such as fashion, music, and relationships all take on greater importance for African-American students in independent schools. Students struggle with questions of "acting White" when they adopt the culture and values dominant at the institution in which they spend at least one third of their waking hours. They face being considered wanna-bes by their peers if they develop close relationships with classmates outside their race. Moreover, African-American students face being called sellouts by family members and friends if they fail to maintain close ties with the youth in their neighborhoods. The social pressures on these young people are enormous (Datnow & Cooper, 1997).

The unique challenges that African-American students encounter in the independent school environment pose several interesting research questions: What factors lead to the resiliency of African-American students in this environment? What is the connection between these factors? In an earlier paper (Datnow & Cooper, 1997), we argued that despite the culture shock experienced by many African-American students when they first enter these institutions, many of them develop strong peer networks to overcome the unique academic, social, and emotional challenges they encounter. Based on data collected during the first 2 years of a 3-year longitudinal study of the Baltimore Educational Scholarship Trust (BEST),[1] this chapter discusses how peer networks, family members, and school support help to explain the academic and social success of African-American students in elite independent schools. Using both qualitative and quantitative data, this chapter seeks to enhance understanding of the overlapping, as well as important individual, contributions of family, school, and peer group in the resiliency of African-American students in elite independent schools.

Three Spheres of Influence Promoting Academic Success

We hypothesize that there are three major spheres of influence that contribute to the resiliency and success of African-Americans students in independent schools: family support and involvement; school structures, climate, and relationships; and peer support networks. Of the three spheres, the influence of the family is perhaps the greatest in the development of resilience among African-American students in the independent school environment.

Although it is widely accepted that family involvement can greatly influence the development and educational achievement of students, the specific family behaviors that enhance school performance are not well understood (Dornbusch, Ritter, Mont-Reynaud, & Chen, 1990). Some research concludes that a family's ability to stimulate, reinforce, and encourage high expectations contributes to student success (Clark, 1983). Other findings underscore the contributions of parental values and attitudes (Sewell & Shah, 1968), and yet others conclude that parental involvement in the school is the most important factor (Lightfoot, 1978). Despite the relatively limited understanding of the ways in which families are important in the schooling process, there is a growing body of research that confirms that family involvement has a critical influence on student achievement, motivation, and other educational outcomes (Epstein & Connors, 1995; Greenwood & Hickman, 1991; Hoover-Dempsey & Sandler, 1995).

For African-American students in predominantly White independent schools, one of the most important ways a family can be involved in the schooling process is by preparing the students to deal with his or her doubly marginalized status at the independent school (Cookson & Persell, 1985).

---

[1]BEST helps to place and fund economically disadvantaged, academically talented African-American students from the Baltimore metropolitan area in 20 local independent schools. The program works with approximately 600 families annually.

Whereas some families confront the issues of race and class differences explicitly, others choose a more subtle approach. However, given the historical legacy of exclusion in independent schools and the fact that exclusion still affects the prevailing climate at these schools today, research suggests that these issues should be confronted openly (Datnow & Cooper, 1996).

Open dialogue regarding racism and classism are critical for African-American students in the independent school environment because despite extensive civil rights efforts, true integration in American society, and to an even lesser degree in independent schools, has yet to be realized. Consequently, American society remains stratified by both race and class (Cooper & Williams, 1998). Research argues that given these social conditions, African-American children must develop a positive sense of ethnic identity to be successful (Boykin, 1968; Johnson, 1981). In a society where being Black has negative connotations and consequences (Peters, 1981), it is important that African-American children see themselves as competent in academic and social circles, and able to enter and graduate college.

The Black church is a social institution in American society where African-American youngsters are given the opportunity to feel successful and valued. In the African-American community, the church has historically been the place where children, regardless of their family background or intellectual ability, are socialized to believe in their God, their family, and themselves (Pattillo-McCoy, 1998). In the religious community, education is seen as the great emancipator and as a vehicle for upward mobility (Allen, 1986; Landry, 1987). From a young age, children are told of the importance of doing well in school. Consequently, the Black church is structured to provide individuals with experiences that are associated with academic achievement: moral lessons (Smith, 1976), social skills and supportive peer networks (Boyd-Franklin, 1989; Hopson & Hopson, 1990), and positive role models (Lincoln & Mamiya, 1990). Contrary to expectations, a recent study found that where a child grows up has no effect on his or her religious socialization (Brown & Lawrence, 1991). Brown concluded that African-American families' ties to the church remain strong whether they live in an urban center, a suburb, or a rural area. Given its historical and contemporary role in the socialization of African-American youth, the Black church can be conceived as an extension of the Black family.

The second sphere of influence in the resilience of African-American students in the independent school environment is the independent school itself. Research suggests that African-Americans look to nonpublic schools because such schools provide a smaller student-teacher ratio, a greater sense of caring, and a higher quality education (Arnez & Jones-Wilson, 1988). Studies indicate that, with superior resources, individualized attention, enhanced nurturing, and somewhat of a shelter from drugs and negative peer pressure, African-American students in private schools achieve at higher levels than do African American students in other school environments (Torry, 1992). Because students spend more waking time in school than anywhere else, including with their families, where students attend school is critical in the development of a positive academic trajectory (Eccles & Harold, 1993).

To carry out their role effectively, predominantly White independent schools have a dual task. They must provide African-American students with a high-quality education in an environment that historically has not respected the scholarship of African-Americans. They also must create an institutional culture that supports the development of a positive racial and cultural identity among African-American students.

The third sphere that promotes the development of resiliency among African-American students in predominantly White independent schools is the relationship students develop with one another. Research repeatedly demonstrates the connections between peer group association and academic performance (Green, Forehand, Beck, & Vosk, 1980). Research suggests that academic performance can be both positively and negatively affected by peer group association, depending on the dominant value within the peer group (Brown, Lohr & McClanahan, 1986; Roberts & Petersen, 1992).

In one of the most well-cited research studies to look at African-American students and peer group influence, Fordham and Ogbu (1986) suggested that many African-American students, responding to the systematic exclusion of African-Americans in the political, social, economic, and educational systems of the larger society, develop an oppositional social identity. They maintain that African-American students refrain from displaying certain behaviors or engaging in certain activities because they characterize White culture. In their study, academic success was viewed as "White people's prerogative" and striving for success in school was viewed as "acting White". Consequently, Fordham and Ogbu maintained, African-American students, for fear of betraying the collective group identity, resisted or opposed the idea of achieving success in their academic pursuits.

In contrast to Fordham and Ogbu, Mehan, Villavueva, Huberman, and Lintz (1996) in a detracking program found that the African-American students in their study were able to confirm their cultural identity while simultaneously recognizing the importance of academic achievement. This study presented data suggesting that the academic ideology of African-American students in the study was neither oppositional nor conformist. Instead of succumbing to the tensions between academic success and the oppositional demands of some of their peers, the African-American students in the study formed new, academically oriented peer groups that also promoted a respect for cultural maintenance (Datnow & Cooper, 1997).

As the just-mentioned literature suggests, each sphere has embedded within it a socialization process by which students come to understand the importance of success in school. Socialization in this context is defined as the process of change or development that occurs as a result of a student's exposure and interactions (Richardson, 1981). Although the relative importance of these socializing agents may change over time, this chapter reports findings that suggest the family, school, and peer group together influence African-American adolescents' success in elite, predominantly White independent schools.

METHODOLOGY

The data presented are both qualitative and quantitative. The quantitative data were derived from a survey mailed out in spring 1996 and 1997 to 11th- and 12th-grade African-American students who attended one of the 20 BEST member independent schools. The 31 returned surveys represent a response rate of approximately 46%.[2] Survey respondents represented 12 schools. Thirty-nine percent of respondents were male, and 61% were female. Forty-two percent of respondents were juniors and 58% were graduating seniors. The mean and standard deviation of the students' grade point averages were 3.2 and .41, respectively, on a 4.0 scale. The range was from 2.3 to 3.9.

The qualitative data were derived from interviews with 42 students in eight different BEST member independent schools. Twenty-eight of the students interviewed were seniors; 17 of these also completed the survey. Interviews were conducted in fall 1995 and spring 1996. With a few exceptions, most of the students interviewed had been enrolled in an independent school for 2 or more years and were in the 10th, 11th, or 12th grade. The semistructured interviews lasted an average of 1 hr. All the interviews were taped and later transcribed.

---

[2]The modest return rate is primarily a function of the timing of the surveys. Surveys were sent to the homes of graduated seniors, many of whom had already relocated to attend college. However, the demographic profile of survey respondents suggests that the sample is representative of the 67 BEST students who graduated in 1996 and 1997.

THE AFRICAN-AMERICAN STUDENT EXPERIENCE IN INDEPENDENT SCHOOLS

Research suggests that independent schools are difficult places for African-American students to feel welcome and fit in (Brookins, 1988; Zweigenhaft & Domhoff, 1991). Consistent with these research findings, students who returned the survey, as well as those interviewed, reported having difficulty acclimating to the independent school environment. Sixty-one percent of the survey respondents reported strong feelings of alienation, 39% reported a lack of belonging, and 35% indicated that they had some difficulty fitting in and often felt like "outsiders within" (Datnow & Cooper, 1997).

Similarly, our interview data indicated that many African-American students felt marginalized by race. David, a sophomore at Lake School[3] said, "Sometimes you might not always feel like you belong...you don't always feel a part of things. [At lunch] you will see all the Blacks sitting together and all the Whites sitting together." This is a particularly common experience for African-American students in the independent school environment with more than three or four students in their cohort. David went on to say that he and his fellow African-American classmates were not surprised by the segregation and isolation they felt because before entering high school they had been forewarned by upper grade students that the dynamics between African-American students and their White classmates changed in high school. They were told, "Don't expect to have the same close friends, don't expect to go to the same parties, don't expect to be as close. . . you become different." Echoing this sentiment was Mary, a student at Orwell School. Mary shared a similar experience and stated that "In the sixth grade, I remember when I came, everyone was just a happy-go-lucky family, and they wanted me to be the new Black kid in the family." However, Mary observed that relationships between Black and White students changed dramatically by high school.

Although racial differences are far more salient on a daily basis for African-American students in independent schools, differences in social class are also a source of much frustration. Although 71% of students who returned the survey reported that they were middle to high income when compared to other families in the greater Baltimore area, 74% considered themselves low income when compared to their classmates at school. Despite the fact that the majority of students indicated that they lived in a two-parent household,

---

[3]To maintain confidentiality, pseudonyms are used for the schools and participants in the study.

students still felt that they had fewer financial resources at their disposal than did their classmates. Although the African-American students surveyed in these schools were BEST students and received some financial assistance, not all African-American students in the participating schools were BEST students and not all African-American students received large financial aid awards.

Interestingly, many of the BEST students in these schools came from highly educated families who made sacrifices to send their children to these schools. Fifty-three percent of the students surveyed reported that their fathers had bachelor of arts degrees, and 20% reported that their fathers had advanced degrees. Furthermore, 61% of the students indicated that their mothers had bachelor of arts degrees, and 36% indicated that their mothers had advanced degrees. Despite the presence of a middle-class African-American student population at most of these schools, our interview data indicated that there was a strong misperception by White students that all African-American students were poor and were on financial aid. Although the reality of being poor and on financial assistance is painful for many of the African-American students to whom it applies, the stigma and connotations attached to it are even more hurtful to the African-American student community at large, reinforcing students' feelings of isolation. Moreover, the perpetuation of this stereotype may create a false sense of entitlement among the White students at these schools.

As shown in Fig. 9.1, despite the difficulties African-American students experienced acclimating to their schooling environments, some demonstrated great resiliency and maintained a strong positive sense of themselves. Ninety-one percent of the students who returned the survey indicated that they felt accomplished, and 96% reported that they felt academically competent.

The tenacity and persistence of African-American students in these environments facilitated the fulfillment of one of their primary goals, enrollment in college. Ninety-seven percent of BEST graduates of the class of 1996 and 96% of the class of 1997 enrolled in a 4-year college or university immediately after graduation. With few exceptions, students indicated that their schooling experience at the independent school gave them the academic training necessary to be successful at institutions of higher learning. When asked about the major advantage of attending an independent school, one BEST student succinctly stated, "It's the college thing."

Participating schools reported that with college enrollment as a goal, many BEST students distinguished themselves by accruing special honors, awards, and academic distinctions. Fifty-five percent of BEST students achieved at least one special honor. These honors included being named to the dean's list or honor roll for high academic achievement, national merit commendations, athletic awards for the most valuable or most improved player, and special awards (often named after particular individuals) given by the school to students who are particularly distinguished for one reason or another. Over half of the BEST graduating seniors from the classes of 1996 and 1997 were distinguished by their ability to obtain awards and honors for their personal achievements and their contributions to their school communities.

Success in Independent Schools:
College Enrollment

This study used college enrollment as a measure of BEST students' academic success. Data reported by participating schools revealed that African-American students enrolled in colleges and universities at rates similar to those for the independent schools as a whole. In the class of 1996, of the BEST students who graduated, 18 enrolled in historically Black colleges

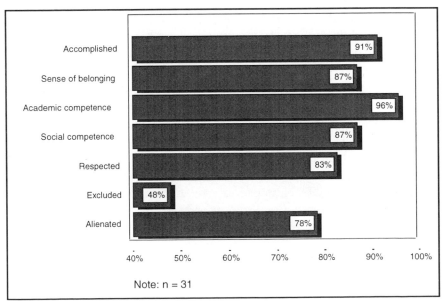

Fig. 9. 1: African-American student experience in Baltimore independent schools.

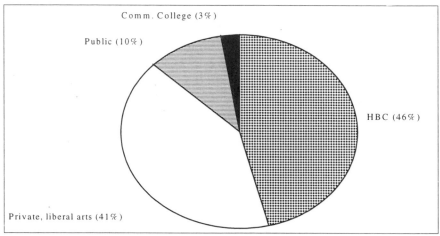

Fig. 9.2: BEST class of 1996 enrollment.

(HBCs), 16 enrolled in private liberal arts colleges, 4 enrolled in traditional public universities, and 1 enrolled in a community college[4] (see Fig. 9.2.; Datnow, Cooper, & Stringfield, 1997).

In the class of 1997, of the 28 BEST students who graduated from independent schools, nearly all attended 4-year colleges and universities. Six (6) attended HBCs, 15 attended private liberal arts colleges, 4 attended traditional public universities, 2 attended military universities (the U.S. Naval Academy), and 1 did not enroll in college immediately after graduation (see Fig. 9.3).

As Figs. 9.2 and 9.3 show, HBCs were a popular choice among BEST students in 1996; however, the percentage of students attending HBCs dropped by half for the class of 1997. Clearly, many BEST students chose to attend college in a predominantly Black setting, a departure from their independent school experience. Students in the class of 1997 were more likely to choose private liberal arts colleges and public universities than were those in the class of 1996. Interestingly, relatively few students in either class chose to attend traditional public universities. This may be a reflection of their positive experience in private school settings.

Research has shown that students from independent schools attend the

---

[4]Note that some of the HBCs that BEST students have chosen to attend are in fact public, such as Howard University. However, for the purposes of this analysis, public HBCs were counted as HBCs to distinguish them from traditional public state universities such as the University of Maryland and the University of North Carolina.

nation's most prestigious and selective colleges and universities at a much higher rate than do students from public schools (Cookson & Persell, 1985). For this reason, we looked into whether the BEST graduates were attending colleges considered to be highly selective. Using selectivity ratings from the *Fiske Guide to Colleges* (Fiske, 1998), we found that 33% of the BEST graduates from the class of 1996 and 25% of the BEST graduates from 1997 enrolled in colleges and universities that admit less than 50% of their applicants, including Williams College, the University of Pennsylvania, Spelman College, Johns Hopkins University, Duke University, Morehouse College, the U.S. Naval Academy, Columbia University, Notre Dame, Emory University, and the University of North Carolina-Chapel Hill.

Supports Fostering Resiliency and Success

Our research suggests that three spheres of influence work together to create resiliency and school success, here defined as college enrollment, among African-American students in independent schools. The presence of such a network helps students cope with the contentious realities of the independent school.

Sphere 1: Family Support/Involvement. Seventy-five percent of the students in our survey indicated that their families were involved in their education. The kinds of involvement discussed by the respondents included

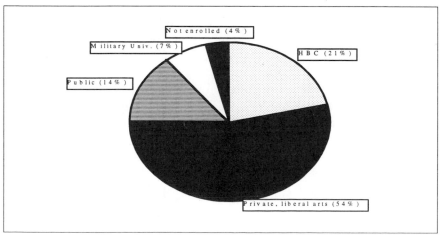

Fig. 9. 3: BEST class of 1997 enrollment.

everything from assistance with homework to assistance in the college selection process. Fifty-eight percent of the students stated that their fathers were important to their success in school. Ninety percent of the students indicated that their mothers were important. One student talked about the strong support from his mother, who was a single parent. He stated:

> My mother's really trying to keep me focused because my brother's in the Navy, and he's not always there to give me that extra push, so my mother's there. You know she's being my brother, my mother and my father, my friend, my best buddy. She's trying to keep me straight so that I don't go off and get off track.

Many students discussed the importance of their families in their school success. They discussed the fact that they felt obligated to do well in school because their parents made sacrifices for them to take advantage of the independent school experience. This appears to function differently for White students in this environment. According to the students we interviewed, White students expressed a sense of entitlement to a good education, whereas African-American students felt a sense of indebtedness to their parents, who had sacrificed to provide them excellent educational opportunities. As a student at Lake School stated, "I don't skip class because of my parents. . . . They'll get to me." He stated that his parents' aspirations for him were "getting a good job and...staying out of trouble. Just being a good person. . . . That's what they stress."

The concept that family extends beyond the traditional nuclear family is one of the important characteristics of the African-American community. In many instances, particularly in urban areas, "family" is a term used to describe relationships with grandparents, aunts, uncles, and play relatives. Thirty percent of the students in the survey reported that family members outside the nucleus also were essential to their current success in school. This illustrates the significant influence that families have on the success of students. Compared to other socializing influences, such as the media or public opinion, arguably the family has the most lasting impact on a child's competencies (Harrison, Wilson, Pine, Chan, & Buriel, 1990).

In the African-American community, one of the most important and consistent aspects of family socialization is church attendance and involvement. To the extent that young people are involved in church or religious activities, they are socialized to a certain world view. Often a student's belief system regarding social and political issues such as abortion, sex, and sexual orientation is developed in the church. Attitudes, opinions and behaviors are developed and influenced by involvement in a social institution that promotes a particular value system (Sanders, 1998; Sanders & Herting, chap. 7, this volume).

Many of the students who were interviewed discussed the importance of church involvement in their success in school. Obviously, church participation was more central for some students than for others. Illustrating the importance of church participation in the development of resiliency among African-American students, one student stated "I believe in God. I believe He's a centerpiece in everything that I do. . . . It helps me to do the right thing...staying out of trouble." We found it significant that 72% of the students in the survey considered themselves religious or spiritual people and 53% of them believed it was important to attend church on a weekly basis. This reinforces our interview data, which suggest that church is an important influence and that value systems promoted through religious activities operate to socialize students' toward school success.

Sphere 2: School Structures, Climate, and Relationships. African-American students who attend elite independent schools undergo a unique experience. It has been argued that African-American students are caught between two cultures (Cookson & Persell, 1991). To be effective with and sensitive to these students, schools must have an explicit commitment to understanding and valuing their unique experiences and perspectives (Pomales, 1986). In our research, we have identified four ways in which independent schools attempt to make their institutions more receptive to African-American students (Datnow & Cooper, chap. 10, this volume), and, in so doing, support their school success.

We found that one of the most important ways independent schools created a positive atmosphere for African-American students was by establishing an explicit institutional commitment to racial diversity. Interviews and observations indicated that schools that embraced diversity and dealt openly with issues of race tended to be places where students felt more comfortable expressing their own racial identity. African-American students expressed greater feelings of belonging and a sense of community in those schools where the awareness of diversity issues was evident early in the admissions process.

Several admissions directors reported asking candid questions about race in interviews (see Datnow & Cooper, chap. 10, this volume). These questions signaled to African-American students and their families that the school understood the unique challenges faced by African-American students in these types of school environments. Conversely, at the schools we visited where faculty and staff took a "color-blind" approach to students, we documented more examples of unhappiness among African-American students. Overall, 74% of the students who responded to the survey indicated that the climate at their school was comfortable, 83% found their school climate friendly, and 73% found their school climate welcoming to their families.

One of the most visible signs of the integration of African-American students into the life and culture of the school was their participation, and also their involvement in leadership roles in school-sponsored clubs and organizations. In fact, the founders of the A Better Chance program, which, like BEST, helps to place and fund African-American students in elite college preparatory schools, made "preparation for future leadership" one of the program's expressed goals for students (Johnson & Anderson, 1992). Creating school environments where African-American students desired to be leaders in their school communities and were accepted by their peers as such was perhaps one of the greatest challenges in making independent schools comfortable and supportive for African-American students.

To the credit of the independent school community and of the students themselves, survey results indicated that some BEST students were engaged in a wide variety of activities ranging from varsity athletics, school plays, dance troupes, and horseback riding to student government, newspaper, yearbook, forensics clubs, and cultural awareness clubs. The mean number of activities the BEST students were involved in during their high school careers was 5.3; the range was from 1 to 18. Ninety percent of the BEST students who returned surveys were involved in two or more school activities. The data also revealed that 42% of the BEST students surveyed were involved in at least one leadership activity. Sixteen percent of these students were engaged in three or more leadership roles in their schools. Leadership activities included holding offices in student government (e.g., student body or class president, class treasurer), acting as official mentors for younger students, serving as officers in student clubs, and leading team sports.

The second way in which independent schools demonstrated their commitment to addressing the needs of African-American students was by providing students with role models with whom to share common life experiences. With many of the independent schools having faculties that were less than 1% African-American, the entire independent school community acknowledged this as a problem. Many schools realized that students benefit from role models with whom they can identify. Even though most students surveyed lacked African-American role models on campus,

73% of these students reported that they felt that their teachers respected African American students. More importantly, 87% of these students indicated that they felt that their teachers cared about them. Although these schools have not been successful in hiring a diverse faculty, both survey results and interview data indicated that at least some have been successful in hiring people who care about all students.

Third, to make the social adjustment to independent schools easier for African-American students, several of the schools tried to generate a "critical mass" of African-American students at each grade level. This was important, given that 53% of the students in the survey reported that their closest friend attended their school and was of the same ethnicity. To be nurturing environments for African-American students, independent schools must continue to find ways to recruit, maintain, and graduate African-American students. As one admissions director explained, "To have one [African-American student] in the sixth grade is not enough. There is power in numbers. Kids should not have to be pioneers." Another stated that "students should have others that they can bond with." However, most were unsure how many African-American students are needed to create a comfortable learning environment for all students.

The final way, according to our data, in which independent schools were trying to embrace African-American students was through the formation of Black student associations. Black student associations appeared to greatly affect the resiliency of African-American students. Eighty-nine percent of the students in the survey reported that having a Black student organization was important at their schools. Although the structure, purpose, importance, and name of these organizations varied across schools, all of these organizations served as a "safe space" for African-American students to explore, discuss and celebrate African-American history and culture (Datnow & Cooper, chap. 10, this volume).

One of the questions confronting independent schools is how to accommodate diversity while still maintaining cohesion within the school community. The school personnel we spoke with all had grappled with this issue, and they shared their concerns with us. One admissions director we spoke with commented that although admitting BEST students (and African-American students in general) was the first step in achieving diversity, there were many more steps schools must take before an authentic multicultural environment could exist.

Sphere 3: Peer Networks. In an earlier analysis of our data, we found that within the context of elite, independent schools, African-American students and their peers placed a high value on academic achievement and hard work (Datnow & Cooper, 1997). Seventy-one percent of the students surveyed indicated that the peers they studied with were academically successful. We also found that the students in our study identified their African-American peer group networks, both formal and informal, as one of the most important factors in helping them to cope in predominantly White school environments and helping to ease their feelings of alienation and isolation. Seventy-two percent of the respondents to the survey reported that their school peers were an important factor in their school success. Additionally, we found that African-American peer networks functioned to simultaneously foster school success and provide a space for students to reaffirm their racial identity. Seventy-two percent of the students in the survey indicated that their ethnic identity was important to their identity at school.

In terms of academic identity, one of the most striking features of the peer networks among African-American students was that these networks encouraged students to be smart, without feeling as though they had to sell out or act White. Our qualitative data suggested that promotion of strong academic identities began as early as the first week of school. David, a sophomore at one of the BEST member schools, indicated that one of the most significant differences in his schooling experience at the independent school was that it was okay to be smart. He stated that "in my other school, it was not really cool to be smart, you know. And here, if you're not smart, you are not cool – like the complete opposite."

Older students often served as role models for the new students. Many students spoke of how older students took them under their wing to acclimate them to the academic and social demands of the school. Our research indicated that for many students in the independent school environment, being cool included being academically successful. Black students who were high achieving were revered by their peers and even regarded as role models. Therefore, Black peer group members were socialized toward academic excellence.

CONCLUSION

This chapter attempts to contribute to a growing body of literature about African-American student experiences in different school settings. It used survey and interview data to give insight into the complex systems of support used by African-American students in elite independent schools to achieve success, as measured by college enrollment. The primary findings of this study suggest that the Black family, including the Black church, the school, and the peer group, influenced the academic success of African-American adolescents in the study.

By exploring African-American students' strategies for success in environments that have been characterized as unwelcoming, educators can design new plans and approaches for better educational environments for African-American students in other school settings. This study suggests that these approaches must recognize the distinct, but overlapping facets of each of the spheres of socialization discussed here. Strategies must be developed to ensure that families are supported by the school and larger community in providing students with the guidance and encouragement required for their resilience and school success. Similarly, families and schools must help students, especially adolescents, to select appropriate peer groups that can support and enhance their academic and social growth and development. Finally, strategies to improve the educational outcomes of African-American students must include ways for schools to work more closely with researchers, educators, families, and communities to create school environments that promote the development of positive academic and racial self-concepts for all students. Such collaborative efforts among families, schools, and communities may provide more students with the support they need to achieve their full potential in both public and private educational institutions.

REFERENCES

Allen, W. (1986). *Gender and campus race differences in Black student academic performance, racial attitude and college satisfaction.* Atlanta, GA: Southern Education Foundation.

Arnez, N. L., & Jones-Wilson, F. C. (1988). A descriptive survey of Black parents in the Greater Washington, D.C., area who chose to send their children to nonpublic schools. In D. T. Slaughter & D. J. Johnson (Eds.), *Visible now: Blacks in private schools* (pp. 209-224). New York: Greenwood.

Boyd-Franklin, N. (1989). *Black families in therapy: A multisystems approach.* New York: Gilford.

Boykin, A. (1968). The triple quandary and the schooling of Afro American children. In U. Neisser (Ed.), *The school achievement of minority children: New perspectives.* Hillsdale, NJ: Lawrence Erlbaum Associates.

Brookins, G. (1988). Making the honor roll: A Black parent's perspective on private education. In D. Slaughter & D. Johnson (Eds.), *Visible now: Blacks in private schools.* (pp. 12-20). Westport, CT: Greenwood.

Brown, B. B., Lohr, M. J., & McClanahan, E. L. (1986). Early adolescents' perceptions of peer pressure. *Journal of Early Adolescence,* 6, 139-154.

Brown, D., & Lawrence, G. (1991). Religious socialization and educational attainment among African-Americans: An empirical assessment. *Journal of Negro Education*, 60(3), 411- 426.

Clark, R. (1983). *Family life and school achievement: Why poor Black children succeed or fail.* Chicago: University of Chicago Press.

Coleman, J., & Hoffer, T. (1987). *Public and private high schools.* New York: Basic Books.

Cookson, P. W., & Persell, C. H. (1985). *Preparing for power: American elite boarding schools.* New York: Basic Books.

Cookson, P. W., & Persell, C. H. (1991). Race and class in America's elite boarding schools: African-Americans as the outsiders within. *Journal of Negro Education*, 60(2), 219-228.

Cooper, R., & Williams, E. (1998). *The salience of race in American education.* Manuscript submitted for publication.

Datnow, A., & Cooper, R. (1996, April). *Coping mechanisms that lead to success for African American students in elite private schools.* Paper presented at the annual meeting of the American Sociological Association, New York.

Datnow, A., & Cooper, R. (1997). Peer networks of African-American students in independent schools: Affirming academic success and racial identity. *Journal of Negro Education*, 66(1), 1-17.

Datnow, A., Cooper, R., & Stringfield, S. (1997). *BEST second year report.* Baltimore: Johns Hopkins University, Center for Social Organization of Schools.

Dornbusch, S. M., Ritter, P. L, Mont-Reynaud, R., & Chen, Z. (1990). Family decision making and academic performance in a diverse high school population. *Journal of Adolescent Research*, 5(2), 143-160.

Eccles, J. & Harold, R. (1993). Parents - school involvement during the early adolescent years. *Teachers College Record*, 94(3), 567 - 587.

Epstein, J. L., & Connors, L. J. (1995). School and family partnerships in the middle grades. In B. Rutherford (Ed.), *Creating school/family partnerships* (pp.137-166). Columbus, OH: National Middle School Association.

Fiske, E. B. (1998). *The Fiske guide to colleges.* New York: Random House.

Fordham, S., & Ogbu, J. (1986). African American students' school success: Coping with the burden of "acting White." *Urban Review*, 18(3), 176-206.

Green, K., Forehand, R., Beck, S., & Vosk, B. (1980). Person - environment congruence as a predictor of adolescent health and behavioral problems. *American Journal of Community Psychology*, 10, 511-526.

Greenwood, G. E., & Hickman, C. W. (1991). Research and practice in parent involvement: Implications for teacher education. *Elementary School Journal*, 91, 279-288.

Harrison, A. O, Wilson, M. N., Pine, C. J., Chan, S. Q., & Buriel, R. (1990). Family ecologies of ethnic minority children. *Child Development*, 53, 87-97.

Hoover-Dempsey, K. V., & Sandler, H. M. (1995). Parental involvement in children's education: Why does it make a difference? *Teacher College Record*, 97 (2), 310-331.

Hopson, D. A., & Hopson, D. S. (1990*). Different and wonderful: Raising Black children in a race-conscious society.* New York: Prentice - Hall.

Johnson, R. (1981). The Black family and Black community development. *Journal of Black Psychology*, 8, 35-52.

Johnson, S., & Anderson, D. K. (1992). Legacies and lessons from independent schools. *Journal of Negro Education*, 61(2), 121-124.

Landry, B. (1987). *The new Black middle class.* Berkeley: University of California Press.

Lightfoot, S. L. (1978). *Worlds apart: Relationship between family and schools.* New York: Basic Books.

Lincoln, C. E., & Mamiya, L. (1990). *The Black church in the African-American experience.*

Durham, NC: Duke University Press.

Mehan, H., Villanueva, I., Huberman, M , & Lintz, A. (1996). *Constructing school success: The consequences of untracking low-achieving students.* Cambridge, UK: Cambridge University Press.

Pattillo-McCoy, P. (1998). Church culture as a strategy of action in the Black community. *American Sociological Review*, 63, 767-784.

Peters, M. (1981). Racial socialization of young Black children. In J. McAdoo (Ed.), *Black children: Social, educational and parental environments* (pp. 159-173). Newbury Park, CA: Sage.

Pomales, J. (1986). Effects of Black students' racial identity on perceptions of white counselors varying in cultural sensitivity. *Journal of Counseling Psychology*, 28, 120-157.

Richardson, B. (1981). *Racism and child rearing: A study of Black mothers.* Unpublished doctoral dissertation, Claremont Graduate School, Claremont, CA.

Roberts, L., & Petersen, A. C. (1992). The relationship between academic achievement and social self-image during early adolescence. *Journal of Early Adolescence*, 12(2), 197-219.

Sanders, M. G. (1998). The effects of school, family and community support on the academic achievement of African-American adolescents. *Urban Education*, 33(3), 385-409.

Sewell, W., & Shah, V. P. (1968). Parents' education and children's educational aspirations and achievement. *American Sociological Review*, 33(2), 191-209.

Smith, J. (1976). *Outstanding Black sermons.* Valley Forge, PA: Judson.

Torry, S. (1992, March 22). Public school - private school debate tugs emotions, purse strings. *The Washington Post*, p. B1.

Zweigenhaft, R., & Domhoff, G. (1991). *Blacks in White establishments.* New Haven, CT: Yale University Press.

10

Creating a Climate for Diversity? The Institutional Response of Predominantly White Independent Schools to African-American Students

AMANDA DATNOW
ROBERT COOPER
Johns Hopkins University

This chapter analyzes the institutional response of predominantly White, elite independent schools to African-American students. Using qualitative data collected in nine independent schools in Baltimore, this chapter shows that although these independent schools are making symbolic commitments to racial diversity, they vary in the degree to which they operationalize those commitments. The schools' climates for racial diversity impact African-American students' educational experiences, as students internalize the messages that are conveyed to them by the schools. This chapter illuminates the structures and cultures that exist within elite private schools, and suggests ways in which such schools can promote the success of African-American students.

Since the 1960s, African-American[1] students have been enrolling in predominantly White, elite independent schools in increasing numbers. Much of the increase in enrollment can be attributed to the efforts of a number of organizations, including A Better Chance, Prep for Prep, Black Student Fund, and the Baltimore Educational Scholarship Trust (BEST), that have initiated and maintained the presence and participation of African-American students in these schools known to prepare students for positions

---

[1] In this chapter, we alternate between the terms African-American and Black. This is because students in our study used both terms in referring to themselves.

of power and leadership (Cookson & Persell, 1985; Johnson & Anderson, 1992). Additionally, the majority of independent schools have enacted policies of nondiscrimination, and a growing number actively recruit minority students in their efforts to create more diverse student populations (Speede-Franklin, 1988).

Despite these efforts, research shows that these White, elite independent schools, with their history of racial exclusion, are often places where African-American students find it difficult to fit in (Brookins, 1988; Datnow & Cooper, 1997; Zweigenhaft & Domhoff, 1991). African-American students in such institutions are sometimes caught between two cultures and, consequently, are doubly marginalized. They often feel alienated from the culture of the school, and from their families and friends, particularly in boarding school environments (Cookson & Persell, 1991). Feelings of alienation also stem from the fact that African-American private school students have substantially fewer family economic resources relative to the school population as a whole (Schneider & Shouse, 1992). Research also suggests that African-American students may have weaker social relationships with their teachers than do other students in such schools, and that this lack of connection may affect their motivation and academic performance (Schneider & Shouse).

These findings suggest that the climate for racial diversity at predominately White, elite independent schools impacts African-American students' educational experiences, as students internalize the messages that are conveyed to them in their school environments. Yet, although schools often make symbolic commitments to racial diversity, they vary in the degree to which they operationalize those commitments. To shed greater light on the response of predominantly White, elite independent schools to African-American students, this chapter[2] uses qualitative interview data to explore the degree to which nine of these schools in Baltimore attempt to create positive climates for diversity. The data collection for this study took place in schools that are members of BEST, an organization that aims to increase the enrollment of African-American students in independent schools.

---

[2] This study was funded by the Abell Foundation in Baltimore, Maryland, as part of a larger evaluation of BEST. Support for the writing of this paper was also provided by a grant from the Office of Educational Research and Improvement, U.S. Department of Education. However, the opinions expressed are the authors' and do not necessarily represent the policies or positions of the funders.

An earlier version of this chapter was presented at the 1997 Annual Meeting of the American Educational Research Association in New York.

INSTITUTIONAL RESPONSES TO DIVERSITY

In the past 30 years, predominantly White independent schools have made significant gains in the area of student diversity. Prior to the 1960s, few of the nation's elite independent schools admitted students of color (Cookson & Persell, 1985). This historical legacy of exclusion undoubtedly affects the prevailing racial climate at these schools. Black students live with an awareness that their parents would not have been able to attend their school. Conversely, White students, who may be children of the school's alumni, often enjoy a privileged status.

Despite the gains in enrollment of Black students in elite independent schools, some argue that Black students at these schools are "token individuals" (Speede-Franklin, 1988). Speede-Franklin argued that recruitment efforts by independent schools in the period from 1955 to 1980 resulted from three basic motivations: (a) a moral imperative based on the idea of *noblesse oblige*; (b) beginning in the 1970s, IRS exemptions for compliance with racially nondiscriminatory policies; and (c) the need for a new student market when school enrollment levels dropped. As further evidence of Black "tokenism" at White, elite independent schools, the author noted that these schools still serve a very small number of Black students, even in cities where these students constitute the majority population (Speede-Franklin).

Regardless of why these schools seek to increase their Black student enrollment, research on Black students in private schools suggests that there are a series of factors that constitute positive institutional responses to diversity (Arnez & Jones-Wilson, 1988; Royal, 1988; Speede-Franklin, 1988). Much of this research focuses on specific actions schools can take to make their schools more comfortable, supportive environments for Black students. For example, Royal recommended that predominantly White independent schools institute support systems for Black students. This includes (a) providing counselors who are sensitive and aware of the needs of Black students; (b) offering academic support services to those in need, without assuming that all minority students require this; (c) providing the entire community with a sense of the history of the non-White population; and (d) actively recruiting faculty of color.

Royal (1988) argued that students of all races are at risk on private school campuses when the curriculum does not address the contributions of non-White ethnic groups, and when schools do not work actively to eliminate the intentional or unintentional perpetuation of stereotypes and racism on their campuses. Royal's conclusions are echoed by Arnez and Jones-Wilson

(1988), who argued that private school officials should consider including more about African-American culture and values in their courses and activities. Speede-Franklin (1988) also argued that "schools must articulate clearly their expectations of staff in promoting diversity, reducing prejudice, and creating an atmosphere of mutual respect" (p. 29).

The extant research on what predominantly White independent schools can do to better accommodate Black students takes a structural perspective, focusing on organizational or systemic changes that schools need to institute. Although these efforts are clearly important, it seems that a broader vision of institutional responses to diversity is also critical. Specifically, the focus must be not only on the structural aspects of an institution's response to diversity, but also on how members within settings socially construct those structures. Thus, a closer look at the sociocultural aspects of the institutions is needed to understand how multiple factors influence institutional responses to diversity.

Research on diversity in institutions of higher education provides insight into both the structural and the sociocultural realms (Hurtado, Milem, Allen, & Clayton-Pederson, 1996). Although this research does deal with a different educational level, the issues involved in diversifying predominantly White, elite colleges and high schools appear to be remarkably similar. Hurtado et al. reported that studies of structural diversity and its impact on students have resulted in three key findings. First, campuses that increase their racial/ethnic enrollments significantly improve the educational experiences of minority students (Hurtado et al.). Institutions that lack diversity often regard minority students as symbols, or as tokens, rather than individuals, and exaggerate intergroup differences (Kanter, 1977). Second, financial aid policies have a strong impact on the presence and persistence of minority students (Orfield, 1992). Finally, the representation faculty of color on campuses benefits students from their particular racial groups.

Hurtado et al. (1996) pointed out, however, that structural policies are inextricably linked to attitudes and practices. In a review of research on the psychological and behavioral dimensions of creating climates for diversity, the authors concluded that cross-group social interaction, discussions about race and diversity, attendance at racial awareness workshops, and enrollment in ethnic studies classes positively impact students' racial understanding. Moreover, they concluded that perceptions of a discriminatory environment and poor intergroup relations impact the success of both students of color and White students. They also reviewed findings of the importance of students receiving validating experiences. Students should not feel like a guest in someone else's house (Turner, 1994). They and their families must feel welcomed and as though they are a significant part of the school. Schools accomplish this both through the mission and values they convey and through the curriculum and programs they sponsor.

We bring this literature to bear as we discuss how predominantly White, elite independent schools create climates for diversity. First, however, we explain the research methods and cases under study.

METHODS

Overview of BEST

This chapter presents data collected in a 3-year study (1995-1998) of the BEST program. BEST is a program that helps to place and fund economically disadvantaged, academically talented African-American students from the Baltimore metropolitan area in 20 local independent schools. BEST recruits qualified applicants, counsels students and families in choosing independent schools, and shepherds them through the application process. Over 600 African-American families seek out BEST's services each year, applying for independent school admission at all grade levels. Approximately 70 new BEST students are enrolled in independent schools each year.

BEST exists within an interesting community context. For the White upper-middle class in Baltimore, it is almost a birthright to attend independent schools, as has been the case for generations. African-American students of all social classes in Baltimore have traditionally attended public schools, and only in the 1960s did the first Baltimore independent schools begin to accept African-American students. Moreover, in Baltimore, most students live in racially segregated neighborhoods and attend relatively segregated schools. Now, due to the efforts of BEST and the schools' own efforts at diversifying, independent schools are among the few sites in which Baltimore students of different racial groups attend school together.

Case Study Design

Case study methodology enables educational researchers to examine a contemporary phenomenon within its real-life context (Yin, 1989). In this study, we investigated the phenomenon of Black students currently attending elite independent schools through BEST. Case study research relies on a triangulation of multiple sources of evidence, including interviews, relevant documents, and observations to establish construct validity. In our study of BEST, we interviewed students, school staff, and parents. We conducted classroom observations, and we reviewed documents produced by each school and by BEST. Finally, case study methodology is the best strategy available for exploring situations in which the intervention being evaluated (i.e., BEST) has no clear, single set of outcomes (Yin).

As coprincipal investigators for this study, we conducted all of the data collection and analysis ourselves and did not employ the use of research assistants. Although there were only two of us, we were a diverse research team in terms of race, gender, and disciplinary background.

All school personnel interviews were conducted individually, while students were interviewed individually and in small groups. A total of 9 admissions directors, 3 school heads, and 42 African-American students in nine different schools were interviewed during the 1995-1996 and 1996-1997 school years. With the exception of a few, all of the students had been enrolled in independent schools for 2 or more years and were in the 10th through 12th grades. In most schools, we were able to interview the entire population of students that fit these criteria. We interviewed a total of 19 males and 23 females, ages 15-18. Of the total number of students interviewed, 37 were graduating seniors, ages 17 and 18.

In all interviews, we used semistructured interview protocols, asking open-ended questions of respondents. Interviews lasted an average of 1 hour, although many were longer. All of the interviews were taped and transcribed at the completion of each school site visit. To encourage participants to respond honestly to our questions, we promised them confidentiality throughout the study.

School Sample

This study, and case study research in general, employs replication, not sampling logic. Application of a statistical sampling logic is inappropriate for case study research in which the goal is to study both a phenomenon of interest and its context (Yin, 1989). For external validity, case studies rely on analytical rather than statistical generalizability, aiming toward generalization of results to a broader theory, and not to the larger universe. That is, cases (in this case, schools) are included because they are likely to produce either similar results or contrary results for predictable reasons, and not because they represent the entire set of available cases (Yin). We focused on a subset of schools to obtain a more indepth picture of what the independent school experience is like for BEST students.

We chose schools after reviewing the relevant literature in the field with regard to the factors that are likely to produce contrary results. Specifically, the nine independent schools where data were collected for this study include a variety of BEST member schools. Some of the nine schools are highly selective and others are moderately selective; some are single-sex, and others are coed; some have a religious affiliation, and others do not; and some of the schools are day schools, and others are boarding schools (see Table 10.1)[3].

All of these schools are members of the National Association of Independent Schools (NAIS) and the Association of Independent Maryland Schools. NAIS member schools are nonprofit, and tax exempt, and maintain fiscal independence from government and church entities. Each school is governed by a board of trustees and subscribes to a policy of nondiscrimination (Speede-Franklin, 1988).

The nine schools in this study are located in and around Baltimore. Although there are obvious size and architectural differences across schools, all of the campuses are physically beautiful, often serene, ideal environments for scholarly pursuits. Grounds are well-manicured and buildings are in excellent condition. All of the schools offer special facilities of some type or other; most have superb athletic and fine arts facilities, as well as high-tech libraries, and several even offer horse-riding facilities.

The schools in our sample range in size from a total enrollment of 180 to 945 students. All but two of the schools offer schooling in kindergarten (K), or pre-first, through Grade 12. The total percentage of African-American

Table 10.1: Sample of Schools*

School Name	Single Sex or Coed	Day or Boarding
The Franklin School	All boys	Day
Highlands School	All boys	Day
The Garland School	All girls	Day
The Brookline School	All girls	Day
Simmons Academy	All girls	Day
The Orwell School	Coed	Day and boarding
The Lake School	Coed	Day
The Harris School	Coed	Day
The Bennett School	All girls	Day and boarding

Note. Information on schools' selectivity and religious affiliation is not included to protect the anonymity and confidentiality of the schools.

---

[3]For purposes of confidentiality, pseudonyms are used for the schools and participants in the study.

students in these schools ranges from a high of approximately 15% to a low of 3%, and possibly lower. These numbers are slightly skewed in schools offering Grades K-12, because lower schools (K-5) tend to have fewer African-American students than do middle and upper schools (9-12).

The approximate annual tuition cost at these independent schools was $11,000 in 1996-1997. Although BEST does assist with the funding of some students, most of the financial aid that BEST students receive comes directly from the schools. Although the majority of BEST students receive financial assistance, a few do not. The average financial award to a BEST student is approximately $6,500, reflecting the fact that some students receive full financial aid and some receive much less than the average. Thus, our sample reflects students from a range of social class backgrounds.

Methods of Data Analysis

As Eisenhardt (1989) suggested, data analysis is the most difficult and least codified part of the case study process. Although there is flexibility, the goal of the analysis is to become intimately familiar with each case under study and with patterns across cases. Thus, in analyzing the interview data we have collected, we drew upon advice and methods detailed by several qualitative methodologists, including Miles and Huberman (1984), Yin (1989), and Strauss and Corbin (1990). Miles and Huberman outlined very specific methods for analyzing qualitative data acquired in a case study, including constructing a matrix of categories, placing evidence within these categories, and creating data displays. The ultimate goal of case study data analysis is to treat evidence fairly, to produce compelling conclusions, and to rule out alternative interpretations (Yin).

During case study data analysis, interview transcripts, field notes, and documents were coded and sorted into sections of a case report outline, forming case files for each school. Case files were prepared after each site visit and were used to guide future data collection. In the process of analysis, the data were brought into an ongoing conversation with our theoretical framework that brought together literature in education and sociology.

FINDINGS

An analysis of the interview and observational data collected at nine independent schools shows that creating a climate that promotes the success of African-American students depends on several factors, including (a) the institutional philosophy regarding the school's responsibility for educating African American students; (b) the alignment of admissions practices with the school's symbolic commitment to racial diversity; and (c) the degree to which the institutional structure and culture embrace and accept diversity. These factors combine to create what is, at one extreme, a school environment that is very supportive of African-American students and, at the other extreme, a school environment that is minimally supportive. Each of these factors is next discussed in detail.

The Institutional Philosophy Regarding the Education of African-American Students

All of the independent schools in this study voluntarily joined BEST, an organization that aims to increase the representation of African-American students in elite, predominantly White independent schools. By participating in BEST, the schools made at least a symbolic commitment to diversifying their school populations. Toward this goal, the major benefit of involvement in BEST for most schools is access to the African-American population in Baltimore. As one admissions director stated, "BEST is out in the community in places where we aren't." Another admissions director reiterated that "BEST is helping us recruit African-American students." Yet, another admissions director further explained the important purposes of BEST:

> It is wonderful that there's an organization that is trusted by the African-American community, not seen largely as robbing the schools of the talented students but rather providing another option for kids. That's something we can't do. An individual school cannot do that no matter who you have making the overtures. It needs to be more broad based than that and trusted.

To the contrary, one admissions director felt that her school attracts a Black population without BEST and that the school participates in BEST "because it is politically correct."

Several admissions directors felt that, in addition to serving the important function of recruitment of African-American students, BEST also serves as a clearinghouse or broker of independent schools for the African-American community. They applauded the fact that BEST provides information. An admissions director explained: "I feel like BEST is enormously helpful, in terms of just informing families about each step of the process, and helping families to really get a handle on what this whole independent school world is about."

Despite some difference of opinion among the nine independent school admissions directors, the key commonality among them was that they were all committed to increasing the representation of Black students at their schools. However, on close investigation, these efforts at diversifying meant different things at different schools. That is, the institutional philosophies regarding the need for diversity varied.

Some school administrators were able to articulate very strong philosophies of how the education of Black students fits in with their overall school mission. The head at the Brookline School, for example, stated that without diversification independent schools, with their histories of racial exclusion, "are in danger of becoming bastions of privilege." She explained:

> The founders of our school who were rebels and revolutionaries were also deeply bigoted people, about Jews and Blacks in particular. The history of integration at this school is one of passion and the commitment of individuals and of people in the community. There has been a long-standing commitment for making this a diverse community and a multicultural community.

She added: "I think to have more diversity is better for the institution. . . . Insofar as we represent the society we're in, the better we are." In sum, this school's commitment to Black students was based on a perceived need to reverse historical patterns of racial and ethnic discrimination, an interest in reflecting society at large, and a belief that independent schools should serve a racially and economically diverse student population. These beliefs were articulated by several admissions directors at other schools as well.

Although the majority of the schools in this study had prior histories of racial exclusion, there were a couple of exceptions. For example, the Harris School was founded "upon a notion of tolerance and respect for individuals." The admissions director explained:

> We were the first school to racially integrate in this city. We were started by a group of Jewish businessmen whose children were denied admission to all of our city's independent schools. So the school was really begun in response, and as an open community for children of any background.

The Lake School has also long maintained a commitment to diversity, and it admitted Black students shortly after the Harris School. The admissions director at the Lake School also articulated a philosophical commitment to admitting Black students and to making sure they are successful. He took a strong personal interest in the issues and concerns of Black students in predominantly White independent schools and was one of the founders of the organization that eventually became BEST. Clearly, the commitment to diversity at these schools has been long standing, and instead of reversing past legacies of exclusion, they were concerned with holding true to their original missions. In these schools, the question was not one of whether to be a racially diverse school, but rather of how the best climate for racial harmony could be achieved.

Some schools appeared to hold the philosophy that admission of Black students helped the White students have more of a "real life" education. For example, the director of admissions at the Franklin School said that the school had gained "wonderful things" from the presence of Black students. At times, the benefits of Black student representation were discussed in terms of how they would add value to the education of the majority White population at the school, not in terms of what the African-American students themselves would gain from an independent school education. Schools, thus, had varied perspectives on why diversity was important.

At these elite independent schools, administrative leadership provided important direction in terms of the schools' institutional commitment to diversity. Several of the schools in this study experienced a turnover in leadership, which often marked a shift toward diversity as a central goal. For example, the headmistress at Garland, new to the school 2 years before, was very forward thinking and had made some important changes at the school to support diversity. She began to offer financial aid to students in the lower grades, broadening the number of African-American applicants eligible for admission. In addition, the board of trustees at this school is unique. Its membership is reflective of the student body in terms of racial and ethnic diversity. This board recently adopted a diversity statement that is included in the school's handbook.

Another example of the impact of administrative leadership on institutional commitment to diversity is the case of the Harris School. The admissions director explained that the middle school's African-American principal created "an immediate credibility in that she was really able to address what it's like for African Americans to come to Harris, which is the bottom line question." She added, of the school's head, who joined the school in the previous year:

> . . . [He] has been very specific and clear about really looking closely at our efforts along the lines of diversity. He has taken over chairing the diversity committee, which is a very important school-wide committee. I think he knows how important it is that this sort of initiative come from the head of the school. The committee has done significant work over the course of the year, and is

very committed to not just looking at numbers, but looking at practice, and
looking at cultures, and how we support those families, and what the messages
are, not just in curriculum, but in all facets of our school and community life.

The impact of a school head's philosophy is clearly important in shaping the
institution's overall philosophical commitment to creating and nurturing a
multiracial student population.

The data presented in this section have shown that the independent schools
in our sample have strong commitments to increasing the number of African-
American students on their campuses. It appears, however, that even though
the schools share this common goal, the individuals we interviewed in these
schools articulated varying levels of commitment to the goal and saw
different reasons for diversity.

The Alignment of Admissions Practices With the School's Symbolic Commitment to Racial Diversity

The philosophical commitment to diversity (for whatever reasons are
articulated) is operationalized in a school's admissions practices for African-
American and other minority students. Symbolic commitments to diversity
that do not translate into practice cannot effect meaningful change. The
admissions policies and processes at the various schools are discussed in this
section.

The BEST member schools vary in their admission procedures. BEST
applicants (all African-American) represent an average of 25% of the
applicant pool for independent schools. At some schools, BEST students are
considered part of the regular applicant pool. At others, BEST applicants are
considered separately, and in some cases they are given preferential
consideration. The admissions director at one school stated that the latter
procedure is "in keeping with their commitment to BEST and their
commitment to Baltimore."

Without exception, a school visit is a required part of the application
process. A prospective BEST student and his or her parent(s) schedule with
the admissions office a day to spend at the school. The student and parent(s)
are interviewed by a member of the admissions office staff. The parent(s)
then typically tours the school with the admissions staff member. The
prospective student attends classes with a student enrolled in the grade to
which the student is applying.

During the school visit and throughout the application process, a few of the
schools give special attention to African-American families, especially those

of highly qualified applicants who are likely to have several options. The admissions director at the Highlands School said that the special attention given to the families has made the school very successful in increasing its African-American student population: "We give them [African-American families] the special attention they need as newcomers to the independent school application process." This involves taking the time to orient them to the admissions procedures and following up after school visits. For example, the school arranges meetings between applying African-American students and families with returning African-American students and families. Later in the admissions process, Highlands holds a dinner for all accepted African-American students, their families, and returning families. The admissions director stated that after this dinner, some parents have approached him and said, "We were waffling over where to send our child, but now we're coming here."

Some school admissions directors directly confronted race issues in their interviews with prospective Black students. For example, at the Lake School, when BEST applicants came in for interviews, the admissions director tried to get an idea of how they might adjust socially. He typically asked up-front questions, such as, "How do you think you're going to feel in a school where you're one of several Black kids? Have you ever been in a school where you were a minority?" Still, he believed that "you can't assume that students of the same color have the same values." That is, he believed that Black middle-class students share little in common with Black low-income students. The admissions director at Garland had a similar philosophy. She explained that she is very up-front with BEST families about the issue of being a minority at the school, but that this was sometimes "tricky," as she does not want to "offend those Black middle-class parents who may have more in common with her than with low-income Blacks." To illustrate, she commented, "The mayor's daughter (who is Black) doesn't need to be oriented. That would be insulting." However, she believed that an orientation of some sort might be helpful to lower-income African-American applicants and their families.

Other admissions directors reported feeling decidedly uncomfortable confronting racial issues with African-American families during the initial interview. The director of admissions at Simmons Academy stated:

> I don't want to offend anybody, and what I usually do is if someone asks me, "What is your African-American population?" I tell them that it's very small. I will ask them if they have a problem with that. I want to find out. I feel very uncomfortable bringing that up.

This approach perhaps did not serve this school well in its recruitment efforts; the school has a 3% Black population, and a parent of a BEST applicant reported feeling very uneasy in the admissions office at this school.

The schools varied in their admissions criteria, with some schools remaining more reliant on objective measures of achievement and others less so. Despite this variation, all admissions directors appeared open to considering a student's special talents and circumstances and most of them also revealed that the admissions process takes a fair amount of intuition on their part. In our interviews with admissions directors, we heard an eclectic set of explanations for how students are chosen. One admissions director told us that they "may admit someone who is a B or C student in a tough school, if they show promise and a strong character," but because the school offers no remedial courses, they feel they cannot accept students whose grades are average or below average. She added that they are "more likely to take 'risks' in admissions at the middle school level, because they have more time to work with the kids."

In contrast, at some schools, the admissions staff looked for students who have demonstrated they can succeed before coming to the independent school. "We are not going to accept a student if we feel that they cannot do our program. We don't think it's fair to them, to put them in a situation where they will struggle, and lose self-esteem," stated one admissions director. Some schools seemed to hold the philosophy that they should educate only very highly qualified African-American students, especially because these students were often receiving financial aid. For example, the admissions director at Orwell stated that financial aid students have to be "better than the average bear" to be accepted. The Simmons Academy admissions director was upset that BEST was steering more qualified applicants to other schools instead of to her school. She noted that "we don't have a support system to be able to accept children with a low IQ."

Admissions personnel at a number of schools were more likely to accept an applicant whose parents they deemed supportive. This did not mean that they would not accept students from single-parent families, although some schools admitted to favoring students from two-parent families. As one admissions director stated, "It's a rare kid that can succeed without family support, although there are exceptions."

To make social adjustment easier, several admissions directors tried to ensure that there was a critical mass of African-American students at each grade level. For example, as the admissions director at Orwell explained, "To have one in sixth grade is not enough. There is power in numbers. Kids shouldn't have to be pioneers." Another admissions director stated that "students should have others that they can bond with." However, most were unsure how critical mass ought to be defined, that is, how many African-American students were necessary to create a comfortable atmosphere. Black students at all of the schools, but particularly those with very low Black enrollments, felt that their schools would be better places were there more Black students. For example, Sara, one of two African-American freshmen at Simmons, stated: "If there were more Black people, I would feel more comfortable."

At most of the schools, racial diversity was the number one priority in financial aid awards. One school's admissions director stated that this was because the school had a reputation as a "WASPy school," and they were working hard to change that. In keeping with their commitment, this school was one of the few independent schools in the area that gave aid in the lower school. The admissions director believed that bringing students in early would give them a greater chance of success: "If we don't get these boys by then it's too late, we lose them to the streets." Although they were committed to providing financial aid to Black students, all of the admissions directors were also very interested in attracting full-paying African-American applicants. One stated that he was concerned that "minorities and financial aid are so strongly linked," and he did not want the school to reinforce the stereotype that all African-Americans are low-income.

Despite the opinion of almost all of the admissions directors that the adjustment issues for African-American students are more socioeconomic than racial, the students we interviewed all emphatically stated that race was a far more salient issue than was social class in their adjustment to these schools. In our interviews and observations, we found that schools that deal with the issue of race directly, from the moment of the admissions interview onward, tended to be places where students feel more comfortable about their own racial identity on arrival at the school. At several of the schools where African-American students reported feeling most comfortable, admissions directors asked questions about racial issues during the interviews. These schools openly embraced multiculturalism and diversity. Conversely, at schools where staff took a color-blind approach to students by not confronting issues of race, we noted more reports of unhappiness among African-American students.

The Degree to Which the Institutional
Structure and Culture Support Diversity

The independent schools in this study were taking a variety of steps to make their schools places where African-American students were comfortable and able to succeed academically. The statement of one admissions director captures the sentiment of many: "We want to create an atmosphere where all kids can fit in." However, schools varied in the degree to which they had achieved this goal. This variation is due, in large part, to differences in how schools' structures and cultures support diversity. First, we look to some of the structural features of schools in assessing their commitment to a positive climate for diversity, focusing primarily on the institutional commitment to African-American student programs and multicultural curricula. Second, we examine some cultural features that make independent schools more welcoming environments for African-American students.

Structural Factors. Schools ranged in the degree to which they had structures in place that created a positive climate for diversity. Accordingly, they ranged in the opportunities they provided for students to learn African-American history and different aspects of African-American culture. These opportunities ranged from offering a number of courses in African-American history and culture, to holding lectures during African-American Heritage Month, to not including African-American history or culture at all. The Franklin School, a pioneer in providing students with opportunities to learn about African-American history and culture, offered several courses as electives for upper school students, including "Black History," "South African History and Literature," "History of the New South," and "The Meaning of the Civil War." These classes also were open to students from Brookline and Garland. By contrast, the Bennett School offered very few opportunities to learn about African-American culture, even about Black authors in literature classes.

Some schools attempted to foster a positive climate for diversity by hiring a coordinator of multicultural affairs. As the admissions director at Garland explained, this person's job was "to make sure that all cultures are reflected in the school's curriculum." The admissions director cited several examples of what was done to reflect diversity: There is Haitian art hanging on the walls of the school and a multicultural resource center in the library supported by a grant from Black alumni. This center includes papers on loan from the Library of Congress that memorialized Juanita Jackson Mitchell, a civil rights activist and school alumnus. The school has also assembled a committee of parents to address multicultural affairs.

Some students at Garland, however, believed that the multicultural coordinator simply "posted little caricatures of the people of many lands on her bulletin board, and that's the extent of it." In contrast, students preferred opportunities to dialogue about race issues. They cited a human relations day when they "talked about race and racial tension." Another student added, "I thought it was helpful; it brought things out into the open." However, despite this open dialogue, they felt as though some of the contributions of Black students were not recognized. For example, one student complained that the all-Black gospel choir "is never included in the holiday concerts" and that the Black Awareness Club was solely responsible for raising money for Black History Month programs. A student explained that "the Black Awareness Club had to put everything together. It should be a whole-school responsibility." She remarked that the Jewish students on campus were not solely responsible for the Holocaust assembly earlier that year.

The schools' sponsoring of Black student associations was very important to the African-American students interviewed. Although the structures, purposes, importance, and names of these organizations varied across the different independent schools, the common denominator was that they served as spaces for African-American students to remain grounded in the culture, history, and struggle of African-American people, and as places of emotional support. It was less the activities of the organizations, and more the symbolic representation of the organizations, that signaled to students that they had a place in the schools.

Students talked about these clubs as being places to address issues pertinent to African-Americans, both among group members and in the school at large. For example, many of the students stated that these organizations were where they discussed the historic Million Man March. Most students also saw it as the club's role to raise awareness about issues pertinent to African-Americans in the school as a whole. Students explained that, in addition to serving as places for the affirmation of cultural identity, the African-American student organizations at their schools serve as places for emotional support.

Recognizing the fact that students benefit from role models with whom they can identify, all of the admissions directors expressed their school's intention to increase the number of African-American faculty members. Some schools actively recruited African-American teachers nationally through various organizations, such as the Multicultural Alliance. However, despite such efforts, several schools still had very low (or no) representation of African-American teachers on their faculties. Highlands was one of the schools that actively tried to recruit African-American teachers but has only 5 on their faculty of 100 teachers. The admissions director believed that "the job candidates are out there, it's just a matter of convincing them to come to the school." Not surprisingly, the number of Black teachers on the faculty had a profound effect on Black students' experiences. As a student at Simmons exclaimed, "there are no Black teachers, and that is a real problem." Several students at Bennett agreed, stating that "we really need an African-American teacher. The only Blacks here work in the cafeteria or cut the grass."

As the data presented in this chapter suggest, the schools in our study are making structural efforts to support African-American students by sponsoring Black student associations, offering multicultural curricula, and recruiting Black teachers. However, their success at meeting these goals varied, and this affected students' experiences and feelings of belonging. In our interviews with students, we learned that students enjoyed opportunities to learn more about the history and contributions of African-Americans, particularly when these opportunities were well integrated into the school and were not seen as add-ons to satisfy a small group of students.

Cultural Factors. School personnel were often uncertain about what kind of institutional climate or culture for diversity they hoped to create. More often than not, they were uncomfortable with any expressions of solidarity among the African-American students at the school. For example, the admissions director at Garland expressed dismay that several years prior there was a group of "militant" students who were promoting "Black power." Similarly, the admissions director at the Orwell School expressed disdain for a group of Black girls who were a "very outspoken negative group." She felt that this type of behavior inhibited the unified feeling of the "Orwell family" that the school worked hard to promote.

This fear of Black student solidarity was also present at the Bennett School and became apparent when Black students moved to create a Black Awareness Club. Over the years, there was hesitancy on the part of the administration to have such a club because of fears it would lead to divisiveness among the students. Eventually, at the end of the 1995-1996 school year, a student was able to push through a proposal for the club by saying that it would be "all encompassing" and "not we versus them." She wrote a formal proposal that was passed by the head. According to the students, the formation of clubs at this school typically was not this formal. There was some contention over the name of the club. The administration favored calling the club the "Rainbow Club" or the "Students of Color Club." The leader of the club surveyed 15 schools and found that "Black" was used in the name of such clubs in all of these schools. Thus, the decision was made that "Black" could be used as part of the name. However, the students had to call themselves a Black "awareness club," not a Black "student union."

Further evidence of the fear of group solidarity and racial divisiveness at Bennett occurred when the verdict of the O.J. Simpson criminal trial was released. School officials made the decision neither to report the verdict to the students nor to discuss it in their classes for fear that it would provoke racial division among students or harmful discussions. Silencing of the verdict was possible in this isolated boarding school environment. Black students found this silencing to be particularly disturbing and revealing of the school's general avoidance of important race issues. Students at Bennett told us that teachers "deliberately avoid" discussing race and "are afraid that we'll bring up racial issues in classes." One student stated: "They give more attention to the Holocaust than to slavery." Overall, the students agreed that the school did little to accommodate Black students. "The school has nothing geared for us," explained one student. Another student reiterated, saying, "It does not seem that our needs are recognized. They could at least ask us what could be changed." She added that "sometimes they ask, but they don't act (on our suggestions)." The students were disgruntled at what they perceived to be a stereotypical impression about Black students among the faculty. One student summed it up: "You're on scholarship, you're Black, you're supposed to be smart." As a result, she added, "if you're average, you get shunned."

Some of the schools appeared to deal openly with racial issues in their school communities, sponsoring forums for students and families to discuss diversity. For example, an admissions director at the Brookline School discussed the fact that her school recently held a multicultural potluck supper, where each family brought a dish of their native culture. A lecturer gave a speech titled "Living in two worlds: Experiences of prejudice." She noted that the school has tried to broaden conceptions of diversity beyond a Black-White issue. Several years ago, the faculty at this school also participated in a race/multicultural self-assessment. As the admissions director described, the direct style of the program, which lasted a full year, "really got people talking." As previously noted, the faculty of the Garland School also attempted to stimulate discussions about race among students and staff.

The Orwell School also attempted to deal openly with racial issues on campus. The admissions director cited several disturbing incidents of racism on the campus last year. After these incidents, a town meeting was held where students voiced their opinions about the racial problems on campus.

They also addressed these issues in a multicultural committee. Now there is renewed vigilance in the school community about racism in the school. Students were pleased at the efforts being made to remediate such problems.

Students at Highlands reported that they felt that the school culture was accepting of diversity and made them feel welcome. When asked why he chose Highlands, one student said that he didn't want to have to go to a school and act differently. "I wanted to be myself," he stated, and he felt he could do that at Highlands. Students agreed that "you shouldn't have to change to fit in." A senior student commented that the "younger brothers try a little too hard to fit in," adding that, "as long as you know who you are, you're okay." When asked what he would tell a new Black student who was coming to the school, one student answered: "Don't be discouraged by the fact that there are only a few Blacks at the school." The students felt as though despite the small number of Blacks, one could still find a niche at the school.

The students at Highlands indicated that there was not animosity between Black and White students at the school, but that some of the White students were ignorant (about Blacks in general) because "their only interaction with Blacks is here." They felt that the faculty and administration were somewhat threatened by the fact that they were a group of all Black students who liked to hang out together and sit together in the lunchroom. A student recounted an incident when a teacher came up to him and his African-American friends in the lunchroom and said, "segregation ended in the sixties," asking the students to split up and integrate with White students in the lunchroom. The students expressed dismay that as Blacks, they were always being asked to integrate, whereas no one asked the White students to come and sit with them.

In summary, the data show that the independent schools in this study varied in the degree to which they created positive and healthy climates or cultures for racial diversity. At schools that dealt openly with issues of race and racism and allowed African-American students to express their racial identity, students felt comfortable with themselves and felt as though they were a valued part of the school community. Where there existed silence about, or avoidance of, race and racial issues, African-American students expressed frustration and discomfort.

CONCLUSION

This chapter illuminates the structures and cultures that support diversity within elite, predominantly White private schools. In so doing, it helps lead to a better understanding of how these schools operationalize their stated commitments to diversity by creating school environments where African-American students can thrive academically and personally. Clearly, institutional cultures and structures influence students' attitudes toward schooling and their own sense of racial identity. An exploration of these important issues gives insight into how to provide better educational environments and options for African-American students, in both private and public schools.

Race is a salient factor in defining institutional cultures and students' social and educational experiences. Nowhere is this more apparent than in the schools of the White, power elite. Although some independent schools are making considerable strides toward creating more positive climates for diversity, the journey is not complete. Structural changes (i.e., admitting African-American students, sponsoring Black student associations, hiring African-American and other faculty of color, etc.) are important steps toward creating positive climates for diversity. However, structural changes do not always lead to changes in the culture of the institution or in the attitudes of individuals so that issues of race can be openly discussed, and blatant or subtle acts of racial discrimination can be fairly and swiftly addressed. To accomplish the latter, school personnel must question their own ideologies about race and diversity, and the ways in which those belief systems are conveyed to students through the institutional culture and structure of schools. Finally, inquiry about race and diversity should be promoted among all members of the school community, students included. For example, one school organized a discussion among faculty members of Tatum's 1997 book, *Why are all the Black kids sitting together in the cafeteria, and other conversations about race.* This promoted an open dialogue about the issues facing Black students in the predominantly White independent school setting.

One admissions director poignantly stated the need for an open, accepting and responsive school environment for all students:

> You can't afford to have admitted students who are different from your majority students and be satisfied with saying, "You're a guest at the table." You have to change table settings; you have to change the institution. Changing independent schools isn't easy and you have to hold onto some things. You can't afford to have it not be recognizable. But you also have to

make it a place where the traditions and the history are acceptable to all the students because otherwise, you're simply a servant for education, but you're not really a community that is multicultural.

REFERENCES

Arnez, N. L., & Jones-Wilson, F. C. (1988). A descriptive survey of Black parents in the greater Washington, D. C., area who chose to send their children to nonpublic schools. In D. Slaughter & D. Johnson (Eds.), *Visible now: Blacks in private schools* (pp. 209-224). Westport, CT: Greenwood.

Brookins, G. (1988). Making the honor roll: A Black parent's perspective on private education. In D. Slaughter & D. Johnson (Eds.), *Visible now: Blacks in private schools* (pp. 12-20). Westport, CT: Greenwood.

Cookson, P. W., & Persell, C. H. (1985). *Preparing for power: America's elite boarding schools*. New York: Basic Books.

Cookson, P. W., & Persell, C. H. (1991). Race and class in America's elite boarding schools: African-Americans as the outsiders within. *Journal of Negro Education*, 60(2), 219-228.

Datnow, A., & Cooper, R. (1997). Peer networks of African-American students in independent schools: Affirming academic success and racial identity. *Journal of Negro Education,*. 66(1), 1-17.

Eisenhardt, K.M. (1989). Building theories from case study research. *Academy of Management Review*, 14(4), 532-550.

Hurtado, S., Milem, J. F., Allen, W. R., & Clayton-Pederson, A. R. (1996). *Improving the climate for racial/ethnic diversity in higher education institutions.* (Final Report to the Lilly Endowment, Inc.). Nashville, TN: Vanderbilt University.

Johnson, S., & Anderson, D. K. (1992). Legacies and lessons from independent schools. *Journal of Negro Education*, 61(2), 121-124.

Kanter, R. (1977). Some effects of proportion on group life: Skewed sex ratios and responses on token women. *American Journal of Sociology*, 82, 965-989.

Miles, M., & Huberman, M. (1984). *Qualitative data analysis*. Beverly Hills, CA: Sage Publications.

Orfield, G. (1992). Money, equity, and college access. *Harvard Educational Review*, 62(3), 337-372.

Royal, C. R. (1988). Support systems for students of color in independent schools. In D. Slaughter & D. Johnson (Eds.), *Visible now: Blacks in private schools* (pp. 55-69). Westport, CT: Greenwood.

Schneider, B., & Shouse, R. (1992). Children of color in independent schools: An analysis of the eighth grade cohort from the National Education Longitudinal Study of 1988. *Journal of Negro Education*, 61(2), 223-234.

Speede-Franklin, W. (1988). Ethnic diverse: Patterns and implications of minorities in independent schools. In D. Slaughter & D. Johnson (Eds.), *Visible now: Blacks in private schools* (pp. 21-31). Westport, CT: Greenwood.

Strauss, A., & Corbin, J. (1990). *Basics of qualitative research: Grounded theory procedures and techniques*. Newbury Park, CA: Sage.

Tatum, B. D. (1997). *'Why are all the Black kids sitting together in the cafeteria,' and other conversations about race.* New York: Basic Books.

Turner, C. (1994). Guests in someone else's house: Students of color. *Review of Higher Education*, 17(4), 355-370.

Yin, R. (1989). *Case study research*. Newbury Park, CA: Sage.

Zweigenhaft, R. L., & Domhoff, G. W. (1991). *Blacks in the White establishment*. New Haven, CT: Yale University Press.

IV

From Research to Practice

11

Toward an Understanding of School Reconstitution as a Strategy to Educate Students Placed at Risk

HEINRICH MINTROP
University of Maryland, College Park

A new get-tough attitude toward habitually low-performing schools has taken hold in recent years as policymakers have raised the stakes in their jurisdictions' accountability systems. School reconstitution is one of these high-stakes accountability measures. Reconstitution is also a part of U.S. Secretary of Education Richard Riley's action agenda. In this chapter, I explore how reconstitution policies might affect teachers' motivation to increase their performance as educators serving in schools with large concentrations of students placed at risk. I base my exploration both on theoretical models that aid in the conceptualization of salient questions and on empirical findings from the first year of a 3-year study that illustrate key theoretical and policy issues. The aim of the chapter is to contribute to an incipient discussion about the role of reconstitution policies in educational reform.

A new "no excuses era" of school reform has dawned, according to Hugh Price, president of the Urban League:

> There are no longer any excuses for the failure of inner-city students to achieve. The landscape of urban public education is dotted with teachers, classrooms, and even entire schools that deliver the goods. The needed innovations have been designed and field-tested, and are now ready for mass market. (Price, 1997)

The urgency for improvement contrasts with the persistent reality of failing public schools, especially in the core of American cities. Chicago recently identified approximately 100 public schools in that city alone that have fewer than 15% of their students reading at the national norm.[1] (Chicago Public Schools, 1997). A new get-tough attitude toward habitually low-performing schools has taken hold in recent years as policymakers have raised the stakes in their jurisdictions' accountability systems. School reconstitution is one of these high-stakes accountability measures. Reconstitution is also a part of U.S. Secretary of Education Richard Riley's action agenda. In his *Fourth Annual State of American Education Address*, he contended that, "we need to stop making excuses and get on with the business of fixing our schools. If a school is bad and can't be changed, reconstitute it or close it down" (Riley, 1997).

In this chapter, I explore how reconstitution policies might affect teachers' motivation to increase their performance as educators serving in schools with large concentrations of students placed at risk. I base my exploration both on theoretical models that aid in the conceptualization of salient questions and on empirical findings from the first year of a 3-year study[2] that illustrate key theoretical and policy issues. The aim of the chapter is to contribute to an incipient discussion about the role of reconstitution policies in educational reform.

RECONSTITUTION DESIGNS

Although the term "reconstitution" in its most general connotation evokes images of accountability coupled with sanctions, actual policies that travel under the guise of reconstitution differ from state to state and from district to district. Some jurisdictions, although engaging in some form of reconstitution, avoid the term altogether (e.g., Kentucky). One of the better known cases of large-scale experimentation with reconstitution is the San Francisco public school system, which has carried out school reconstitutions since 1984 as a means by which to increase the academic achievement of its Hispanic and African-American student populations. In San Francisco, the policy set in motion a process whereby persistently failing schools, primarily

---

[1]This is measured by the Iowa Basic Skills Test.

[2]This research is supported by the U.S. Department of Education, Office of Educational Research and Improvement. The opinions expressed are the author's and do not necessarily represent OERI positions or policies.

serving underprivileged student populations, were closed and reopened with newly composed faculties, sometimes under different names and often with more decidedly academic missions. In schools under reconstitution, faculty members lost their building seniority and were forced to reapply for their old positions. In a later version of reconstitution, called the "Comprehensive School Improvement Program," schools identified as failing through a mix of quantitative and qualitative indicators were put on probation. Each year, a small number of bottom-ranked schools unable to improve their performance were reconstituted; that is, the faculty were subjected to reapplication. Currently the system is again being revamped in negotiations between the San Francisco Unified School District and teachers' unions.

Other states experimenting with fairly systematic reconstitution-type policies are Kentucky and Maryland, trailblazers in the standards-based systemic reform movement. In these states, school accountability coupled with sanctions (i.e., reconstitution) has become legislated as part of wider school performance assessment programs. In the Maryland state accountability system, reconstitution entails the identification of schools that have produced persistently low and declining test scores on the state's performance-based assessment test.[3] These schools are designated as "reconstitution-eligible" (RE) (Maryland State Department of Education, 1997). Actual reconstitution, the final sanction, is envisioned as a state takeover of local schools from local jurisdictions. To date, only three schools have been subjected to this final stage.

Maryland, like San Francisco, targets the lowest performing schools. However, the Maryland sanctions apply as strongly to individual schools as to local districts, which may lose jurisdiction over their persistently failing schools. In so far as a high concentration of students placed at risk is present in schools that find themselves in the lowest performance ranks, reconstitution in Maryland and San Francisco targets the education of students placed at risk by affecting the education schools placed at risk offer.

This is not necessarily the case in Kentucky's accountability system (Guskey, 1994; Petrosko, 1996). As in Maryland and San Francisco, the Kentucky system is multistaged, with a probationary stage ("school in decline") and a stage at which full sanctions apply ("school in crisis"). The Kentucky system, however, focuses on schools that fail to meet their predetermined performance growth targets, regardless of rank. Hence, the

---

[3] The performance-based assessment test (MSPAP, Maryland School Performance Assessment Program) is not given in high schools. Other tests and qualitative measures are included in a school's performance index.

Kentucky accountability system less explicitly affects schools with large concentrations of students placed at risk. Many more jurisdictions are currently implementing accountability policies akin to reconstitution, among them Chicago (Wong & Anagnostopoulos, 1997; Wong, Anagnostopoulos & Rutledge, 1998) and New York (Ascher, Ikeda, & Fruchter, 1997). In each case, different target populations, procedures, and sanctions, as well as a different mix of threats and capacity building measures, make up the accountability system.

Despite its growing popularity, there is scant evidence of the benefits of such policy. Only one jurisdiction, the San Francisco Unified School District, has any extensive or long-term experience in vacating the professionals in a school and starting over. The scant extant data on reconstitution and its effects, therefore, come primarily from San Francisco. Orfield et al. (1992), in their evaluation of that district's "first wave" of reconstitutions deemed the policy successful and suggested that the district reconstitute a number of bottom-performing schools every year "until the task is completed" (p. 56). But San Francisco's first wave of reconstitutions was unique in that not only faculties but also student bodies were recomposed, for example, by reclassifying the schools from neighborhood to magnet schools. In addition, the reorganization effort was accompanied by a substantial infusion of additional funds. No systematic evaluation from San Francisco is available on subsequent waves of reconstitution, which were carried out with different sets of policies and with less auspicious support (Goldstein, Kelemen, & Koski, 1998). A similar lack of systematic evaluation exists in other jurisdictions where reconstitution policies and accountability systems are in more nascent stages. But policy making does not move at the speed of research. Policy making sometimes moves more slowly when research suggests solutions that run against the grain of public sentiment. It sometimes moves more swiftly than research when a policy measure makes intuitive sense as a sorely needed solution to a seemingly intractable problem that policymakers feel compelled to address.

RECONSTITUTION AS PROBATION

Reconstitution in its various forms is an accountability scheme that has been designed for high stakes. This chapter takes a closer look at how it might help to improve the education of students placed at risk. Reconstitution adds an element of sanctions to standards-based accountability and may work in several ways. The measure may communicate to the public that something is being done about failing schools; decoupled from forceful action, it serves a largely symbolic function. It may pose a distant threat of sanctions to schools that perform fairly well. Although in all likelihood these schools will not encounter actual imposition of sanctions, they may nevertheless increase their performance to preempt such an unlikely event. Reconstitution may pose an imminent threat of sanctions to schools that persistently fail to meet their performance target. If as a result the school is put on probation, this imminent threat is particularly poignant. Finally, to schools failing their probation, reconstitution stands as a draconian school reorganization that is coupled with penalties for personnel, such as loss of building seniority or even tenure. Schools serving large numbers of students placed at risk may be primary targets for probation and reorganization.

Of these two strategies, probation is the more feasible and, heretofore, more frequently implemented. In many systems (e.g., a state, county, or local district), schools that persistently fail (Meyer & Zucker, 1989) are not evenly distributed, but tend to come in clusters that coincide with poverty and often with concentrations of underprivileged ethnic minorities. When a system begins to apply stringent accountability measures (test scores, attendance rates, etc.) across all schools under its jurisdiction, these clusters become visible. In the state of Maryland, for example, most reconstitution-eligible schools identified by the state are located in Baltimore, which has seen about half of its schools identified as reconstitution-eligible, that is, on probation. The numbers of identified schools on probation concentrated in Chicago are staggering as well. It seems likely that the system's capacity would be overtaxed if, within a reasonable time frame, all of these schools were targeted for drastic reorganization or overhaul. If all of these schools' faculties, for example, were subjected to a reapplication process, actual reconstitution of schools in systems of high failure concentration might lead to drastic personnel turnover and create a burgeoning system-internal labor market. Personnel likely would be reshuffled in a grand scheme among the failing schools that post openings, whereas high-performing schools might pursue talented teachers and otherwise shield themselves from the stigmatized applicant pool.

In systems of high-failure concentration, then, a massive and swift overhaul strategy through reconstitution does not appear practical or feasible. To execute such an overhaul, a system must be able to terminate low-performing teachers' tenure or take advantage of precipitated retirement waves, and count on a sufficient supply of new applicants who are better educated and more motivated to take over tough assignments than the previous teaching cadre. The latter condition may be doubtful in some areas of high-failure concentration, given the difficulty of recruiting and retaining young, poorly paid, and untenured educators in these assignments (Argetsinger, 1998). Thus, in systems encountering high concentrations of failing schools, the success of reconstitution as a strategy of school improvement seems to hinge on its impact as a credible threat. In other words, the large majority of schools on probation in such systems must improve by working to avert reconstitution, rather than through actual reconstitution.

Although reconstitution designs differ across experimenting jurisdictions, most probation designs are a combination of the following mandates and incentives: standards, sanctions, group accountability, goal clarity, school management mandates, and capacity-building measures. The performance of a school on probation is assessed by student achievement tests or other indicators. Schools are threatened with sanctions such as drastic reorganization, loss of tenure, or state takeover when they fail to improve. Whole faculties, rather than individual teachers, are held accountable for increasing the school's organizational performance. The assessment system provides the school clear goals that center on student learning. Most designs mandate schools, on being identified as on probation, to undergo a formal process of school improvement. These designs also frequently stipulate that schools must compile school improvement plans, form responsible bodies for coordinated action such as school improvement teams, and monitor the implementation of school improvement plans. Reconstitution designs differ in the degree to which they offer additional resources for capacity building.

The combination of mandates and incentives contained in any probation design aims at motivating a school's educators to channel school activities into a rational (i.e., goal-oriented and coherent) process of organizational learning and coordination. It also aims to restructure and intensify curriculum and instruction through teacher learning and instructional change. Thus, a study of probation designs looks at three key aspects of performance (a) educators' motivation, (b) effective school management, and (c) instructional technology, as well as the capacity to increase student performance as measured by the assessment instruments. In this chapter, I discuss only the aspect of educators' motivation: How might reconstitution as imminent threat work to boost the motivation of individual educators and whole faculties to increase their professional effort?

INDIVIDUAL MOTIVATION

The threat of reconstitution causes initial discomfort, dissatisfaction, and often resistance among educators at identified sites. If events in San

Francisco (Ruenzel, 1997) and Philadelphia (Jones, 1997) are any indication, reconstitution policies can be contentious and divisive, potentially pitting state, local districts, unions, schools, administrators, and teachers against one another. These policies can, therefore, upset the kind of consensus between policymakers and educators that scholars of earlier stages of school reform postulated to be essential for success (Elmore, 1990).

Although diminished satisfaction may disrupt labor peace, it may not necessarily translate into diminished job performance. Studies in the tradition of behaviorist industrial psychology have not found a clear relationship between job satisfaction and job performance (Lawler, 1973; Mohrman, Mohrman, & Odden, 1996). Job satisfaction is seen as related to commitment expressed in phenomena such as turnover and absenteeism. Performance motivation, however, is often conceptualized in relationship to sense of efficacy (Ashton & Webb, 1986), internal control (Weiner, 1986), clear goal setting (Locke, 1968), and expectancy of rewards (Lawler). These varied, though related, sources of motivation (Rowan, Chiang, & Miller, 1997) are assumed to increase teachers' performance if teachers (a) believe that the task is in their control and they have the requisite competence for its execution, (b) see a connection between individual effort and expected reward, and (c) value the reward itself.

Kelley and Protsik (1997) used this approach to explain teachers' response to the Kentucky accountability system and its incentive programs, which included pay rewards for successful schools and the threat of drastic sanctions for persistently failing schools. In their sample of six schools that successfully improved performance, they found evidence for the motivating influence of the Kentucky incentives. Interviewed teachers saw their school's target score on the performance-based test (Kentucky Instructional Results Information System) as clear, and attainment within their control. Teachers said they had changed their practice so that test and instructional formats would better match, although some bemoaned the neglect of basic skills. Teachers in these award-winning schools felt able and competent to achieve their goal. Interestingly, despite their schools' performance success, they were more motivated by fear of sanctions than by reception of monetary rewards. As noted by the authors, their study had limitations. Most notably, their sample of schools did not contain persistently failing schools, nor did the study provide information on the schools' educational load (poverty, at-risk population, etc.). Moreover, the study was conducted a posteriori so that teacher interviews may very well have been biased toward rationalizing and attributing success to one's own control and ability.

Responses of teachers working in situations less conducive to success can be expected to differ when viewed in light of the literature on teacher burnout, a phenomenon more commonly encountered in inner-city schools with large numbers of poor and minority students (Dworkin, 1987; LeCompte & Dworkin, 1991). Whereas previously cited models of job performance motivation view challenge, discomfort, and perhaps even stress as potentially positive stimuli for increased energy output, research on burnout centers on the role of commitment and the negative role of job dissatisfaction on teacher behavior. Burnout occurs when, in response to job stress and dissatisfaction, teachers experience a loss of idealism and enthusiasm for their work; their efficacy and sense of control is low; and they feel a sense of powerlessness, meaninglessness, normlessness, and isolation in their work. As a result, they withdraw and externalize blame for their failure to their students by whom they often feel victimized. Many burnt out teachers desire to leave their jobs, but when no exit options are readily available, they become "entrapped" (Dworkin).

Dworkin and others in this research tradition identify low morale and commitment as the key problem besetting schools in this milieu. They contend that any hope of improving schools depends on finding ways to nurture a sense of dignity, professionalism, and support among dispirited faculties. Intrinsic rewards, sense of meaningfulness in teaching, autonomy or reduction of external intrusion especially in urban environments, and collegial support from the principal all have been identified as helping to prevent low morale and burnout.

How might accountability policies impact teachers' commitment in this context? LeCompte and Dworkin (1991) analyzed teachers' responses to mandatory competency testing as part of the Texas school reform effort of the mid-1980s. They demonstrated that Texas' across-the-board approach to implementing more rigorous standards for teacher competence increased burnout levels. Prior to the reform, burnout rates were especially high among novice teachers and tended to fall with additional years of experience. However, the reform triggered a sharp increase of burnout among senior teachers with 10-15 years of experience, an increase that only partially abated in subsequent years after the furor over the reform had died down. Thus, the reform adversely affected those teachers presumed to have the highest work commitment and vestedness in the system, the very group on which solid school improvement strategies in all likelihood must bank. Although the thrust of high-stakes accountability measures is different from teacher competency testing, the two have in common that they impose external standards on teachers, and do so regardless of individual performance or experience.

The relationship between job motivation and performance, on the one hand, and job satisfaction and commitment, on the other hand, is far from clear in light of the discussed models. Yet, it seems quite possible that the same incentives and sanctions that researchers recommend as means to increase performance, particularly sanctions in case of nonperformance, may be detrimental to teachers' commitment to remaining in workplaces where they feel unappreciated and powerless to begin with. Accountability measures, then, can have two consequences. On the one hand, they can challenge teachers to reach a defined and attainable goal, the accomplishment of which promises reward or aversion of penalties. In this case, the teacher is likely to increase his or her performance. On the other hand, accountability measures can cause a teacher to feel further victimized by the system. In this case, ritual compliance, disengagement, and entrapment prevail unless the teacher chooses to exit an embattled school that has been put on probation. It is therefore crucial, particularly for schools with high educational loads (e.g., poverty, special needs students), in which educational talent tends to be relatively low (National Commission on Teaching & America's Future, 1996), that the accountability system and its incentives be appropriate to the situation lest they do more harm than good.

Shamir (1991), in an insightful theoretical synthesis of research on motivation, criticized motivation theories that view the individual as "rational maximizer of personal utility" on the grounds that these theories are not sensitive to the situation of educators at schools. In Shamir's view, expectancy and goal-setting models of motivation presuppose "strong situations" (i.e., situations structured by clear and specific goals); reward expectancies; and clearly identifiable relationships between increased effort, performance, and reward. In "weak situations" where rewards are less abundant, where there is less tendency to differentiate among individuals on the basis of work performance because of collective orientations, or where links between performance and rewards are more difficult to construct, "point of action" theories of motivation, as Shamir called them, are less adequate. These models of motivation are useful in predicting discrete task behavior, but they are less powerful in explaining a "diffuse and open-ended concept of commitment" that refers to a "shifting number and range of rather ill-delineated performances rather than to ironclad and numerically constant behaviors having clearly defined parameters that everyone knows" (Shamir, p. 408).

GROUP ACCOUNTABILITY

In most high-stakes accountability designs, a whole school faculty is held accountable, and, on failure to meet performance expectations a whole school faculty is put on probation. Very little is known about how group accountability might work in the context of schools (Hanushek, 1994; Malen, 1999). Bolstered by a plethora of research on effective schools, the key assumption underlying this group approach is that schools as organizations are the most suitable strategic units for educational improvement. Some authors believe that group accountability may be a way "to motivate teachers and administrators to enact their jobs in a manner that leads to significantly higher student achievement, *sometimes without a commensurate increase in expenditures*" [italics added] (Mohrman et al., 1996, p. 54). Tying the fate of teachers to organizational performance has been suggested by a number of researchers (Conley & Odden, 1995; Elmore, Abelmann & Fuhrman, 1996; Mohrman et al., 1996; Odden & Conley, 1992). Because little empirical material is available (Kelley & Protsik 1997), the scholarly discussion borrows heavily from experiences in private industry. In light of these experiences, group accountability is seen as a means to motivate performance increases, to channel performance efforts toward strategic goals of the organization, and to generate high involvement of employees in the life of the organization. Group performance systems are believed to remedy the reported divisiveness that earlier, largely failed, attempts of individual merit pay schemes induced in faculties (Malen, 1999; Malen, Murphy, & Hart, 1987). In this way, they may strengthen collegiality and a sense of collective responsibility. These potentially positive effects may be mitigated, however, by negative effects that could be of particular salience for schools on probation serving large numbers of traditionally underprivileged student populations. Next, I discuss some of these potentially negative effects.

Control and Commitment

There seems to be consensus among scholars that for group performance incentives to work the goals need to be clear and attainable, and the performing unit "should have control over a product, a defined set of services, or services for a defined population" (Mohrman et al., 1996, p. 67). With regard to these criteria, schools on probation with high educational loads are in a special situation. If the system's performance targets are applied equally across all schools and are ambitious enough so that high- and average-performing schools are challenged to increase productivity to meet these targets, then persistently low-performing schools may face unrealistic growth expectations. In the case of low-performing schools, then, the expectation of success diminishes, the incentives lose their positive quality, and the aversion of penalties (e.g., reorganization, takeover, loss of tenure) becomes an uphill battle.

Moreover, if administrator, teacher, and student mobility rates are high, teachers may lack a sense of control. At a certain level of faculty turnover, school operations become ephemeral and the maintenance of basic routine operations becomes the first line of defense. The school site ceases to be the strategic unit of educational improvement. In this case, schools on probation may need baseline stabilization first, before they can hope to undertake ambitious instructional reform projects. In most cases, the strategic unit for such baseline stabilization is not the school as an effective organization, but the district or state as an organization that provides the necessary externally induced stability or, as often happens, instability (Page, 1995).

With a switch from individual to group performance incentives, rewards and sanctions operate less successfully as the loop between employees' efforts and expected rewards is spun more loosely (Shamir, 1991). As a result, performance motivation must tap into teachers' more broad-based and diffuse commitment to the organization. This is necessary because the chain from effort to reward for the individual teacher runs through the behavior of students, over which he or she has limited control in the classroom; through the behavior of colleagues at the site, over which he or she has no control due to the spatial organization of schools and traditional norms of autonomy; and through the behavior of the system itself, the orderly functioning of which he or she cannot take for granted in many instances. Hence, the threat of reconstitution may not trigger a direct performance response from the individual teacher even when the teacher is driven by a reward calculus.

Free Riding

Individual teachers must have at least some trust in the enforcement capacity of the leadership and in the commitment of a sizable number of colleagues at the site. Trust in leadership and colleagues decreases the fear of free riders in the organization, a phenomenon that Olson (1965) identified as detrimental to all collective action. Olson argued that individuals, as rational reward-maximizing actors, will not commit to an organization if their action does not have an immediate benefit for them and if they can hope to obtain desired goods without exerting individual effort. Free riding, for example, may occur when a middle school's performance is measured based on eighth-grade students' test performance. When student mobility is high, seventh-grade teachers may be able to benefit from eighth-grade teachers' efforts without increasing their own performance.

Two organizational responses could overcome the free rider problem. One response is increased collegiality, a hope that advocates of group accountability nurture. In this case, teachers and administrators depart from norms of autonomy and assumptions of individual performance and develop collective responsibility for performance. External performance expectations, then, are internalized. Another response to the free rider problem takes the approach that site leadership visibly enforces individual performance standards, assuring faculty members of the containment of free riding. In the second case, group accountability leads to a strengthening of hierarchy and compliance with, rather than internalization of, external standards. Therefore, a baseline of capable leadership or collegiality is a precondition for group accountability to work.

Retaining High-Performing Teachers

To increase the performance of their organizations, managers of organizational renewal are faced with the key problem, according to Schein (1991), of retaining high-performing employees and either raising performance levels of low performers or separating from them. In private industry, obvious instruments used to achieve this are pay, promotion, and dismissal. According to Schein, increases in authority, recognition, and commitment to the process of organizational change are levers of intrinsic motivation that make it harder for high-performing employees to leave. Moreover, in expectancy models of motivation, motivation depends not only on actual rewards received but also on the level of rewards the employee perceives to deserve based on the performance of a "comparison other." Hence, for higher performing employees to remain satisfied and thus committed to the organization, their "perceived equitable reward level" (Lawler, 1973, p. 83) must be higher.

Regardless the reasons, it has been notoriously difficult for schools to reward high-performing employees differentially. However, the blanket declaration of a whole school as failure and the threat of subjecting all employees to sanctions, such as reapplication and screening, regardless of perceived performance levels, may communicate to high-performing teachers that their higher performance is not recognized by the accountability agency. Furthermore, these actions may communicate that good performance does not count when it is carried out in association with lower performing colleagues or in exacerbating social circumstances. Thus, one could expect higher performing teachers, the very teacher cadres that need to be retained and mobilized for organizational renewal, to be particularly dissatisfied with this method of performance assessment.

At minimum, then, higher performing teachers need to be reassured that they are less affected and that at some point in the process individual performance differences, recognized by knowledgeable insiders, will count. The blanket threat of reconstitution regardless of performance differences, on the other hand, may in the long run only increase the flight of better qualified teachers to schools or districts with more job security or workplace stability (Darling-Hammond, 1994; 1997). Alternatively, commitment of high-performing teachers to their school may offset exit tendencies, but the source of this commitment appears to be not a rational reward-maximizing calculation, but rather an ingrained collective work orientation, the expectation of psychic rewards, commitment to students, and perhaps idealism.

Finally, in the previously cited literature on high-performance organizations, the group as accountability unit is usually understood as the basis for rewards or bonuses for good performance rather than as the unit that may have to absorb sanctions and penalties. The response of work units to sanctions, perhaps involving high personal stakes, may flow from individual and organizational processes that are quite different from those at work in high-performance or high-involvement organizations. The former may be more adequately captured by a different line of inquiry that places the failing organization and its crisis in the center.

INDUCED CRISIS AND ORGANIZATIONAL LEARNING

If accountability systems, such as the ones in Maryland or San Francisco, target those schools for probation that are the lowest performing and have experienced slippage in recent times, in all likelihood the policy design will have to deal with schools that have a long record of serious underperformance and decline. According to some theories of organizational decline (Meyer & Zucker, 1989), organizations continuously decline when they lose sight of their primary objective, such as profitmaking in the private sector or the efficient delivery of a service in the public sector, but are kept alive by powerful groups that derive benefits from the mere existence of the organization. Interest groups, such as employees, governments, or community groups, divert the organization toward other goals, such as job security or easing public pressure. When this happens, the theory says, the organization is left to decline, but will nevertheless be maintained. In this situation, arresting the decline requires a strong and dramatic signal from management or external forces that throws the organization into crisis until it has resumed its primary objective. In applying this model to failing or persistently declining schools, external agencies induce crisis and threaten the existence of the faculty or the organization in order to redirect the effort of leadership and employees toward student learning and achievement.

Induced crisis can motivate an organization to learn. Bennett and Ferlie (1994) described the opportunity scenario in vivid terms:

> A crisis moves awkward issues up agendas. . . . We are likely to see continuing pressure from pioneers, the formation of special groups that seek to evangelize the rest of the organization, high energy and commitment levels and a period of organizational plasticity (p.11).

Dynamic principals and groups of highly involved teachers inside the organization, or community pressure groups and change agents external to the organization, could provide the ferment in the micropolitics of the school site. One should probably conceive of this kind of organizational learning as a political act involving the redistribution of power at the site (Ball, 1990), rather than as an administrative procedure or managerial project. For internal forces to unfreeze, the threat must not be too great, but crisis must be clearly orchestrated (Bennett & Ferlie, p. 112). The initiative should move to high-performing and highly motivated, perhaps even maverick, groups of teachers and administrators without overwhelming low performers with anxiety.

External threat and induced crisis, however, are not automatic triggers of learning (Levine, Rubin, & Wolohojian, 1982). According to Staw's threat-rigidity model (Staw, Lance, & Dutton, 1981), negative sanctions (in the case examined here potentially generated by reconstitution) can influence performance in two ways: they can induce either performance decrement or performance increment. Individuals who are threatened by the environment develop anxiety and stress, which leads to restriction in information processing, reliance on well-learned behavior, and increases in drive and energy. According to this model, when the dominant behavior patterns of the individual are appropriate to the situation, performance increment occurs. When such patterns are inappropriate, performance decrement occurs.

A review of studies on group behavior suggests a similarly binary response. Staw et al. (1981) suggested that two organizational responses to threat are likely. If the group believes in the likelihood of success in meeting the new demand from the environment, cohesiveness increases as does support for leadership, but there is also a tendency to move toward uniformity. If the group believes in the likelihood of failure, cohesiveness decreases, leadership becomes unstable, and dissension arises (Staw et al.). The organization is then unable to turn itself around, and often leadership is replaced or personnel depart. In this case, probation would have failed. Again, as in the case of individual responses, without people who possess the skills with which to manage the crisis of the organization, sanctions become counterproductive. However, according to this model, even organizations that successfully respond to new stressful external demands tend to reinforce dominant patterns of operation, rather than learn new things.

Thus, theoretical models of motivation speak to the potential success as well as failure of probation incentive designs. In the following section, I present preliminary findings from a study of reconstitution as probation that has been conducted in Maryland, Kentucky, and San Francisco. Data presented here come from schools in Maryland. In this chapter, these early findings are meant to illustrate some of the theoretical points I have discussed thus far. I address three questions in my descriptions: (a) Do the stigma and the threat of sanctions motivate individual teachers to increase work effort? (b) Does group accountability motivate the faculty to increase cohesion by enhancing either collegiality or hierarchy? and (c) Does induced crisis lead to productive or counterproductive responses on the part of the organization under threat? I first look at the overall system to search for broad parameters for increased school performance due to probation, which is called "reconstitution eligibility" in Maryland. I then describe one school to give a vivid example of what kinds of issues come to the fore in schools on probation.

SCHOOL PROBATION IN MARYLAND

The Maryland school accountability system was implemented in 1993 and, unlike systems in other jurisdictions, has been fairly stable since then. In Maryland, the state superintendent and board of education designate schools that are performing in the bottom rank and that have had declining performance records in previous years as RE. The heart of the Maryland accountability system for elementary and middle schools, in addition to attendance rates and basic skills test scores, is the performance-based test MSPAP, which assesses students' ability to perform a broad range of complex activities that often have real-life applications. On identification as RE, the school is required to submit a school improvement plan for the state's approval. Review panels and state monitors visit the school to help in the diagnosis of needs and the implementation of the plan. Funding and organization of capacity-building measures for individual school sites are largely left to local districts which, in the case of Maryland, tend to be large and congruent with counties.

As of October 1998, the state has put 89 schools on probation. Most of these schools perform in the bottom rank with recently declining test scores and are faced with high educational loads. Of the 82 elementary and middle schools on probation, the percentage of students who qualify for free and reduced price lunch ranges from 32 to 100%, with a median of 77%. Most of the RE schools in Maryland serve an African-American student population (over 80% of the enrollment in most RE schools); the overwhelming majority (more than 80%) of RE schools are located in the state's largest city, 10% are located in another local jurisdiction with a majority African-American population, and only two schools are located in majority White counties. Mean percentages of students who pass the MSPAP with satisfactory performance are 8.9% in math and 8.7% in reading among RE elementary schools, and 10.9% in math and 7.6% in reading among RE middle schools. The state considers 70% of students scoring satisfactory on the MSPAP an acceptable benchmark. Up until 1998, none of the RE schools had successfully exited the system, nor had final sanctions been applied to any of these schools. Reconstitution eligibility in Maryland, rather than a transitory stage, appears to be a protracted period of probation for schools that face exceptionally arduous challenges.

It is too early to tell whether Maryland's accountability system works for schools on probation. Most schools have only been part of the program for a few years, presumably too short a timespan to see a turnaround. Moreover, little systematic research and evaluation are available; research efforts that inform the author are in their infancy stage. These cautionary remarks notwithstanding, figures from the state's accountability system available at this point[4] are worth exploring. I next present data from elementary and middle schools whose performance is measured by the state's MSPAP test, given to third-, fifth-, and eighth-grade students every year.

---

[5]I wish to acknowledge the contribution of Ann MacLellan, research assistant in the Project on the Study of School Reconstitution, to the quantitative analysis.

Table 11.1 displays mean MSPAP scores as a percentage of students passing in a satisfactory manner for the RE elementary and middle schools identified in 1996. At present, the 1996 cohort is the most suitable group for analysis. It provides a fairly large number of cases with pre- and postidentification performance scores. The 1995 MSPAP scores, the basis for identification in 1996, and the 1997 MSPAP scores, attained 1.5 years after identification, are listed. Comparison of these two scores provides a sense of growth for this short time period. The 1996 RE cohort (n=33) is compared with two groups: all schools in Maryland, and all schools in Maryland that have a similar educational load as indicated by at least 50% of students receiving free and reduced lunch meals. All 33 RE elementary and middle schools in the 1996 RE cohort are in the "above 50% free and reduced lunch" bracket. This comparison provides a sense of how growth on MSPAP in RE schools stacks up to growth in schools in the rest of the state and schools with similar educational loads.

Table 11.1 shows that, overall, yearly growth on the MSPAP for all Maryland schools has been modest, as indicated by the percentage of students passing the reading and mathematics portion of the MSPAP test at a satisfactory level ("percentage satisfactory"). The percentage of students scoring "satisfactory" increased in both elementary school math (+3.4 points)

Table 11.1: Performance Changes on MSPAP- Scores "Percent Satisfactory" in 1995 and 1997 for Elementary and Middle Schools in Maryland

		Mean Scores 1995	Mean Scores 1997	Point Difference
			(Percentages)	
1996 cohort of	Elementary math	7.1	9.9	2.8
reconstitution	Elementary reading	6.4	9.7	3.3
eligible schools	Middle math	10.7	14.6	3.9
(N=33)	Middle reading	6.6	11.3	4.7
All Maryland	Elementary math	23.7	24.3	0.6
schools with 50%	Elementary reading	13.5	18.7	5.2
or more students in	Middle math	17.1	18.1	10.0
free/reduced-lunch program	Middle reading	9.9	10.9	1.0
All Maryland	Elementary math	43.6	47.0	3.4
schools	Elementary reading	28.6	34.5	5.9
	Middle math	40.9	44.2	3.3
	Middle reading	26.9	25.2	-1.7

Note. Fifth-grade scores are used for elementary school averages, and eighth-grade scores are used for middle school averages.

Table 11.2: Reversal of Decline- Mean Differences of Change 1994/95 and 1995/97 (1996 RE Cohort)

MSPAP Math Scores			*MSPAP Reading Scores*		
1996 RE Elementary/ Middle Schools in Highest Decline 1994-1995	*Mean Difference 1994/1995 (%)*	*Mean Difference 1995/1997 (%)*	*1996 RE Elementary/Middle Schools in Highest Decline 1994-1995*	*Mean Difference 1994/1995 (%)*	*Mean Difference 1995/1997 (%)*
School 1	-15.2	15.1	School 1	-8.5	14.0
School 2	-13.6	8.0	School 2	-7.4	7.4
School 3	-11.9	16.1	School 3	-9.9	-0.9
School 4	-7.1	-2.9	School 4	-13.6	3.0
School 5	-4.9	-6.8	School 5	-9.0	7.5
School 6	-5.6	-2.0	School 6	-8.6	1.4
School 7	-7.9	0.0	School 7	-8.4	5.5
School 8	-6.6	10.8	School 8	-6.1	4.1
School 9	-8.5	1.7	School 9	-7.6	13.8

and reading (+5.9 points) statewide. Among the middle schools across the state, satisfactory math scores increased by 3.3 points, and middle school reading scores posted a small decline (-1.7 points).

By comparison, the mean differences between 1995 and 1997 scores for the 1996 RE cohort of elementary and middle schools are similar to those of the rest of the state; in some areas RE school performance grew slightly more, in some areas slightly less. Comparison of the 1995 and 1997 means of the 1996 RE cohort with means from schools that had to deal with similar educational loads (as indicated by the percentage of students qualifying for free and reduced lunch meals) shows that RE schools perform below the mean of all Maryland schools with a similar educational load. Growth on MSPAP in RE schools was in some cases smaller, and in others larger than that of schools with similar poverty situations. Thus, these figures do not suggest that probationary status for reconstitution triggers clearly marked above average performance growth. At the same time, RE schools, clearly bottom performers, are at least keeping pace with the state as a whole.

In many respects, probation may first and foremost be a tool for arresting decline and stagnation in persistently failing schools given that the state targets schools for probation whose performance record indicates negative change. Table 11.2 illustrates whether such a reversal of decline has occurred in RE schools on probation. The table displays 10 of the 33 schools from the 1996 RE cohort that had the largest drop in performance as indicated by the difference between means of "percentage satisfactory" in math and reading in the year prior to identification (i.e., 1994-95). The difference between 1995 and 1997 scores (the last scores available at this time) indicates whether these exceptionally troubled schools were able to reverse their decline. Table 11.2 suggests that 9 of the 10 schools were able to reverse declining scores in both reading and math. In many instances, reversal exceeded a mere reversal of the sign, and substantial gains were made. Clearly, probationary status for reconstitution had a positive effect on these troubled and declining schools.

What are realistic growth expectations for schools on probation? Probationary status in Maryland (reconstitution eligibility), as indicated by the admittedly crude figures provided here, does not seem to elicit performance increases exceeding those for the rest of the state. Although they are not closing the gap, schools on probation may at least improve. There are indications that schools with especially low performance records and marked deterioration may respond favorably to the incentive of probation and may be able to reverse the worst decline. Thus, the Maryland figures presented here tell a tale of caution and muted expectation, but also of hope. Next, I present findings from one school that illustrate why perhaps low performing schools that serve large numbers of students placed at risk are at once motivated and constrained by reconstitution.

THE TALE OF ONE SCHOOL ON PROBATION

A glimpse into the life of one school may serve as a tale of caution and hope. This school is taking part in the 3-year study of high-stakes accountability in three U.S. jurisdictions. Although the research project has not systematically analyzed interview and observation material from all the schools, unfolding events at the described school are not atypical for many of the schools that participated in the study. In the following description, I concentrate on the issue of motivation framed by the three previously stated questions regarding threat, collegiality, and productivity of induced crisis. Given the stage of my research, I do not attempt to give final answers; rather the description should be read as an open-ended and illustrative lead into lines of inquiry the project will further pursue.

Educational Load

The school serves about 800 students in the seventh and eighth grades, the overwhelming majority of which are African-American. About one half of the student body qualifies for free and reduced price lunches; hence the school lies at the lower end of RE schools in this indicator of educational load. The faculty is three fourths African-American. In the school year 1997-1998, when research at the school began, 40% of the 59 faculty members had less than 6 years of job experience, 20% had 6-15 years, and another 40% had more than 15 years experience. Thus, the school is heavily staffed by young and old teachers, and not many mid-career teachers. Prior to the year of identification, the school had experienced declining MSPAP test scores. For example, from 1994 to 1997 reading test scores declined from 13 to 10% of students scoring at a satisfactory level. Mathematics scores declined during the same period from 28 to 14% of students scoring at a satisfactory level on the MSPAP.

School Year 1 (1997-1998)

The school year began with a new administration that was charged to reverse the existing decline. In February, the state announced that the school would become RE. I gained access to the school in April 1998. I began to observe faculty and school-based management team (SBMT) meetings and to conduct interviews with administrators and teachers, initially focusing on teachers highly involved in the affairs of the school. Both these teachers and the principal accepted the state's verdict as beyond their control, expressed relief that local and state authorities were de-emphasizing the punitiveness of the measure, hoped that reconstitution-eligibility might be a chance for the school to pull together, and assured the interviewer that the school would successfully master the challenge and improve.

The immediate challenge for the principal, however, was to understand the new external demands that new managerial mandates imposed on the school. Foremost, upon identification the school had to design and write a substantial school improvement plan (called the transition plan) based on a template furnished by district administrators. The plan had to be compiled within 2 months and submitted to the state board of education. The principal assembled a small group of four or five teachers, at least one of them on released time, who she felt had the ability to write such a plan. This was an unusual and enormous task for the writing team, especially given that the principal was new to the school. In this initial stage, reconstitution consisted of compiling a plan that could meet approval first by local officials and then by the state board. This became the overriding concern for administration and involved teachers. Although the designers of the plan conversed with other faculty about various elements of the plan, no systematic effort was launched to involve faculty on a broad scale. The school managed to write a plan that won praise from local administrators, but internally it was introduced to the SBMT as *fait accompli*. No broad-based discussion about the plan among faculty ensued. In fact, SBMT members were invited to view the plan in the principal's office, whereas teachers did not receive a copy of the plan until the following school year.

While the principal and the small teacher core concentrated on designing steps for school improvement, regular school operations slowly deteriorated, primarily due to mounting discipline problems. During class periods, the halls were filled with roaming students. Some teachers complained about being threatened by students, and being unable to keep student disruptions and violent behavior under control. In informal short response interviews, teachers blamed the inexperience of their administrators for this sorry state of affairs.

Toward the end of the school year, morale was low, expectations for performance improvement had evaporated, and dissension had reached the administrative team. One of the vice principals voiced her helplessness and her disapproval of the principal's lack of skill as a disciplinarian. The school year ended with a mass exodus of slightly less than half the staff, most of whom were seasoned teachers, including a large number of science teachers credentialed in their field, some highly involved teachers, and at least one plan writer. Most teachers who volunteered for exit interviews were beginning teachers. Prevalent reasons for their leaving were lack of student discipline, an inept administration, and better career options elsewhere. Reconstitution was mentioned, but paled in the face of problems these exiting teachers faced in their classrooms everyday. One teacher who chose to stay commented, "Nobody wants to be associated with a sinking ship."

School Year 2 (1998-1999)

In the following school year, the district installed a new principal in the school. The new principal had a track record of having previously achieved performance improvements in a similar school. She was not given much choice as to her new assignment, but she was allowed to assemble her own administrative team: two assistant principals, a master teacher, and a coordinator for school improvement activities whose position is funded out of a local reconstitution budget. She immediately set out to tackle the school's discipline problems. In a faculty meeting early in the year, she introduced her plan to the faculty. The plan involved a strict hall pass, escort, and lunch supervision system. When one of the teachers who had been at the school the previous year wanted to voice a concern with the plan, this teacher was interrupted and told in no uncertain terms "to follow the policy." All discussion abated thereafter. The new discipline policies were set in motion, carried out by a compliant faculty, and enforced by a determined administration. In time, student discipline improved. The principal succeeded in imposing a sense of orderly conduct on the school that had previously been absent – no small feat. But she accomplished this by determined top-down action and the vigilance of the new administrative team. Little involvement and participation of the old building faculty was sought.

A similar pattern was observable in other areas of school improvement. At a staff development day early in the year, the staff was finally handed a copy of the school improvement plan that had been approved by the state board of education, and thus, was considered a binding document, although the school had a completely new administration as well as a faculty with about 40% new teachers. The coordinator for the school improvement process wanted to use the staff development day to familiarize staff with the plan's content and particularly convey the plan's unique format. To this end, groups of teachers were given assignments to search for the linkages between goals, needs assessments, activities, and responsibilities in various areas of school operations as they were described in the plan. The teams were given a worksheet that required them to fill in content and page numbers for the various categories. The team I observed carried out the task with little luster. Finally, one of the teachers caught on to the task. Her worksheet was subsequently copied and given to the rest of the workgroup. At no time during the observed staff development session was there a discussion among faculty about the actual goals and ideas that they were expected to carry out. In subsequent interviews, whenever I asked how familiar informants felt with the plan – presumably the blueprint design for their improvement effort - they pointed to this particular staff development day.

During the early part of the 1998-1999 school year, about one fourth of the faculty was interviewed. The prevailing view in these interviews was that reconstitution was not a real threat. Teachers felt confident about their personal future. "There is always a place for a competent teacher," one teacher said. They called the state's tactic "a bluff" or "scare tactics." "Let the state come and take over, and then we'll see if they can do it better," was a sentiment echoed in many interviews. At the same time, teachers conceded that the state was right to point out performance deficiencies. Although the fairness of the accountability process was doubted on account that "the MSPAP is too hard for our students" and that teachers "are doing the best they can, given what they are up against," most teachers accepted responsibility for improvements, while at the same time they complained that the state placed too much blame on teachers. Teachers expressed a willingness to contribute to the school's success, although they rarely volunteered with concrete suggestions for their own classrooms. Optimism again prevailed in the school's second year of probation. As reasons for their optimism, teachers mentioned the improvement in discipline and the help the school had received and would continue to receive as a result of reconstitution. This year the local district provided additional resources for two staff positions and extensive staff development to reconstitution-eligible schools.

The school began Year 2 of probation with a committed senior staff and a large number of new teachers at the school. Senior teachers pointed out that after the mass exodus of the previous year, only staff who knew the situation of the school and who really wanted to be there remained. In contrast, interviewed first-year teachers were not sure what reconstitution eligibility entailed. Oblivious to the concerns of the school as a whole, they felt absorbed by the day-to-day challenges of managing students and instruction. The more seasoned teachers, although more astute about whole-school affairs, pointed to their students when asked why they chose to stay. Some expressed commitment explicitly to "this type of student," the "difficult" age group, or the community served by the middle school. Most teachers conveyed that they felt competent and that they, therefore, had something to offer to students and the community. In no case was it fear of sanctions, or the raising of test scores, per se, that motivated teachers to put forth greater effort. Rather, the school's probationary status was seen as a wake-up call to renew and reaffirm teachers' commitment to their students.

The school was abuzz with improvement activities. Teachers became participants in various committees that concentrated on specific areas of the school's operation. In SBMT meetings, teachers reported on their successes. The master teacher made the 20 or so first-year teachers her focus. The school improvement and test coordinators helped classroom teachers with centrally administered test preparation technology and practice. Staff development focused on performance-based pedagogy and lesson delivery. The administrative team conveyed to the staff in no uncertain terms what "they" (i.e., the state as well as visiting state and local monitors and coaches) expected teachers to do. For example, posting MSPAP words at eye level, posting objectives for each lesson, writing lesson plans for each lesson, displaying the district curriculum guide on the teachers' desks opened at the appropriate page for the day were all demands that the administrative team made on teachers, invoking expectations of external authorities.

Thus, in the second year, a strong administration, bolstered by accountability mandates, was able to tackle discipline problems, instill hope for success, and involve a growing number of teachers in the prescribed improvement process. Although teachers seemed to accept the need for improvement and were ready to comply, concrete steps were palpably driven by external demands. By November of Year 2, there were indications of trouble. Teachers began to complain that there were too many meetings. A copy of a passage from the union contract, implying that administrators' demands on teachers' time were out of compliance with the contract, was anonymously put in teachers' mailboxes. No teacher had volunteered to become the union representative for the year. In a few interviews with particularly vocal teachers, complaints that the principal, despite having improved student discipline, was insensitive to her staff and not interested in their voices were aired. A few teachers, one of them highly involved in the improvement process, confided that they would exit immediately if they only could. The principal's "tight ship," bolstered by the requirements of the new accountability system, seemed to have alienated a presumably small group of vocal and highly involved classroom teachers.

Interpretation of the Narrative

What does the glimpse from this school reveal about the effect of sanctions on motivation, the effect of group accountability on faculty cohesion, and the effect of induced crisis on the overall response of the organization? Because as mentioned earlier, I am reporting on a research project in progress, I cannot produce corroborated findings. However, in the hope that it might be of use for those thinking about the issue of high-stakes accountability for schools placed at risk, I offer some hunches that have been informed by the data, and that inform my theory building as I continue my research. Probation (i.e., reconstitution-eligibility in Maryland) does trigger in teachers a willingness to increase their performance, at least initially when the signal is still fresh, as reactions in newly identified schools indicate. This increase in motivation, however, is not due to the threat of sanctions. Particularly among teachers who become highly involved, probationary status renews commitment to their students and appeals to their sense of professional responsibility, even though they may feel hurt and, to a degree, unfairly judged.

Although a diffuse optimism and hope for success seems important – an optimism that teachers link more to the expectation of outside help than to a change in their own performance – more important for teachers' involvement is the sense of commitment triggered by probation, despite the discomfort it brings. Thus, it may not be clarity of goals or a defined expectation of valued rewards that mobilizes teachers who become involved, but rather a sense of professional pride, commitment, and perhaps idealism. Thus, reconstitution as probation may succeed in increasing teacher motivation, at least initially, but for reasons not predicted by a get tough accountability logic that assumes that teachers are rational, goal-oriented, and reward-maximizing actors. Instead, school improvement under an externally imposed accountability system must tap into teachers' commitment to their school and their students.

In the described school, as well as in other observed schools, reconstitution as probation is accompanied by a strong hierarchization of school management. School administrators are often the only ones in the school who have the requisite know-how to fulfill the requirements and expectations of the new accountability system, who channel external demands to their faculties, and who enhance their standing in the school with borrowed authority from the accountability agency. At the same time, their own performance pressures have increased palpably. As a result of probationary status, teachers come together in more frequent meetings, but rather than deliberating the school's vision, goals, and strategies, they more often conduct meetings in the spirit of fulfilling external expectations.

At this point, no systematic data on the differential impact of probation on various teacher groups are available. I hypothesized earlier that, in the logic of a rational model of motivation, high-performing teachers may expect commensurably higher rewards for their efforts; such expectations must be frustrated when the school's performance is measured by the group's performance. Although this scenario may have played a role in the mass exodus that coincided with reconstitution eligibility, it does not seem to have played a large role based on interviews in Year 2. Instead, probation was observed to mobilize the commitment of highly engaged and competent teachers to their (often challenging) students and schools, perhaps overriding concerns for differential rewards. This commitment may need to be nourished by opportunities for these teachers to exercise their voice in the affairs of the school. Here, a school administration, such as the one previously described, reacting to external accountability demands and the pressures of induced crisis with rigid central control, may alienate the very group of active and highly involved teachers on which success of the school improvement effort hinges.

Did the induced crisis elicit a productive response from the organization? Clearly, in Year 1 of probation, crisis in the described school was exacerbated. From the beginning, reconstitution, was an affair delegated to the principal, who relied on a small group of capable teachers. Time pressures in meeting the requirements of the accountability system were paramount. Likewise, escalating discipline problems were not taken up as a collective challenge, but responsibility rested with the administration. As the school year came to an end, hope of improvement yielded to expectation of further deterioration. Morale sank, dissension rose, though not openly, eventually spreading to the administrative team, while top-down operations became more rigid. According to the previously described threat-rigidity model, threat resulted in fragmentation and partial dissolution. The organization lost both its leadership and a good portion of its seasoned faculty.

Whether Year 2 will bring about a more productive response remains to be seen. The year began with a new strong administrative team and a less experienced faculty, as exiting seasoned teachers were replaced by novices who now make up about two fifths of the faculty. Hope for success resurfaced, school operations tightened up, and the core of highly involved teachers expanded, but it is the administrative team that is clearly in charge of the process. The school may succeed to the degree that the administration overcomes the spirit of top-down accountability and balances control with strategies that bolster teachers' commitment to their school and their students.

CONCLUSION

I argued earlier that, as far as the improvement of seriously underperforming schools placed at risk is concerned, the feasibility of reconstitution designs hinges on the probationary stage. In many reconstitution designs, a mix of mandates and incentives consisting of clear goals and standards, sanctions, group accountability, and school management mandates bears on the school during the probationary stage. Reconstitution as probation is directed at increasing motivation, making organizations more effective, and inducing instructional changes. Here, I focused on the affective response of individual educators and organizations to high-stakes accountability. I looked at competing models of teacher motivation, one stressing rational aspects of the work process, the other stressing the moral and expressive side of educators in schools. I attempted to discern contradictory tendencies inherent in group accountability, and I proposed possible scenarios of organizational response to crisis.

Summary data from the Maryland accountability system illustrated that reconstitution targets schools with arduous educational loads and challenging populations of poor and minority students. The data also suggested that realistic expectations for school improvement must be set, in all likelihood, within very modest parameters. The descriptive and interpretive analysis of events at one school out of a larger sample depicted some of the reasons that reconstitution as probation might at once have positive and negative effects on targeted schools, undercutting the full impetus of accountability. Events at the school, I suggested, demonstrate the positive impact of the external accountability agency in sending a wake-up call to the declining school organization, and in challenging teachers' professional pride and self-concept (although the risk of fragmenting the organization even further through this challenge is high). Expectation of success is a key ingredient in teachers' actions, but above all, it is the recurrence of the theme of teachers' commitment to their school and their students that is striking. In this area, reconstitution policies are weak for three reasons: they are only loosely tied to the provision of additional assistance; they tend to tap into a more rational calculation of quantitative goal, effort, and reward; and they reinforce a hierarchical management model that seems to alienate outspoken and potentially high-involvement workers. Whether and how jurisdictions modify reconstitution policies to encourage and deepen teachers' professional commitment may ultimately determine how successful these policies are in improving schools placed at risk.

REFERENCES

Argetsinger, A. (1998, October 28). Maryland superintendent unveils plan to lure new teachers; impending shortage prompts $50 million proposal. *The Washington Post*, p. B01.

Ascher, C., Ikeda, K., & Fruchter, N. (1997). *Schools on notice — A policy study of New York State's 1996-1997 schools under registration review process.* New York: New York State Education Department.

Ashton, P., & Webb, R. (1986). *Making a difference: Teachers' sense of efficacy and student achievement.* New York: Longman.

Ball, S. (1990). *The micro-politics of the school: Towards a theory of school organization.* London: Routledge.

Bennett, C., & Ferlie, E. (1994). *Managing crisis and change in health care: The organizational response.* Philadelphia: Open University Press.

Chicago Public Schools (1997) *School Probation Information Packet.* Chicago: Office of

Accountability

Conley, S., & Odden, A. (1995). Linking teacher compensation to teacher career development. *Educational Evaluation and Policy Analysis, 17*, 219-237.

Darling-Hammond, L. (1994). Performance-based assessment and educational equity. *Harvard Educational Review, 64*(1), 5-31.

Darling-Hammond, L. (1997). School reform at the crossroads: confronting the central issues of teaching. *Educational Policy*, 11(2), 151-166.

Dworkin, A. (1987). *Teacher burnout in the public schools: Structural causes and consequences for children*. Albany: State University of New York Press.

Elmore, R. (1990). *Restructuring schools: The next generation of educational reform* (1st ed.). San Francisco: Jossey-Bass.

Elmore, R., Abelmann, C., & Fuhrman, S. (1996). The new accountability in state education reform: From process to performance. In H. Ladd (Ed.), *Holding schools accountable: Performance-based reform in education* (pp. 65-98). Washington, DC: Brookings Institute.

Goldstein, J., Kelemen, M., & Koski, W. S. (1998, April). *Reconstitution in theory and practice: The experience of San Francisco* . Paper presented at the annual conference of the American Educational Research Association, San Diego, CA.

Guskey, T. (Ed.). (1994). *High stakes performance assessment: Perspectives on Kentucky's reform*. Thousand Oaks, CA: Corwin.

Hanushek, E. (1994). *Making schools work: Improving performance and controlling costs*. Washington, D C: Brookings Institute.

Jones, R. (1997, February 19). Teachers head to court, students hit streets to protest school plan. *The Philadelphia Inquirer*, p. B-1.

Kelley, C., & Protsik, J. (1997). Risk and reward: Perspectives on the implementation of Kentucky's school-based performance award program. *Educational Administration Quarterly, 33*(4), 474-505.

Lawler, E. (1973). *Motivation in work organizations*. San Francisco: Jossey-Bass.

LeCompte, M., & Dworkin, A. (1991) *Giving up on school: Student dropouts and teacher burnouts*. Thousand Oaks, CA: Corwin.

Levine, C., Rubin, I., & Wolohojian, G. (1982). Managing organizational retrenchment: Preconditions, deficiencies, and adaptations in the public sector. *Administration and Society, 14*(1), 101-136.

Locke, E. (1968). Toward a theory of task motivation and incentives. *Organizational Behavior and Human Performance, 3*, 157-189.

Malen, B. (1999). On rewards, punishments and possibilities: Teacher compensation as an instrument for education reform. *Journal of Personnel Evaluation in Education, 12* (4), 387-394.

Malen, B., Murphy, M., & Hart, A. (1987). Restructuring teacher compensation systems: An analysis of three incentive strategies. In K. Alexander, K. & D. Monk, (Eds.), *Attracting and compensating for America's teacher*. (p. 91-142). Cambridge, MA: Ballinger.

Maryland State Department of Education. (1997). *Criteria for Reconstitution*. Baltimore: Author.

Meyer, M., & Zucker, L. (1989). *Permanently failing organizations*. Thousand Oaks, CA: Sage.

Mohrman, A., Mohrman, S. & Odden, A. (1996). Aligning teacher compensation with systemic school reform: Skill -based pay and group-based performance rewards. *Educational Evaluation and Policy Analysis, 18*(1), 51-71.

National Commission on Teaching & America's Future. (1996). *What matters most: Teaching for America's future*. New York: Author.

Odden, A., & Conley, S. (1992). *Restructuring teacher compensation.* San Francisco: Jossey - Bass.

Olson, M. (1965). *The logic of collective action: Public goods and the theory of groups.* New York: Schocken.

Orfield, G., Cohen, B., Foster, G., Green, R. Lawrence, P., Tatel, D., & Tempes, F. (1992). *Desegregation and educational change in San Francisco: Findings and recommendations on consent decree implementation.* Report submitted to Judge William H. Orrick, U.S. District Court. San Francisco.

Page, R. (1995). Who systematizes the systematizers? Policy and practice interactions in a case of state-level systemic reform. *Theory into Practice, 34*(1), 21-29.

Petrosko, J. M. (1996). Assessment and accountability. In J. Lindle, J. Petrosko, & R. Pankratz (Eds.), *1996 Review of Research on the Kentucky Education Reform Act* (pp. 3-51). Frankfort: Kentucky Institute for Education Research.

Price, H. (1997, August). *'No Excuses' era of urban school reform.* Keynote address delivered at the Urban League. New York: Urban League.

Riley, R. (1997). *Fourth annual state of American education address: Putting standards of excellence in action.* Speech delivered at the Carter Center. Atlanta, GA: Carter Center.

Rowan, B., Chiang, F. S., & Miller, R. L. (1997). Using research on employees' performance to study the effect of teachers on student performance. *Sociology of Education, 70*(4), 256-284.

Ruenzel, D. (1997). Do or die. *Teacher Magazine, 8,* 24-30.

Schein, E. (1991). *Organizational culture and leadership.* San Francisco: Jossey - Bass.

Shamir, B. (1991). Meaning, self and motivation in organizations. *Organization Studies, 12*(3), 405-424.

Staw, B., Lance, E., & Dutton, J. (1981). Threat-rigidity effects in organizational behavior: A multilevel analysis. *Administrative Science Quarterly, 26,* 501-524.

Weiner, B. (1986). *An attributional theory of motivation and emotion.* New York: Springer.

Wong, K. K., & Anagnostopoulos, D. (1997). *Can system-wide accountability standards be implemented? Lessons learned from the probation policy in low-performing Chicago high schools.* Unpublished manuscript.

Wong, K., Anagnostopoulos, D., & Rutledge, S. (1998, October). *Accommodation and conflict: The implementation of Chicago's probation and reconstitution policies.* Paper presented at the annual meeting of the Association for Public Policy Analysis and Management, New York.

12

Talent Development Middle Schools: Blueprint and Results for a Comprehensive Whole School Reform Model

DOUGLAS J. MACIVER
MARTHA A. MACIVER
ROBERT BALFANZ
STEPHEN B. PLANK
ALLEN RUBY
Johns Hopkins University

The Center for Research on the Education of Students Placed At Risk has been working since 1994 to develop, implement, and evaluate the talent development middle school (TDMS) model. The goal of the TDMS model is to build on structural reform recommendations and to establish the curriculum, instruction, school organization, and professional development needed for all students to learn challenging academic materials and prepare for successful futures. In this chapter, we discuss (a) the TDMS model's development, (b) the implementation of the model in several Philadelphia middle schools and plans for more widespread implementation, and (c) research findings on student attitudes and achievement gains that suggest the model is making a difference in the lives of young adolescents placed at risk.

The signature practices for middle grades education that grew out of the middle school movement, including detracking, cooperative learning, exploratory classes, flexible scheduling, and the establishment of closer relationships between students and teachers through advisory and interdisciplinary teacher team approaches (Carnegie Council on Adolescent

Development, 1989; Epstein & MacIver, 1990; Hough, 1997, National Middle School Association, 1995), provided a necessary foundation for middle school reform. However, these practices by themselves have proven insufficient to help low-performing middle schools that serve poor and minority students to turn themselves around and become "beacons of improvement" characterized by large numbers of students who become proficient in the knowledge and skills that middle school students need in order to have strong "future prospects" (Lipsitz, Mizell, Jackson, & Austin, 1997; Madhere & MacIver, 1996). Middle schools that serve primarily poor and minority students have been especially open to adopting the signature practices of the middle school movement because they are desperate to reduce the number of young adolescents in their schools who do not fare well (MacIver & Epstein, 1990). Yet, very few of these schools have succeeded in defying society's stereotypes about the unreachability and unteachability of the young adolescents that they serve.

What are some of the elements missing from the blueprint provided by the signature practices? Although the establishment of interdisciplinary teaming and a teacher advisory program may ensure that each student in a middle school will have more support from (and more meaningful relationships with) caring adults at the school than in the stereotypical junior high schools of the past (Arhar, 1997; MacIver, 1990; MacIver & Epstein, 1991); it is nonetheless true that interpersonal ties between students and teachers in most middle schools are still incredibly weak (Darling-Hammond, 1997, McLaughlin & Doda, 1997). This is a consequence of the typical middle school's approach to staffing and school organization. Ninety-two percent of U.S. seventh-grade students and 97% of the nation's eighth-grade students have a different teacher for each of the major academic subjects (McPartland, 1990). This team of teachers usually changes each year as students progress through middle school (e.g., students are passed on from a seventh-grade teaching team to an eighth-grade teaching team). As a result, in most middle schools, the typical student and the typical teacher are together for just one period a day for approximately 180 days. The superficial and fleeting nature of student-teacher relationships (and parent-teacher relationships) in most middle schools is exacerbated by each teacher's being responsible for so many different students (e.g., five different sections of students). These relationships are undoubtedly too weak to motivate either teachers or students to "do whatever it takes" to reach new heights of teaching and learning (Wilson & Corbett, 1998).

Thus, middle schools need to do much more to help teachers, students, and families establish strong bonds and close, productive relationships. The existing literature on student achievement indicates that middle schools must do even more than establish and nurture these close relationships. To create an environment in which every student can achieve a high level of intellectual proficiency, middle schools must also improve four related aspects of the social organization of learning: the curriculum, instructional and peer assistance strategies, assessment, and professional development.

THE CURRICULUM

Middle school students need to be engaged by a common core curriculum that is coherent, focused, and challenging. Simply put, students usually do not learn what they are not taught or given a structured opportunity to acquire (Knapp, 1995). In addition, there is growing evidence that student engagement is higher when academic tasks are more complex (Bruer, 1994; Stodolsky, 1988). Student engagement, in turn, has been shown to be a key element in the rate and level of learning (Means, Chelemer, & Knapp, 1991). Unfortunately, international comparisons, national surveys, and case studies all indicate that the middle grades in the United States currently fall short on one and often all of these features (Balfanz, 1997; Corbett & Wilson, 1997; Knapp, 1995; National Center for Educational Statistics [NCES], 1996; Stevenson & Stigler, 1992). Tracked middle schools typically deny students in the lower tracks the opportunity to acquire and master higher order competencies (Oakes, Gamoran, & Page, 1992). The existing middle school curriculum is often fragmented and repetitive. As a result, students are not afforded the opportunity to acquire new knowledge in an organized and systematic fashion. In the recent Third International Mathematics and Science Study (TIMSS), for example, U.S. students ranked 23rd of 27 in the rate of growth of mathematical knowledge between seventh and eighth grade (Beaton et al., 1996). Researchers attribute much of this low ranking to a curriculum that is "a mile wide and an inch thick" (Schmidt, McKnight, & Raizen, 1996). Both the earlier work of Stevenson and Stigler and the more recent TIMSS research argue that high levels of academic achievement are attained in nations where classroom instruction is supported by curricula that introduce advanced skills and concepts to all middle grade students in a thoughtful, focused, and active manner.

INSTRUCTIONAL STRATEGIES

By itself, a coherent, focused, and challenging core curriculum is not enough to dramatically increase the number of middle school students who achieve a high level of academic excellence. Detracking, inclusion, and the changing demographics of the student population in the United States have led to middle school classrooms that are populated with students who are from more diverse backgrounds and who have a wider range of prior academic success and preparation than in the past (Natriello, McDill, & Pallas, 1990). Heterogeneous secondary school classrooms, for instance, can contain students at five or more instructional levels (Mevarech & Kramarski, 1997). This shift in the distribution of student characteristics at the classroom level from a narrow range of instructional levels and prior experiences to a more varied one has increased the complexity of middle school instruction. Fuchs, Fuchs, Mathes, and Simmons (1997) argued that in the absence of new instructional strategies that enable teachers to effectively structure learning in this more complex environment, teachers will simplify the instructional challenge. They accomplish this by focusing on the students they consider "teachable" and eliminating the "difficult to teach students from consciousness." In other words, unless the organization of instruction in middle schools is expanded to include a repertoire of instructional strategies that are effective in heterogeneous classes, the elimination of tracking and the institution of a common core curriculum still may not improve the learning of a sizable number of students.

Fortunately, a number of instructional strategies have shown promise in delivering high-level instruction to heterogeneous classes. These include but are not limited to reciprocal teaching (Palincsar & Klenk, 1991), classwide peer tutoring (Fuchs et al., 1997), the East Asian whole class method (Stevenson & Lee, 1995), and several variations of cooperative learning (King, 1994; Mevarech & Kramarski, 1997; Slavin, 1995; Webb & Farivar, 1994). The common threads that run through these approaches are the use of peer-assisted learning, explicit mechanisms for providing students with essential background knowledge, an emphasis on developing metacognitve strategies, and materials or strategies that actively engage students with questions that provoke higher order thinking. What remains to be shown is that these strategies or other effective methods of teaching in heterogeneous classes can be implemented and sustained across the core subjects and throughout the middle grades.

ASSESSMENT

The existing literature suggests that increasing the number of middle school students who acquire advanced academic skills also requires several reforms in assessment. First, few points have been as clearly made and abundantly disseminated in the past as that of than the need to align classroom instruction and assessment (e.g., American Federation of Teachers, 1992; Glaser & Silver, 1994). Yet in practice, because of the multiplicity of authorities to whom schools, teachers, and students are accountable, this remains a difficult task. Second, at the classroom level, students need to be provided with continual corrective feedback on their work (Locke & Latham, 1990). Seatwork, however, which has traditionally occupied much of students' time in the middle grades, commonly goes unchecked and uncorrected (Stevenson & Stigler, 1992). Third, assessments at the classroom level need to facilitate or at least support a classroom environment in which every student is encouraged and motivated to put forth solid effort (MacIver & Reuman, 1993; MacIver, Reuman, & Main, 1995). Fourth, assessments should feature performance tasks that are "essential, integrative, rich, engaging, active, and feasible" (Forgione, 1990, p. 3).

PROFESSIONAL DEVELOPMENT

Sustained, schoolwide, and curriculum-specific professional development is needed to realize the improvements sought in curriculum, instructional strategies, and assessment in the middle grades. Existing research on what constitutes effective professional development (McLaughlin & Oberman, 1996) is sparse but it has made several key points. First, Cohen, Wilson, and Hill (1997) in a survey of elementary mathematics teachers in California found that generic staff development (sessions on using manipulatives or conducting standards-based mathematics lessons, for example) had no effect on teacher self-reports of classroom practice or district achievement scores. Curriculum-specific sessions, on the other hand, which provided teachers with content knowledge (operating with fractions, for example) and which prepared them to teach actual replacement units incorporating standards-based lessons, had a positive effect on both teacher self-reports of classroom practice and classroom achievement. As the authors stated:

> This is a terrifically important result, if it stands up, for it suggests that when teachers have significant opportunities to learn the content that students will

learn in ways that seem to enable them to learn more about teaching the material – and when assessments are linked to the students' and teachers' curriculum – teachers' opportunities to learn pay off for their students' learning. (p. 61)

The importance of continual technical assistance and follow-up has also been noted (Fuchs et al., 1997). In particular, any innovation that requires substantial change in teacher practice needs to be supported with in-classroom implementation assistance (Balfanz & MacIver, 1998). Finally, there is growing evidence of the need to involve the entire teaching staff in a focused and collaborative effort to improve teaching and learning in a school (Elmore, Peterson, & McCarthey, 1996; Nelson & Hammerman, 1996). Professional development efforts that target a handful of teachers or a particular subject in a particular grade may lead to "pockets of excellence" (Corbett & Wilson, 1997) but they do not create successful learning communities (Knapp, 1995).

The challenge then for the middle grades is not simply to improve curriculum, instruction, assessment, and professional development but to do it throughout the school, across grades and across subjects. This is a tall order. It is made even taller by the fact that it needs to occur not only in middle schools where the conditions for reform may be favorable, but also in all other middle schools, including those often found in our nation's inner cities, which face the extreme conditions of large class sizes, high student and faculty mobility, and high concentrations of poverty (Knapp, 1995).

THE TALENT DEVELOPMENT MIDDLE SCHOOL BLUEPRINT

Since 1994, the goal of the talent development middle school (TDMS) model has been to build on structural reform recommendations and to establish the curriculum, instruction, school organization, and professional development needed for all students to learn challenging academic materials and prepare for successful futures. Talent development (TD) is a philosophy about the excellence schools and students can achieve as well as a blueprint for how to attain such excellence. Not all of the components have been created from scratch. Many draw from the best practices that have emerged during the past decade of middle school reform. What we believe is most innovative and promising about the TD effort is the way in which the components fit together as a whole, to support and facilitate one another as a model for whole school reform. The eight key components of TDMS model can be summarized as follows.

Structural Foundation

Communal Organization. When teachers are asked, "What matters for teaching?" – one of the factors that they emphasize is the importance of close, sustained relationships with students. Such relationships are important for knowing students well, motivating them, taking account of their prior knowledge and interests in planning how to approach a lesson, and adjusting plans as needed in light of students' responses (Darling-Hammond, 1997). Likewise, the TDMS model asserts that the establishment of close, caring relationships between teachers and their students is not a frill but is a necessary condition to support teaching and learning for understanding. Because deep learning does not occur unless students contribute effort and cooperation, teaching is inherently a risky endeavor (Cohen, 1996; Lortie, 1975; Means et al., 1991). As Darling-Hammond noted, "These risks are increased when teachers aim for ambitious learning rather than settling for rote work, which is more easily controlled" (p. 80). To enable middle school teachers to be daring in their classroom instruction – that is, to make it safe for them to use active teaching strategies that prompt students to inquire, discover, and apply knowledge – TD middle schools implement innovative approaches to school organization and staffing that allow teachers and students to establish strong bonds and a shared sense of purpose. *Looping* (assigning teachers to the same students for 2 or 3 years) is one of these innovative approaches.

In addition, in TD middle schools, small learning communities that serve 200 to 300 students, occupy their own parts of the building, and endure for at least 3 years are established. Also, teachers are encouraged to teach at least two subjects (semidepartmentalization), which allows them to establish stronger relationships with a smaller number of students (MacIver & Plank, 1997b). Finally, teachers are organized into two- or three-person interdisciplinary teams so that they can confer with one another and respond to the students whom they share.

Detracking of Instruction. For too long, middle and high schools have been driven by a sorting paradigm in which some students receive high-level instruction while others are relegated to lower quality education and lower quality futures. The TDMS model asserts that all children are capable of succeeding in demanding college-preparatory courses when given the right types of support.

Because tracking causes gross inequalities in students' access to knowledge, instructional resources, and well-qualified teaching, TDMS students are heterogeneously grouped for their core academic classes. This eliminates nightmare sections – those lower track sections that no one wants to teach and that typically feature a slow pace and dumbed-down content.

To help teachers manage these heterogeneous classes effectively and teach in ways that help students learn, TDMS staff provide them with focused and coherent professional development in the use of subject-specific cooperative learning and teaching-for-understanding instructional methods, as well as classroom management techniques designed for diverse classrooms. By combining heterogeneous classrooms with effective cooperative learning approaches that feature guided peer tutoring and peer discussion of high-level content, TD schools cultivate the conceptual learning of all students. This use of structured cooperative learning is also quite effective in building peer support for achievement in the classroom so that positive peer pressure leads students to embrace academic aspirations and encourage other students who are not giving their best effort to work harder.

Instructional Edifice

A Demanding Core Curriculum for All. In TD schools, every student completes a research-and-standards-based core curriculum in the major subject areas. In each of the major subject areas, the curriculum emphasizes active learning, the acquisition of essential foundational knowledge, and the development of higher order competencies. Our goal is to provide all students with access to curriculum that can be universally recognized as the centerpiece of a world-class education. All eighth-grade students, for example, will study algebra, read and analyze great literature, perform hands-on science experiments, and interpret original documents from U.S. history.

Reading/English/language arts (RELA) is taught as a double-period block each day using student team literature (Jones & Shaw, 1998, MacIver, Plank, & Balfanz, 1997, Stevens & Durkin, 1992), an innovative, thoroughly tested, and highly effective cooperative learning approach to teaching and learning in RELA. In this approach, students read award-winning novels, plays, and poems that serve as a springboard for vocabulary and reading comprehension exercises and literature-based writing, all of which are pursued via peer-assisted learning techniques.

The research-and-standards-based mathematics curriculum in TD schools is built around materials developed by the University of Chicago School Mathematics Project (UCSMP, 1998). It blends skill building with problem solving and is designed to enable all students to succeed in algebra in the eighth grade (Balfanz, Plank, MacIver, & Ryan, in press).

In science, TDMS staff from Johns Hopkins University help schools take advantage of the recent developments occurring in science education by (a) working with the science faculty of each TD school to modify their curriculum so that it becomes aligned with the national science standards and with benchmarks developed by the National Science Foundation and the American Association for the Advancement of Science, (b) providing professional development, and (c) working with teachers to implement effective new science modules. In doing so, TDMS staff draw from a number of recently developed curricula that meet the national standards including *Science and Technology for Children, Full Option Science System, Science Education for Public Understanding Program, INSIGHTS, Science Plus, FACETS, Project Wet,* and *Project Atmosphere.* Such a program helps teachers implement modules from these curricula and adapt portions of their school's existing curriculum to meet the standards (Ruby, in press).

The TDMS U.S. history program includes (a) a coherent, comprehensive set of curricular materials designed to assist all students in understanding the most important primary sources of information about American history, such as the Declaration of Independence and the U.S. Constitution, as well as outstanding secondary sources of information, especially volumes from Joy Hakim's award-winning *A History of Us* series, and (b) instructional practices, peer assistance processes, writing assignments, enriching extension activities, simulations, and assessments (Dangel, Garriott, & Perkins, 1998).

Supports for Teachers

The demanding core curriculum is supported by high-caliber, curriculum-specific professional development. The instructional edifice in TD schools is further supported by curriculum coaches, in-school support staff, and Hopkins-based instructional facilitators.

Ongoing, Subject-Specific Staff Development. In each subject area, teachers engage in a multiyear sequence of professional development that focuses on instructional strategies, content knowledge, assessment tools, and modeling and previewing upcoming lessons.

Curriculum Coaches. A curriculum coach in each subject area provides follow-up support to accompany the ongoing staff development in that subject. These coaches are skilled and intensively trained school district teachers who are placed on special assignment to the TD program. Each curriculum coach typically works with three schools at a time during implementation years and spends 1 to 2 days a week at each school, providing in-classroom support (including modeling, troubleshooting, peer coaching, meeting with small groups of teachers to go over upcoming lessons, and making sure that teachers have the supplies and materials necessary to implement the program).

In-School Support Staff. School-level personnel provide another tier of teacher support. At least two teachers in each major subject area in the school are trained during the implementation year to become the in-school support staff. Over time, these teachers play increasingly larger roles in ongoing professional development, sustaining the program within the building, and training new teachers.

Hopkins-Based Instructional Facilitators. The Johns Hopkins TD staff provides the final tier of teacher support. This staff is composed of expert teachers in each instructional program who stay in weekly phone contact with the curriculum coaches and school-level personnel. The Johns Hopkins TD staff work with these coaches and other personnel to plan and organize the ongoing staff development and to solve problems that arise. They also make several annual visits to the school to review the progress being made in implementation, assist with staff development, and assist in planning.

Supports for Students

Extra Help, Enrichment, and Recognition. When a school dismantles tracking and exposes all students to the same demanding core curriculum, some students will need extra help and other students, especially top achievers, will be inspired to seek additional advanced learning opportunities. Without reinventing the sorting paradigm, there are good ways to provide this extra help and enrichment. In TD schools, "extra-dose" classes can replace another elective course for 10 weeks to give intensive extra help to those who need it and focused opportunities for enrichment to those ready for even more advanced work. These classes use cooperative groups and computers to provide intensive individualized learning experiences. Both students needing extra help to meet high standards and those seeking enrichment have responded enthusiastically to these extra-dose classes even though the students miss an elective class for 10 weeks in order to participate (MacIver, Balfanz, & Plank, 1998).

These extra-dose classes help make detracking work well because the teachers of the regular classes feel no pressure to dumb down or slow down the curriculum. The teachers know that intensive extra help will be received by all students who need additional time and instruction to master the material.

In addition to extra help, many students need extra opportunities to earn recognition if thcy are to give their best efforts. When a child has received Cs and Ds for years, he or she has seldom received academic accolades and may perceive success in school as unattainable. In an effort to change this situation, TD schools use growth-oriented evaluation that recognizes individual improvement and progress toward high standards in addition to giving students realistic, unambiguous feedback concerning how their performance compares to national norms and performance standards (MacIver & Reuman, 1993; MacIver, Reuman, & Main, 1995).

Career and Education Exploration. Middle school is the right time for students to learn about different career paths; form high aspirations; and make decisions about middle school, high school, and even postsecondary schooling. In TD schools, students complete a 3-year course that meets weekly. The career exploration and educational decision-making curriculum is designed to (a) provide students with opportunities to find out about careers in which they are interested through a variety of activities, including reading, role playing, interviewing, researching, and listening to career representatives in person and on video; (b) enable students to develop and view their own career aspirations in light of their interests and academic strengths; (c) give students facts about types of high schools and colleges, including entrance requirements and courses of study available to them; and (d) lead students to connect their current academic performance to the behaviors that help or hinder it, so they can achieve academic goals that will enable them to realize their career aspirations.

Cultural Relevance. TD curricular materials and professional development emphasize culturally relevant materials and teaching practices (Ladson-Billings, 1994). This component of the program recognizes that students will work harder and learn more if instruction is attentive to the student population's cultural patterns and norms, promotes cross-cultural understanding, and helps students connect to and interpret cultural traditions.

School-Family-Community Partnerships. TD schools participate in the National Network of Partnership schools (Epstein, Coates, Salinas, Sanders, & Simon, 1996; Sanders & Epstein, chap. 15, this volume). The network, established by researchers at Johns Hopkins University, brings together schools, districts, and states that are committed to developing and maintaining comprehensive programs of school-family-community partnerships. As part of the network, TD schools establish action teams that plan, carry out, and evaluate school, parent, and community partnership activities that support students' learning and school success.

IMPLEMENTATION OF THE TALENT DEVELOPMENT MODEL

Central East Middle School in Philadelphia became the first TDMS during spring 1995. Two more Philadelphia schools – Cooke and Beeber Middle Schools – became TDMSs in fall 1997, with Cooke following a "rapid start" implementation plan and Beeber adopting a "gradual start" implementation schedule. Two additional schools – Shoemaker and Clemente Middle Schools – became TD schools in fall 1998. Taken together, these five middle schools in Philadelphia serve a total of 5,600 students and represent every middle school in the two clusters targeted by this initiative. Plans are underway to begin a national field test of the TDMS model in fall 1999. Twelve additional schools in four districts in different areas of the United States will be selected for this field test.

We have assessed implementation of the components of the TDMS model using several methods: student surveys (in which students were asked the extent to which they experienced instructional activities inherent in the model), informal classroom observations by instructional facilitators and curriculum coaches, and teacher focus groups. Surveys also were conducted among students at a matched comparison school to determine the extent to which instructional components of the TDMS model occurred more frequently at the experimental school.

As noted earlier, the RELA curriculum in the TDMS model uses student team literature instructional methods and materials developed by TD curriculum writers. These materials support the teaching of award-winning novels; plays; poems; and nonfictional literature such as biographies, autobiographies, and narrative historical accounts. After only one semester of implementation, we found highly significant differences between the experimental and control schools on how frequently the components of student team literature occurred in classrooms (overall effect size of .68) (MacIver & Plank, 1996). Analyses using hierarchical linear modeling (HLM) indicated that the variable, *School*, was a significant predictor of classroom means on six of the nine items in the student team literature implementation measure. Students in the experimental school experienced more frequent opportunities to compose meaningful sentences using vocabulary words from the novel they were reading, do story-related writing, work in teams to master the vocabulary used in a novel, discuss a novel with a partner, explain answers to their teammates and check to make sure that all their teammates understood the material, and make predictions about what might happen in the rest of the story. In contrast, the variable, *School*, was not a significant predictor of using team awards for progress, partner reading, or partner questioning.

Six focus groups, conducted in December 1997 by the director of research for the Philadelphia Educational Fund with teachers at two of the TDMSs in Philadelphia, yielded the following conclusions:

> Teachers' responses to the Talent Development training, materials, and instructional approach are generally favorable, with some components coming in for more praise than others. The intensive and sustained nature of the training model along with the multiple levels of support – from CRESPAR [Center for Research on the Education of Students Placed At Risk] trainers, teacher leaders in the school, and a teacher on special assignment in math – appear to provide a highly effective package of professional development services. Opposition to potentially controversial aspects of the initiative – cooperative learning and de-tracking – was voiced by just a few teachers. While acknowledging their students' shaky levels of performance, teachers seemed willing to forge ahead, believing that a continuous schoolwide approach will produce better student achievement. (Useem, 1998)

The impact of implementation of the TD model on teacher's use of exemplary teaching practices across all major subject areas has been confirmed by an independent longitudinal study. This study seeks to detail the impact on middle school students of the school district of Philadelphia's introduction of content and performance standards. Qualitative researchers Corbett and Wilson (1997) interviewed students in five middle schools each year as the students progressed through their 3 years in middle school. These researchers recently added, as a sixth school, the first TDMS, Central East. Interviewing a sample of eighth-grade students, they sought to determine whether the TD school has succeeded – where five similar Philadelphia middle schools have not – in offering a high-quality education with substantial standards-driven classwork, and consistently excellent and caring teachers. In a preliminary report, Corbett summarized their strikingly positive interviews at Central East:

> The Central East students value the same qualities in teachers that we found in the other five middle schools (willingness to help, ability and willingness to explain clearly, and being strict). What was different was these qualities were found in almost all of their major classes whereas in the other schools such distribution was rare. Moreover, and more significantly, students described classwork that was substantial and clearly related to the changes CRESPAR is encouraging. Students also generally believed that most students got along with

one another. While students in all the schools similarly felt they were getting a good education, the students at Central East described a different education than the others. Essentially most students trust teachers to do what's best for their futures; Central East seems to be living up to that trust dramatically better than the others. (Corbett, personal communication)

In the final report, Wilson and Corbett (1999) let the students at Central East speak for themselves:

Serendipity allowed us to interview five females and one male at School #6 [Central East] who had previously attended two of the five original schools in the sample. Therefore, we were able to solicit, firsthand, the differences they encountered between the two schools. Their observations seemed to bear out the hints of a different tone to the school [characterized by more demanding and appropriate learning opportunities] that were alluded to earlier. (p.71)

They cite the following exchange as one example:

Student: The work is challenging.
Interviewer: Do you like doing hard work?
Student: I like doing work at my level. The work here is much harder
                  than at School #3.
Interviewer: Was School #3 too easy for you?
Student: I was beyond the work at School #3. Here the work is much
                  harder and more like what I can do.

EVIDENCE OF EFFECTIVENESS

Impact on Reading Achievement

After 1 year of implementation of the student team literature program, a significant advantage in reading comprehension improvement was observed in 21 classes at the first TDMS relative to 25 classes in a closely matched comparison site. The improvements in reading comprehension at Central East were substantial (MacIver et al., 1997). In analyses that controlled for prior achievement and current grade level, the typical Central East student outperformed his or her counterpart at the comparison school on the Stanford 9 multiple choice test of reading comprehension by almost 12 scale score points. The difference between a typical seventh-grade student and an eighth-grade student at these two schools is only six points. The student team literature program helped Central East's students to achieve almost twice this much learning. It is as though every student at Central East were given 2 years of extra growth in reading comprehension. Students with the highest prior achievement benefited even more from student team literature. They outperformed the students with the highest prior achievement from the comparison school by 17 scale score points in reading comprehension. The observed effect size of .51 is quite large compared to the impact of other educational reforms and is of the magnitude needed to achieve serious academic gains (Mosteller, Light, & Sachs, 1996).

The data also indicate that it was not just the typical student who improved. Some analyses suggest that it was the high achievers who made the greatest absolute gains in reading achievement. Yet, the reported mean gains appear to be, in part, the result of increasing the number of students in the upper reaches of the achievement distribution and decreasing the number of students in the lower reaches. In short, improvements in reading comprehension were widespread. The student team literature instructional program in the context of the TDMS model appears, on average, not merely to have benefitted just low, middle, or top achievers but rather to have demonstrated a "common school effect" (Bryk, Lee, & Holland, 1993). Almost all of the students at Central East felt its positive impact.

The achievement gains in reading continued in the second year (1996-1997). For example, eighth-grade students at Central East Middle School witnessed a 10.9 percentage point gain in the percent of students scoring better than basic in reading and an 8.4 percentage point decline in the percent of students scoring below basic. Of 17 other large middle schools in Philadelphia that are comparable to Central East, with poverty rates between the high 70% and low 90% mark, only one school showed progress similar to that demonstrated by Central East in reading achievement.

Findings from Central East and its comparison site can now be supplemented by data from Cooke Middle School, the second school in Philadelphia to implement the TD model, and its comparison site. A first step toward assessing the feasibility of effectively scaling up the TD model to multiple sites is noting whether the positive and significant first-year effects of student team literature on achievement observed at Central East also were realized at Cooke.

After Cooke Middle School's first year of implementation, fifth- and sixth-grade students also showed notable achievement gains in reading, in fact, much greater than those attained at Cooke's comparison school (See Table

Table 12.1: Achievement Gains in Reading at Cooke Middle School and its Comparison School						
	Cooke Middle School			Comparison School		
	9/97	4/98	Difference	10/97	4/98	Difference
	Fifth grade total reading achievement					
Number tested	182	179	-3	190	218	28
Mean scaled score	583	620.9	37.9	600.6	619	18.4
Median grade equivalent	2.8	3.9	1.1	3.5	3.9	0.4
Below basic (%)	79	50	-29	54	54	0
Basic (%)	17	42	25	36	42	6
Proficient or advanced (%)	4	8	4	9	5	-4
	Sixth grade total reading achievement					
Number tested	243	234	-9	167	223	56
Mean scaled score	610.1	627.9	17.8	621.9	633.1	11.2
Median grade equivalent	3.5	4.2	0.7	3.9	4.5	0.6
Below basic (%)	62	56	-6	50	48	-2
Basic (%)	34	38	4	42	45	3
Proficient or advanced (%)	4	6	2	8	7	-1

12.1). As can be seen in the second row of Table 12.1, the mean scale score for fifth-grade students at Cooke Middle School in total reading increased by almost 38 points, whereas the mean scale score in the comparison school increased by only about 18 points. Note that Cooke fifth-grade students started out significantly behind their peers at the comparison school, but overtook them during the course of Cooke's first year as a TD school. Between fall and spring, the median grade equivalent of Cooke fifth-grade students increased from second grade, eighth month to third grade, ninth month, and the percentage of fifth-grade students scoring below basic in reading declined by 29% (from 79% to 50%). As can be seen in the lower half of Table 12.1, sixth-grade students at Cooke also outgained their counterparts at the comparison school, although the difference was not as large as that for fifth-grade students. Recent research (Plank & Young, 1999) indicates that. Therefore, we do not yet know whether Cooke Middle School students also outgained comparison school students at the seventh- and eighth-grade levels.

Impact on Mathematics Achievement

Table 12.2 shows the gain achieved in mathematics at Central East in 1996 -1997. The school achieved higher gains than the control school even though the TD mathematics program was only partially implemented at Central East in1996-1997. (The extra-help lab has been in full operation since the first year of implementation. During the second year of implementation, we began to transition to the standards-based curriculum by introducing a monthly schoolwide, open-ended problem to every classroom, and by piloting the new curriculum in selected classes. The standards-based curriculum was fully implemented during the third year of the program in fall 1997.)

Preliminary data for fifth- and sixth-grade students from Cooke Middle School also show notable achievement gains in mathematics. These gains are greater than those attained at Cooke's comparison school (See Table 12.3).

Improved mathematics achievement among Central East students needing extra help in mathematics has also resulted from implementation of an extra-dose class, the computer- and team-assisted mathematics acceleration course (CATAMA). CATAMA is an innovative combination of computer-assisted instruction and structured cooperative learning that students receive in addition to their regular math course for about 10 weeks during the school year. High levels of student engagement and cooperation were observed among participants, and interviews revealed that students liked being in CATAMA and working with a partner and a computer to strengthen their procedural knowledge and skills (MacIver, et al., 1998). Analyses comparing seventh-grade students who participated in CATAMA during the 1996-1997 school year with a matched sample of seventh-grade students at a control

Table 12.2: Percent of Eighth-Grade Students Scoring at or Above Basic Performance in Math on Stanford 9 Achievement Test (Composite Measure–Multiple Choice and Open-Ended)

School Year	Central East	Control School
1995 - 1996	8.5%	6.7%
1996 - 1997	16.4%	9.2%

Note. Results are for implementation years 1 and 2.

Table 12.3: Total Math Achievement at Cooke Middle School and its Comparison School

	Cooke Middle School			Comparison School		
	9/97	4/98	Difference	10/97	4/98	Difference
Fifth Grade Total Math Achievement						
Number tested	191	177	-14	184	221	37
Mean scaled score	582.2	616.7	34.5	601.6	615.8	14.2
Median grade equivalent	3.0	4.4	1.4	3.8	4.3	0.5
Below basic (%)	74	71	-3	51	68	17
Basic (%)	22	23	1	38	26	-12
Proficient or advanced (%)	4	7	3	12	6	-6
Sixth Grade Total Math Achievement						
Number tested	242	217	-25	213	224	11
Mean scaled score	601.6	631.1	29.5	619.3	636.2	16.9
Median grade equivalent	3.9	4.8	0.9	4.6	5.2	0.6
Below basic (%)	85	74	-11	61	66	5
Basic (%)	15	24	9	33	27	-6
Proficient or advanced (%)	0	2	2	6	8	2

school indicate that growth in mathematics procedures achievement was about one half a standard deviation higher for CATAMA participants than for students in the comparison sample (see Table 12.4). This effect of CATAMA participation on mathematics procedures scale scores translates into an 11 point advantage in students' end-of-year national percentile ranks. The typical CATAMA participant was boosted to the 54th national percentile in math procedures achievement, whereas the typical student from the matched comparison sample reached only the 43rd national percentile.

CATAMA participants outgained nonparticipants across the entire prior achievement spectrum, except for the four participants and four nonparticipants with the lowest starting points (those whose total math scale scores from the previous spring were between 585 and 624). Table 12.5 summarizes the mean growth in math procedures scale scores obtained by participants and nonparticipants for these 8 cases (with prior total math scale scores below 625) and for the other 88 cases (with scores above 625). For the 88 cases with starting points on the total math scale over 625, CATAMA participants grew by 28.6 points on average (outgaining nonparticipants by almost 18 points). The CATAMA participants with starting points on the total math scale that were below 625 also showed dramatic growth (growing

37.3 points on average). However, these four CATAMA participants were outgained by their 4 matches from the comparison sample by about 24 points. It may be that the 4 seventh-grade students from the comparison school with the lowest starting points received one-on-one tutoring or some other similarly intense form of help.

The CATAMA program also helped significantly more seventh-grade students (compared to the control school) to boost their end-of-year mathematics procedures test scores on the Stanford 9 to at least the 85th local percentile, a level required by many of the special admissions high schools in Philadelphia. Eighteen of 48 CATAMA participants reached the 85th citywide percentile on their mathematics procedures test, as opposed to only 7 of the 48 matched students from the comparison sample (χ^2 (1) = 6.54, $p<.01$).

Effects of Student Team Literature and Looping on Student Attitudes

Evidence from student surveys after just one semester of implementing student team literature in the first TDMS, Central East, indicated that student team literature had significant effects on 7 of 10 attitudinal measures shown by previous research to be associated with higher academic achievement. These measures are student perceptions of peer support for achievement (effect size=.65), teacher caring (effect size=.58), working to meet adults' standards (effect size =.44), utility value of English/language arts (effect size=.41), effort (effect size=.36), self-concept of ability (effect size=.34), and giving one's best (effect size=.31).

Table 12. 4: Multiple Regression Model to Predict Seventh-Grade Students' End-of-Year Mathematics Procedures Scale Scores on the Stanford 9 Achievement Test (N = 96)

Predictor	b	SE	p-value	Standardized Coefficients
Intercept	674.57	3.27	0.00	
Prior math achievement	0.62	0.14	0.00	β = 0.47
CATAMA participant	12.16	4.62	0.01	delta = 0.49
Prior x CATAMA	0.40	0.20	0.05	

Note. Prior Math Achievement is grand-mean-centered. R^2 = 0.46

Table 12.5: Growth in Math Procedures Scale Scores for CATAMA Participants and
Nonparticipants Whose Prior Total Math Achievement Scale Scores were Greater or Less Than 625

Group	Number	Mean Growth[a]	SD
Prior total math achievement greater than 625			
CATAMA participants	44	28.6	28.7
Nonparticipants	44	10.9	23.0
Prior total math achievement less than 625			
CATAMA participants	4	37.3	11.6
Nonparticipants	4	61.5	8.2

[a] Growth between spring 1996 and spring 1997.

In contrast, a teacher's use of student team literature is not a significant predictor of student outcomes on the intrinsic value of RELA, antiacademic norms, or teacher showing disrespect for students.

After two years of implementation, evidence from Central East shows the power of looping. The purpose of looping is to create positive learning environments characterized by (a) caring (atypically warm and productive student-teacher relationships), (b) daring (increased use of nontraditional and active learning and cooperative learning instructional techniques aimed at teaching and learning for understanding), and (c) unusual levels of student enthusiasm. Students were surveyed three times. First, a survey that focused on teacher caring, teacher daring, and student motivation in RELA was conducted in February 1996 (before looping had occurred). Second, a similar survey that focused on mathematics was conducted in May 1996 (before looping had occurred). Finally, a survey that encompassed both RELA and math was conducted in June 1997 (after looping had occurred in Intervention Group 1).

Longitudinal multiple regression analyses compare the composite scores of students in Intervention Group 1 (who experienced both looping and the other communal organization components) with those in Intervention Group 2 (students from the same school who did not experience looping but did experience other communal organization components) and the matched school comparison group while controlling for students' prior status on these composites. The adjusted means and significance tests derived from these analyses are summarized in Tables 12.6 through 12.9.

As can be seen in Table 12.6, the analyses reveal that students in Intervention Group 1 perceived their math teachers as both more caring and more daring than did students in either one of the other groups. Students in Intervention Group 1 were also less likely than those in the matched school comparison group to report that their teacher emphasized traditional math methods and were more likely to indicate that they were regularly asked to explain their math work.

As Table 12.7 shows, the self-ratings of effort and ability by students in Intervention Group 1 were generally higher than those in the other groups (three out of the four relevant comparisons indicated statistically significant differences in favor of this group). Students in Intervention Group 1 also perceived math to be more exciting (than did the matched school comparison group) and more useful (than did students in both other groups).

Students in Intervention Group 1 also perceived their RELA teachers to be more caring and more daring (when it comes to implementing cooperative learning) than did students in the matched comparison group (see Table 12.8). However, students in Intervention Group 2, which did not experience looping but did experience other communal organization components, indicated that their RELA teachers were also caring and moderately daring.

Table 12.6: Student Reports of Math Teacher's Caring and Support and Frequency of Traditional and Nontraditional Math Instruction in Winter 1997			
	Intervention Group 1[a]	*Intervention Group 2[b]*	*Matched School Comparison[c]*
Teacher cares	-.80	-1.17***	-1.11***
Traditional math	-.27	-.15	-.06**
Math teacher dares	.08	-.06*	-.10***
Students explain math	.25	.19	-.38***

Note. Table entries are adjusted means derived from multiple regression analyses controlling for student reports from spring of the prior school year.
*   Mean is different from mean of Intervention Group 1, $p<.05$.
** Mean is different from mean of Intervention Group 1, $p<.01$.
***Mean is different from mean of Intervention Group 1, $p<.001$.
[a] Looping plus other communal organization components. $N = 134$.
[b] No looping, but otherwise similar to Group 1. $N = 151$.
[c] Not looped, nor communally organized. $N = 236$.

Table 12.7:Student Reports of Their Effort and Ability in Math, and Their Rating of How
Exciting/Interesting/Enjoyable and how Useful Math is to Them

	Intervention Group 1[a]	Intervention Group 2[b]	Matched School Comparison[c]
My effort in math class	.11	-.12*	.04
My ability in math	.15	-.04*	.00*
Math is exciting/interesting/ enjoyable	.09	.07	-.12**
Math is useful	.26	.10*	.02***

Note. Table entries are adjusted means derived from multiple regression analyses controlling for
student reports from spring of the prior school year.
*   Mean is different from mean of Intervention Group 1, $p<.05$.
**   Mean is different from mean of Intervention Group 1, $p<.01$.
***Mean is different from mean of Intervention Group 1, $p<.001$.
[a] Looping plus other communal organization components. $N = 134$.
[b] No looping, but otherwise similar to Group 1. $N = 151$.
[c] Not looped, nor communally organized. $N = 236$.

As can be seen in Table 12.9, a student's group membership was a
significant predictor neither of students' reports of their effort and ability in
RELA nor of their ratings of how exciting or useful RELA is to them. Taken
together, these results suggest that looping may help teachers to be more
daring, that is, to use practices that are recommended by education reformers
more frequently. There is also evidence that looping may contribute to
higher ratings of teacher caring and other positive motivational outcomes for
students in math (but not in RELA). One reason for the differences between
the RELA analyses and the math analyses may be that students in all groups
had RELA as a double-period class (90 minutes), whereas math was a single-
period class. It may be that spending twice the amount of time in RELA
class each week helped teachers and students develop sufficiently close
relationships and positive attitudes even in those groups where looping was
not practiced.

Effects of Career Exploration
and Educational Decision-Making Curriculum

Analyses have shown large and significant effects of the career exploration and educational decision-making lessons on students' self-reported career understanding and belief in the importance of making educational and career plans during middle school (MacIver & Plank, 1997a). Significant effects are also seen on seventh-grade students' educational attainment goals (in analyses that account for their prior goals as sixth-grade students). As we continue our research, we hope that the career exploration and educational decision-making activities will also facilitate (a) high levels of accurate knowledge about adult work and education, (b) successful transitions to high school, (c) persistence in high school, and (d) successful transitions to college and work.

Table 12.8: Student Reports of Reading/English/Language Arts (RELA) Teachers' Caring and Support, and Frequency of Effective Cooperative Learning Practices in RELA Class, Winter 1997			
	Intervention Group 1[a]	*Intervention Group 2[b]*	*Matched School Comparison[c]*
Teacher cares	.02	.09	-.18*
RELA teacher dares	.22	.08^	-.24***

Note. Table entries are adjusted means derived from multiple regression analyses controlling for student reports from February of the prior school year.
* Mean is different from mean of Intervention Group 1, $p<.05$.
** Mean is different from mean of Intervention Group 1, $p<.01$.
***Mean is different from mean of Intervention Group 1, $p<.001$.
[a] Looping plus other communal organization components. $N = 137$.
[b] No looping, but otherwise similar to Group 1. $N = 160$.
[c] Not looped, nor communally organized. $N = 256$.

Table 12.9: Student Reports of Their Effort and Ability in RELA and Their Rating of How
Exciting/Interesting/Enjoyable and How Useful RELA is to Them in Winter 1997

	Intervention Group 1[a]	Intervention Group 2[b]	Matched School Comparison[c]
My effort in RELA class	.01	-.04	.04
My ability in RELA	.00	.05	.05
RELA is exciting/interesting enjoyable	.03	.05	-.04
RELA is useful	.04	-.01	-.07

Note. Table entries are adjusted means derived from multiple regression analyses controlling for
student reports from February of the prior school year.
*   Mean is different from mean of Intervention Group 1, $p<.05$.
** Mean is different from mean of Intervention Group 1, $p<.01$.
***Mean is different from mean of Intervention Group 1, $p<.001$.
[a] Looping plus other communal organization components. $N = 137$.
[b] No looping, but otherwise similar to Group 1. $N = 160$.
[c] Not looped, nor communally organized. $N = 256$.

CONCLUSION

Evidence from the first two TDMSs demonstrates that it is possible to
implement a demanding core curriculum in a detracked school and to create
a situation in which students at all levels of the achievement distribution
make significant and substantial gains in academic performance. The initial
results also indicate that it is possible to create a supportive middle school
environment that enables teachers to be both caring and daring, and provide
students with the motivation and assistance they need to be engaged by
school. In short, the early indications are that the TD model provides urban
middle schools with a blueprint for organizational and instructional reforms,
which provide students with the "algebra and sympathy" (McGrath, 1998)
that they need in order to excel.

These results, moreover, were obtained in inner city middle schools with
characteristics (class sizes greater than 27, high mobility, and concentrated
poverty) that Knapp (1995) found to dramatically limit "teaching for
meaning." The strong gains in reading comprehension and mathematical

proficiency provide an initial validation of the TDMS model and its belief that a challenging instructional program, sufficiently supported and implemented schoolwide, can lead to large and widely distributed achievement gains in schools that serve young adolescents placed at risk.

Consequently, these early results leave us hopeful that challenges raised by the leaders of the major middle school reform initiatives can be met. It will not be easy. Our own experience confirms that it will require constant attention at multiple levels (Useem, Christman, Gold, & Simon, 1997) to assure that all students are provided with the learning opportunities, support, and motivation they need in order to succeed. However, our experience also shows that it can be done. The challenge remaining is to produce the same encouraging achievement results elsewhere as this school reform model is extended to more middle schools.

REFERENCES

American Federation of Teachers. (1992). U.S. education: The task before us. *American Educator*, 16(4), 19-30.

Arhar, J. (1997). The effects of interdisciplinary teaming on teachers and students. In J.L. Irvin (Ed.), *What current research says to the middle level practitioner* (pp. 49-56). Columbus, OH: National Middle School Association.

Balfanz, R. (1997, March). *Mathematics for all in two urban schools: A view from the trenches.* Paper presented at the annual meeting of the American Educational Research Association, Chicago.

Balfanz, R., & MacIver, D. (1998). *The school district's role in creating high performing urban middle schools.* Baltimore: Center for Research on the Education of Students Placed at Risk.

Balfanz, R., Plank, S. B., MacIver, D. J., & Ryan, D. (In press). *Achieving algebra for all with a facilitated instructional program: First year results of the talent development middle school mathematics program..* Baltimore: Johns Hopkins University, Center for Social Organization of Schools.

Beaton, A. E., Mullis, I. V. S., Martin, M. O., Gonzalez, E. J., Kelly, D. L., & Smith, T. A. (1996). *Mathematics achievement in the middle school years.* Chestnut Hill, MA: Boston College's TIMSS International Study Center.

Bruer, J. T. (1994). *Schools for thought: A science of learning in the classroom.* Cambridge, MA: MIT Press.

Bryk, A. S., Lee, L. E., & Holland, P. B. (1993). *Catholic schools and the common good.* Cambridge, MA: Harvard University Press.

Carnegie Council on Adolescent Development. (1989). *Turning points: Preparing American youth for the 21st century.* Washington, DC: Carnegie Council on Adolescent Development.

Cohen, D. K. (1996). Rewarding teachers for student performance. In S.H. Fuhrman & J.A. O'Day (Eds.), *Rewards and reform: Creating educational incentives that work* (pp. 60-112). San Francisco: Jossey-Bass.

Cohen, D. K., Wilson, S., & Hill, H. (1997, March). *Teaching and learning mathematics in California.* Paper presented at the annual meeting of the American Educational Research

Association, Chicago.

Corbett, H. D., & Wilson B. L. (1997). *Urban students' perspectives on middle school: The sixth grade year in five Philadelphia middle schools.* Philadelphia: Philadelphia Education Fund.

Dangel, S., Garriott, M. D., & Perkins, S. (1998). *Talent development U.S. history curriculum for eighth-grade* (Pilot ed.). Baltimore: Johns Hopkins University, Center for Social Organization of Schools.

Darling-Hammond, L. (1997). *The right to learn: A blueprint for creating schools that work.* San Francisco: Jossey-Bass.

Elmore, R. F., Peterson, P. L., & McCarthey, S. J. (1996). *Restructuring in the classroom: Teaching, learning, and school organization.* San Francisco: Jossey-Bass.

Epstein, J. L., Coates, L., Salinas, K. C., Sanders, M. G., & Simon, B. S. (1996). *Partnership 2000 schools manual: Improving school-family-community connections.* Baltimore: Johns Hopkins University, Center on Families, Communities, Schools.

Epstein, J. L., & MacIver, D. J. (1990). *Education in the middle grades: National practices and trends.* Columbus, OH: National Middle School Association.

Forgione, P. (1990). *Accountability and assessment: The Connecticut approach.* Paper presented at the Public Education Forum, Baltimore.

Fuchs, D., Fuchs, L. S., Mathes, P. G., & Simmons, D. C. (1997). Peer-assisted learning strategies: Making classrooms more responsive to diversity. *American Educational Research Journal, 34,* 174-206.

Glaser, R., & Silver, E. (1994). Assessment, testing, and instruction: Retrospect and prospect. *Review of Research in Education, 20,* 393-419.

Hough, D. (1997). A bona fide middle school: Programs, policy, practice, and grade span configurations. In J.L. Irvin (Ed.), *What current research says to the middle level practitioner* (pp. 285-294). Columbus, OH: National Middle School Association.

Jones, L., & Shaw, A. (1998). *Student team literature teacher's manual* (2nd ed.). Baltimore: Center for Social Organization of Schools.

King, A. (1994). Guiding knowledge construction in the classroom: Effects of teaching children how to question and how to explain. *American Educational Research Journal, 31*(2), 338-368.

Knapp, M. S. (1995). *Teaching for meaning in high-poverty classrooms.* New York: Teachers College Press.

Ladson-Billings, G. (1994). *The dreamkeepers: Successful teachers of African American children.* San Francisco: Jossey-Bass.

Lipsitz, J., Mizell, M. H., Jackson, A. W., & Austin, L. M. (1997, March). Speaking with one voice: A manifesto for middle-grades reform. *Phi Delta Kappan, 58,* 533-540.

Locke, E. A., & Latham, G. P. (1990). *A theory of goal setting and task performance.* Englewood Cliffs, NJ: Prentice Hall.

Lortie, D. C. (1975). *Schoolteacher: A sociological study.* Chicago: University of Chicago Press.

MacIver, D. J. (1990). Meeting the needs of young adolescents: Advisory groups, interdisciplinary teams of teachers, and school transition programs. *Phi Delta Kappan, 71*(6), 458-464.

MacIver, D. J., Balfanz, R. & Plank, S. B. (1998). An elective replacement approach to providing extra help in math: The talent development middle schools' computer and team-assisted mathematics acceleration (CATAMA) program. *Research in Middle Level Education Quarterly, 22*(2), 1-23.

MacIver, D. J., & Epstein, J. L. (1990). *How equal are opportunities for learning in the middle grades in disadvantaged and advantaged schools?* (Rep. 7). Baltimore: The Johns Hopkins University, Center for Research on Effective Schooling for Disadvantaged Students.

MacIver, D. J., & Epstein, J. L. (1991). Responsive practices in the middle grades: Teacher teams, advisory groups, remedial instruction, and school transition programs. *American Journal of Education,* 99, 587-622.

MacIver, D. J., & Plank, S. B. (1996). *Creating a motivational climate conducive to talent development in middle schools: Implementation and effects of student team reading.* (Rep. 4). Baltimore/ Washington, DC: Center for Research on the Education of Students Placed at Risk.

MacIver, D. J., & Plank, S. B. (1997a, March). *From "at-risk" to "on target": Effects of participation in career exploration activities on urban middle school students.* Paper presented at the annual meeting of the American Educational Research Association (AERA), Chicago.

MacIver, D., & Plank, S. (1997b). Improving urban schools: Developing the talents of students placed at risk. In J. L. Irvin (Ed.), *What current research says to the middle level practitioner* (pp.243 - 256). Columbus, OH: National Middle School Association.

MacIver, D. J., Plank, S. B., & Balfanz, R. (1997). *Working together to become proficient readers: Early impact of the talent development middle school's student team literature program* (Rep. 15). Baltimore/Washington, DC: Center for Research on the Education of Students Placed at Risk.

MacIver, D. J., & Reuman, D. A. (1993). Giving their best: Grading and recognition practices that motivate students to work hard. *American Educator,* 17(4), 24-31.

MacIver, D. J., Reuman, D. A., & Main, S. (1995). Social structuring of the school. In M. R. Rosenzweig & L. W. Porter (Eds.), *Annual Review of Psychology*: (Vol. 46, pp. 375-400). Palo Alto, CA.: Annual Reviews.

Madhere, S., &. MacIver, D. J. (1996). *The talent development middle school: Essential components.* Baltimore/Washington, DC: Center for Research on the Education of Students Placed at Risk.

McGrath, A. (1998, April). Algebra and sympathy: In a tough world, teachers increasingly offer some of both. *U.S. News and World Report,* 124(15), 57-58.

McLaughlin, H. J., & Doda, N. M. (1997). Teaching with time on your side: Developing long-term relationships in schools. In J. Irvin (Ed.), *What current research says to the middle level practitioner* (pp.57 - 72). Columbus, OH: National Middle School Association.

McLaughlin, M. W., & Oberman, I. (Eds.). (1996). *Teacher learning: New policies, new practices.* New York: Teachers College Press.

McPartland, J. M. (1990). Staffing decisions in the middle grades. *Phi Delta Kappan,* 71(6), 438-444.

Means, B., Chelemer, C., & Knapp, M. S. (Eds.). (1991). *Teaching advanced skills to at-risk students.* San Francisco: Jossey-Bass.

Mevarech, Z. R., & Kramarski, B. (1997). IMPROVE: A multidimensional method for teaching mathematics in heterogeneous classrooms. *American Educational Research Journal,* 34(2), 365 - 394.

Mosteller, F. D., Light, R. J., & Sachs, J. A. (1996). Sustained inquiry in education: Lessons from skill grouping and class size. *Harvard Education Review,* 66(4), 797-842.

National Center for Education Statistics (1996). *Pursuing excellence.* Washington DC: Author.

National Middle School Association. (1995). *This we believe: Developmentally responsive middle level schools.* Columbus, OH: Author.

Natriello, G., McDill, E. L., & Pallas, A. M. (1990). *Schooling disadvantaged children:*

Racing against catastrophe. New York: Teachers College Press.

Nelson, B. S., & Hammerman, J. K. (1996). Reconceptualizing teaching: Moving toward the creation of intellectual communities of students, teachers, and teacher educators. In M.W. McLaughlin & I. Oberman (Eds.), *Teacher learning: New policies, new practices* (pp. 3-21). New York: Teachers College Press.

Oakes, J., Gamoran, A., & Page, R. (1992) Curriculum differentiation: Opportunities, outcomes, and meanings. In P. W. Jackson (Ed.), *Handbook of Research on Curriculum* (pp. 570-608). New York: Macmillan.

Palincsar, A. S., & Klenk, L. J. (1991) Dialogues promoting reading comprehension. In B. Means, C. Chelemer & M. Knapp (Eds.), *Teaching advanced skills to at-risk students* (pp. 112-130). San Francisco: Jossey-Bass.

Plank, S. B. & Young, E. (1999). *To scale or not to scale? Evaluations of the talent development middle school's student team literature program.* Baltimore/Washington, D.C.: Center for Research on the Education of Students Placed at Risk.

Ruby, A. (In press). *An implementable curriculum approach to improving science instruction in urban middle schools.* Baltimore: Johns Hopkins University, Center for Social Organization of Schools.

Schmidt, W. H., McKinght, C. C., & Raizen, S. A. (1996). *A splintered vision: An investigation of U.S. science and mathematics education.* Boston: Kluwer.

Slavin, R. E. (1995). *Cooperative learning: Theory, research, and practice* (2nd ed.). Boston: Allyn & Bacon.

Stevens, R. J., & Durkin, S. (1992). *Using student team reading and student team writing in middle schools.* Baltimore: Center for Research on Effective Schooling for Disadvantaged Students.

Stevenson, H. W., & Lee, S. (1995). The East Asian version of whole-class teaching. *Educational Policy,* 9(2), 152-168.

Stevenson, H. W., & Stigler J. W. (1992). *The learning gap.* New York: Summit.

Stodolsky, S. (1988). *The subject matters.* Chicago: University of Chicago Press.

University of Chicago School Mathematics Project. (1998). *The University of Chicago School Mathematics Project.* Chicago: Author.

Useem, E. L. (1998). *Teachers' appraisals of talent development middle school training, materials, and student progress: Results from focus groups.* (Rep. 20). Baltimore/Washington, DC: Center for Research on the Education of Students Placed at Risk.

Useem, E. L., Christman J. B., Gold, E., & Simon, E. (1997). Reforming alone: Barriers to organizational learning in urban school change initiatives. *Journal of Education for Students Placed at Risk,* 2(1), 55-78.

Webb, N. M., & Farivar, S. (1994). Promoting helping behavior in cooperative small groups in middle school mathematics. *American Educational Research Journal,* 31(2), 369-395.

Wilson, B., & Corbett, H. (1999). *"No excuses": The eighth grade year in six Philadelphia middle schools.* Philadelphia: Philadelphia Education Fund.

13

Fostering Resilience in High School Classrooms: A Study of the PASS Program (Promoting Achievement in School Through Sport)

CRYSTAL MCCLENDON
SAUNDRA MURRAY NETTLES
ALLAN WIGFIELD
University of Maryland, College Park

A diverse array of school reforms and youth development programs are attempting to mobilize processes that foster resilience among students placed at risk. Among these is Promoting Achievement in School Through Sport (PASS), an elective, year-long class designed to assist learners in transferring to the academic arena skills learned through playing sports. An implicit goal of the program is to engage students, teachers, coaches, families, and communities in building protective environments for youth. In this chapter we (a) describe the PASS program, (b) present research findings that suggest that the program has a positive impact on student achievement, and (c) discuss features of the PASS classroom that may explain its impact on student achievement and resilience.

The lack of academic success among some minority students continues to be a serious problem of great urgency. A large proportion of poor African-American and Hispanic students comprise those considered to be at risk for negative educational outcomes, such as illiteracy and school dropout (Nettles, 1991). The educational picture is particularly dismal for African-Americans. As African-American students go through school, some fall behind Whites in major academic areas such as mathematics, writing, and reading. Statistics from the Education Commission of the States reveal that the average African-American student answered about 45% of the mathematics items on the National Assessment of Educational Progress test correctly, in contrast to the average White student who answered 63% correctly (National Center for Educational Statistics [NCES], 1997). Furthermore, according to the National Institute of Education, only 66% of African-American 17-year-olds were reading at an intermediate level or higher, in contrast to 89% of their White counterparts (NCES). Forty-five percent of 17-year-old White students were adept readers according to National Assessment of Educational Progress tests, whereas only about one sixth (16%) of African-American students were categorized as adept.

Explanations for the lack of academic success among some African-American students have focused on a variety of processes. Some researchers have emphasized cognitive processes and learning style differences among different groups, and argued that schools do not deal well with the learning styles of African-American students (e.g., Hale-Benson, 1986). Others have focused on motivational issues, with some researchers arguing that African-American students have low expectations for success, experience feelings of hopelessness, deny the importance of individual effort, and lack persistence in the face of failure, all of which lower their achievement (see Graham, 1994, for review). Yet, Graham noted that many researchers have found that African American students often are very motivated to achieve. Therefore, factors other than motivational and cognitive processes must be considered in order to understand the achievement gap between African-American and White students. A number of broader social factors are important to consider. Incompatible home-school environments, exposure to violence, racism and discrimination, drugs and poverty, low socioeconomic status, low teacher expectations, and lack of person-environment fit are a few of the risk factors that contribute to negative school outcomes for African-American students (see Ogbu, 1985; Portes, 1996; Spencer & Markstrom-Adams, 1990, for further discussion).

Another of the many factors that affect academic performance is the school climate in which students are expected to learn. School climate involves the physical facility, places, programs, policies, and people that comprise the student's learning and emotional environment (Brookover et al., 1978; Edmonds, 1979; Walberg, 1985). The influence of educational environments on student development and outcomes has been an important line of inquiry (e.g., Astin, 1968; Gottfredson, 1987; Moos, 1979; Walberg). Researchers have stressed that school climate has a significant effect on academic achievement, asserting that schools that have positive, caring, and orderly climates and that recognize the individuality of students enhance students' social, emotional, and intellectual growth (Comer et al., 1985; Edmonds, 1979; Perry & College, 1993; Purkey & Smith, 1983; Rutter, Maughan, Mortimore, & Ouston, 1979). Many research studies have also identified student perceptions of the school climate as a primary factor in student achievement (Dezmon, 1996).

Rutter et al. (1979) conducted a landmark study of effective schools in which he tracked students over a 5-year period. They concluded that schools where the students had consistent successful outcomes (e.g., behavior, attendance, and grades) had marked institutional characteristics. These characteristics included an emphasis on academic work, flexibility, systems of incentives and rewards, and arrangements whereby students could take responsibility for their own behavior. Rutter et al. found that success was not related to the size of the school or the physical characteristics. Instead, they found that the whole ethos of the social institution, commonly referred to as *school climate*, was more significant than the sum of its parts.

Efforts to identify important features of classroom climate that influence student outcomes have been made. For example, Soloman, Watson, Battistich, Schaps, and Delucchi (1992) characterized caring classroom environments as those in which a feeling of mutual concern between the teacher and students exists, and in which all students are contributing members. Other researchers have added that these classrooms are depicted by teachers who show concern and interest in students' ideas, projects, and experiences (see Lewis, Schaps, & Watson, 1995; Phelan, Davidson, & Cao, 1992). Students' academic performance is enhanced when they perceive their teachers and other school personnel to be supportive and helpful (Patchen, 1982; Sanders & Jordan, chap. 4, this volume; Skinner & Belmont, 1993; Wentzel, 1997).

Using the "caring classrooms" framework, Kinney (1995) examined classroom climate by conducting case studies that identified teacher strategies and student perceptions and experiences of a particular curriculum in an urban, vocational high school. The outcomes targeted in this study were student academic engagement and motivation. The sample for this study consisted of 78% Hispanic, 15% African-American, 6% Southeast Asian, and 1% White students in the 9th to the 12th grades. These students attended a large public high school ($N = 2,900$) in a neighborhood characterized by high levels of unemployment, abandoned factories, empty lots, dilapidated housing, and frequent crime.

Summarizing case studies from these classrooms, Kinney (1995) identified recurring themes, one of which was teacher support. A major finding was that teachers created a comfortable learning environment by working individually with students, listening attentively to their questions and concerns, and exhibiting sensitivity to students from economically disadvantaged backgrounds. Another theme was learner-centered instruction. Teachers in this study indicated that they tailored most instructional activities to students' experiences and interests. Moreover, teachers viewed the classroom climate as the foundation for other strategies they used to encourage motivation and achievement. The students in these classrooms exhibited academic engagement and motivation, as well as a great deal of respect and support of other students' hard work and dedication. Kinney concluded that the students in this study expressed high levels of motivation in combination with strong aspirations.

In recent years, both research on educational environments and a second line of inquiry, studies of resilience, have led to a reconceptualization of ways in which schools can foster academic and socioemotional competence. Resilience refers to an individual's response to risk. It has been linked to effective school climate via an emphasis on protection against risk, that is, the notion that environments can foster qualities in individuals that are linked to successful adaptation despite risk (Masten, Best, & Garmezy, 1990; Nettles, 1991; Werner, 1990; Winfield, 1991; Zimmerman & Arunkumar, 1994). Benard (1991) identified social competence, problem-solving skills, autonomy, and a sense of purpose and future as four main characteristics that resilient children possess. Lewis et al. (1995) speculated that educators who nurture these elements of resilience by offering students a curriculum that is challenging and relevant to their future goals are more likely to help students become motivated, lifelong learners. Krovetz and Speck (1995) argued that for a school to be successful in fostering student resilience, teachers need to create a caring environment where students feel they have the necessary support to reach their goals. As reviewed by Benard, schools can play an essential role in reducing risk by providing environments characterized by three key features: high expectations, caring and support, and opportunities for participation.

A diverse array of school reforms and youth development programs are attempting to mobilize protective processes. Among these is Promoting Achievement in School Through Sport (PASS), an elective, year-long class designed to assist learners in transferring to the academic arena skills learned through playing sports. As described in what follows, an implicit goal of the program is to engage students, teachers, coaches, families, and communities in building protective environments for youth. This chapter reports findings from an evaluation of the PASS program[1].

PROMOTING ACHIEVEMENT IN SCHOOL THROUGH SPORT

The PASS program was created by the American Sports Institute (ASI), a nonprofit educational organization, and is designed for middle and high school students who want to improve their grades and physical performance. Although most PASS students are athletes seeking to regain their athletic eligibility, other students also participate in PASS. The PASS program seeks to facilitate students' attainment of important personal academic and social goals by teaching them various ways to regulate their behavior, motivate themselves, and remain focused on their goals.

The PASS program helps students accomplish eight major objectives, which correspond to the eight fundamentals of athletic mastery (FAMs) developed by ASI. In both academic and physical pursuits, students are expected to improve their ability to (a) concentrate over a prolonged period of time, being able to focus on the task at hand and block out distractions and negative thoughts; (b) be balanced when physically active and to balance their time, both in school and outside of school; (c) relax and stay in control when in class, taking tests, doing homework, and participating in physical activities; (d) exert appropriate amounts of power without undue stress; (e) establish rhythm by maintaining regular schedules and activities; (f) be flexible in order to establish better relationships with teachers and classmates, be open to new ideas, and remain injury free; (g) trust and act on instinct in order to enhance test scores, creativity, decision making, and reactions; and (h) develop an attitude consisting of patience, perseverance, and staying positive in order to see things through to their completion (ASI, 1992).

PASS is offered as an elective class. The class is self-paced, mastery based, and project oriented. Students identify the FAMs, develop principles related to them, and apply these principles to an action plan they create to achieve individualized goals they set for improving their grade point averages (GPA)

[1]This chapter is based on a dissertation completed by Crystal McClendon under the direction of Allan Wigfield and Saundra Nettles. The authors would like to thank colleagues in the PASS program for their cooperation in the completion of this study. The study was supported, in part, by a grant from the Department of Education, Office of Educational Research.

and physical performance. Once the action plan is developed and implementation begins, students regularly monitor and evaluate their progress toward these goals. Through this process, students develop skills that translate into increased success in their classwork, and better preparation for college and work.

As in any classroom, the role of the PASS teacher is crucial to the program's success. In recognition of this, ASI conducts a comprehensive, 3-week, summer-teacher training institute for new PASS teachers. During the institute, PASS teachers are introduced to the PASS curriculum that includes, in addition to learning modules, explicit instructions as to how the physical environment of the PASS classroom is structured. Teachers also become familiar with students' roles (for example, the "groundskeeper" is in charge of leading PASS routines), feedback for performance (e.g., "drunken monkey counts" are given for inappropriate behaviors such as tardiness), and classroom rituals (for example, the "clap-in," a nonverbal signal given by the groundskeeper is used at the beginning of the class period). ASI also conducts site visits, evaluations, and other follow-up for new and experienced PASS teachers.

Prior PASS Evaluations

In a 4-year impact study (ASI, 1996), data gathered from 1991 through 1995 showed that over a 4-year period, students in PASS classes consistently earned better grades at the end of the school year than did comparison group students. In the 1991-1992 school year, PASS students did 19% better than the comparison students; in 1992-1993, PASS students did 17% better; in 93-94, PASS students did 18% better; and in 94-95, PASS students did 14% better than their comparison group counterparts (ASI, 1996). Overall, in a 4-year composite, PASS students did 17% better than the comparison group students. During this period, 47% more PASS students than comparison students increased their grades. For those athletes who wished to regain eligibility to participate in sports (looking at students with 2.0 GPA or lower), PASS students were 85% more likely than the comparison group students to actually regain their academic eligibility. Of that same group, on average, twice as many PASS students as comparison group students increased their GPAs by a full grade point or more.

PURPOSE OF THIS STUDY

A major purpose of the study reported in this chapter was to further evaluate the effects of the PASS program on academic performance. Although PASS enrolls a diverse population of students, we were particularly interested in PASS' impact on the academic achievement of African-American students. A secondary goal of the study was to identify features of the PASS classroom that may foster student resilience, one of the implicit outcomes of the program. Thus, our interest was to explore the ways in which the PASS classroom offers a protective environment for participants.

The study tested three hypotheses. The first was that PASS students would have significantly higher post-GPAs than would non-PASS (comparison group) students. The second hypothesis was that African-Americans in the PASS group would have significantly higher post-GPAs than would African-Americans in the comparison group. The final hypothesis was that PASS classrooms would render more examples of social support for student achievement, connectedness to the world beyond the classroom, academic engagement, higher order thinking, substantive conversation, and depth of knowledge than would non-PASS classrooms as measured by Madison scores for authentic instruction.

METHODS

Sample

Students. The population from which the sample was drawn consisted of high school students from two large metropolitan areas in the United States. Five school districts (one in the midwest and four in the west), located in low- to middle-income communities, participated in the PASS program and were included in this study. The schools represented in this study were selected based on the amount of time each school had participated in the PASS program (at least 1 year). Both the midwestern and western areas were diverse in terms of the race/ethnicity, socioeconomic status, and academic achievement levels of the students. The total sample consisted of 900 students from 16 high schools in the west and midwest.

Of the entire sample, 22 students (2.4%) were freshmen, 205 (23%) were sophomores, 346 (38%) were juniors, and 327 (36%) were seniors in high school. Most of the students (608, or 68%) were male; 292 (32%) were female. African Americans comprised 54% of the sample ($N = 489$). There were 196 White students (22%), 170 Latinos (19%), and 45 students (5%) of other racial/ethnic groups.

The study also included a comparison group. The comparison group consisted of students who were enrolled in the same schools as the PASS students, but who were not participating in PASS activities. At the start of the school year, PASS teachers selected a comparison student for each student who enrolled in PASS. The comparison group student was matched with the PASS student using as criteria GPA, race/ethnicity, gender, grade level, and involvement in extracurricular activities. The comparison students were not involved in any way either in the intervention or in the study, except to compare their end-of-year grades with those of PASS students.

Classrooms. Classroom observations at six schools were used to provide a description of what occurs in PASS and non-PASS classrooms. A purposive sample of 11 classrooms (8 PASS and 3 non-PASS) was selected from six schools. One of the non-PASS classes was taught by a teacher of one of the PASS classes that was observed. Other non-PASS classrooms were a social studies class and a gym class. Observations were conducted during the 1997-1998 school year.

Measures

Student Grades. The primary student outcome used in this study was the cumulative GPA for each PASS and comparison student, based on all course subjects. For the entire sample, grade point averages were obtained at two time points: year-end grades from the previous year, 1995-1996, and year-end grades from the year of the program, 1996-1997. GPAs were calculated on a point scale of one to four (A = 4, B = 3, C = 2, D = 1, F = 0). They were collected for both the PASS students and the comparison group at the beginning of the school year and at the end of the school year. The grades were collected by the PASS instructor. Comparisons of these GPAs were conducted to examine the effects of PASS on student achievement.

Classroom Observations. The first author used a form developed by ASI, an aspect of technical support provided to PASS teachers, to record observations. The observations consisted of four main areas: PASS room ambiance, PASS routines, teacher presentation, and PASS support. In each PASS class, diverse aspects of teaching and learning such as material on bulletin boards, what the students were doing, instructions given by the teacher, and group work and interactions were rated.

Observations of three non-PASS classrooms within the same schools as the PASS classes were also conducted by the first author. An observation form was developed to capture similar characteristics featured within the PASS class and record basic classroom dynamics such as class control. The non-

PASS observation form was similar to the PASS form, with the exception of PASS activities, curriculum, and routine, which typically would not be found in non-PASS classrooms. For each observation, the observer documented the number of instructional cues, symbols, displays, and bulletin boards found in the classroom. A measure of class control constituted one component of the observation. The researcher tallied the number of times the teacher had to redirect the class to remain on task or assert other forms of discipline. The researcher took field notes including the instructional styles of the teacher (e.g., lecture vs lecture and discussion). Part of the observation involved tallying the number of times students worked together on tasks (for a full description of classroom observations, see McClendon, 1998).

To score the classroom observation data, the Madison framework for authentic instruction (Newmann, Secada, & Wehlage, 1995) was used. Although teachers in both PASS and non-PASS classrooms were not specifically using the Madison framework, this method for scoring classroom observations was used because it emphasizes authentic student achievement. The goal of authentic student achievement is to assess complex, important, real-life outcomes (see Hambleton, 1996; Worthen, 1993). This method also helped to identify the type(s) of instruction that took place in PASS and non-PASS classrooms.

The Madison framework assesses six dimensions of classroom life: higher order thinking (HOT), depth of knowledge and student understanding (DK), connectedness to the world beyond the classroom (CWC), substantive conversation (SC), social support for student achievement (SSSA), and academic engagement (AE). Within each of the six dimensions, there are five standards for rating instruction used in this framework. Newmann, Secada and Wehlage (1995) conceptualized these standards as continuous constructs from less to more of a quality rather than as a categorical (yes or no) variable. Each standard is expressed as a dimensional construct on a five-point Likert scale. To score classroom observations using this scoring rubric, researchers are instructed to distinguish between high- and low-scoring lessons and then offer examples of criteria for specific ratings. Furthermore, raters are asked to consider both the number of students to which the criterion applies and the proportion of class time during which it applies.

Two independent raters (the first author and a doctoral student) scored each classroom on each of the six dimensions. Each classroom was rated on each dimension based on the criteria mentioned previously, using specific sections of both the PASS and the non-PASS observation form. Scores were tabulated, and mean scores were computed for each dimension for PASS (N = 8) and non-PASS (N = 3) classes. To establish interrater agreement, the total number of matching and adjacent (scores that are one point away from each other) scores for each dimension in each class was calculated. These scores were then divided into the sum of scores for all 11 classrooms. For the scoring of all 11 classes on the six dimensions, the proportion of total inter-rater agreement was 66%, and the proportion of adjacent agreements was 86%.

RESULTS

Differences in Grades:
PASS and Comparison Groups

To test the first hypothesis regarding the effects of the PASS program on student grades, a repeated measures analysis of variance (ANOVA) was conducted. In this first analysis, there was one within-subjects factor, time of measurement, and two between-subjects factors, group (two levels) and race/ethnicity (four levels). Results from the tests of between-subjects effects did not reveal a significant group effect, $F(1, 887) = .00$, $p>.05$. This indicates that there were no significant differences between the combined pre- and post-GPAs of PASS and non-PASS students. Results from tests of within-subject effects found no significant time effect, $F(1, 887) = .01$, $p > .05$. However, there was a significant interaction effect between time and group on students' grades $F(1, 887) = 5.61$, $p<.05$ which means that the pattern of change for the PASS and non-PASS students' grades was different, these two groups differed significantly either at posttest or at pretest, or both. The means and standard deviations for the interaction are presented in Table 13.1.

To explore the interaction further, post hoc analyses (one-way ANOVAs) were conducted. These analyses showed that there were significant group differences at posttest, $F(1, 893) = 8.83$, $p<.05$, but not at pretest, $F(1, 893) = .917$, $p>.05$. Thus, PASS students had significantly higher posttest grades than did the comparison group. However, for PASS students, post hoc analyses do not indicate any significant differences in pre- and posttest grades over the school year, $F(1, 457) = .50$, $p>.05$. Thus, although PASS

Table 13. 1: Means and Standard Deviations of PASS and Comparison Groups Students: Pre and Post				
	Pre		*Post*	
	M	SD	M	SD
PASS	2.44	0.82	2.48	0.88
Comparison	2.37	0.91	2.30	0.94

students' grades increased over the school year, the change was not statistically significant. The comparison group's GPA significantly declined over the academic year, $F(1, 436) = 4.85$, $p<.05$.

Within-Race Effects
for African-Americans

The second set of analyses examined whether African-Americans in the PASS program had higher grades than did African-Americans not enrolled in the PASS program. To test the second hypothesis, a 2(time) x 2(group) ANOVA was conducted on the pre- and posttest grades of African-American students in the two groups (PASS and non-PASS). There was a significant group effect, $F(1, 486) = 6.67$, $p<.05$, which means that, averaged across time, PASS and non-PASS African-American students differed on grades. African-American PASS students achieved significantly higher post-GPAs than did comparison students. No significant time or group by time effects were found in this analysis. The mean scores and standard deviations for PASS and non-PASS African-American participants' pre- and post-GPAs are displayed in Table 13.2.

One-way ANOVAs were conducted to follow up this analysis. A significant group effect was found at posttest GPA, $F(1, 486) = 8.52$, $p<.05$. This finding reveals that African-American students in PASS had significantly higher post-GPAs than did African-American students in the comparison group. There were no significant group differences in pretest GPAs, $F(1, 486) = 2.72$, $p>.05$.

Classroom Observations:
Results of Qualitative Analyses

The final research hypothesis involves the comparison of PASS and non-PASS classes on six dimensions: HOT, DK, SC, CWC, SSSA, and AE. Madison scores for authentic instruction assessment were used. This section presents the results for the PASS classes first (by dimension) followed by the results for the non-PASS classes. In conjunction with the reporting of these scores, we offer specific examples that characterize recurring themes found in the PASS and non-PASS classes to give the reader a clear sense of the activities in these classrooms. A summary of the average scores (by dimension) on the Madison assessment is shown for PASS and non-PASS classes in Table 13.3.

On the HOT dimension, the eight PASS classes received a score of 3.5. This indicates that PASS students engaged in both lower order thinking (LOT) and HOT, but that there is at least one significant question or activity in which some students perform some HOT operations. Nearly all the PASS classes observed had at least one activity that involved specific HOT skills. For example, one class was observed in an exercise to illustrate flexibility, one of the FAMs. Following routines to engage students' attention and concentration, the student groundskeeper led the class in exercises to promote flexibility, for example, step-on, step-off line. During this physical activity, students worked in pairs, practicing a mock strike toward the other's midsection by first stepping on line and then off line. While students were engaged in this practice, the teacher reminded students to use what they already knew about focusing on their center, breathing, concentrating, and the like. These students practiced several techniques in an effort to understand what happens when you strike both on and off line. HOT was manifested here through student problem-solving, evaluation, and implementation of new strategies that accompanied successful completion of this activity.

For DK, PASS classes received a mean score of 3.7, which indicates that these teachers either structured their lessons so that students demonstrated their understanding of the problematic nature of information and ideas or explained how they solved a relatively complex problem. A routine activity in many classes was completion of the "feasibility" worksheet. During this activity, students were split into small groups to discuss individual academic and athletic goals, and the relative feasibility of attaining those goals. This exercise required students to operate with a clear definition of what

Table 13. 2: Means and Standard Deviations of African-American Students' Pre- and Post-GPAs				
	Pre		Post	
	M	SD	M	SD
PASS	2.21	1.44	2.27	.086
Comparison	2.11	0.86	2.04	0.90

Table 13.3. Madison Scores for Authentic Instruction, PASS and Non-PASS					
		Six Dimensions			
HOT	*DK*	*CWC*	*SC*	*SSSA*	*AE*
PASS *(N=8)*					
3.5	3.7	4.0	3.5	4.5	4.0
Non-PASS *(N=3)*					
2.0	2.0	2.5	3.0	3.0	3.0
1.5	1.7	1.5	0.5	1.5	1.0

Note. The scores are average scores for each dimension. The scores range from 1 to 5, 5 being the highest.

HOT, higher order thinking; DK, depth of knowledge; CWC, connectedness to the world beyond the classroom; SC, substantive conversation; SSSA, social support for student achievement; AE, academic engagement.

feasibility means in the context of goal-setting. Students also were expected to consider factors pertinent to the attainment of goals to assess the feasibility of their goals and the goals of others. Finally, after the group activity, individuals reported the results of this exercise in relation to their goals. In this way, students were asked to use present knowledge to hypothesize future outcomes, and to move out of their own experience and help others assess whether their goals were feasible.

For the third dimension, CWC, PASS classrooms received an average score of 4, which indicates that there was a connection between classroom knowledge and situations outside the classroom. This score also reflects the fact that PASS students explored these connections in ways that created personal meaning and significance, in addition to knowledge and skill attainment.

One exchange used as an example of the criteria for connectedness occurred as follows: The student groundskeeper led a discussion of a quote by Grantland Rice, who said, "For when the one great scorer comes to write against your name, he marks not that you won or lost but how you played the game." (This quote represents the philosophy of the PASS program and hangs as a banner in each PASS classroom.) One student responded, "...I won one battle but I lost the war. I improved athletically but did terrible academically. You could have all the talent in the world but you will go nowhere if you don't do well in school."

SC within PASS classes obtained an overall rating of 3.5, which translated into relatively high levels of sustained student conversation about the subject matter. This score also reflected at least three consecutive interchanges, each of which included a statement by one person and a response by another. One illustration of sustained conversation between students was the FAM challenges (exercises). This activity involved students working in small groups to practice such activities as push-ups, ball toss, white and black crane, energy handstand, stretch, and balance. During these exercises, students recorded the outcomes of each exercise for their partner, provided verbal feedback to their partner, and assessed whether the other student reached his or her goal(s). This evidence signified that there was a significant amount of sustained conversation.

The extent to which the classroom is characterized by an atmosphere of mutual respect and support among teacher and students is the question posed for SSSA, the fifth dimension. PASS classrooms received a 4.5 score overall, which suggests that social support was strong as demonstrated by both teacher and students. This high score also signified that the teacher engaged in forms of expression that conveyed high expectations for all students. Social support was reflected in the PASS class in two major ways: athlete of the day and groundskeeper duties and responsibilities. In each PASS class, the name of the athlete of the day was posted on the wall and that person received special recognition. The PASS teacher acknowledged this student with accolades and encouraged each student to say something good about the athlete of the day. Mutual respect was also demonstrated by class attentiveness and responsiveness to the student groundskeeper who directed some of the classroom activities. Students recognized this individual by remaining "on-task," attentive, and motivated to work. The students did not show disruptiveness, disrespect, or lack of interest. These examples also corresponded to the final dimension, AE.

For PASS classes, the AE dimension received an overall score of 4. This score reflects the widespread academic engagement of most PASS students. Most of the PASS students were on task, pursuing the substance of the lesson most of the time. PASS routines such as concentration, clap-in, physical warm-up, and hands-down were activities that invited student engagement. Also in-class assignments such as group work and FAM challenges were other windows through which to witness students' on-task behaviors. Within the eight classrooms observed, only one drunken monkey count (feedback given for inappropriate behavior, tardiness, or other off-task behaviors) was observed. This feedback was given to a student who did not bring proper academic materials to class. Overall, PASS classes flowed smoothly from the clap-in to the clap-out.

In general, in non-PASS classes students used LOT. An example of this was observed in a math class where students were constantly given instructions on how to solve math problems (rounding decimals), what the rules were, and where their mistakes occurred. The class primarily consisted of the teacher calling on students to give their answers to problems. Another non-PASS class was a traditional physical education class wherein students were instructed on how to play volleyball. In this class, too, LOT was predominant. Providing the exception to the rule, one non-PASS class participated in a mock trial where students were required to apply subject matter to a real-life situation, that is, a court case. In this instance, students were able to manipulate two sets of information and create a meaningful class experience. Despite this exception, students in non-PASS classes were primarily engaged in routine LOT operations as reflected by an overall score of 2 for the HOT dimension.

As reflected by the mean DK score of 2, the non-PASS classrooms were characterized by a mix of superficial and deep knowledge. In these classes, at least one significant idea might be presented in depth and its significance grasped, but in general the focus was not sustained. For the most part, these classes were characterized by shallow knowledge, with the exception of the social studies class. In this class, students were asked to integrate historical knowledge, personal interpretation, and court law. This activity required complex and relatively deep understandings. However, the other classes maintained less than one significant idea that would be considered deep.

In general, students in non-PASS classes encountered a topic, problem, or issue that the teacher tried to connect to students' experiences or to contemporary public situations. In these classrooms, the teacher may or may not have succeeded in making this connection (mean score = 2.5). It is unclear whether the physical education and math classes were able to connect subject content beyond the class to the world. These two classes consisted of rote assignments and the practice of procedural routines. However, the mock trial experience was directly connected to students' real-life experiences, and it was plausible that this experience held great meaning and value for these students.

Non-PASS classrooms received an overall score of 3 for the fourth dimension, SC. This indicates that there were some instances of sharing ideas, applying information, or making distinctions. This also indicates that there was at least one example of sustained conversation (at least three consecutive interchanges). During each of these classes, there were several examples of teachers and students engaged in conversations related to the subject matter.

SSSA was neutral or mildly positive in non-PASS classrooms, as indicated by the mean score of 3. Evidence of social support came mainly in the form of verbal approval from the teacher for student effort and work. (Students who were reluctant participants, or less articulate or skilled in the subject areas were less likely to receive this support.) The social studies teacher was able to combine instructions with expectations of mutual respect, participation, and challenging thinking. The physical education teacher also created a positive climate by encouraging teamwork, risk-taking, and mutual respect.

Non-PASS classrooms received a mean score of 3 for AE, as well. These classrooms were characterized by sporadic or episodic engagement. Although some students in the gym and social studies classes were actively involved in class activities, most of the students in the non-PASS classes were not engaged. The math class was observed to have the highest number of students participating in off-task behaviors such as talking, making rude remarks to other students, reading unrelated material, not paying attention, and laughing at others.

DISCUSSION AND CONCLUSION

GPAs of PASS and comparison group students were nearly identical at the onset of the intervention. However, our findings suggest that PASS students were able to stabilize and, to some extent, improve their grades over the course of the school year, whereas non-PASS students' GPAs declined over the school year. However, despite these gains, our analysis did not reveal a statistically significant change in PASS student grades over the course of 1 year. This finding is in direct contrast to ASI's 4-year impact study (ASI, 1996), which reported that PASS students achieved significantly higher post-GPAs when compared to pre-GPAs. This contrast could be explained by comparing the methodology and analysis of both this study and the 4-year impact study. Compared to the ASI study, this study analyzed a much smaller sample of students and analyzed fewer school years. However, both studies revealed that, on average, PASS students' grades improved over 1 school year.

Of further interest, our analyses suggest that although African-American students received lower grades than did other racial/ethnic groups in the study, African-American students' involvement in the PASS program was important in enabling them to sustain and improve their grades. One explanation for this finding centers around the authentic scores of instruction. It is clear that the PASS classrooms have more indicators of authentic instruction than do non-PASS classrooms. Thus, one can hypothesize that if there is more authentic instruction taking place in one classroom environment (PASS) than in another (non-PASS) and achievement is higher in the PASS environment, then authentic instruction may be linked to achievement outcomes, such as grades. Perhaps stronger evidence (for predicting the relationship between grades and authentic instruction) may be gained by additional studies that use the school classroom as the unit of analysis.

Results from this study also reveal that PASS classes score higher on all six dimensions of the Madison scores for authentic instruction. This result implies that the instructional settings of PASS and non-PASS classes are different. It may be the features and routines embedded within the PASS classroom that account, at least in part, for the variance found in the grades of PASS versus non-PASS students. Quantitative and qualitative observations suggest that there are specific features, for example, instructional strategies and social support, embedded within the PASS class (which differs from non-PASS classes) that may impact learning. Observations show that PASS classrooms are interesting and meaningful to students, which may help them achieve higher grades than non-PASS students.

These results are consistent with the key assumptions of Benard's (1991) characterization of protective factors within the school. PASS classrooms feature caring and support, high expectations, problem-solving strategies and skills, opportunities for youth participation, engagement, and involvement as witnessed in the classroom observations. Overall, these results indicate that the PASS classroom provides an excellent model of what a protective environment looks like for all students, especially those who are at risk for academic failure.

REFERENCES

American Sports Institute. (1992). *PASS-Promoting achievement in school through sport: A teacher's guide.* Mill Valley, CA: Author.

American Sports Institute. (1996). *4-year impact study.* Mill Valley, CA: Author.

Astin, A.W. (1968). *The college environment.* Washington, DC: American Council on Education.

Benard, B. (1991). *Fostering resiliency in kids: Protective factors in the family, school, and community.* Denver, CO: Western Regional Center for Drug-Free Schools and Communities.

Brookover, W., Schweitzer, J., Schneider, J., Brady, C., Flood, P., & Wisenbaker, J. (1978). Elementary school social climate and school achievement. *American Educational Research Journal, 15*(2), 301-318.

Comer, J., Haynes, N., Norris, M., Hamilton-Lee, M., Boger, J. M., & Rollock, D. (1985). *Psychosocial and academic effects of an intervention program among minority school children.* New Haven, CT: Yale University, Child Study Center. (ERIC Document Reproduction Service No. ED 286 946).

Dezmon, B. (1996). *Perceptions of school climate: A comparison of high achieving and low achieving and low achieving African-American suburban middle school students.* Unpublished dissertation, University of Maryland, College Park.

Edmonds, R. (1979). Effective Schools for the urban poor. *Educational Leadership,* 37(1), 15-24.

Gottfredson, G. (1987). American education: American delinquency. *Today's Delinquent,* 6, 5-71.

Graham, S. (1994). Motivation in African Americans. *Review of Educational Research,* 64(1), 55-117.

Hale-Benson, J. (1986). *Black children: Their roots, culture, and learning style.* Provo, UT: Brigham Young University Press.

Hambleton, R. K.(1996). Advances in assessment models, methods, and practices. In D.C. Berliner & R. C. Calfee (Eds.), *Handbook of educational psychology* (pp. 899-925). New York: Macmillan.

Kinney, D. A. (1995, August). *Nurturing urban adolescents' motivation to learn: A teacher's strategies and his students' perceptions.* Paper presented at the annual meeting of the American Sociological Association, Washington, D.C.

Krovetz, M., & Speck, M. (1995, December/January). Student resiliency: Toward educational equity. *The High School Journal,* 111-114.

Lewis, C., Schaps, E., & Watson, M. (1995, March). Beyond the pendulum. *Phi Delta Kappan,* 547-554.

Masten, A., Best, K., & Garmezy, N. (1990). Resilience and development: Contributions from the study of children who overcome adversity. *Development and Psychopathology,* 2, 425-444.

McClendon, C. (1998). *Promoting achievement in school through sport (PASS): An evaluation study.* Unpublished dissertation, University of Maryland, College Park.

Moos, R. H. (1979). *Evaluating educational environments.* San Francisco: Jossey - Bass.

National Center for Education Statistics. (1997). *NAEP 1996 trends in academic progress.* Washington, DC: U.S. Department of Education, Office of Educational Research and Improvement.

Nettles, S. M. (1991). Community involvement and disadvantaged students: A review. *Review of Educational Research,* 61(3), 379-406.

Newmann, F., Secada, W. & Wehlage, G. (1995). *A guide to authentic instruction and assessment: Vision, standards, and scoring.* Madison: Center on Organization and Restructuring of Schools, Wisconsin Center for Education Research, University of Wisconsin.

Ogbu, J. U. (1985). A cultural ecology of competence among inner-city blacks. In M. B. Spencer, G. K. Brookins, & W. R. Allen (Eds.), *Beginnings: The social and affective development of black children* (pp. 45-60). Hillsdale, NJ: Lawrence Erlbaum Associates.

Patchen, M. (1982). *Black-White contact in schools: Its social and academic effects.* West LaFayette, IN: Purdue University Press.

Perry, T., & College, W. (1993). *Toward a theory of African-American school achievement:* (Rep. 16). Boston: Center on Families, Communities, Schools, & Children's Learning.

Phelan, P., Davidson, A., & Cao, H. T. (1992). Speaking up: Students' perspectives on school. *Phi Delta Kappan,* 73(9), 695-704.

Portes, P. (1996). Ethnicity and culture in educational psychology. In D. Berliner & R. Calfee (Eds.), *Handbook of educational psychology* (pp. 331-357). New York: Macmillan.

Purkey, S. C., & Smith, M. S. (1983). Effective schools: A review. *Elementary School Journal*, 83, 426-452.

Rutter, M., Maughan, B., Mortimore, P., & Ouston, J. (1979). *Fifteen thousand hours: Secondary schools and their effects on children*. Cambridge, MA: Harvard University Press.

Skinner, E., & Belmont, M. (1993). Motivation in the classroom: Reciprocal effects of teacher behavior and student engagement across the school year. *Journal of Educational Psychology*, 85, 571-581.

Soloman, D., Watson, M., Battistich, V., Schaps, E., & Delucchi, K. (1992). Creating a caring community: Educational practices that promote children's prosocial development. In F. Oser, A. Dick, & J. Patry (Eds.), *Effective and responsible teaching: The new synthesis* (pp. 383-396). San Francisco: Jossey-Bass.

Spencer, M., & Markstrom-Adams, C. (1990). Identity processes among racial and ethnic minority children in America. *Child Development*, 61, 290-310.

Walberg, H. (1985). Effective schools: A quantitative synthesis of constructs. *Journal of Classroom Interaction*, 20(2), 12-17.

Wentzel, K. (1997). Student motivation in middle school: The role of perceived pedagogical caring. *Journal of Educational Psychology*, 89, 411-419.

Werner, E. E. (1990). Protective factors and individual resilience. In S. J. Meisel, & J. P. Shonkoff (Eds.), *Handbook of early childhood intervention* (pp. 331-357). New York: Cambridge University Press.

Winfield, L. F. (1991). Resilience, schooling, and development in African-American youth: A conceptual framework. *Education and Urban Society*, 24(1), 5-14.

Worthen, B. R. (1993). Critical issues that will determine the future of alternative assessment. *Phi Delta Kappan*, 74, 444-457.

Zimmerman, M. A., & Arinkumar, R. (1994). Resiliency research: Implications for schools and policy. *Society for Research in Child Development*, 8(4), 1-17.

14

Small Learning Communities Meet School-To-Work: Whole School Restructuring for Urban Comprehensive High Schools

NETTIE E. LEGTERS
Johns Hopkins University

This chapter describes specific reform practices schools are implementing to realize the vision for high schools in the United States set forth in Breaking ranks, a report published by the National Association of Secondary School Principals. The first section of this chapter reviews a general critique of public high schools articulated in the 1980s and describes the reform practices that have emerged over the past decade in response to this critique. The second section offers examples of schools that have pulled together a number of such reforms into a comprehensive school restructuring effort, focusing on one school in depth. The third section identifies challenges schools can expect to encounter when implementing the set of reforms. This section draws on the experiences of several schools the author and a research team at Johns Hopkins CRESPAR have worked with since 1994 as part of the Talent Development High Schools project.

The opening scene of the 1989 film *Lean on Me* is designed to shock. It portrays a gritty urban high school filled with thugs, drugs, and overt violence. The fast-moving clip ends with the hospitalization of a teacher who tried to break up a student fight as the graffiti-filled hallways echo with a student crying, "Somebody help!"

If you ask real urban high school students what they think of that scene (which a colleague and I did in recent focus group interviews), most will say that it is Hollywood hype.[1] Some even allude to racist and classist overtones that permeate media representations of inner-city schools, promoting fear and reinforcing stereotypes of urban pathology and "otherness." In fact, many of the complaints that these students expressed about their school – boring classes, lack of caring adults, too few engaging activities – are very common criticisms of most large comprehensive high schools, urban and nonurban alike (Sizer, 1984).

Our students go on to say, however, that many of the problems highlighted in the film do exist in their school, albeit in less exaggerated form. They speak of neighborhood gang rivalries that make the school and surrounding area feel unsafe, of students hustling for money, becoming teen parents, and engaging in other activities that distract them from getting an education; and of their sense that students often seem more in control of the school than do the adults who are running it. They share a collective sense that they are not receiving as good an education as students who attend selective magnet schools or suburban schools. Their stories are told with sparks of anger and resentment tempered by an underlying resignation that recalls their school's motto – "Hope and Endure."

These students' experiences reveal the dual challenge of urban high school reform. As with most large, comprehensive high schools, urban high schools face the blight of anachronism brought on by a rapidly changing world. Structured to provide a college-bound education for only a few students, high schools have been widely criticized for leaving too many students woefully unprepared for increasingly technological workplaces that are demanding not only a high school diploma, but high-level skills and postsecondary training as well. At the same time, urban high schools face the additional challenge of economic and demographic changes that have brought an unprecedented concentration of poor and linguistically and ethnically diverse students to their doors – students who have always had more difficulty succeeding in traditional high schools. Although large city school leaders report improving trends (Council of the Great City Schools, 1998a; 1998b), data from urban districts show that students continue to fail and drop out of urban high schools at much higher rates than in nonurban areas (Education Week/Pew Charitable Trust, 1998).

Buffeted by change and under pressure to reform, urban comprehensive high schools have engaged in a growing amount of experimentation with new approaches over the past decade. One strand of experimentation encourages

---

[1]Focus group interviews were conducted by the author and Professor Lory J. Dance, Department of Sociology, University of Maryland-College Park.

schools to adopt strategies from the middle school movement (see MacIver, et. al., chap.13, this volume) and from restructuring efforts in industry and government to replace large, highly standardized, and bureaucratic organizational structures with smaller, more responsive, and flexible learning communities (Lee, Bryk, & Smith, 1993). Another strand promotes curriculum and instructional practices developed through an emerging national school-to-career movement that emphasizes work as an important context for learning at the secondary level (Olson, 1997). In an increasing number of schools, these two strands are being merged to create small career academies, magnet programs, and other forms of focused small learning communities or schools-within-a-school (Fine, 1994; Stern, Raby, & Dayton, 1992). Unfortunately, much of the experimentation in urban high schools has touched very few students to date. Programs often are piecemeal, and selective, and have come under fire for exacerbating educational inequity in urban districts by "creaming off" the most academically motivated students and most talented teachers (Jeter, 1998).

Despite these drawbacks, experimentation in urban high schools has played a crucial role in laying the groundwork for more ambitious ventures. Spurred on by new state standards and reconstitution orders (see Mintrop, chap.11, this volume), more failing high schools are beginning to explore whole-school restructuring with an eye on providing all students with opportunities to learn relevant, high-level curriculum in a safe climate of caring and support. These efforts have both stimulated and been supported by a renewed national focus on restructuring high schools, as discussed in the recent report, *Breaking ranks*. This report calls for changes in curriculum, instruction, assessment, school organization, professional development, community partnerships, and leadership in U.S. high schools (National Association of Secondary School Principals/Carnegie Foundation, 1996). *Breaking ranks* promotes a vision of high schools that are broken down into smaller units; that emphasize a common curriculum and interdisciplinary instruction; that embrace diversity as a strength; that integrate technology into all aspects of learning; and that provide teachers and administrators with the time, resources, and support they need to improve their school.

The purpose of this chapter is to describe specific reform practices schools are implementing to realize the vision set forth in *Breaking ranks*. Furthermore, this chapter shows how some high schools are pulling together a number of these specific reform practices to form a schoolwide approach to improving failing comprehensive high schools. The first section reviews a general critique of public high schools articulated in the 1980s and describes the reform practices that have emerged over the past decade in response to this critique. The second section offers examples of schools that have pulled together a number of reforms into a comprehensive school restructuring effort, focusing on one school in depth. The third section identifies challenges schools can expect to encounter when implementing the set of reforms. This section draws on the experiences of several schools I and a research team at Johns Hopkins CRESPAR have worked with since 1994 as part of the talent development high schools project.[2]

COMPREHENSIVE HIGH SCHOOLS: PROBLEMS AND SOLUTIONS

I turned around and looked just in time to see the fellas bopping around the corner, heading out of the building. They left and never came back. They dropped out of school, just like that. I understood why it was so easy for them to quit. There was little in the classes we took that seemed even remotely relevant to our world. I couldn't figure out how learning all that stuff would translate into helping us form a better life. (McCall, 1994)

Common Critique and the Urban Challenge

A series of studies and national reports released in the 1980s identified many shortcomings to the organization, curriculum, and instructional practices found in traditional comprehensive public high schools (Boyer, 1983; Carnegie Forum, 1986; Goodlad, 1984; Oakes, 1985; Powell, Farrar & Cohen, 1985; Sizer, 1984). In general, researchers found what practitioners had known for years – that many students (as well as teachers and administrators) felt apathetic and alienated from school; that the curriculum was fragmented, superficial, and increasingly disconnected from the changing world beyond school; and that high schools offered students highly differentiated and unequal learning opportunities. One study compared high schools with shopping malls that offer quality service and products only to those students with the resources to demand them while allowing the majority of students to pass through an unfocused, watered-down curriculum with very little effort (Powell et al.). Even well-funded, elite public high

[2]This research was supported by the U.S. Department of Education, Office of Educational Research and Improvement (OERI). The opinions expressed are the author's and do not necessarily represent OERI positions or policies.

schools have been found to offer vastly unequal learning opportunities to different groups of students (Mathews, 1998).

General criticisms of comprehensive public high schools are magnified in urban districts contending with the educational consequences of middle-class flight, social and financial disinvestment, and a recent wave of immigration. Louis and Miles (1990) aptly extended the shopping mall analogy to urban districts by comparing urban high schools to inner-city minimarts:

> Run-down and overpriced, they often present a limited selection of shoddy goods for their customers . . . . The customer is often poor and usually has neither the resources to go elsewhere in search of better merchandise, nor the assertiveness to demand improved service. (p. 3)

The particular challenges urban high schools face are many. National data show stark achievement gaps among pre-high school students in math, science, and reading, with far more urban students scoring below "basic" than their nonurban counterparts (Education Week Pew Charitable Trust, 1998). This means that most students are entering urban high schools with extremely poor prior preparation. A high concentration of poverty among students and in surrounding neighborhoods also means that issues of health, safety, and early transitions into adult roles loom larger in the daily operation of urban high schools.[3] In addition, urban high schools face higher levels of academic, linguistic, and cultural diversity than do nonurban high schools. This diversity results in larger numbers of students who require special or individualized services, and places demands on teachers to teach highly heterogeneous groups. The typical neighborhood high school in Baltimore, for example, must provide special education services to 20% of its students, compared with 12% statewide and less than 1% in the city's magnet high schools (Baltimore City Public School System, 1997). Finally, many urban city school systems are very large and are mired in bureaucratic inertia, complicated politics and short-lived leadership, leaving high schools both unsupported and subject to constantly shifting priorities (Education Week/Pew Charitable Trust, 1998; Louis & Miles, 1990).

Given these challenges, it is not surprising that urban high schools fare

---

[3]Poverty rates have nearly doubled in many large cities since the early 1980s, making urban students more than twice as likely to attend high-poverty schools (schools in which more than half the students qualify for free or reduced-price lunch) than their non-urban counterparts. Not only poor, but minority students are overrepresented in urban schools; although urban school districts enroll only one quarter of public school children in the United States, over one third of the nation's poor students and nearly half its minority students attend school in urban areas (Education Week/Pew Charitable Trust, 1998).

worse than their nonurban counterparts on most measures, including achievement and dropout and graduation rates. Only from one third to less than one half of students in urban districts score at the basic level or higher in reading, mathematics, and science, compared with over two thirds of students in nonurban districts. High schools in urban districts on average lose over half of their students between the freshman and senior years, compared to a nationwide average of less than one third. At just under 10%, the single-year dropout rate for urban districts is nearly twice the national average; some urban districts struggle with single year dropout rates as high as 20% (Education Week/Pew Charitable Trust, 1998). These numbers spell disaster for young adults who typically need post-high school education credentials to find living wage employment in an economy where low-skill jobs are becoming increasingly scarce (Singh, 1994).

Research has traced the malaise of high schooling – general apathy, fragmented curriculum, and unequal learning opportunities that lead to poor achievement and high dropout rates – to several specific features of high schools that are especially problematic in urban contexts. These features include large size, rigid curricular tracking, departmentalization, disjointed curriculum that lacks relevance, lockstep scheduling, and unsupported transitions. Fortunately, reforms have been developed and are being tested in each area. The remainder of this section discusses these features and outlines the reform responses. These features and corresponding reforms are summarized in Table 14.1.

Specific Problems and
Corresponding Solutions

Size. The large size of most public high schools was once viewed as an advantage because a large, comprehensive high school had more resources, could offer more varied courses, and served as a focal point of pride and social activity in a community (Conant, 1959). More recently, however, a growing body of evidence has revealed the deleterious effects of large schools on a host of student outcomes, including achievement, attendance, involvement in school activities and dropout rates (Fowler, 1992; Lee & Smith, 1995;1997; Oxley, 1994). These effects are typically attributed to the difficulty that students and adults have in getting to know one another well in large schools. Impersonal relationships breed a sense of anonymity, making it easier for students to act out and more difficult for adults to curb adolescent tendencies to defy adult directives. Providing services and enforcing rules in a fair and consistent manner to hundreds of students each

Table 14.1: Criticisms of Comprehensive High Schools and Reform Responses

Criticisms	Reform Responses
Large size	Small Schools Schools-within-a-school (houses, clusters, small learning communities
Curriculum tracking and unequal learning opportunities	Common core curriculum
Departmentalization	Interdisciplinary teaming
Lack of relevance	School-to-work focus Career academies Multicultural curriculum
Rigid schedule	Flexible block scheduling Longer class periods Extra help opportunities (flex school, Saturday school, summer school)
Teacher-centered instruction	Active instructional techniques (cooperative learning, project-based learning, integrating technology)
Unaided transition to high school	Orientation and summer transition programs Advisories and special classes for freshmen Ninth-grade academies Alternative and after-school settings

day overwhelms the patience and talents of even the most committed teachers, administrators, and counselors. Students who feel that no one cares about them or their performance in school are more likely to act out or become disengaged and drop out of school (Klonsky, 1995).

Because nearly all urban high school students attend large high schools, problems attributed to large size affect them more than their suburban and rural counterparts.[4] Personalized relationships are likely to be even more important in schools serving large numbers of poor and minority students, given that a greater proportion of students require more adult attention and special services. Moreover, as young adolescents developing an awareness of their own social identities, poor and minority students also may need personal attachments to persist in what they may view as a White, middle-class establishment to which they feel they do not belong (Fordham & Ogbu, 1986).

---

[4]In 1995, 85% of high school students in urban districts attended schools that enrolled 900 or more students, compared with the U.S. average of 68% (Education Week/Pew Charitable Trust, 1998).

Research on school size has spawned a widespread movement toward smaller schools and the creation of self-contained "houses," "charters," or small learning communities (SLCs) within large high schools. Inspired by the widely publicized success of Central Park East in New York and strongly influenced by Sizer's Coalition for Essential Schools, SLCs have spread to high schools in Boston; Rochester, New York; Columbus, Ohio; Philadelphia; Chicago; Baltimore; parts of California; and other areas. In general, SLCs have been found to have positive effects on students' relationships with peers, teachers, and staff; extracurricular participation; and the sense of community and teamwork among staff. Students participating in SLCs also have been found to have better attendance and course passage rates and fewer suspensions than demographically similar students in more traditional high school settings. These same studies show, however, that the major change in organizational structure, combined with local politics, lack of leadership, and scarce resources, makes it difficult to achieve strong implementation of SLCs on a district-wide scale. These studies further show that weak implementation limits positive outcomes for students and staff (Fine, 1994; Oxley, 1990).

Curricular Tracking. High schools traditionally have been organized into separate curricular tracks – college preparatory, general, and vocational. This structure has been widely criticized for creating unequal learning opportunities for high school students and reinforcing social and economic stratification in society at large (Oakes, 1985; Yonezawa, chap. 6, this volume). Studies show that most high school students are tracked, that students in the lower track classes are disproportionately minority, and that general track students experience a less demanding, watered-down curriculum and much less stimulating instruction than do their high track counterparts (Braddock, 1990; Goodlad, 1984; Oakes & Lipton, 1990).

Tracking is especially problematic in urban schools, where a larger proportion of students perform below grade level and fall below the national average on basic reading, math, and science tests. Most of these students are relegated to a general track, where they have little opportunity to learn higher order skills or take the courses they need to get into college.[5] High dropout rates and poor attendance are partly attributed to tracking: students in general education courses are often bored, know that they are not college bound, and

---

[5]Six out of every ten urban students fail to perform at basic levels in reading, math and science, compared to only one third of non-urban students. In some states, ninety percent of urban students fail to pass basic 8th grade math and science tests (Education Week, 1998).

see little reason to persist in school. A study using national data found that sophomores enrolled in general and vocational tracks are three to four times more likely to drop out than are students in academic programs (Barro & Kolstad, 1987). Lee and Eckstrom (1987) found that students in general and vocational tracks are less likely to have access to a guidance counselor to help with course selection and post-high school planning.

A central feature of restructuring urban high schools is detracking instruction in favor of a common core curriculum in which all students take the same set of college preparatory courses (Lee & Smith, 1995; Newmann & Wehlage, 1995). A core curriculum typically consists of 4 years of English, and 3 or more years each of mathematics, social studies, and science. The strongest arguments in favor of a common core curriculum in urban schools are found in research on Catholic and private schools. Studies show not only that students achieve more in schools that expect all students to succeed in the same set of core academic courses, but also that achievement is distributed more equitably across socioeconomic class within those schools (Bryk, Lee, & Holland, 1993; Coleman, Hoffer, & Kilgore, 1982). Other studies that examine learning opportunities and course taking in high schools support these findings (Council of the Great City Schools, 1998b; Lee, Smith & Croninger, 1997; for review, see McPartland & Schneider, 1996). A recent study of detracking initiatives suggests, however, that the forces of academic differentiation run deep in high schools. Powerful parents and conflicts with the stratified nature of higher education systems can pose substantial barriers to detracking efforts (Wells & Oakes, 1996).

Departmentalization. A universal feature of traditional secondary schooling is organization into subject-area departments. Specialization in a particular subject area enables secondary teachers to know a subject well and hence teach the higher level instructional content required for older students. Departmentalization, however, has been criticized for producing a superficial and fragmented curriculum that fails to engage many students. Research evidence also suggests that instructional benefits of departmentalized staffing may be offset by the ways in which departmentalization detracts from a school's ability to provide an environment of caring and support for its students (Bryk, Lee, & Smith, 1990; McPartland, 1990). Departmentalization can interfere with positive teacher-student relations by putting up procedural, psychological, and logistical barriers between teachers and students. Because secondary teachers' professional identities are more closely bound to the standards of a particular subject area (and often strict curricular guidelines), they may be more likely to fail students who do not meet the course requirements without feeling a personal need to help students overcome their difficulties. High school teachers typically teach five or six different classes per day with little or no interaction with teachers in other subjects who may teach those students, which makes it very difficult for them to know any individual student and his or her capabilities well (LaPoint, Jordan, McPartland, & Penn Towns, 1996).

To preserve the benefits of subject-area specialization but eliminate its isolating and potentially alienating aspects, restructuring high schools are experimenting with interdisciplinary teacher teaming (Lee & Smith, 1995; Newmann & Wehlage, 1995). Better known as a middle school practice, the most prevalent form of interdisciplinary teaming is a four-teacher team made up of a math, an English, a science, and a social studies teacher. These teachers share responsibility for the curriculum, instruction, evaluation, and often the scheduling and discipline of a group of 100-150 students (Alexander & George, 1981; Arhar, 1992; MacIver & Epstein, 1991). As with SLCs, this arrangement is designed to help personalize the learning environment by increasing knowledge and communication among teachers, students, and parents about students' successes and problems in each subject. This sharing of students is supposed not only to provide teachers, parents, and students with a more integrated view of students' progress, but also to help students feel that there is a group of concerned adults looking out for them.

Interdisciplinary teaming also can lend more coherence and depth to the traditional academic curriculum by enabling teachers to integrate lessons across subject areas and focus on thematic units. This aspect of teaming, however, requires curricular flexibility as well as training and time for teachers to plan together. Leaders of one high school teaming experiment suggested that "changing structures and relationships precedes changing curriculum" (Ashby & Ducett, 1995/1996).

Relevance of Schoolwork. High dropout rates, poor attendance, and poor performance among students in vocational and general tracks are indicators that many students are disengaged and care little about school. This is attributed, in part, to teacher-centered, textbook-bound, skill and drill instructional techniques that dominate teaching in general track classes, especially in urban comprehensive high schools serving high-poverty students (Haberman, 1996). Apathy among students also has been attributed to a lack of connection between schoolwork and the world beyond school. Since employers do not require transcripts or other evidence of school performance, it is unclear to students who do not see themselves as college bound how doing well in school makes a difference for their futures (Bishop, 1989). Most business leaders believe that high schools do little to prepare students for the teamwork, communication, decision-making, technological, and computing skills required in changing workplaces (Secretary's Commission on Achieving Necessary Skills, 1991). Poor and minority students, moreover, are even more prone to apathy in a traditional high school curriculum because they are less likely to see their experience or heritage represented in curricular materials, and often lack role models and other motivational supports for academic performance.

An emerging school-to-work or school-to-career movement is one of the most prominent reform efforts aimed at making schoolwork more relevant and engaging more students in school. Inspired by European systems and supported by the 1994 School to Work Opportunities Act, many states across the country have developed technology preparation, shadowing, apprenticeship, internship, and other work-based learning programs for high school-aged youths (Olson, 1997; Stern, Finkelstein, Stone, Latting, & Dornsife, 1995). High schools also are experimenting with integrating academic and vocational curricula to form focused career majors, clusters, pathways, or academies (Grubb, 1995).

Career academies present a potentially powerful manifestation of school-to-work efforts because they combine the relevance of a career focus with the personalized environment of a self-contained SLC. Career academies have been found to have positive effects on student performance, dropout prevention, and college attendance (Stern et al., 1992). Early evidence from an evaluation of 10 career academy programs indicates that career academy students are more motivated to attend school and view schoolwork as more relevant to their futures, and that job satisfaction and sense of belonging to a strong professional community are higher among academy teachers (Kemple, 1997). Most high schools that experiment with career academies, however, have only one academy that serves a small group of students. Grubb (1995) pointed to the potential for all students in a high school to participate in a career-focused program, noting the added benefit of having students actually choose their own program and hence increasing their attachment to school. Very few high schools are implementing multiple career academies, clusters, or majors, however, and research studies are scant.

Compared with the school-to-work movement, efforts to make schooling and schoolwork more relevant to students' cultural background and experiences are less developed, especially at the high school level. Scholars argue that minority students are more likely to excel in educational environments that acknowledge and respect their language, history and culture (Boykin, 1994; Hale, 1994; Hale-Benson, 1986; Ladson-Billings, 1994). For example, recent studies suggest that African-American students are more engaged and learn more in communal and cooperative group settings than in more traditional individual and competitive learning environments (Boykin). Boykin offers nine dimensions of an "Afro-cultural ethos" that, taken together, offer a rich heuristic framework for rethinking the education of African American students. To date, however, studies of pedagogical approaches that might be more responsive to students' different cultural backgrounds have focused primarily on elementary grade students, leaving open the question of what culturally relevant pedagogy might look like for students in a later developmental stage. Multicultural curricula and language experiments (e.g., ESOL, ebonics) in general have proved controversial, and there is a great need for further experimentation and research in this area.

Schedule and Instruction. A broad critique of traditional uses of time for schooling has recently emerged (National Education Commission on Time and Learning, 1994). The rigid, "factory" model of students moving from class to class six to eight times per day is another aspect of high school organization that impedes the development of close relationships between teachers and students. Periods that are 45-50 minutes in length also make it difficult for teachers to complete lessons, present material in a variety of ways so that more students understand, or implement innovative approaches such as project-based, technology-based, and cooperative learning strategies. Finally, the traditional high school schedule reinforces content coverage over depth of understanding, and inhibits strategic and flexible grouping of students who need extra help in a particular area.

In an effort to move away from fragmented instruction and impersonal, factory-like environments, high schools are experimenting with alternative forms of scheduling (O'Neil, 1995). Foremost among these are the 4 x 4 and alternate day block schedules. Each of these models structures the school day around four 90-minute periods. In the 4 x 4 plan, students take the same four classes each day and complete them in one semester. In the alternate day plan, students take half their classes in extended periods one day, and the other half of their classes the next day, with the pattern repeating throughout the school year (Canady & Rettig, 1995). Flexible block scheduling is often used to support SLCs and interdisciplinary teaming because it gives team teachers the opportunity to change the schedule from week to week or even daily, to meet the particular and changing needs of their students.

Research on block scheduling from around the country indicates that the practice is on the rise. In one study, the number of high schools increased from just over 1% (6 schools) to 35% (130 schools) between 1992 and 1995 (Public Schools of North Carolina, 1998). The same study showed that students in block scheduled schools are more likely to be poor, but that they scored significantly higher on standardized subject tests than did students in nonblocked schools after adjusting for starting point, parental educational level, and homework time. Another study attributed increases in on-time graduation rates, college attendance, and improved test scores to block scheduling reforms (Langland, 1997). The author's observations and research in high schools in Baltimore suggest that block scheduling helps reduce discipline referrals and class tardiness, in part because students spend less time in the halls during the day.

Transitions. When students make the transition into high school in the ninth grade, they must negotiate a new physical space, new relationships with adults and peers, and more challenging academic demands. Most high schools are large, bureaucratic organizations characterized by more formal rules and impersonal relationships than middle or elementary schools. Research on school transitions shows that many students struggle with the transition to high school (see Roderick, 1993, for review). Among all high school students, ninth-grade students tend to have the lowest grade point averages, greatest number of disciplinary problems, and highest failure rates. In her study of one school district, Roderick found that average grades declined by 18% following the move from middle to high school. She also showed that academic failure is more likely for many students during their first year of high school. Moreover, she demonstrated that academic failure during that year has a greater impact on students' decisions to persist in school because they are in the process of determining whether they fit in high school.

Successfully integrating into a traditionally organized high school is likely to be more difficult for poor and minority students. These students, generally, are more oriented toward work life than toward academics, tend to be placed in less engaging lower track classes, and are more likely to experience conflicts between their student role and other roles (parent, worker, translator, gang member) they play outside of school (Bryk & Thum, 1989; Eckstrom, Goertz, Pollack & Rock, 1987; Fine, 1985; 1987; Oakes, 1985). With little personal attachment or access to extra help, many ninth-grade students fail courses, fall further and further behind, and ultimately become disengaged and drop out.

Roderick (1993) reviewed a number of programmatic approaches designed to ease students' transition into high school. These include orientation and summer transition programs such as STEP, and targeted remediation programs that introduce students to the high school environment and provide extra help with academic course work (see also Natriello, McDill, & Pallas, 1990). Other approaches involve creating advisories or special classes for ninth-grade students that emphasize personal contact between students and teachers and that focus on social support, life skills, and career awareness. Some districts are experimenting with more radical approaches that involve separating ninth-grade students from the rest of the school for all or part of the school day through the use of interdisciplinary teams, schools-within-a-school, or altogether separate schools (Beyers, 1997; McPartland, Jordan, Legters, & Balfanz, 1997). Other strategies include alternative settings and after-school programs that provide extra help for students or that enable students to continue earning credits toward graduation while working or while addressing legal or personal problems that make it difficult for them to attend regular day school.

PUTTING IT TOGETHER

A small group of high schools across the country have been recognized for their successful experimentation with the reform strategies described in the previous section. In May 1996, as part of the New American High School Project, the U.S. Department of Education and the National Center for Research in Vocational Education identified 10 exemplary high schools committed to comprehensive restructuring. These schools have been acknowledged primarily for their emphasis on college and career preparation achieved through organizing around a single career theme, incorporating career clusters or pathways, or implementing small, self-contained, career-focused academies (Stern & Hallinan, 1997). The New Urban High School initiative, also sponsored by the U.S. Department of Education, has identified four additional exemplary sites of comprehensive, whole school reform in large, urban districts that include many of the same elements (Rosenstock, 1998).[6] Many of these 14 high schools, as well as others in more nascent

---

[6]One school, William Turner Technical Arts High School in Miami, Florida, was identified as exemplary in both the New American High Schools and New Urban High Schools projects.

stages of reform, are linked to collaboratives designed to stimulate and support reform.[7]

Even among these exemplary high schools, only a handful are pulling together most or all of the reform components just described into a comprehensive plan for whole school restructuring. Those that are putting the pieces together are in the early phases of implementation, and very little research evidence is available to attest to their success. Some promising early results are emerging, however, as the following case illustrates.

Patterson High School. Located in a deindustrialized part of Baltimore, Patterson High School had suffered the effects of increased unemployment and consequent poverty that have plagued many working-class, urban neighborhoods over the past two decades. Once known as a "good school," by the early 1990s its plummeting achievement, dropout rates rising to over 50%, and increasing truancy and violence had earned this school a reputation for being disorderly and ineffective. Initial site visits prior to the implementation of the reform program confirmed this perception:

> The school learning environment was in chaos. Small groups of unruly students were constantly roaming the halls and stairways, and repeated faculty efforts to bring order to the building were unsuccessful. Teachers unable to maintain peace in the halls retreated to their classrooms where they tried to do their best with the few students in their own rooms. They kept the doors of their rooms closed, and many papered over their door windows to shut out the outside confusion. (McPartland, Legters, Jordan, & McDill, 1996)

Patterson is a large high school, with over 2,000 students. As with many urban schools, the student population has changed over the past 30 years. Once a school with a majority population of White, middle-class students, Patterson's current student body is about 60% African-American; 30% White (most of whom live in working class neighborhoods of Greek, Polish, and Italian heritage); and 10% Native American, Asian, and Hispanic. As with many inner cities attempting to stem middle-class flight, Baltimore has several high schools with special programs and entrance requirements that draw students from throughout the city. In contrast, Patterson is a nonselective school that receives all the students within a specified geographical zone who are not accepted into one of the selective citywide

---

[7] These collaboratives include the Coalition of Essential Schools, the High Schools that Work Network, the California and Philadelphia Partnership Academies, the Philadephia Schools Collaborative, and the CRESPAR Talent Development Project.

high schools.

In 1993, the Maryland State Board of Education took unprecedented action to force improvement in the failing schools across the state by adopting regulations that set forth procedures for school "reconstitution." In January 1994 (and in each January of subsequent years), local school systems received a list of schools that the state board deemed eligible for reconstitution because they were not meeting state standards and were declining or not making adequate progress toward the standards. Reconstitution eligible schools were required to submit a comprehensive plan for substantial change in their administration, staff, organization, or instructional program. The plans were required to address the specific concerns of the state monitors and be approved by the state board. On approval of their plans, schools were given 3-5 years to implement the proposed changes. Although the state board has yet to spell out exactly what steps it will take at the end of the implementation period, the implication is that the state will take over schools that fail to improve during the allotted time.

Patterson was one of the first high schools in its district threatened with reconstitution if it did not produce significant changes to improve its dropout and attendance rates and student performance on state functional tests. In response, the school underwent an improvement planning process in 1994-1995 and began implementing several reforms in fall 1995. These reforms included the following:

- Dividing the school into five smaller schools-within-a-school. With a total enrollment of 2,170 students and 110 full-time faculty (as of fall 1995), Patterson is one of the largest high schools in its district. In Grades 10-12, students now attend one of four smaller, career-focused academies. In the 9th grade, students attend a self-contained academy called the Ninth Grade Success Academy. Each academy is located in a separate part of the school with its own entrance and an administrative team made up of an academy principal and an academy leader. Subject-area departments have been officially disbanded under the new organization, although teachers still meet in subject-area groups to discuss curricular objectives.

- Reorganizing the schedule into four extended periods of 90 minutes (4 x 4 block) to provide more time for in-depth instruction and flexibility in scheduling and teaching methods.

- Organizing teachers in the Ninth Grade Success Academy into interdisciplinary teacher teams (made up of four teachers – a math, an English, a science, and a social studies teacher – called a MESS team) who share the same students and have a common 90-minute planning period built into the daily schedule.

- Instituting a twilight school, an after-hours program for students who have serious attendance or discipline problems, or who are entering the school after being suspended from another school or released from incarceration. Students may be admitted into (or back into) day school by doing well and earning credits in the twilight program.

- Releasing students at noon every Wednesday to provide time for academies and teams to meet, plan and participate in professional development activities.

- Installing computer labs, classroom phones, and other state-of-the-art equipment to upgrade the school's technology and communication systems.

Following a tension-filled planning process that resulted in some teachers leaving the school, the remaining teachers and administrators at Patterson came together to implement the reform process with a marked spirit of cooperation and teacher involvement. The academies were initiated and designed by teachers who emerged as leaders in the planning process. Teachers and administrators formed ad hoc committees to carry out various elements of the plan, many of which had to be implemented immediately or over a period of only a few months. These plans included making structural changes to the school building, coordinating the faculty and student academy selection processes, selecting and purchasing technological equipment, planning a kickoff faculty retreat, and – what turned out to be one of the most challenging tasks – scheduling teachers and students for classes according to the new organization.

A research team from the Johns Hopkins CRESPAR was asked to assist Patterson in its school improvement process. The CRESPAR team surveyed students and teachers several times throughout the planning and implementation process, and also collected qualitative interview and observation data to gain a deeper and more nuanced understanding of changes occurring in the school. Johns Hopkins CRESPAR also obtained attendance, promotion, and achievement data from the school district.

Effects of the Reforms. The most dramatic result of the reform effort at Patterson has been a marked improvement in overall school climate and in teachers' and students' perceptions of their school[8]. For example, prior to implementation of the reforms, the vast majority of teachers (80-90 percent) reported that the school's learning environment was not conducive to achievement, that student misbehavior interfered with their teaching, and that the school lacked close relations among staff. After the first year of reform, these numbers dropped to 20-30%, indicating an almost complete turnaround in teachers' experiences at Patterson. Compared to a match control school, students at Patterson were much more likely to report improvement in their school on a variety of climate indicators such as students roaming the halls, overall school safety, and fairness of school rules. During a visit to the school, a nationally known educator asked a random group of students in the hall what they thought of the new Patterson. Although some students complained that the school became more strict after the reorganization, their comments suggested that they appreciated the more disciplined environment and the sense that they were attending "a real school." One student then proudly pointed out that Patterson was able to reduce the number of security guards from three to one after implementation. She laughingly told her teacher that students called the lone guard the "Maytag Man," referring to the appliance mechanic whose machines work so well that he is left with nothing to do.

Attendance and promotion data also improved at Patterson. Over a 3-year period (spring 1994 to spring 1997) consisting of 1 planning year and 2 implementation years, Patterson raised its attendance rate by 10% for the entire school and by 15% for its ninth-grade students. Over the same period, the average attendance rate in Baltimore's other high schools declined three percentage points. In part because they were attending more regularly, more students at Patterson were promoted to the next grade than had been in the past. In fall of the planning year (1994-1995), there were 2.5 times as many ninth-grade students as juniors and seniors combined in the school. By fall 1998, the number of juniors and seniors combined equaled the number of ninth-grade students. Increased passing rates were not the result of social promotion or a watered-down curriculum. In 1997, Patterson had the highest number of graduates who met the course requirements for the University of Maryland system among Baltimore's nine nonselective comprehensive high schools.

---

[8] For more in-depth analysis of Patterson data, see McPartland, Balfanz, Jordan and Legters (1998).

In the area of achievement, focused efforts within the ninth-grade transition program resulted in a 20 percentage point increase in the number of students passing the Maryland state functional math exam, and a 12 percentage point increase in the number of students passing the state's functional writing exam. This gave Patterson the highest pass rate in math among the city's nine neighborhood high schools and the third highest pass rate in writing. Recall that the state's decision to identify Patterson as a reconstitution-eligible school was based partly on the school's performance on these exams. Maryland uses a school performance index based on attendance, retention, and functional test scores to rate and compare schools. In 1994-1995, when it became reconstitution eligible, Patterson had the second worst school performance index among the nine zoned comprehensive high schools in Baltimore. By 1996-1997, after their second year of implementing the reforms, Patterson had the second highest index score among those high schools and the highest among the eight largest schools.

Other Sites. By breaking the school down into smaller schools, moving to an extended period, offering a career focus, providing a special program for ninth-grade students, and other efforts, the faculty and staff at Patterson were successful in creating a much improved school. In part because of Patterson's growing reputation as a "turn around" school, the Baltimore City Public School System is investing in the movement of all of its zoned, comprehensive schools to a schoolwide academy approach. A look around the country indicates that other high schools and districts are implementing reform models that look strikingly similar to the whole school approach being implemented in Baltimore.

The Oakland School District, for example, is investing heavily in the same model of "wall-to-wall" career academies with ninth-grade transition programs and flexible block scheduling, building on the success that single-career academies have had in that district. Virtually the same model being implemented at Patterson can be found among the high schools identified as exemplary in the New American High School Project, including Encina High School in Sacramento, California; the Chicago Vocational Career Academy School; and William H. Turner Technical Arts High School, in Miami, Florida. Bell Multicultural High School in Washington, DC, serving low-income students who come from 50 different countries, has organized into a ninth-grade "prep cluster" and four career-focused clusters. In Rio Rancho, New Mexico, a large grant from the Intel Corporation has supported a high end version of the model. Struggling with the all too familiar problems of apathy and low achievement, Rio Rancho educators built a new school from the ground up that included separate buildings for the ninth-grade academy and each career academy (Hornblower, 1997).

Although still in their beginning stages, these ambitious efforts show promise for providing a viable alternative for high schools that want to provide all students with access to a college preparatory curriculum, adequate academic support, and a community of caring adults who hold high expectations for their success. Transforming an entire high school along these lines is no easy task, however. The following section outlines a number of challenges that schools are likely to encounter as they implement this package of reforms.

CHALLENGES TO WHOLE-SCHOOL HIGH SCHOOL RESTRUCTURING

Through our experience working with reforming high schools in Baltimore, the Johns Hopkins CRESPAR team has identified a number of challenges to implementing the set of reforms that Patterson and other schools are implementing. These challenges fall into three main categories: learning opportunities, technical difficulties, and professional community.

Learning Opportunities

Committing to a Common Core Curriculum with High Standards for all Students. When reorganizing a comprehensive high school into multiple career-focused academies, it is important to ensure that all academies, in both perception and reality, provide all students with college-preparatory course work. The forces of academic differentiation run so deep in high schools that tracking may be sustained in subtle ways; for example, one academy may be designed in such a way that it draws the college bound students, whereas others become dumping grounds for less motivated students. Schools loathe to eliminate special programs (for either accelerated or at-risk students), and in the process of restructuring may attempt to preserve those programs by shifting them "whole hog" into one academy or another during reorganization. Though this may be necessary during a transitional period, schools must be prepared to evaluate, reorganize and even eliminate programs that compete with the goal of providing high level academic coursework to all students.

Another challenge schools will face in this area is the development of teaching resources to teach a common core of college-preparatory academic classes in each academy. Many high school teachers not only are specialized by subject area but have developed further specialization within their subject, with strengths in teaching algebra or chemistry, for example. In failing urban high schools, many teachers have not had experience teaching high-level courses because so few students have populated college-preparatory tracks. Breaking up departments of teachers and distributing them to multiple academies throughout the school means that all teachers must be trained and feel confident teaching at various levels within their disciplines. Transitional structures, again, may be necessary, with upper-grade students crossing academies for upper-level courses such as physics and calculus until teachers for those courses can be placed in their academies. Schools also are using distance learning and early enrollment in community college courses to place students in advanced courses.

Committing to Integrated Curriculum and Work-Based Learning. The great strength of the career academy approach is the connection between academic and work-based learning. This connection is achieved by involving industry partners in designing the academy curriculum and by ensuring that students have exposure to the workplace through job shadowing, internships, and actual paid work experiences. Realizing and sustaining these elements requires a great deal of time, training, energy, and commitment on the part of school- and industry-based staff. These elements do not materialize overnight and will never be developed if schools and districts rely on academy leaders or principals who have teaching or traditional administrative duties. Among the New Urban High Schools, Rosenstock (1998) found that the barriers to developing work-based learning opportunities exist primarily on the school side, where schools lack the knowledge and resources to establish and sustain strong partnerships. In Baltimore and Philadelphia, school-to-work initiatives at the district level are now being implemented to facilitate the development of industry advisory boards and provide high school academy staff with the training and facilitation needed to "put the career" in their career academies.

Creating work-based learning opportunities also must mean more than finding jobs for students. Research has actually found a negative relationship between working more than 15-20 hours a week and performance in high school (see Stern, 1997, for review). Although students who work fewer hours perform better than students who work long hours, research is mixed on whether working fewer hours per week has benefits for students' academic performance. Evidence indicates that school support and supervision mitigate the negative impact work may have on student performance. This suggests that supportive linkages between students' classroom learning and work-based learning are necessary for students to reap the full benefits of work experience. Such linkages will require academic teachers to revisit curricula, and develop and monitor their students' work-based learning experiences.

Committing to Revitalized Instruction. Many reformers have learned that structural reforms (school-within-a-school, interdisciplinary teams, extended periods) are necessary but not sufficient conditions for improvements in teaching and learning. Teaching in a 4 x 4, block schedule with 80-90 minute periods enables teachers to use varied instructional techniques, cooperative learning, alternative assessment, technology, project-based learning, and more student-directed, hands-on activities. However, unless teachers are trained in these techniques and in using the longer period effectively, instruction will remain unchanged no matter how many minutes are given for a class period.

Professional development for improved instruction must not be modeled after traditional forms of in-service training in which isolated teachers learn generalized skills primarily through fragmented, one-shot training workshops that are part of district-level, one-size-fits-all programs. Fortunately, education reform efforts are forcing the emergence of new models of professional development. These professional development models emphasize the need for teachers to take an active role in their own growth, and the importance of learning opportunities that are coherent; long range; and closely linked to immediate classroom contexts, school goals, and real curricula (Corcoran, 1995; Little, 1993; National Commission on Teaching and America's Future, 1996; National Foundation for the Improvement of Education, 1996). This kind of professional development must be supported by ongoing relationships with trainers and facilitators, and by peer coaching networks within and among schools.

Human and Technical
Challenges of Reorganization

As with any comprehensive, schoolwide change, planning is absolutely critical to successful implementation of the package of reforms described in the previous section. Schools cannot expect to completely reorganize overnight or even over a summer. Indeed, Johns Hopkins CRESPAR recommends that schools take an entire year to plan once they have committed to implementing this set of reforms. This is because the effective implementation of a ninth-grade academy and multiple career-focused academics requires the participation of the entire faculty and staff. Ownership of the SLCs comes when faculty have had a hand in creating them and have had a chance to select which one they want to join. There also must be time for faculty to market the academies to the students and their families, and for students to undergo a self-assessment process and ultimately choose their academy. Without these elements of participation and choice, the multiple-academy model can quickly deteriorate into contrived structural reform with all of the cynicism and resistance that typically accompanies such top-down change efforts.

A planning year also is necessary to work through the technical challenges that accompany the transformation of a comprehensive high school into multiple, self-contained SLCs, especially in the areas of facilities changes, staffing, and scheduling. For SLCs to be self-contained, each must be equipped with its own entrance, offices, faculty work rooms, and labs – not a trivial task for high schools long organized around subject-area departments and a scattering of special program areas. Staffing also presents a challenge in this labor-intensive model. Not only must each academy be outfitted with its own administrative team and support staff, but each must have enough teachers to teach all of the core academic subjects and electives to its students. Schools moving to this model also experience scheduling challenges due, in part, to the lack of computerized software available to generate the matrices necessary to develop a master schedule for multiple schools-within-a-school. Schedulers working within a 4 x 4 block schedule must be especially creative with year-long electives such as band or chorus that involve students from throughout the school.

Professional Community

Ideally, implementing the reforms that make up the new vision for high schooling set forth here help foster a more student-centered professional community among faculty and staff. Survey and observation evidence from Baltimore high schools suggests that proximity and a common focus on interdisciplinary teams within a ninth-grade academy and within upper-grade career academies engender more frequent interactions among teachers about students and, to a lesser extent, about professional practice (Legters, 1996). However, the new structures can create divisions among faculty as well. In one school, ninth grade academy teachers expressed feelings of being not only separated from but also looked down on by upper-grade academy teachers. By disbanding subject-area departments, teachers also are separated from their subject-area peers, requiring schools to institute different kinds of support for (and monitoring of) novice teachers.

Professional community also can be enhanced or strained depending on how clearly schools are able to develop the new leadership structures required to operate a multiple, wall-to-wall academy concept. In general, the success of multiple academies rests in part on the ability of the whole school principal to delegate authority and allow each academy to run itself on a daily basis. In Baltimore high schools, academies have both an academy principal (typically an assistant principal) and an academy leader (often a former department head). In the ninth-grade academy, interdisciplinary teams also have a team leader. Because they are not full-fledged administrators and because they are now general instructional leaders with responsibilities for teachers from a variety of subject areas rather than a subject area in which they have some expertise, academy leaders and team leaders experience high levels of uncertainty and ambiguity in their positions. Tensions arise when, for example, an academy principal overrules disciplinary decisions made by ninth-grade team leaders, or when an academy leader with a math background conducts an observation of an English teacher. Teachers express concern that the whole school principal is removed and out of touch with their academy and hence does not serve as an effective mediator of these tensions. Lacking proven models, schools that adopt these reforms must negotiate new systems of leadership and evaluation that meet the challenges of the new structures.

The foregoing discussion by no means represents an exhaustive list of the challenges and barriers high schools will face when attempting to implement the package of reforms presented here as a model for whole school change. Other challenges urban schools are likely to face include competing with magnet and suburban schools for teaching and financial resources, effectively integrating special education students into the reforms, and convincing districts wedded to outmoded models of professional development to provide adequate time and resources for reform (see Legters, 1998). Additional challenges are certain to be identified as high schools continue their efforts and as more high schools adopt the reforms. There is no doubt that restructuring comprehensive high schools is a very difficult task that requires tremendous coordination of effort and resources. Just because it is hard does not mean that it should not be attempted, however. The United States, and especially our inner cities, can ill afford the social and economic consequences of maintaining the status quo.

CONCLUSION

Whole school reform is finally taking center stage in the education arena. More and more educators are understanding that piecemeal reform too often produces a confusing and inefficient proliferation of programs that generate resource battles, reinforce inequity, and ultimately help only a few students. Nowhere is this more apparent than in large, urban comprehensive high schools where a complex, loosely coupled, and often highly politicized organizational structure has encouraged a Band-Aid approach to the growing social and academic challenges these schools face. Although headway has been made at the elementary- and middle-grade levels (Legters & McDill, 1994; Slavin & Fashola, 1998), most inner-city high schools remain in need of sustained comprehensive reform.

This chapter has shown that reform ideas for high schools exist and that some schools are putting these ideas together in an approach to whole school reform. Because these efforts are still in their infancy, research evidence showing positive effects remains more suggestive than conclusive. Perhaps most notable about these efforts, to date, is simply the level of convergence of the reform strategies adopted by restructuring high schools. That restructuring high schools appear to be embracing so many of the same reform strategies suggests that the time may be ripe for a national high school restructuring movement. Such a movement would lend added coherence to the efforts of high schools around the country and better enable practitioners, researchers, and policymakers to learn from these efforts.

REFERENCES

Alexander, W. M., & George, P. S. (1981). *The exemplary middle school.* New York: Holt, Rinehart & Winston.

Arhar, J. M. (1992). Interdisciplinary teaming and the social bonding of middle level students. In J.L. Irvin (Ed.), *Transforming middle level education: Perspectives and possibilities* (pp. 139-161). Boston: Allyn & Bacon.

Ashby, D., & Ducett, W. (1995/1996, December/January). Building interdisciplinary teams: Ten things you should know before beginning. *High School Magazine, 3*(2), 12-18.

Baltimore City Public School System. (1997). *Maryland school performance program report.* Baltimore: Author.

Barro, S., & Kolstad, A. (1987). *Who drops out of high school? Findings from high school and beyond* (Rep. No. CS87-397c). Washington, DC: U.S. Department of Education, National Center for Education Statistics.

Beyers, D. (January 31, 1997). For freshmen, a false start: Perils of ninth grade prompt freshmen to try new approaches. *The Washington Post*, pp. A1, A10.

Bishop, J. H. (1989). Why the apathy in American high schools? *Educational Researcher,*

18(1), 6-10.

Boyer, E. L. (1983). *High school: A report on secondary education in America.* New York: Harper & Row.

Boykin, A. W. (1994). Harvesting talent and culture: African-American children and educational reform. In R. J. Rossi (Ed.), *Schools and students at risk: Context and framework for positive change* (pp. 116-140). New York: Teachers College Press.

Braddock, J. H. II (1990). *Tracking: Implications for student race-ethnic subgroups* (Rep. No. 2). Baltimore: Johns Hopkins University, Center for Research on Effective Schooling for Disadvantaged Students.

Bryk, A. S., Lee, V. E., & Holland, P. B. (1993). *Catholic schools and the common good.* Cambridge, MA: Harvard University Press.

Bryk, A. S., Lee, V. E., & Smith, J. B. (1990). High school organization and its effects on teachers and students: An interpretive summary of the research. In W.H. Cline & J.F. Witte (Eds.), *Choice and control in American education* (pp.135-226). New York: Falmer Press.

Bryk, A. S., & Thum, Y. (1989). The effect of high school organization on dropping out: An exploratory investigation. *American Educational Research Journal, 26*(3), 353-383.

Canady, R. L., & Rettig, M. D. (1995). *Block scheduling: A catalyst for change in high schools.* Princeton, NJ: Eye on Education.

Carnegie Forum on Education and the Economy: Task Force on Teaching as a Profession. (1986). *A nation prepared: Teachers for the 21st century.* New York: Carnegie Corporation of New York.

Coleman, J. S., Hoffer, T., & Kilgore, S. B. (1982). *High school achievement: Public and private schools compared.* New York: Basic Books.

Conant, J. (1959). *The revolutionary transformation of the American high school.* Cambridge, MA: Harvard University Press.

Corcoran, T. B. (1995). *Helping teachers teach well: Transforming professional development.* New Brunswick, NJ: Consortium for Policy Research in Education.

Council of the Great City Schools. (1998a). *Signs of progress: Preliminary evidence of urban school comeback.* Washington, D C: Author.

Council of the Great City Schools. (1998b). *Charting the right course: A report on urban student achievement and course-taking.* Washington, DC: Author.

Eckstrom, R. B., Goertz, M. S., Pollack, J. M., & Rock, D. A. (1987). Who drops out of high school and why? Findings from a national study. In G. Natriello (Ed.), *School dropout: Patterns and policies* (pp. 52-69). New York: Teachers College Press.

Education Week/Pew Charitable Trust. (1998). *Quality counts '98: The urban challenge -- Public education in the 50 states* (Vol.17). Washington, DC: Author.

Fine, M. (1985). Dropping out of high school: An inside look. *Social Policy, 16*(2), 43-50.

Fine, M. (1987). Why urban adolescents drop into and out of public high schools. In G. Natriello (Ed.), *School dropout: Patterns and policies* (pp. 89-105). New York: Teachers College Press.

Fine, M. (1994). *Chartering urban school reform.* New York: Teachers College Press.

Fordham, S., & Ogbu, J. U. (1986). Black students' school success: Coping with the burden of "acting white." *Urban Review,* 18(3), 176-206.

Fowler, W. J. (1992, April). *What do we know about school size? What should we know?* Paper presented at the annual meeting of the American Educational Research Association, San Francisco.

Goodlad, J. I. (1984). *A place called school: Prospects for the future.* New York: McGraw-Hill.

Grubb, W. N. (1995). Coherence for all students: High schools with career clusters and majors.

In W. N. Grubb (Ed.), *Education Through Occupations in American High Schools* (pp. 97-113), New York: Teachers College Press.

Haberman, M. (1996). The pedagogy of poverty versus good teaching. In W. Ayers & P. Ford (Eds.), *City kids, city teachers: Reports from the front row* (pp. 118-130). New York: The New Press.

Hale, J. E. (1994). *Unbank the fire: Visions for the education of African American children.* Baltimore: Johns Hopkins University Press.

Hale-Benson, J. (1986). *Black children: Their roots, culture, and learning styles.* Baltimore: Johns Hopkins University Press.

Hornblower, M. (1997, October). Rio Ranch, N.M.: Pointing the way toward a practical future. *Time*, 150(7), 84-85.

Jeter, M. (February 13, 1998). Integrated magnet school leaves students poles apart. *The Washington Post*, pp. A1, A12.

Kemple, J., (1997) *Career academies: Communities of support for students and teachers.* New York: Manpower Demonstration Research Corporation.

Klonsky, M. (1995). *Small schools: The numbers tell a story.* The Small Schools Workshop. Chicago: Illinois University College of Education.

Ladson-Billings, G. (1994). *The dreamkeepers: Successful teachers of African American children.* San Francisco: Jossey-Bass.

Langland, C. (February 10, 1997). Longer classes help learning, school's study finds. *The Philadelphia Inquirer*, p. B2.

LaPoint, V., Jordan, W., McPartland, J. M., & Penn Towns, D. (1996). *The talent development high school: Essential components* (Rep. No. 1). Baltimore: Johns Hopkins University/Howard University, Center for Research on the Education of Students Placed at Risk.

Lee, V. E., Bryk, A. S., & Smith, J. B. (1993). The organization of effective secondary schools. In L. Darling-Hammond (Ed.), *Review of research in education* (pp. 171-267). Washington, DC: American Educational Research Association.

Lee, V. E., & Eckstrom, R. (1987). Student access to guidance counseling in high school. *American Educational Research Journal*, 42(2), 287-310.

Lee, V. E., & Smith, J. B. (1995). Effects of high school restructuring and size on early gains in achievement and engagement. *Sociology of Education, 68*(4), 241-270.

Lee, V. E., & Smith, J. B. (1997, Fall). High school size: Which works best and for whom? *Educational Evaluation and Policy Analysis*, 19(3), 205-227.

Lee, V. E., Smith, J. B., & Croninger, R. G. (1997). How high school organization influences the equitable distribution of learning in mathematics and science. *Sociology of Education*, 70(2), 128-150.

Legters, N. E. (1996). *Intensification or professionalization: High school restructuring and teachers' work experiences.* Unpublished doctoral dissertation, Johns Hopkins University, Baltimore.

Legters, N. E. (December 7, 1998). Boosting high school reform (Opinion editorial). *The Baltimore Sun*, p. 15A.

Legters, N. E., & McDill, E. L. (1994). Rising to the challenge: Emerging strategies for educating at-risk youth. In R. J. Rossi (Ed.) *Schools and students at risk: Context and framework for positive change* (pp.23-50). New York: Teachers College Press.

Little, J. W. (1993). Teachers' professional development in a climate of educational reform. *Educational Evaluation and Policy Analysis, 15*(2), 129-151.

Louis, K., & Miles, M. (1990). *Improving the urban high school: What works and why.* New York: Teachers College Press.

MacIver, D. J., & Epstein, J. L. (1991). Responsive practices in the middle grades: Teacher teams, advisory groups, remedial instruction, and school transition programs. *American Journal of Education, 99*(4), 587-622.

Mathews, J. (1998). *Class struggle: What's wrong (and right) with America's best public high schools.* New York: Times Books.

McCall, N. (1994). *Makes me wanna holler: A young Black man in America.* New York: Vintage Books.

McPartland, J. M. (1990). Staffing decisions in the middle grades: Balancing quality instruction and teacher/student relations. *Phi Delta Kappan, 71,* 465-469.

McPartland, J. M., Balfanz, R., Jordan, W., & Legters, N. (1998). Improving climate and achievement in a troubled urban high school through the talent development model. *Journal of the Education of Students Placed at Risk, 3*(4), 337-361.

McPartland, J. M., Jordan, W., Legters, N., & Balfanz, R. (1997). Finding safety in small numbers. *Educational Leadership,* 55:14-17.

McPartland, J. M., Legters, N., Jordan, W., & McDill, E. (1996). *The talent development high school: Early evidence of impact on school climate, attendance, and student promotion* (Rep. No. 2). Baltimore, MD: Johns Hopkins & Howard University Center for Research on the Education of Students Placed at Risk.

McPartland, J. M., & Schneider, B. (1996). Opportunities to learn and student diversity: Prospects and pitfalls of a common core curriculum. *Sociology of Education, Extra Issue,* 66-81.

National Association of Secondary School Principals/Carnegie Foundation. (1996). *Breaking ranks: Changing an American institution.* Reston, VA: Author.

National Commission on Teaching and America's Future. (1996). *What matters most: Teaching for America's future.* New York: Author.

National Education Commission on Time and Learning. (1994). *Prisoners of time.* Washington, DC: Author.

National Foundation for the Improvement of Education. (1996). *Teachers take charge of their learning.* Washington, DC: Author.

Natriello, G., McDill, E. L., & Pallas, A. M. (1990). *Schooling disadvantaged children: Racing against catastrophe.* New York: Teachers College Press.

Newmann, F. M., & Wehlage, G. G. (1995). *Successful school restructuring.* Madison, WI: Center on Organization and Restructuring of Schools.

Oakes, J. (1985). *Keeping track: How schools structure inequality.* New Haven, CT: Yale University Press.

Oakes, J., & Lipton, M. (1990). Tracking and ability grouping: A structural barrier to access and achievement. In J.I. Goodlad & P. Keating (Eds.), *Access to knowledge: An agenda for our nation's schools* (pp. 43-58). New York: College Entrance Examination Board.

Olson, L. (1997). *School to work revolution.* Reading, MA: Addisson - Wesley.

O'Neil, J. (1995). Finding time to learn. *Educational Leadership,* 53(3), 11-15.

Oxley, D. (1990). *An analysis of house systems in New York City neighborhood high schools.* Philadelphia: Temple University, Center for Research in Human Development and Education.

Oxley, D. (1994). Organizing schools into small units: Alternatives to homogeneous grouping. *Phi Delta Kappan,* 75(7), 521-526.

Powell, A., Farrar, E., & Cohen, D. (1985). *The shopping mall high school.* New York: Houghton Mifflin.

Public Schools of North Carolina. (1998, March). *Block scheduling in North Carolina: Implementation, teaching and impact issues − 1997 survey results.* Raleigh, NC: Author.

Roderick, M. (1993). *The path to dropping out.* Westport, CT: Auburn House.

Rosenstock, L. (1998, April). *Changing the subject: The new urban high school.* Paper presented at the annual meeting of the American Educational Research Association. San Diego, CA.

Secretary's Commission on Achieving Necessary Skills. (1991). *What work requires of schools: A SCANS report for America 2000.* Washington, DC: U.S. Department of Labor.

Singh, V. P. (1994). The underclass in the united states: Some correlates of economic change. In J. Kretovics & E. Nussel, (Eds.). *Transforming urban education* (pp. 57-72). Boston: Allyn & Bacon.

Sizer, T. R. (1984). *Horace's compromise: The dilemma of the American high school.* Boston: Houghton Mifflin.

Slavin, R. E., & Fashola, O. S. (1998). *Show me the evidence! Proven and promising programs for America's schools.* Thousand Oaks, CA: Corwin Press.

Stern, D. (1997, November). The continuing promise of work-based learning. *Centerfocus*, No. 18. Berkeley, CA: National Center for Research in Vocational Education.

Stern, D., Finkelstein, N., Stone, J. III, Latting, J., & Dornsife, C. (1995). School to work: Research on programs in the United States. Washington, DC: Falmer Press.

Stern, D., & Hallinan, M. T. (1997). The high schools, they are a-changin'. *Center Work* (Tenth Anniversary Issue), 8(4). Berkeley, CA: National Center for Research in Vocational Education.

Stern, D., Raby, M., & Dayton, C. (1992). *Career academies.* San Francisco: Jossey-Bass.

Wells, A. S., & Oakes, J. (1996). Potential pitfalls of systemic reform: Early lessons from detracking research. *Sociology of Education, Extra Issue,* 135-143.

15

Building School-Family-Community Partnerships in Middle and High Schools

MAVIS G. SANDERS
JOYCE L. EPSTEIN
Johns Hopkins University

To better understand how some secondary schools are working to develop school, family, and community partnerships, 22 educators, parents, and students at two middle schools and two high schools were interviewed. The four schools are members of the National Network of Partnership Schools, which brings together and provides technical assistance to schools, districts, and states committed to developing comprehensive and permanent programs of school-family-community partnership. This chapter is organized into seven sections. The first section discusses social networks, social capital, and a theory of overlapping spheres of influence to elucidate the conceptual foundation for school, family, and community partnerships. The second section outlines and discusses essential elements of a comprehensive program of school, family, and community partnership. This section describes a framework of six types of family and community involvement and an action team approach to partnerships. The third section outlines the methods used in this study. The fourth and fifth sections of this chapter describe partnership programs at two middle schools and two high schools, respectively. These sections report the schools' progress and the challenges they face in developing schoolwide programs of partnership. These sections are followed by a general discussion of this study. The final section situates the study's findings within the broader context of current literature on school-family-community partnerships at the secondary level.

Schools are institutions that are responsible for the formal education of children and youth. However, schools that carry out this responsibility most effectively understand themselves and their students to be part of a larger social system that includes families, and communities. Research conducted for over a decade indicates that when schools, families and communities work together as partners, students benefit. Partnerships between schools, families, and communities can create safer school environments, strengthen parenting skills, encourage community service, improve academic skills, and achieve other desired goals that benefit students (see summaries of studies in Epstein, 1992; Henderson & Berla, 1994; Rutherford, Anderson, & Billig, 1997). The inclusion of family involvement in the Goals 2000: Educate America Act (see Mitchell, chap. 8, this volume) is evidence of a growing national recognition about the importance of families and communities for students at all ages and grade levels.

Yet, despite the importance of families' active involvement in their children's education throughout their schooling, involvement for many families decreases as their children progress from elementary to middle and high school. This decline occurs despite studies that illustrate the importance of parental involvement for the school success of middle and high school students (Dornbusch and Ritter, 1988; Duncan, 1969; Eccles & Harold, 1993; Lee, 1994).

To better understand how some secondary schools are working to reverse this decline, administrators, teachers, and parents at two middle schools and two high schools were interviewed.[1,2] The four schools are members of the National Network of Partnership Schools, which brings together and provides technical assistance to schools, districts, and states committed to developing comprehensive and permanent programs of school, family, and community partnership (Epstein, Coates, Salinas, Sanders and Simon, 1997).[3]

This chapter is organized into seven sections. The first section discusses social networks, social capital, and a theory of overlapping spheres of influence that combine to provide a conceptual foundation for school, family, and community partnership. The second section outlines and discusses essential elements of a comprehensive program of school, family, and community partnerships. This section describes a framework of six types of involvement and an action team approach to partnerships. The third section outlines the methods used in this study. The fourth and fifth sections of the paper describe partnership programs at two middle schools and two

[1]This research was supported by the U.S. Department of Education, Office of Educational Research and Improvement (OERI). The opinions expressed are the authors' and do not necessarily represent OERI positions or policies.

[2]The authors would like to thank the teachers, principals, parents, and students who graciously consented to participate in this study.

[3]Portions of this chapter have been published in the *Middle School Journal* 31(2): 35-39; and the *High School Magazine*, 5(3): 38-49.

high schools, respectively. These sections report the schools' progress and the challenges they face in developing schoolwide programs of partnership. These sections are followed by a general discussion of this study. The final section situates the study's findings within the broader context of current literature on school, family, and community partnerships at the secondary level.

THEORETICAL SUPPORT
FOR SCHOOL-FAMILY-COMMUNITY PARTNERSHIPS

In the past decade, developments in social theory have provided greater insight into how strong connections between schools, families, and communities enhance children's learning and social and emotional growth and well-being. As Epstein (1995) noted, current theory on school, family, and community partnerships alters earlier understandings of the influence that each of these institutions has on children. It was commonly thought that there was a sequential influence of family, school, and community on the growth and development of a child. The family was viewed as being primarily responsible for nurturing the child and laying the foundation for his or her entry into school. The school was seen as the socializing agent that prepared the child for his or her role in the larger community (see, e.g., Parsons, 1985). Recent syntheses of many studies, however, indicate that from early childhood, the home, school and community simultaneously affect children's growth and development (Wasik & Karweit, 1994; Young & Marx, 1992). The continued importance of these contexts through each stage of a child's development is delineated by a number of related perspectives. These include the social network paradigm, Coleman's concept of social capital, and Epstein's theory of overlapping spheres of influence.

The social network paradigm highlights the importance of significant others in an individual's social system who provide support and resources such as information and money (Barnes, 1972; Blau, 1964; Leinhart, 1977). Although there are several definitions of social networks, the most common reference is to the linkages between individuals, groups, and institutions with which a person has contact and on which a person perceives he or she can depend for support (Bott, 1971). One of the primary functions of an individual's social network is to provide a buffer against negative stresses, thereby promoting greater psychological and personal well-being (D'Abbs, 1982).

In educational research, it has been found that children with well-developed social networks have more positive educational outcomes than do children without them (Coates, 1987). Clark (1991) wrote that social networks provide social support defined as the "availability of people on whom we can rely, people who let us know that they care about, value, and love us" (p.45). Clark contended that the greater an adolescent's social support is, the greater is the likelihood that he or she will succeed in school.

Coleman (1987) referred to social networks as an integral part of social capital. Social capital is the information, attitudinal and behavioral norms, and skills that individuals can spend or invest to improve their chances for success in societal institutions, such as schools. Individuals gain social capital through their social networks. Coleman, Hoffer, and Kilgore (1982) reported that students in Catholic and other private schools achieve at a higher level in mathematics and verbal skills than do students in public schools largely because of the transmission of common messages, expectations, and norms from the family, church, and school. In this example, a social network comprising family, church, and school provides youths in Catholic schools with the social capital necessary for school success.

Epstein's (1987) theory of overlapping spheres of influence also emphasizes the importance of schools, families, and communities working together to meet the needs of children. This theory integrates educational, sociological, and psychological perspectives on social organizations, as well as research on the effects of family, school, and community environments on educational outcomes. A central principle of this theory is that certain goals, such as student academic success, are of mutual interest to people in each of these institutions, and are best achieved through their cooperative action and support (Epstein, 1992). The relative relationship between these institutions is determined by the attitudes and practices of individuals within each context. When school, family, and community members develop networks, the results of their interactions are acquired and stored as social capital. Thus, social networks are strengthened and social capital is increased when partnership activities that enable families, educators, and community members to work cooperatively around children's growth and development are implemented (Epstein & Sanders, 1996).

FROM THEORY TO PRACTICE: THE NATIONAL NETWORK OF PARTNERSHIP SCHOOLS

Based on the theoretical concepts just described and years of research in schools across the country, a framework of six types of school, family and community involvement was created (Epstein, 1995; Sanders & Epstein, in press). The six types of involvement are (a) parenting, helping all families establish home environments that support children as students; (b) communicating, designing and conducting effective forms of communication about school programs and children's progress; (c) volunteering, recruiting and organizing help and support for school functions and activities; (d) learning at home, providing information and ideas to families about how to help students at home with school work and related activities; (e) decision making, including parents in school decisions; and (f) collaborating with the community, identifying and integrating resources and services from the community to strengthen and support schools, students, and their families. Different practices can be implemented to foster each of the six types of involvement. The objective, however, is for schools, families, and their surrounding communities to aid one another in rearing healthy, successful children.

To further assist schools in developing comprehensive and permanent programs of partnership, an action team approach for school-family-community partnerships was developed (Epstein et al., 1997). Action teams for school-family-community partnerships consist of 6-12 members including family members, teachers, administrators, other school staff (i.e., counselors, nurses, parent liaisons), community representatives, and students in the upper grades. The action team approach ensures that school, family, and community representatives share responsibility for the development, implementation and evaluation of partnership practices. To organize its work, an action team selects a chair or cochairs to coordinate and schedule meetings and to share information with the rest of the school community about partnership activities. Committee chairs or cochairs oversee work and progress on each of the six types of involvement, ensuring that at least one practice for each type of involvement is implemented or improved each year.

These two developments – the framework of six types of involvement and the action team for school-family-community partnerships – are the cornerstones of the National Network of Partnership Schools begun in 1996. Each school in the national network strengthens its program by addressing the six types of involvement and by using the action team approach. The four schools in the present study have been members of the National Network of Partnership Schools since its inception. The middle schools, however, have been working on partnership activities using the framework of six types of involvement and the action team approach for 3 years as part of a research program that preceded the formation of the national network.

The present study uses interview data to examine how the four schools are working to develop stronger partnerships with their families and communities. More specifically, this study explores how these middle and high schools articulate, implement, and seek to improve school-family-community partnerships to better serve their student populations.

METHODS AND ANALYSIS

In April 1997, four urban schools – Southbend Middle School, Harbortown Middle School, Northshore High School, and University Park High School[4] – were selected to learn how middle and high schools are working to develop stronger school, family, and community connections. These schools were selected based on their reports of progress shared at an annual partnership program celebration and planning workshop, and the recommendations of district facilitators for school-family-community partnerships who support and assist the schools in their work.

These schools were visited during May and June 1997. At each school visit, interviews were conducted, and when available, supporting documents were reviewed. The interviews were face-to-face and lasted approximately 1 hr. At each school, the chair of the action team was interviewed. In addition, other members of the school community who are either working on or affected by school-family-community partnerships were also interviewed. At Southbend Middle School, the principal, the parent liaison, and two volunteers were interviewed. At Harbortown Middle School, the parent liaison and an assistant principal were interviewed. At Northshore High School, an assistant principal, two teachers, three students and a parent member of the Parent-Teacher Association (PTA) were interviewed. At University Park High School, an assistant principal, a student, and two teachers, one a member of the action team, were interviewed.

The interviews followed a semistructured design to ensure that specific topics were covered, and that unique or individual factors were also allowed to emerge. Precautions were taken to "avoid imposing . . . interests" on the participants (Seidman, 1991). The 22 participants were encouraged to elaborate on questions in order to provide more accurate and comprehensive descriptions of the goals, activities, challenges, and outcomes of their programs of school-family-community partnership. To avoid the distractions

---

[4] Pseudonyms are used to ensure the anonymity of the participating schools and the individuals interviewed.

that often accompany taking detailed descriptive notes, interviews were audiotaped with respondents' permission and later transcribed.

The raw data generated from the 22 respondents, which consisted of over 100 pages of written text, were coded and analyzed. Data analysis was an ongoing and iterative process. It consisted of reading the written text to identify emerging themes related to the schools' development of partnership programs, and finding distinctions and connections among identified themes across the schools. The themes identified through this process are organized and discussed in narrative form first for middle schools and then for high schools.

MIDDLE SCHOOLS

Southbend Middle School. Southbend Middle School is located in a poor, industrial section of the city. It serves 412 students in Grades 6 through 8. About 74% of its students receive free or reduced-price lunches, and 23% receive special education services. Approximately 40% of the student population is African-American and 60% is White. The mobility rate is high, with about 14% of the student population entering and 36% withdrawing from the school during the 1995-1996 school year. The student average daily attendance rate is about 85%.

For three decades, Southbend Middle School has had a reputation for vandalism, poor achievement, and high dropout. These features are seen as contributing factors to the school's historically low level of parental and community participation. The new principal, Ms. Harris, is working to improve the school's climate and reputation through a number of reforms to enhance student behavior, achievement, and attendance. According to Ms. Harris, school-family-community partnerships and the school improvement efforts that she has initiated must occur simultaneously. She states, "I think that family and community involvement and school improvement should be joint efforts. I really don't want one to happen without the other. I think they support each other. I think that they go hand in hand. . . ."

Harbortown Middle School. Harbortown Middle School has more than double the population of Southbend, serving 861 African-American students in Grades 6 through 8. About 86% of its students receive free or reduced-price lunches, and 18% receive special education services. The school's mobility rate is high, with about 16% of the student population entering and 26% withdrawing from the school during the 1995-1996 school year.

Average daily student attendance is about 82%. The school is located in an economically depressed area close to a growing cultural and commercial center.

Like Southbend, Harbortown Middle School is also facing change. As a result of school closings and subsequent rezoning, most students live outside the immediate area and are bussed to the school. Traveling to and from the school is difficult for many of Harbortown's families, which negatively affects parental volunteering and attendance at school meetings. Public housing reform and school restructuring promise to keep the school's student population in a state of flux. Effectively educating students in this uncertain environment is the school's mission, as well as its challenge. Ms. Ross, the school's assistant principal, sees school-family-community partnerships as central to achieving this goal, saying, "[they are] the only way that we can succeed really. The families and the community people are the ones who drive the image of the school. They're your spokespersons. The way people talk about the school outside is the impression that people will get . . . ."

Putting Words Into Action

Educators and parents interviewed for this study agreed that school-family-community partnerships are important for student success. The respondents had a very broad definition of the term "partnerships." The breadth of their definition reflects the range of family and community involvement included in the framework of six types of involvement. Although the schools have not yet implemented activities for each of the six types of involvement, each school has made substantial progress toward the development of a comprehensive program of partnership.

Type 1: Parenting. Type 1 activities assist families with parenting and child-rearing skills, understanding child and adolescent development, and setting home conditions that support children as students. For example, parents play a key role in helping students get to school on time every day. Schools can help families understand and carry out this parenting responsibility in a number of ways. Southbend Middle School has hired two of its volunteers as paid attendance monitors. These volunteers – Ms. Stevens, a community member, and Ms. George, a parent – now work with students, teachers, and especially families to help improve student attendance. According to Ms. Stevens:

> We do a lot of things as attendance monitors. We make home visits, and we call parents to find out why the child is not in school. We also call to encourage parents, and to let them know that they are the first and primary educators of their children. We encourage them to come in and volunteer time, find out why the child does not want to attend school, find out what the problem is.

This is the first year that Southbend Middle School has implemented this Type 1 activity and the school is pleased with the results. Ms. Stevens reports that students have responded well to this partnership activity and are aware that the school is working closely with their families to encourage regular school attendance.

Harbortown Middle School has also implemented Type 1 activities. To help families develop skills that they can use to improve their own educational and professional opportunities, and, ultimately, opportunities for their children, the school has a computer class for parents every Tuesday. The action team chairperson, Ms. Gunthrie, reports that attendance at the computer class was good during the first semester of the school year, but tapered off during the second semester. She and others on the action team are working with a community group to find better ways to inform parents about the class and other services that the school offers.

Type 2: Communicating. Type 2 activities include school-to-home and home-to-school communications about school programs and students' progress. Harbortown knows the importance of good communication with its families. It found that communicating with families helped the school to improve students' attendance and test scores. According to Ms. Ross:

> We did a lot of communicating with parents for both those things. For all of the major testing sessions, parents were notified about what their children needed to do to prepare, and what parents could do to help them prepare.

Harbortown Middle School is also proud of its telecommunications system, which permits important information to be communicated efficiently to all families. As Ms. Green, the parent liaison, who is also a member of the action team, explains, "We can feed school information to the system, and it will automatically call every parent in the school and provide that information." The action team chairperson for Harbortown, Ms. Gunthrie, further explains that, "once a month everything that is happening for the month that needs to be publicized, like immunizations, is on the Parentel [the school's telecommunications system]. Our Parentel will dial parents until it gets an answer."

Because Southbend is working to change its long-standing negative reputation, communication with its students' families is very important. But how does the school communicate with families who are unwilling to come to the school? Southbend decided to go to the families. Southbend school teacher and action team chairperson, Ms. Carl, describes the "Get to Know the Principal" teas as one of the school's most important partnership activities. To give families from the three different communities around the school the opportunity to meet and talk with the new principal, the action team for school-family-community partnerships planned a series of teas. One tea was held at a health center, another at a recreational center, and the third at a local church.

Type 3: Volunteering. Type 3 activities enable families to give their time and talents to support schools, teachers, and children. The framework of six types of involvement includes attendance at school events and activities as a form of Type 3 involvement because family members are volunteering their time to celebrate the accomplishments and talents of students. Harbortown has very little trouble with this type of family and community volunteerism. The parent liaison and action team member, Ms. Green, explains that although families may hesitate to volunteer their services at the school, they enjoy watching their children perform. When discussing how to get more families to volunteer as classroom helpers, cafeteria monitors, and in other ways, Ms. Green states:

> To really get them more involved, we have to first let the children perform. Then, [we] talk to parents about other things we would like for them to become involved in, and explain those things so that they can better understand them.

It is important for schools to identify volunteer opportunities that help provide students with meaningful learning opportunities in safe, nurturing environments. Southbend Middle School has developed, for example, a parent patrol. The school had a discipline problem and many students walked the halls when they should have been in their classrooms. The parent liaison and action team member, Ms. Taylor, believed that parents could assist school personnel in monitoring the hallways. She began a parent patrol program by training 25 volunteers. When describing the initial results of the program, Ms. Taylor states that "when the kids found out that their parents were coming to school volunteering, there was a big turnaround. And, it wasn't just fear, some of the students were proud that their parents were a part of the school." Southbend is planning a volunteer celebration for the families who assisted the school in monitoring the halls and other activities. The celebration is the school's way of thanking volunteers for making a difference.

Type 4: Learning at Home. The type of involvement that families are most interested in is how they can help their children with learning at home (Epstein, 1995). Research in the United States (Hoover-Dempsey & Sandler, 1995; Lee, 1984); and abroad (see research summaries in Sanders & Epstein, 1998) has shown that when families become involved with students' learning at home, students' attitudes toward learning and school performance improve.

At this time, Southbend does not have well-developed Type 4 activities. Harbortown, on the other hand, has been able to implement a successful activity to assist families in monitoring their children's homework. The school has established a homework line. Each teacher in the school has a code number that parents are given at the beginning of the school year. When a parent wants to know his or her child's homework assignment, the parent can call the homework line and enter the teacher's code number. The school hopes that over time, more families will use the homework line. According to Ms. Gunthrie, the action team chair at Harbortown Middle School, "Some parents use the homework line, but for those parents who need more encouragement, we will focus on them next year."

Type 5: Decision Making. Type 5 activities enable families to participate in school decisions that affect their own and other children. Family representatives on school councils, committees and other decision making bodies, and in the PTA, Parent-Teacher Organization (PTO), and other parent organizations ensure that parents' voices are heard and incorporated into school decisions. Southbend and Harbortown have parent representatives on their school improvement teams and on their action teams for school-family-community partnerships, but would like to reestablish strong PTOs to encourage more family involvement in school decision making. The parent liaison at Southbend, Ms. Taylor, plans to use the school's volunteer celebration to identify parents interested in establishing a PTO.

Harbortown Middle School is also working to reestablish its PTO. According to one of the school's assistant principals, Ms. Ross, the school has not had an active PTO in over a year. Harbortown is working to revive the PTO through other Type 5 activities, such as its community meetings. When the school had problems with student discipline on the school bus, it held meetings in the community to decide how to resolve the issue. Ms.

Gunthrie, the action team chairperson at Harbortown Middle School, hopes to "build a resource list" from participants at the community meetings. From the list, she hopes to recruit members to re-establish a PTO at the school.

Type 6: Collaborating with the Community. Type 6 activities facilitate cooperation and collaboration among schools, families, and community groups, agencies and individuals. Harbortown and Southbend have developed productive community connections. For example, Southbend worked with a national volunteer organization, Americorp, to create a beautiful parent room where parents can meet and volunteers can work or relax with a cup of coffee (Johnson, 1993). The room is freshly painted with colorful decorations that create a warm and inviting atmosphere. Above the room's large windows is a banner that reads, "VOLUNTEERS MAKE THE DIFFERENCE." The room has a bulletin board listing the latest school news, a large work table, and books on child development. The room also has a refrigerator, a soda machine, and a microwave oven. Southbend Middle School also has been able to provide students with additional counseling services through its partnerships with a local university and a counseling agency. The school's principal, Ms. Harris, plans to continue to reach out to community agencies and organizations to provide needed resources for Southbend's students and families.

Harbortown's community connections also have been beneficial to the school, its students, and their families. The school works closely with a team of individuals from several institutions, including a local college and the juvenile justice system. This team has worked with the school to survey families to better understand their needs and concerns, to plan community meetings, and to mentor students. In addition, the school has developed connections with a local high school, which has proven mutually beneficial. Ms. Gunthrie, the action team chairperson, explains:

> As a part of our community involvement, high school students, especially those who . . . attended [Harbortown Middle School], . . . earn their service credits by working with our students and tutoring them. Or, if we have an affair and want parents to come, we let them help with babysitting.

Harbortown has other community connections, including a partnership with a local church, that have resulted in the school's being repainted, students being tutored, and parents being taught more about managing household budgets. However, the school's assistant principal hopes for still greater participation from the surrounding community, "so that the kids can see that others are taking an interest."

Improving the Process

Southbend and Harbortown Middle Schools have implemented a variety of worthwhile partnership activities. Although these activities are not uncommon at the elementary school level, they are atypical at the middle school level and symbolic of these schools' growing awareness of and commitment to school-family-community partnerships. However, there is room for improvement in each school's program. For example, each of the schools could add to the activities it now conducts to ensure that its program has at least one well-designed activity for each of the six types of involvement and that the activities implemented are linked to specific school improvement goals. Furthermore, each school could improve how it currently meets the challenges for each type of involvement (Epstein, 1995) such as providing information to families who cannot attend school meetings and activities; providing families with regular, two-way forms of communication about school activities and concerns in a language that they can readily understand; and implementing a regular schedule of interactive homework to encourage family participation in children's learning at home (Epstein, Salinas, & Jackson, 1995). Each school has acknowledged the gaps in its partnership program and has expressed the desire to make improvements.

A large part of each school's progress will be determined by the quality of its action team for school-family-community partnerships, the action arm of the partnership program. A well-functioning action team ensures that planning, implemention and evaluation of partnership activities are responsibilities shared by administrators, teachers, parents, and others in the school and surrounding community (Sanders, 1999). The team approach also reduces the likelihood of individual burnout and increases the likelihood that programs become permanent. However, developing a well-functioning action team is a process that takes time, commitment, organization and excellent communication.

For example, Southbend's action team has faced a number of challenges because the chairperson of the action team did not know of her position until after the school year had begun. As a result, she found it difficult to coordinate the team and delegate to its members specific roles and responsibilities. Because Southbend's current principal, Ms. Harris, is committed to improving the partnership program, she is working with a district facilitator for school-family-community partnerships to carefully identify and train a new action team. She also is working to schedule time during the summer when the team can create a 3-year outline and the required 1-year action plan for the upcoming school year. By establishing a common agenda and clarifying goals, roles, and responsibilities of team members prior to the beginning of the academic year, Southbend's action team will be much better prepared to develop and carry out an effective and comprehensive program of partnership.

Harbortown Middle School's action team has been more stable than Southbend's. The action team chairperson, Ms. Gunthrie, has been in her position for 3 years and has learned much about the process during that time. When describing her growth as action team chairperson, she states:

> I have learned from meeting with [the district facilitator] how to delegate authority rather than trying to take it on as a one man show, and so its gotten a bit easier. Now we have a chair for each of the types of involvement and that makes it easier. I oversee it all and just monitor what the team is doing.

Harbortown's action team, however, still has areas in which it can improve. For example, some members of the team do not know the names, positions, or responsibilities of other members. All members of the action team for school-family-community partnership should be able to articulate its structure, functions, and activities as well as the chairperson. Furthermore, each team member should be aware of all planned activities. Achievement of these goals requires that the action team chairperson develop a regular meeting schedule to improve team awareness, planning, and communication.

HIGH SCHOOLS

University Park High School. University Park High School serves 1, 900 students in Grades 9 through 12. About 57% of its students receive free or reduced-price lunches, and 22% receive special education services. Approximately 60% of the student population is African-American, 35% is White, and 5% is Asian-American and Latino. The mobility rate is high, with about 13% of the student population entering and 39% withdrawing from the school during the 1995-1996 school year. The student average daily attendance rate is about 77%.

Northshore High School. Northshore High School serves 2, 300 African-American students in Grades 9 through 12. About 52% of its students receive free or reduced-price lunches, and 17% receive special education services. The mobility rate is moderately high, with about 10% of the student population entering and 25% withdrawing from the school during the 1995

-1996 school year. The student average daily attendance rate is about 72%. Both high schools have developed a schools-within-school approach to improve student attendance and achievement (see Legters, chap. 4, this volume). When students enter the ninth grade, they are assigned to a team and a mentor. The teams and mentors work with ninth-grade students to help them successfully transition into high school. During the second semester, ninth-grade students take a career inventory and engage in a number of activities designed to help them select one of the several career schools offered. In 1996, these schools became members of the National Network of Partnership Schools to develop school-family-community partnerships that further encourage students' intellectual, social, and emotional development.

The Importance of School-Family-Community Partnerships

Educators, parents, and students at University Park and Northshore agreed that family and community participation in students' education is important. Their reasons varied, as did each individual's notion of the ideal relationship between the school, the family, the community, and students. The word that resurfaced time and again as the respondents discussed the importance of partnerships was "support." Respondents agreed that high school is an important, but difficult time in a student's educational career and that support from significant adults is important for helping students successfully navigate this period. Respondents also agreed that communication and cooperation between individuals in a student's home, school, and community increased the likelihood that the student would receive the support needed to transition into the workplace, a postsecondary institution, or both. According to Ms. Smith, a teacher at Northshore:

> High school is where students are preparing to go out there and do something with their lives, whether it is work, whether it is a post-secondary institution or whether it is a technical school. . . . Someone or some people need to be there for support, to say, "Now, come on you can do it. You can do it. I know you can. Now, what do I need to help you with?"

The 10th-grade students who were interviewed see family involvement as important to their success at Northshore. The following dialogue serves as illustration.

Interviewer: Do you think that family involvement is important to your success?

Respondents: Yes, (all students)

Interviewer: Why?

Patricia: Because my mother encourages me to go to school, and I go. But if I had a parent who didn't encourage me, I don't think that I'd go.

Interviewer: Okay, Shaun?

Shaun: Parent involvement is important because if you don't have a parent to encourage you and support you – ask you about how you're doing – then you'd think they didn't care. Then you wouldn't have that motivation to go out there and try to get a 100 or a 90; you'll take whatever you get because no one else is interested.

Students, faculty, and administrators at Northshore and University Park High Schools agree that school-family-community partnerships are important at the secondary level. To ensure that all students receive the benefits associated with stronger connections between schools, families, and communities, each school is currently working to develop a well-designed partnership program. The schools have begun the process of developing comprehensive programs of partnership by concentrating on a few practices to bring school personnel, students, families and communities closer together.

Practices of School-Family-Community Partnerships

University Park and Northshore are in their first year of membership in the National Network of Partnership Schools. As such, they are just beginning to develop schoolwide programs of partnership that include activities for each of the six types of involvement: parenting, communicating, volunteering, learning at home, decision making and collaborating with the community. These activities are planned and implemented by an action team for school-family-community partnerships.

Each school has made progress in developing its program of school-family-community partnerships. Northshore's action team planned and implemented "parents night" an occasion designed to provide families with information on their teen's course of study and the school's need for volunteers. The school offered student incentives to increase parental attendance. The homerooms that had the most parents received pizza parties. Action team members are currently evaluating the event to plan for the next year's open house.

The Type 2 activity just described is a good event on which to build stronger relationships between the school and families. Good communication is the basis for any successful program of partnerships. The action team at

University Park High School also conducted a Type 2 activity as its major event for the year. The activity, Park Fest, was a carnival held at the school, and its goal was to encourage positive, fun interaction between students, educators, parents, and the community. Mr. Douglas, a faculty member on the action team, and Ms. Waters, the action team chair, believe that Park Fest was a successful event and a giant step forward for partnerships at University Park. They evaluated the activity and identified several ways to improve the school's next such event.

Planning, implementing, evaluating, and improving activities are the steps schools take to develop well-designed, comprehensive programs of school-family-community partnership. These processes occur within the context of a long-range vision that guides each school's progress.

Visions of School-Family-Community Partnerships

Parents, teachers, administrators, and students have clear ideas about the types of partnership activities they would like to see implemented at Northshore and University Park. At both high schools, teachers, parents, students, and administrators express the need for better communication between home and school. In addition, teachers and administrators envision developing a comprehensive volunteer program. The respondents believe that family and community volunteers are needed to help phone teens who are absent from school; develop a monthly school newsletter to inform parents of important programs and events; tutor and mentor students, and carry out other important activities at school and in other locations to support students. The schools also would like to enhance and expand their Type 5 activities. Mr. Keith, a parent member of the PTA at Northshore, would like to see the PTA and the school's action team for school-family-community partnerships work more closely together to involve families and communities in the education and development of Northshore's students. Mr. King, assistant principal at Northshore, feels that a more active PTA would provide a forum from which parents could advocate for increasing and improving school resources. He states:

> We were short in some areas that I thought were critical. I work for the city; no matter how much I scream and yell that we need this or that, that is not going to get the kind of response that a parent group would get. I pointed to other schools where just parents being visible, we do not need a whole lot of parents, just parents being visible and being vigilant and saying "I want this for my son or daughter" makes a big difference. That is the kind of ideal situation that I . . . envision.

Obstacles to School-Family-Community Partnerships

There are obstacles for Northshore and University Park to overcome in order to develop the types of partnership programs that they envision. According to teachers, parents, administrators, and students, the primary barriers to improved school-family-community partnerships are misguided attitudes and lack of time. The respondents agreed that some parents have the attitude that family involvement at the high school level is unnecessary. Administrators and teachers further acknowledged that some school personnel are not yet open to family involvement. Furthermore, the respondents felt that many families did not have the time to become more involved in school activities. As Mr. Douglas, action team member at University Park, explains;

> Most parents have so many other things going on, they don't have the time to volunteer at the school. Like my son's school, they ask me to do a lot of things, and I haven't had the time to do them.

These barriers can be overcome with a comprehensive partnership program that includes activities for the six types of involvement and meets key challenges for successful activities. Studies and field tests in the United States and other nations indicate that negative attitudes that teachers and families hold about each other become more positive after partnership practices are initiated (Epstein, 1986; Sanders & Epstein, 1998). A well-designed partnership program ensures that all families, even those with limited time, are given opportunities and information needed to be involved in their teen's education in a variety of meaningful ways. To develop comprehensive programs of partnership, however, schools require the efforts and leadership of a core group of parents, teachers, students, and administrators to serve on the action team for school-family-community partnerships.

Continued Development of School-Family-Community Partnerships

The action team approach ensures that the work of developing a partnership program is shared by many, which is important when time is limited. Action team members at Northshore and University Park High Schools state that the action team approach to partnerships is the best way to ensure that a comprehensive program of partnerships develops and grows. However, modifications are necessary for their action teams to be most effective.

University Park High School's action team needs more members, especially family and community representatives. Team members agree that adding members will increase their ability to carry out, monitor, and evaluate more partnership activities. Candace, a student at University Park, emphasizes that student representation on the action team is important, "so that teachers and parents can get . . . [students'] views on things and on what is going on."

The action team at University Park and Northshore also must determine the organizational structure that will function most effectively in large high schools organized into separate career schools or academies. During their first year in the National Network of Partnership Schools, University Park's and Northshore's action teams decided to modify the basic action team structure. Specifically, action teams at both schools independently decided that each academy or career school should have an action team that plans and implements academy-specific partnership activities. Representatives from each academy's action team sit on a schoolwide action team to share ideas and coordinate schoolwide activities.

Northshore's action team is in the process of determining who will represent each career school on the schoolwide action team, when and how often they will meet, and what specific activities they will implement. Ms. Kennedy, the chair of the action team, is optimistic about the partnership program's continued improvement and growth. She believes that the first year of attention to partnerships has helped the school reach a point of "readiness" to develop a more structured and comprehensive program. According to Ms. Kennedy, "I think that across the board we are at a different level for embracing everything. It can work."

DISCUSSION

The educators, parents, and students interviewed at the schools in this study strongly believe that school-family-community partnerships are as important for adolescents as they are for children in elementary schools. The middle schools in the study have been using the framework of six types of involvement and the action team approach to partnerships for 3 years. The high schools in the study have been working on developing partnership programs for only 1 year as members of the National Network of Partnership Schools.

It is interesting to note that many of the partnership activities that middle and high school teachers and administrators in the study identify as important are very similar to the activities that many elementary schools implement.

Teachers and administrators in middle and high schools need assistance with monitoring attendance as much as do teachers and administrators at elementary schools. Similarly, teachers and administrators in middle and high schools need to communicate more regularly with families about students' performance and school programs. Middle and high schools also need families' input into school decisions as much as do elementary schools. Although the respondents recognize that adolescents need more independence than do children in the lower grades, they also recognize that they need the guidance and support of caring adults in the home, school, and community. Accordingly, they continue to improve their programs of partnership.

Program improvement, however, is an incremental and often nonlinear process. The schools in this study face challenges such as personnel changes, shifting student populations, limited resources, and the misguided attitudes that many parents and professional educators have toward school-family-community partnerships for adolescents. To overcome these challenges, schools need well-functioning action teams that are thoughtfully selected; well-organized; and trained to plan, implement, evaluate and continually improve programs of school-family-community partnership. With well-functioning action teams and time, these middle and high schools will be able to develop partnership programs that include activities for each of the six types of involvement, that are linked to school goals, and that enhance students' learning and development (Sanders & Simon, 1999).

CONCLUSION

Family involvement practices at home and at school have been found to influence middle and high school students' academic achievement (Clark, 1983; Ginsburg, & Hanson, 1986); school attendance (Astone and McLanahan, 1991; Epstein & Lee, 1993); homework effort (Keith, Reimers, Fehrman, Pottebaum, & Aubey, 1986); and graduation and college matriculation rates (Conklin & Dailey, 1981; Delgado-Gaitan, 1988). As in these previous research findings, this study's respondents highlight the importance of family participation in the education of youth. The students, parents, teachers, community members, and administrators interviewed reported that school, family, and community connections are essential for students' personal and educational success.

Research suggests that the decline in parental involvement in the education of adolescents reflects, in part, weaker family involvement practices at the secondary school level. Dornbusch and Ritter (1988), for example, found that the majority (60%) of high school teachers reported contacting almost no or few parents. Of the contacts made, most were with parents of students who were academically successful or those who were at risk of failure or described as discipline problems. Similarly, Purnell and Gott (1985) found that secondary teachers, though noting its importance, felt that they did not have sufficient time to implement effective practices of family involvement.

This study, too, finds that professional educators and families feel that time is limited for their work on partnerships. This study also suggests that the attitudes of educators and families can present obstacles to effective school-home-community partnerships. It further indicates, however, that with the right support, a framework of involvement, and a team approach for action, teachers, administrators, parents, students, and community members can work together to build effective programs of partnership.

Schools cannot expect to have their ideal programs overnight. This study shows that even middle schools that have been working on their partnership programs for 3 years have areas in which they can improve. Through annual action plans, improvements in the effectiveness of their action teams, and regular evaluation of their activities, the partnership programs at each of the schools should continue to grow and improve. Incremental progress of this kind has been observed and reported in other schools (Sanders, 1996a; 1996b).

The four schools in this study are among 1,000 schools, 100 school districts and 10 state education agencies in the National Network of Partnership Schools at Johns Hopkins University that are working to build permanent and effective school, family and community partnerships. This network enables educators and parents to learn from each other about successful practices and solutions to major challenges. Participating schools share information, concerns, and best practices so that each school can continue to improve its program of partnership. Members of the national network also have opportunities to participate in research on how programs of partnership affect student outcomes. Increasing numbers of elementary, middle, and high schools are working hard to build successful partnerships because they know from theory, research, and practice that schools cannot effectively educate students at any age or grade level without the help and support of families and communities.

REFERENCES

Astone, N. M., & McLanahan, S. S. (1991). Family structure, parental practices, and high school completion. *American Sociological Review*, 56(3), 309-320.

Barnes, J. A. (1972). *Social networks*. Reading, MA: Addison-Wesley.

Blau, P. M. (1964). *Exchange and power in social life*. New York: Wiley.

Bott, E. (1971). *Family and social network.* London: Tavistock.

Clark, M. L. (1991). Social Identity, Peer Relations, and Academic Competence of African-American Adolescent. *Education and Urban Society,* 24(1): 41-52.

Clark, R. (1983). *Family life and school achievement: Why poor Black children succeed or fail.* Chicago: University of Chicago Press.

Coates, D. L. (1987). Gender differences in the structure and support characteristics of Black adolescents' social networks. *Sex Roles,* 17 (11/12), 667-687.

Coleman, J. S. (1987). Families and schools. *Educational Researcher.* 16(6), 32-38.

Coleman, J. S., Hoffer, T., & Kilgore, S. (1982). *High school achievement.* New York: Basic Books.

Conklin, M. E., & Dailey, A. R. (1981). Does consistency of parental encouragement matter for secondary students? *Sociology of Education,* 54, 254-262.

D'Abbs, P. (1982). *Social support networks: A critical review of models and findings.* Melbourne, FL: Institute of Family Studies. (Eric Document Reproduction Service No. 232 111).

Delgado-Gaitan, C. (1988). The value of conformity: Learning to stay in school. *Anthropology and Education Quarterly,* 19(4), 354-381.

Dornbusch, S. M., & Ritter, P. L. (1988). Parents of high school students: A neglected resource. *Educational Horizons,* 66 (2): 75-77.

Duncan, L. (1969). *Parent-Counselor Conferences Make a Difference.* St. Petersburg, FL: St. Petersburg Junior College. (Eric Document Reproduction Service No. 031 743).

Eccles, J. S., & Harold, R. D. (1993). Parent-school involvement during the early adolescent years. *Teachers College Record,* 94(3), 568-587.

Epstein, J. L. (1986). Parents' reactions to teacher practices of parent involvement, *The Elementary School Journal,* 86(3), 277-294.

Epstein J. L, (1987). Toward a theory of family-school connections: Teacher practices and parent involvement. In K. Hurrelmann, F. Kaufmann, F. Losel (Eds.) *Social intervention: Potential and constraints,* (pp. 121-136). New York: DeGruyter.

Epstein, J. L. (1992). School and family partnerships. In M. Alkin (Ed.), *Encyclopedia of Educational Research,* (6th ed., pp. 1139-1151). New York: Macmillan.

Epstein, J. L. (1995). School/family/community Partnerships: Caring for the children we share. *Phi Delta Kappan,* 76(9), 701-712.

Epstein J. L., Coates L., Salinas K. C., Sanders M. G., & Simon B. (1997). *School, family, community partnerships: Your handbook for action.* Thousand Oaks, CA: Corwin Press.

Epstein, J. L., & Lee, S. (1993). *Effects of school practices to involve families on parents and students in the middle grades: A view from the schools.* Paper presented at the annual meeting of the American Sociological Association, Miami, FL.

Epstein J. L., Salinas, K. C., & Jackson, V. E. (1995). *TIPS: Teachers involve parents in schoolwork - Manual for teachers.* Baltimore: Johns Hopkins University, Center on Families, Communities, Schools and Children's Learning.

Epstein, J. L., & Sanders, M. G. (1996). School, family, community partnerships: Overview and new directions. In D. L. Levinson, A. R. Sadovnik, P. W. Cookson, Jr. (Ed.) *Education and sociology: An encyclopedia,* New York: Garland.

Ginsburg, A. L., & Hanson, S. L. (1986). *Values and educational sources among disadvantaged students.* Washington, D C: U.S. Department of Education.

Henderson, A. T., & Berla, N. (1994). *A new generation of evidence: The family is critical to student achievement.* Washington, D C: National Committee for Citizens in Education.

Hoover-Dempsey, K. V., & Sandler, H. M. (1995). Parental involvement in children's education: Why does it make a difference? *Teachers College Record,* 97(2), 310-331.

Johnson, V. (1993, September). *Parent/family centers in school: Expanding outreach and promoting collaboration* (Rep. No. 20.) Center on Families, Communities, Schools and Children's Learning. Baltimore: Johns Hopkins University.

Keith, T. Z., Reimers, T. M., Fehrman, P. G., Pottebaum, S. M., & Aubey, L. W. (1986). Parental involvement, homework, and TV time: Direct and indirect effects on high school achievement. *Journal of Educational Psychology*, 78(5), 373-380.

Lee, C. C. (1984). An investigation of psychosocial variables related to academic success for rural Black adolescents. *Journal of Negro Education*, 53(4), 424-434.

Lee, S. (1994). *Family-school connections and students' education: Continuity and change in family involvement from the middle grades to high school.* Unpublished dissertation, Johns Hopkins University: Baltimore.

Leinhart, S. (1977). Social networks: A developing paradigm. In S. Leinhart (Ed.), *Social networks: A developing paradigm.* New York: Academic Press.

Parsons, T. (1985). The school class as a social system: Some of its functions in American society. In J. H. Ballantine (Ed.), *School and society: A reader in education and sociology* (pp. 179-197). Palo Alto, CA: Mayfield.

Purnell, R. F., & Gott, E. E. (1985). *Preparation and role of school personnel for effective school - family relations.* Paper presented at the annual meeting of the American Educational Research Association, Chicago.

Rutherford, B., Anderson, B., & Billig, S. (1997). *Parent and community involvement in education,* Washington DC: U.S Department of Education, Office of Educational Research and Improvement.

Sanders, M. G. (1996a). Action teams in action : Interviews and observations in three schools in the Baltimore school-family-community partnership program. *Journal of Education for Students Placed at Risk*, 1(3), 249-262.

Sanders M. G. (1996b). Building family partnerships that last. *Educational Leadership*, 54(3), 61-66.

Sanders M. G. (1999).School membership in the National Network of Partnership Schools: Progress, challenges and next steps. *The Journal of Educational Research*, 92(4), 220-230.

Sanders, M. G., & Epstein, J. L. (1998). School-family-community partnerships and educational change: International perspectives. In A. Hargreaves, A. Lieberman, M. Fullan and D. Hopkins (Eds.), *International Handbook of Educational Change*, (pp. 482-502). Amsterdam: Kluwer Academic.

Sanders, M.G., & Epstein, J. L. (In press).The National Network of Partnership Schools: How research influences educational practice. *Journal of Education for Students Placed at Risk*, 5(1&2), 61-76.

Sanders, M. G., & Simon, B. S. (1999, April). *Progress and challenges: Comparing elementary, middle and high schools in the National Network of Partnership Schools.* Paper presented at the annual meeting of the American Educational Research Association, Montreal.

Seidman, I. E. (1991). *Interviewing as qualitative research: A guide for researchers in education and the social sciences.* New York: Teachers College Press.

Wasik, B. A., & Karweit, N. (1994). Off to a good start: Effects of birth-to-three interventions on early school success. In R. Slavin, N. Karweit, B. Wasik (Eds.), *Preventing Early School Failure* (pp. 13-57). New York: Longwood.

Young, K. T., & Marx, E. (1992). *What does learning mean for infants and toddlers? The contributions of the child, family, and community* (Rep. 3). Baltimore: Johns Hopkins University, Center on Families, Communities, Schools, and Children's Learning.

Conclusion: Effective Schooling for Poor and Minority Adolescents: Refining the Focus

MAVIS G. SANDERS
Johns Hopkins University

The preceding chapters provide insight into, and raise issues and questions about the effective schooling of poor and minority adolescents in the United States. Through the use of quantitative and qualitative methods, large national data sets, and surveys of targeted populations, these chapters collectively illustrate the value of research in the process of educational reform. A primary conclusion that can be drawn from this collection is that with the right support, schools, families, and communities have the potential to create schools where all students, most especially those who have been underserved by U.S. schools, thrive. These chapters further suggest that whether schools live up to this potential has a great deal to do with the attention that educators, researchers, and concerned citizens in students' families and communities direct toward five key areas.

The first of these areas is school expenditures. To address past inequities in educational opportunities that have resulted in unequal outcomes for poor and minority students, additional resources must be directed toward schools that serve large numbers of these students. It is not sufficient to have equal inputs because, as shown by Balfanz, Mintrop, and Legters, schools that serve poor and minority students have needs that far exceed those of schools that serve more advantaged populations. Furthermore, as Balfanz contends, these additional resources must be committed for extended periods of time to have lasting effects on student outcomes. Students whose parents, grandparents and great-grandparents were provided rich educational opportunities are more likely to succeed in school than are students whose forebears were not provided such opportunities (Miller, 1995).

It is clear that the competition for educational resources is fierce. This competition, however, does not diminish the fact that to improve educational opportunities and outcomes for poor and minority students, sufficient resources to address historical and contemporary inequities are necessary (Anyon, 1997). Given the current political climate, the securing of these funds for extended periods will be a difficult struggle that requires commitment and creativity. Despite its difficulty, however, this is a struggle in which advocates for educational equality must engage.

Intricately linked to educational expenditures is educational policy, a second area that requires further attention if effective educational reform for all youths is to take place. Mitchell's chapter on federal education policies documents how educational policy is often diluted during the political process. This dilution leads to policies that cannot fully meet their intended goals because schools, and local and state educational agencies do not have the technical assistance and support necessary to implement them effectively. Mitchell's account of the changes in the Goals 2000 legislation shows that its final version – which omitted opportunity-to-learn standards, and the National Education Standards and Improvement Council, a council to provide technical expertise to states undertaking reform – was weaker than its original version. This weakened legislation has left some states without the guidance, tools, and support needed to implement and effectively evaluate comprehensive improvements in the educational opportunities provided to poor and minority youth.

Mintrop provides an example of how educational policies can fall short of their intended goals at the school level when schools are not provided the support and technical assistance they need to implement reforms effectively. Although hailed as an important component of systemic reform, school reconstitution efforts may fall short of improving student outcomes when schools are not provided with the tools and professional development necessary to build internal capacity for and commitment to change. Educational policies, then, translate into improved practice and outcomes only when they are securely linked to appropriate, context-sensitive resources.

A third area in educational research and practice that requires further attention is the quality of schooling. Research (Fine, 1991; Oakes, 1988), including several chapters in this book, shows that poor and minority students can attend the same schools as White and more economically advantaged students, and have very different experiences. Yonezawa's case studies illustrate how students of different racial and social class backgrounds can have different counseling experiences while attending the same high school. Datnow and Cooper show that Black and White students in elite, private schools may have very different experiences within the same educational institutions. Future research, then, must seek to identify factors that cause differential school experiences. Educational reforms, in turn, must seek to address factors that may negatively impact students' quality of schooling, which ultimately affect student outcomes. Without attention to this area in education, poor and minority students may continue to be deprived of educational opportunities that are experienced by the more advantaged students to whom they are often compared.

A fourth area that requires greater attention in education is the role of families and communities in the educational process. Franklin calls for a shift to a new construct for understanding what places students at risk, and what protects them from risk and promotes resilience. To do so, he argues, a wholistic view of students, which requires understanding and connecting with their families and communities, is needed. The importance of families to students' learning and school success emerges in several of the chapters included in this book. Jordan and Plank discuss the importance of families in students' postsecondary planning. Students whose families can and do discuss college attendance and requirements, and students' future goals and ambitions with them are more likely to attend institutions of higher learning than are students whose families do not. Yonezawa shows how families can also influence the courses that their adolescents take in high school and how this process can affect students' preparation for postsecondary schooling. Sanders and Herting show how families and members of students' communities influence key attitudes that are directly linked to school achievement. Cooper and Datnow, likewise, show that African-American students' family and church involvement positively influences their ability to thrive in the academically rigorous environment of elite, private schools.

It is clear through the research included in these chapters, and research that has accumulated over several decades (Epstein, 1992) that students' families and communities are important in the educational process. Sanders and Epstein report on how schools across the country are attempting to forge closer connections with students' families and communities to better serve students at all grade levels. The authors also show that there are challenges that schools, especially middle and high schools, must face to create successful school, family, and community partnership programs. More research on how middle and high schools can overcome these challenges to create family and community partnership practices that promote adolescents' success in school is needed. Such information would improve the design of many school improvement projects that are currently being implemented, as well as those that will be developed and implemented in the future.

A fifth vital issue raised in this book is the importance of teacher education and professional development. Good schools require many things and central among them are good teachers. Sanders and Jordan illustrate how important teachers who support and have high expectations for their students are to adolescents' engagement in high school. Mitchell's chapter on exemplary African-American teachers also shows how good teachers can make a difference in the schooling experience of youth. Without competent teachers committed to providing a quality education to all students, regardless of race or linguistic and socioeconomic background, no educational policy, no school reform, and no amount of money will improve educational opportunities and outcomes for poor and minority students.

Successful implementation of the educational reforms discussed in the final section of this book depends on the commitment and knowledge of teachers and administrators. To effectively utilize extended class periods, partner with students' families and communities, creatively deliver new curricula, or preside over innovative classroom reforms, teachers need to be well-prepared, and their professional development needs to be well-conceived, well-designed, and long term (American Association of Colleges for Teacher Education; Wood & Thompson, 1993). Balfanz details the challenges faced by teachers and other school personnel in schools that serve large numbers of poor and minority adolescents. Mintrop, too, draws attention to the overwhelming responsibilities of teachers in such schools. Without appropriate professional development and ongoing support, these teachers cannot be expected to successfully carry out meaningful school reforms. However with the right support, including excellent, ongoing professional development, teachers can embrace promising school reforms, and make a difference in the learning opportunities and outcomes of poor and minority students (see Legters, chap. 14, this volume; MacIver, MacIver, Balfanz, Plank, & Ruby, chap. 12, this volume; McClendon, Nettles & Wigfield, chap. 13, this volume).

Effective professional development cannot and should not be a top-down process, however. Teachers have a wealth of experience and expertise, and should be actively involved in the professional development they receive. For example, Mitchell contends that the competencies possessed by the African-American teachers in her study helped these teachers reach and effectively educate many poor and minority adolescents. She further argues that teachers should be given opportunities to share their competencies with others in their professional communities through ongoing professional development. Greater attention to teacher preparation and professional development greatly increases the likelihood of improved schooling experiences for poor and minority students.

In summary, the chapters in this book highlight the need for focused attention to five areas in education: school expenditures; educational policies; quality of school experience; school, family and community connections; and teacher education and professional development. If the debate on differential student outcomes focused more on these issues and less on racial and social class stereotypes and biases, then greater progress would be made in improving the educational outcomes of historically underserved youth. The attainment of this goal is crucial not only for poor and minority students, but for the economic, political, and social well-being of the larger society as well.

REFERENCES

American Association of Colleges for Teacher Education. (1995). *RATE: Teaching teachers: Facts and figures.* Washington, DC: Author.

Anyon, J. (1997). *Ghetto schooling: A political economy of urban educational reform.* New York: Teachers College Press.

Epstein, J. L. (1992). School and family partnerships. In M. Alkin (Ed.), *Encyclopedia of educational research* (6th ed., pp. 1139-1151). New York: MacMillan.

Fine, M. (1991). *Framing dropouts: Notes on the politics of an urban public high school.* Albany, NY: State University of New York Press.

Miller, L. S. (1995). *An American imperative: Accelerating minority educational advancement.* New Haven, CT: Yale University Press.

Oakes, J. (1988). Tracking in mathematics and science education: A structural contribution to unequal schooling. In L. Weis (Ed.), *Class, race and gender in American education*, (pp. 106-125). Albany, NY: State University of New York Press.

Wood, F. H., & Thompson, S. R. (1993). Assumptions about staff development based on research and best practice. *Journal of Staff Development*, 7(1), 52-66.

Author Index

Subject Index